AMONG THE CITIES

JAN MORRIS

AMONG THE CITIES

OXFORD UNIVERSITY PRESS
New York   Oxford

Oxford University Press

Oxford   New York   Toronto
Delhi   Bombay   Calcutta   Madras   Karachi
Petaling Jaya   Singapore   Hong Kong   Tokyo
Nairobi   Dar es Salaam   Cape Town
Melbourne   Auckland

and associated companies in
Berlin   Ibadan

Library of Congress Cataloging in Publication Data
Morris, Jan, 1926–
Among the cities.
Essays originally appeared
in various publications, 1961–1985.
1. Cities and towns.   I. Title.
G140.M65   1985   909   85-13739
ISBN 0-19-520489-1
ISBN 0-19-505662-0 (pbk.)

British Library Cataloguing in Publication Data
Morris, Jan
Among the cities.
1. Cities and towns   I. Title
910'.091732   G140
ISBN 0-670-80146-1

2 4 6 8 10 9 7 5 3 1

Printed in the United States of America

For
TWM and LYNDA
a wedding present

CONTENTS

PREFACE

Years and years ago, observing that nobody in the history of man had ever seen and described the entire urban world, I resolved to do it myself; and in 1983, standing at last in the great square of Tiantanmen in the city of Beijing, I felt this perhaps jejune ambition to have been fulfilled. I had visited and portrayed, during thirty years of more or less constant travel, all the chief cities of the earth.

This book is a by-product of the experience. As time passed I put it into words in a couple of hundred essays, commissioned originally by a dozen or more magazines in Europe and the United States. Some of these were republished in five collected volumes – *Cities*, *Places*, *Travels*, *Destinations* and *Journeys* – and now that I have completed the odyssey, for what it is worth, I have put together a selection of those selections, thirty-seven pieces from among so many, to form a retrospective exhibition, so to speak, of a lifetime's work.

I have chosen them partly for chronology's sake (the first from 1956, the last from 1984), partly for geographical range, partly to reflect changes of history over those three decades, and partly to illustrate the shifting responses of a single mind, faced with the slow unfolding of the planet. They are not *entirely* urban – two are about islands, two about regions – but they do not illustrate travel in any adventurous kind. It was city life that interested me, and living as I myself always have deep in the countryside, it was above all among the cities, those most fascinating of all creations of human energy and ingenuity, that my long journey took me.

First to last, the world never ceased to astonish me, and I hope at least a little of that power to amaze, if nothing more profound, may be found between the covers of this book.

Trefan Morys, 1985

AMONG THE CITIES

1

'A DAY IS HARDLY ENOUGH'

Alexandria, 1966

I had first known Alexandria at the end of the Second World War, when it was still full of Greeks, Englishmen, Egyptian pashas and a gallimaufry of miscellaneous cosmopolitans. Twenty years later I found it, under the autocracy of Gamal Abdel Nasser, suggestively changed.

Our grandfathers, like Baedeker or Napoleon, inspected Alexandria from the front – from the north, from Greece, Italy or the P. and O. Seen from the familiar Mediterranean, the city looks classically self-evident – an ancient and most famous seaport, sweeping spaciously around its bays, and drawn with a Grecian clarity.

From the south, things look very different, for there the port is circumscribed by that queer expanse of brackish water, part salt, part fresh, called Maryût – fragrant with wild flowers in the spring, malodorous in high summer, with fishermen poling themselves about in frail spindly canoes, and boorish fish of monstrous size. A shambled, cluttered townscape is reflected in Maryût, ringed with shacks and railway lines, for here you are seeing Alex out of Egypt. Behind you the desert road has run its forlorn way across the wasteland – nothing since Cairo but a petrol station and a gloomy café: and behind that again all Africa seems to be squatting, breathing its hot breath across the sands.

In the great days of Egyptian travel nobody dreamt of viewing Alexandria from here. This was, to every cultured sightseer, a great city of the Mediterranean, linked indissolubly with Europe by glorious strands of scholarship, celebrated throughout civilization for the schools and libraries of its classical antiquity, its philosophers, astronomers and mathematicians, its associations with men like Euclid, Theocritus, Caesar and even Homer –

'there is an island called Pharos in the rolling seas, off the mouth of the Nile'.

Today the rump view is more apposite, and that queer jumbled image in the surface of Maryût is a true paradigm of the place. Alexandria has wrenched itself free of Europe, and disowns the values of the Grand Tour. Cleopatra, Queen of Egypt, has won. Once the second city of the Roman Empire, now this is only a provincial centre of the Arab world, no longer even Egypt's summer capital, only a port and a holiday resort. The marble serenity has vanished, to be replaced by a pungent but violent new energy – the energy of Egypt itself, restless and inconsequential, full of humour but never at peace, like the fevered state of irritable excitement that overcomes people during a sandstorm.

Grandfather's view of Alexandria still has a pathetic majesty. Legend says that Alexander the Great, who personally decreed the shape of the city, is buried somewhere beneath its streets, intact in a crystal coffin, and a few years ago a dedicated Greek waiter arrived from the Piraeus to unearth him. Night and day his fanatic figure was to be seen at work, digging away behind advertising hoardings, peering into manholes, and sometimes so disrupting the traffic by pursuing his researches in the middle of main streets that in the end the tolerant city authorities had to expel him.

For even now there is a magnetism to the old grandeur of Alexandria. Only a few hidden stones are left of the Pharos, seventh wonder of the world, and over them the Arabs long ago built the fort of Qait Bey: but the very knowledge of their existence is enough, and from the imaginary shadow of that metaphysical lighthouse – once 400 feet high, with a gigantic figure of Poseidon on top – the eye sweeps respectfully around one of the grandest of all waterfronts. The corniche at Alexandria is ten miles long, and never seems to peter out: it is lined with block after block of massive four-square buildings, white or sandy-coloured, and is so fuzzed about with balconies that from a distance it seems to be permanently in scaffolding. There is an ex-royal palace at each end: Ras el Tin serene in the west, from whose quay King Farouk sailed away into exile in his own yacht, Montazah flamboyantly in the east, a turreted ogre's lair in a park, set about with lascivious legend.

From one to the other runs that magnificent promenade, with no particular structure to strike the eye, only a fine sweep and a sense of consequence. Alexandria is not a city of notable monuments – 'a day', says Hachette's guidebook hopefully, 'is hardly enough for a visit of the city'. But as you stand there in the salty sunshine, with a gusty wind from Asia Minor blowing out of the sea, you can scarcely forget that over there the Canopic Way ran straight as a die between a thousand pillars from the Moon Gate to the Sun Gate, and that in the harbour at your feet Mark Antony's triremes came to anchor. A sentry of the Egyptian Army stands sentinel at Pompey's Pillar, an indeterminate monument of antiquity on a hillock near the station, as if to show that even the severe republicans of modern Egypt retain a respect for the imperial splendours: and when, not long ago, they discovered an enchanting little Greek theatre beneath a building site in the centre of the city, the roughest urchins of the back streets, momentarily tamed by its unearthly grace, were to be seen loitering in silent wonder on the edge of the excavation, gazing down upon that white prodigy beneath.

The scale and some of the pride survive. Alexandria is haunted by superb ghosts – queens, admirals, sages, poets. During the Muslim fast of Ramadan the sunset gun is fired each evening from the mole of Qait Bey: and across the silence of the Eastern Harbour, in that brief pearled hush of the Egyptian twilight, its white puff of smoke drifts mystically and disperses, long after the bang, as though virgins are sacrificing to their gods out there, or they are stoking up the Pharos.

To the post-Baedeker generation, emancipated from pith helmets and classical educations, Alexandria was a city of the nearer Orient – a modern Phoenicia. The concert of this city, as Lawrence Durrell heard it, was polyglot and slithery: essentially a Levantine music, sometimes reedy, sometimes harsh, with classical strains to it still, but a soft Arab drumbeat somewhere in the bass.

Thirty years ago this still was a metropolis of the eastern Mediterranean, the capital of Egyptian cotton, the summer capital of the Egyptian government, gifted, wealthy, cynical, with entrepreneurs in sumptuous villas and a dozen jealous national communities living side by side. All the Powers of the world were represented in this cosmopolitan place, and their Consulates still stand there regretfully, monuments to a lost society. The French gazes sternly across the harbour towards the source of all civilization, f.o.b. Marseilles. The Italian is properly touched with the rococo, an *Aida* in stone. The German has become the local headquarters of the Food and Agricultural Organization, and looks a little priggish. The British towers above the tram terminus, with fine wide terraces for gins and tonics, and shady lawns for bird-watching. Churches of diverse kinds, too, stand witness to old certainties – churches of the Melchites, the Syrians, the Armenians, the Greek Catholics, the Maronites, the Chaldeans, the Scots and the Orthodox Copts, who are in communion with the churches of Ethiopia, and have their own Alexandrine Pope.

These were the several poles of Alexandria, not so long ago, and around them little worlds separately revolved. Sometimes you may still taste the tang of that vanished city. Sit with some elderly Copt, for example, in the shade of his suburban garden, and as his clipped dry voice murmurs on, with musty jokes and caustic reminiscences, so you may imagine that the lost society of the pashas still proliferates outside, with all its intricate meshwork of cousinhoods and family ownership, its cocktails at the Yacht Club and its delicious gossip about the scandals at Montazah. Or accept the chaperonage of one of the young University intellectuals, and allow yourself to be shown the city through a blur of persiflage, *non sequiturs* and comical innuendo – the sly oblique humour of the Levant. Or go to the Patriarchate on a Sunday morning, and watch the Orthodox Copts assembling for worship. The Pope may not be on duty, but the elders of the church will be waiting in turbans and grey gallabiyahs on the cathedral steps, and down their long grave line the worshippers will pass, with respectful handshakes and lowered heads, to disappear into the maw of gold vestments and tinny chanting that is the interior of the fane.

Or stand beneath the plaque that marks the home of C. P. Cavafy, with the traffic rumbling and clanking all around you, and the small boys standing stock still to stare, and you may still be snared by the cadences of that great Greek poet, the laureate of the Levant:

> Something they said beside me directed
> my attention toward the café entrance.
> And I saw the beautiful body that looked
> as if Eros had made it from his consummate experience –
> joyfully modelling its symmetrical limbs:

heightening sculpturally its stature:
modelling the face with emotion
and imparting by the touch of his hands
a feeling on the brow, on the eyes, on the lips.

One day I entered a restaurant on the corniche to gloat over a copy of Forster's *Guide to Alexandria*, picked up for a fairly expensive song from the library of a dispossessed plutocrat – a handsome signed copy of that rare and delightful work, printed in 1938, and published, as it were out of a dead age, under the auspices of the Royal Archaeological Society of Alexandria. Clutching this treasure, I ordered prawns and Stella beer – and found myself, as I lovingly opened the yellow covers of the book, miraculously back within its pages, in the 'towsled, unsmartened' Levantine city that Forster knew himself.

A brilliant white sun shone through the windows off the sea, but the restaurant was gently hazed with cigar smoke, steam and cooking fat. It smelt partly of heavy blossom, and partly of shish-kebab. Vases of ageing flowers decorated its tables, dangling glass ornaments hung around its walls, and framed near the door was the statutory price list in Arabic, with fiscal stamps all over it. A dark bored girl in a blue blouse sat dispiritedly at the cash desk. Distracted waiters rushed about with trays, like a chorus of barmen in a musical.

And all around me the Greeks were at their food. Their mothers-in-law were there in fustian black. Their children were there in elaborate frills. A sprawling family unit sat slunched over its victuals at each table, talking loudly in Greek with its mouths full, greeting friends with expansive napkined gestures, and sometimes abruptly propelling small boys in tight-buttoned suits towards the lavatories behind the velvet curtain. With that light, and those prawns, and the thick Arabic cries that came from the kitchen quarters, and the tinkle of glass beads when a gust of wind came through the door – with E. M. Forster beside me on the tablecloth that day, I could be nowhere else in the world but Alexandria.

But melancholy ruled – with the fiscal stamps. Animated though the scene was, those Greeks seemed dispossessed. The city outside was no longer theirs, and their world had shrunk with the centuries, smaller and smaller from the great Hellenic world of the ancients to a plate of pilaf with the children on

Saturday. Levantine Alexandria is a shabby white city now, its
sensuality dullened, its sybarites long since banished or
reformed. Its sun is white, its walls are dingy white, even its
remarks are pallid with nostalgia. 'Ah, you should have been
here twenty years ago!' Or: 'Before the war, now, this was the
happiest city in the world – and look at us now!' Or, most
inescapably of all, that plaintive inquiry of the ill-used everywhere: *'What have we done to deserve it?'*

Alexandria has lost its old meaning and panache, and the
great European communities of the place are dwindled or
subdued. The café life of Alex, which once linked this city so
intimately with the mores of southern Europe, is almost dead,
and the coffee houses themselves, once alive with prattling
matrons, nannies and essayists, are now reduced to frayed
stained tablecloths, weedy flower-beds beneath the trellises, and
waiters pottering desultorily about with feather brushes.

The streets around the Cotton Exchange were once an affluent
amalgam of commerce and high finance, cramped heavy
thoroughfares with small expensive shops – 'something of the
brilliant narrowness of Bond Street', Ronald Storrs thought in
1905. Now the Exchange itself is peeling and deserted, with
vast political slogans often attached to its façade, and a glowering
policeman with a rifle outside its doors; and those once-enticing
streets are sadly faded, stocked with Egyptian-made toothpastes
and greyish indigenous fashions. 'Maybe after two hours' is the
mechanical reply of the concierge at the Cecil Hotel, when he is
asked when the water will be coming on: and somewhere
upstairs there lives one last old English couple, relics of the
summery thirties – the wife blind and bedridden, the husband
still sometimes to be encountered descending the dark staircase
with a careful soldierly tread.

Only a few of the tarboosh shops survive, their brass moulds
glimpsed through clouds of ironing steam, and the palatial waiting rooms of the British Consulate-General, where once the cotton
magnates impatiently thrummed the table, are now haunted
mostly by poor Maltese, demanding their passports. The past is
gliding into literature. I went to the Greek cemetery to look for
Cavafy's grave, and was received most courteously by an elderly
guardian sitting on a chair outside the mortuary chapel. He took
me to the register of burials kept in a cupboard behind the altar,
and ran his finger conscientiously through the quill-pen list of

names, murmuring their polysyllables under his breath: but in
the end he had to close the book with a reverent thud, and confess
himself defeated. Cavafy, that solitary genius of Levantine Alexandria, was forgotten. 'Was he a local man?' the caretaker asked
me sympathetically. 'The name seems familiar.'

The palm trees in Liberation Square are layered with dust, as
though they need a good brush-down, and all over the Levantine
city an air of seedy neglect lies like a blight. The visitor
wandering off the main thoroughfares may suddenly find
himself crossing the bar of a stagnant, silent, private backwater,
listlessly declining there in the afternoon. Drain-hatches are
blocked with sand and dust. Pavement slabs are irregularly
tilted. Three or four men are drinking coffee on the sidewalk,
straddling their chairs and exchanging sporadic gloomy grunts.
Outside his door lounges a single prickly Greek, sucking a
cheroot and wearing a shirt with a brass collar-stud, but no
collar. On a balcony high above a woman in a pink housecoat
yawns, looks languidly right and left, runs her fingers through
her hair and lights a cigarette. A shrouded scavenger, muffled
eerily about the head, scuffles about for fag-ends, and at the end
of the shadowy little street the blinding sun stands there like an
insulating wall, criss-crossed with trams.

Beggars still infest the centre of Alexandria, and chill the
susceptible stranger with compassionate loathing. I was walking
home in Alex one evening when I felt, rather than actually saw,
a legless beggar observing my passage from across the street. He
was strapped to a low wooden trolley, which he pushed along
with his hands, and made an object at once heart-rending and
abhorrent to see: but I had no money on me, neither a pound
nor a piastre, so I quickened my step self-consciously and
hurried down Zaghloul Street towards my hotel.

Behind me I could hear the whirr of his roller-skate wheels,
as he pursued me through the town – a thump when he eased
himself off the sidewalk, a clanking when he crossed the
tramlines, a change of pitch when he left the tarmac for the
flagstones. Faster and faster I walked through the evening
crowds, but I could never escape those whirring wheels: over
the low wall into Zaghloul Square: across the little garden, and
I could hear them skidding down the path, closer than ever
behind my back, so that I could hear the poor man's panting

breath, too; until at last, breaking into a run, I threw myself into the revolving door of the Cecil. The wheels came to a sudden stop on the sidewalk outside, and a curse bade me good night.

Legendary on the seafront; torpid in the centre; the vitality of Alexandria is all at the back. The pallor of this city is the pallor of a hiatus – a pause in history, at a point where civilizations meet. Europe has withdrawn from this African seaport, leaving nostalgia and bitterness behind: but from the back Egypt herself comes flooding in, like fresh blood into desiccated veins – as though Maryût itself has burst its banks, and is inundating the city with muddy life. Baedeker's view and Durrell's music are both illusory now: today you must look at Alex out of the desert, and allow for a lot of noise.

'The Arab town' or 'the Native quarter' is what they used to call the cluttered area between the harbours, where only the most scabrous sort of European normally lived. From Qait Bey it shows only as a kind of blur in the grand symmetry of the waterfront, as though your binoculars are not in focus: but when you enter Alex by way of Maryût, it greets you with indescribable colour, vigour, squalor and variety. Then you know you are entering an Islamic city of Africa, conquered long ago by Arabs – a city that cares little for Athens or Imperial Rome, but is related by blood or religion to Baghdad, Amman and even Addis Ababa. Its energy is terrific, its face is unbeautiful, and already it seems to overawe the faded streets of the Levantine bourgeoisie.

It is mostly a maze of crumbled mud streets, sordid in the daytime, evocatively sinister at night, like the ill-lit lanes of a medieval European city. In and out the winding alleys go, with powerful suggestions of rats and pox, with silent watchmen sitting on stools in dark doorways; and sometimes, through a half-open door, you may see flitting white figures in lamplight, like pale hallucinations, or unhappy infant whores. Sometimes there is a sudden splurge of Arab voices, shrill and vicious above the roar of the city, as though behind those shuttered casements some crime of deviate passion has just been committed. Sometimes there is a sizzle of cooking-fat from a backyard, or a sudden flash of laughter and smiles, as a covey of raggety children darts out of one alley and into another.

Every now and then the labyrinth abruptly opens into a full-blown Arab square – deafening and tumultuous, spiced, dirty,

genial and desperately overcrowded. The white mass of a
mosque rises in the background, illuminated by the street lights,
and out of every window the radios seem to blare, perpetually
fortissimo, with fruity announcers' voices and slithery nasal
quarter-tones. All is nervous noise and movement – sidewalk
buskers, sweetmeat sellers, sailors, hilarious students shooting
at explosive caps with airguns at sidestalls. Ramshackle taxis
rock and shudder across the square. Single-decker trams pull
double-decker trams through the babel. Army officers in padded
greatcoats step from official cars and disappear portentously
into tenements. Down narrow bazaars, ablaze with light, you
may glimpse a shimmer of pots and pans, a violence of yellow
nylon, stacks of pop bottles and trays of wizened herbs.

Where the Arab quarter meets the sea the graceful boats of the
fishermen, felucca-rigged, lie aslant upon the shingle. It is as
though the Egyptians have forced their way through to the
Mediterranean, cutting a corridor among the aliens. Today the
whole quarter seems to be expanding like a ghetto set free –
spilling across the corniche, where the little Egyptians race each
other precariously along the parapet, overwhelming the haughty
purlieus of Ras el Tin, seeping around the forlorn Cotton
Exchange towards the grand suburbs of the east. One day, I do
not doubt, this irresistible vigour will revivify all Alexandria in
a coarser kind, and the city will look out across the Mediterranean with an altogether different confidence – not as it used to,
with an almost proprietorial bow towards Europe, but far more
assertively, as something new and powerful out of Africa.

So expectancy tempers dejection, and one dynamic succeeds
another. I was wandering the streets of the Arab quarter one
day – 'the best way to see it', Forster says, 'is to wander aimlessly
about' – when I happened to catch the eye of a wrinkled cabby
with a towel wrapped round his head, high behind his poor
Rosinante on the seat of his garry. On the impulse of the
moment I winked: and instantly there crossed his face an
expression of indescribable knowingness and complicity, half
comic, half conspiratorial – as though between us, he, the city
and I, we had plumbed the depths of human and historical
experience, and were still coming wryly up for more.

2

A SEPARATE PEOPLE

The Basque Country, 1968

Perhaps the most peculiar people in Europe, certainly among the most resilient, the Basques were relatively quiescent when I went to write about them in the 1960s. Soon afterwards, with the death of the dictator General Franco, they were to resume their violent campaigns of nationalist defiance, and win back some of their political autonomy (though never enough for the fiercest of their patriots).

As the traveller approaches the western foothills of the Pyrenees, whether he is coming from the French side or the Spanish, he is likely to notice something funny happening to the street signs. Some very odd names are creeping in. *X*s and *Z*s abound in the patronymics of greengrocers, villages become less pronounceable with each passing mile, and for once the fading syntax of a classical education is no help at all. The stranger may be forgiven for supposing, as he hastily avoids the turning to Itxassou or Oxocelhaya, that he has somehow strayed off the map of Europe, and is entering some separate and more esoteric continent.

In fact he is entering the country of the Basques, a separate and distinctly esoteric people. Some of them are French by nationality, some Spanish, and they live on both flanks of the Pyrenees: but through all the vicissitudes of European history they have maintained their own character, their own appearance, their own customs and above all their own words. Any description of the Basques must begin with their language, just as any introduction to their homeland starts with those arcane road signs, for the Basques more than anyone depend upon their language for their existence as a race. Without it they would long ago have been absorbed into wider ethnic patterns.

With it they have remained one of the most pungent and forcible minorities in Europe, one of the very few small peoples of the West to defy all the threats and briberies of ethnic conformity.

Basque is one of the world's more alarming languages. Only a handful of adult foreigners, they say, have ever managed to learn it. The Devil tried once and mastered only three words – profanities, I assume. Basque is apparently related to no other language, except perhaps one of the lesser Hungarian dialects. It has a congested look to it, is technically described as agglutinative and polysynthetic, and is full of preoccupied words like *Lerdokiztatu*, *Edantxar* or *Xintxuketa*. One must think in an altogether different way, to talk Basque, for each transitive verb has fourteen different forms; one word means 'she gives it to him', another 'they give it to us', another 'you give it to them', not to speak of those for 'she will give it to us', or 'you would have given it to me' or even (I suppose, for I am getting out of my depth now) 'it might have been given by us to her'. To make a plural in Basque you add the suffix *k*. The Basque word for 'philanthropy', my dictionary tells me, is *Gizadi-Ontzaletasun*. The Basque word for 'almost' is *Ya-Ya*.

I am hardly qualified to write about the Basques, because I do not understand this nerve-wracking language: but as no other English-speaking professional writer understands it either, I fear you will have to make do with me.

The Basques inhabit a moist bumpy country on the shores of the Bay of Biscay. Of the seven traditionally Basque provinces, three are in France, four in Spain: perhaps half a million Basques are Spanish citizens, and another 100,000 Frenchmen. The Basque ethos is strongest in the Spanish coastal provinces of Guipúzcoa and Vizcaya, and it peters away gradually east, west and south, the language fading, the customs losing their tang, under the influence of France and Castile. On the perimeters the Basques are scarcely distinguishable as a people. In the centre they are absolutely unmistakable.

They achieve a daily summit of Basqueness on the waterfront of San Sebastian, the provincial capital of Guipúzcoa. This is an international resort, full of snobbery and starched nursemaids, and for a couple of months in high summer it is actually the capital of Spain, the Government moving up from Madrid in haughty panoply. It is also, though, a busy Basque fishing port, and along the esplanade from the grand hotels the fishing people conduct their affairs with an old and earthy gusto. The trawlers side-step skilfully through the narrow harbour entrance, their stocky crews cast to a Victorian mould of seamanship. The longshoremen clatter about with high-wheeled barrows full of ice. Shuddering diesel trucks load up with lobsters, mullet or baby eels for the insatiable gourmets of Madrid. And on the quayside, any morning when the catch comes in, the Basque fishwives sit at auction.

There are few more formidable sights in Europe than a full-blooded San Sebastian beldame selling fish upon that waterfront. Tourists gape, policemen sheepishly perambulate, fishermen in blue denims trundle to and fro with trays of fish, a calculating throng of restaurateurs and fishmongers sucks its pencils and fingers its wallets: in the centre of it all, supreme, unchallengeable, Basque womanhood enormously presides.

The auctioneer is flanked by cronies, sitting brawnily on kitchen-chairs like a gangster's bodyguard. She herself stands in the middle with a microphone around her neck, wearing a blue anorak, a pink chiffon scarf, white ankle socks and a suggestion of innumerable underclothes. She is in her sixties, perhaps. Her face is heavy-jowled, her wrists are very muscular, and she is built like a boxer, but there is a rich urbanity to her voice as she intones the price of the sardines. The crowd is altogether at her command. The seamen stumble in with their fish-trays like acolytes in an archiepiscopal presence. The cronies laugh at every joke. The policemen shuffle about. The customers never dare to argue. But sometimes that empress of the fish-market, pausing to scribble a price upon her pad, notices a baby in somebody's arms, and looks up unexpectedly with the sweetest of grandmotherly smiles, a twiddle of cod-scaled fingers and what I take to be the Basque equivalent of 'Iddums-didums'.

I know of no exact equivalent to this character anywhere else in the world (her nearest relatives are perhaps the bowler-hatted market-women of Bolivia). She seems to be at once Gothic and Latin, with a perceptible oriental streak as well. In a Catholic region of traditional piety, where men and women still sit separately in church, she appears to be altogether emancipated.

Across the harbour from one of the most sophisticated resorts in Europe, she might have swaggered straight out of some medieval tavern. In all this she is very Basque. Nobody quite knows who the Basques are, or how they first came to their corner of the Pyrenees. They are of distinctive appearance – dark, thick, beak-nosed – and highly individual character: and like the fishwife, they seem to have no peers.

They are an able people – money-people, organizers, builders and great sailors. On the French side of the Pyrenees the Basque country is mostly pastoral, conveniently laced with tourism. On the Spanish side its tone is set by the great iron-fields around Bilbao, the basis of many industries and an economic mainstay of Spain. On both sides the atmosphere is one of astute competence – the kind of acumen that does not bother with fiddly details, checking a passport or charging for a tyre valve, but drives straight to the profitable heart of things, an immediate trade-in price or a meeting with the board of directors at eleven o'clock sharp. Few cities of southern Europe are so punctual and industrious as Bilbao, the economic capital of the Basques, where every other building seems to be a bank, and eight miles of riverfront clank with derricks, ships and warehouses. The Hispanophile must look elsewhere for his orange-blossom idylls: Bilbao is more like Hamburg than Seville, and in its restaurants groups of businessmen perpetually discuss the stock prices, in sober grey suits over plates of eel-spawn.

The Basques have been historically successful at enterprises requiring drive more than meditation – garlic, as their cooks prefer it, more than thyme. They were organized whalers at least as early as the twelfth century, their boats ranging clear across the Atlantic to the Newfoundland grounds, and throughout their history they have been tremendous explorers and colonizers. The first man to sail around the world was a Basque, Juan Sebastian Elcano, who took over the command when Magellan died in the Philippines. Simon Bolivar was a Basque, and so was de Lesseps of the Suez Canal. The two supreme Basque saints were both men of forceful initiative: St Francis Xavier, who took the Cross to Japan, and St Ignatius Loyola, first general of the Jesuits. Basques have always been excellent settlers, always ready to travel: their colonies thrive still in Mexico, in Nevada and on the River Plate, and a familiar sight of the southern French roads is another busload of Basques bouncing in their black berets, stacked around with packages and baskets, towards the profitable opportunities of Paris.

On the high and gloomy pass of Roncevalles, between France and Spain, I sat on the grass one afternoon and read the legend of Roland's death: for it was through this morose defile that Charlemagne and his knights withdrew from Spain in 778, savaged by the vindictive locals, and somewhere up here that the chivalrous Roland fought his last. It all seemed very close to me: the giants and the magic swords, the noble knights and the chargers, the call of the great horn Olivant which plucked the birds dead from their flight: and closest of all, I uncomfortably thought, the black shaggy forms of the Basque guerrillas, whooping weirdly out of the sun and rolling gigantic boulders down the mountainsides.

If the Basques were bloody-minded then, they are hardly more tractable today. Their most noted characteristic down the ages has been a fierce independence. They rolled stones on Charlemagne, they disconcerted Wellington, they were among General Franco's toughest opponents in the Spanish Civil War. If you drive towards the coast from Bilbao, through the lush foothills of Vizcaya, swathed in dark green timber and speckled with white farms, presently you will come to a small market town in a valley – cosily settled there, with kerchiefed women working in its fields as in the travel posters, and the scudding clouds of this Atlantic shore-line driving their shadows up and down the valley floor. It looks at first sight like many another Basque town, neither untowardly ugly nor exceptionally attractive, but you may recognize the name emblazoned at the civic limits: Guernica.

Guernica has been from time immemorial the shrine of Basque liberties. It is their Runnymede. Under the ancient Spanish kings the Basques won for themselves a condition of semi-independence: they elected their own representatives, village by village, to an assembly that met in the shade of a symbolic oak tree in Guernica, and each Spanish king swore upon his accession to respect the privileges of the Basques. Every Basque was officially a nobleman, though the nobility did not always show: as the Englishman Richard Ford wrote in the 1840s, 'although the Basque Provinces may typify the three Graces of Spain, the natives sacrifice but little to maintain those types of amiable humanity'.

The Spanish Basques lost most of their privileges when they rose against the Spanish Crown in the Carlist war of the 1830s, and they lost the rest when they backed the losing side in the Spanish Civil War. As for the French Basques, they long since sank their fortunes in those of France. Even so, nationalist feeling rides high on both sides of the frontier. 'We are a nation,' you will be told, 'not a region, not a group of provinces, not a language, not a folk tradition, but a nation, Euzkadi, the nation of the Basques.' For a few months at the beginning of the Spanish Civil War this resolution was actually embodied in a Basque Republic, formed of three Spanish provinces: it was established after a plebiscite with the blessing of the Republican Government in Madrid, and it had its own stamps and currencies, its flag, its President and all the protocol of sovereignty.

Its memory lingers, and in France there is still, thirty years later, a sad assembly of politicians calling itself the Basque Government in Exile. In houses and museums, or among the bric-à-brac of conversation, you may still trip over relics of its brief pride: a faded patriotic poster, with a virile young Basque in a beret, chest out on a hillside; or a queer forgotten banknote at the back of a drawer, about as worthless as a currency can be; or an old soldier's tale of the ramparts before Bilbao, when Franco's cavalry was storming up from the south. Or you may still see for yourself the sacred oak tree of Guernica.

Hitler's bombers, flying on Franco's behalf, destroyed the centre of Guernica one afternoon in April 1937, in an exploit which was to disturb the conscience of the world. The burning of the town symbolized the end of Basque independence. When, after the Civil War, the Basque Provinces were reunited with Franco's Spain, all vestiges of the old privileges were expunged. Navarre, historically another Basque province, had fought on Franco's side, and was rewarded with an unusual degree of autonomy: the three northern provinces had fought for the Republicans, and they were treated as conquered territories.

In the event Basqueness has proved indestructible, and though General Franco has never restored the privileges of the Basques, his regime has perceptibly relaxed its old disapproval of the language. This is partly because Madrid has come to recognize the tourist appeal of regional cultures, but chiefly because the Basques themselves, led often by their priests, have kept their racial loyalty intact. In France and in Spain the

Basques argue on. In Spain one hears of rallies broken up by the police, fiery sermons, priests imprisoned, strikes that are really nationalist protests. In France, where nobody is going to lock you up for your opinions, a slogan commonly scrawled on railway bridges is *Euzkadi 7 = 1* – a gnomic plea for the union of the seven Basque provinces.

So Guernica retains the wistful allure of might-have-been. For centuries its heart was the oak tree, the supreme token of Basque nationality, beneath whose hoary boughs the elected elders of the nation met in legislature. Successive oaks have been destroyed and planted, but there have been records of their existence on the same spot at least since the fourteenth century. In the place of the oak at Guernica Isabel and Ferdinand, the first monarchs of united Spain, swore in 1476 to uphold the privileges of the Basques: and there too the Basque Parliament held its sessions, in a modest pavilion beside the tree.

The place of the oak miraculously survived the German bombing, but now there could hardly be a sadder place. The present oak sapling stands in a ceremonial enclosure, but it looks dusty and lifeless. The stone seats around it are permanently untenanted, the grass is unloved, the proud hopes of the Parliament House have decayed into dingy municipal deliberations. Over the oak tree there hangs, summer or winter, an air of failure: as if, having tried so hard for so many generations, the spirit of the place has lost heart.

Yet some magic lingers there. This is a site possessed by some penetrating quality of experience or emotion, and if you had never heard of the Basques, and knew nothing of the tree, or Basque history, or the bombing, still I think the place of the oak at Guernica would strike you as haunted. This is a sensation common in Basque country. The Basques are not the best-looking people in Europe, and to my mind there is a certain balefulness to their landscapes, but mystery gives them a powerful fascination. Their annals are full of mystery – not merely the mystery of their origins, but eerie embellishments of legends and history too, devils and ghosts and arcane occurrences. In the spring the farmers of the Pyrenean foothills burn the bracken in their fields: and when at night you see the villages of the Basques illuminated from the slopes above by clumps of fire, blood-red smoke and a ghostly glow from the mountainside, you may be reminded of that queer heritage, and remember that no part of medieval Europe was more infested with witches.

The modern strangeness is largely age. The Basques have inhabited their country for a very long time indeed. Some scholars believe them to be the original inhabitants of the Iberian peninsula, squeezed over the centuries into this northern enclave. They were never conquered by the Moors who overran the rest of Spain, so that their blood remained unusually pure – they used to be considered the ultimate Spaniards, the gentry of gentry. Matters of pedigree have always been dear to them, and many a modest farmhouse in the hills brags an elaborate escutcheon above the door. Hundreds of thousands of aliens have migrated to the Basque provinces in the past half-century, but there is still an inbred feeling to the country: the extraordinary language, the romantic history, bind the people with a private subtlety. Basque architecture, too, gives a meshed flavour to the provinces. The old buildings are intricately half-timbered, and the new ones show a hereditary leaning towards the criss-crossed and the cantilevered, as though their designers would really like to fence them in with iron bars against the intrusion of outsiders.

Inside those houses, moreover, a mystic privacy often seems to reign. The Basques are not a gregarious Mediterranean people, though their genius often takes a hearty turn: theirs is a family society, based fundamentally upon isolated rural dwelling-houses. A Basque farm is thus a little world of its own. It is built to an Alpine pattern, and looks very like a Swiss chalet – living-rooms upstairs, working-rooms below, with the lush green grass sidling up to its front door, and the odd pyramidical haystacks of the Basques paraded down its meadows like troops of African dancers.

Every part of such a house seems to be full and active, and as the doors are opened for your inspection the members of the family are revealed as in some *tableau vivant*, each at work upon a speciality. In the kitchen, grandmother, all in black, is stirring a soup. In the workshop, father is oiling a scythe. The daughter of the house is sewing in the living-room, surrounded by potted plants and oleographs: in a bedroom, the son is at his homework. And as the lady of the house places her hand upon the wooden latch of the last room of all, a distant secret look crosses her face – a madonna look, as in an old painting: a sweet smell of straw and warmth reaches you as the door creaks open, the light inside is dim, and there in the core of the farmhouse you see the last members of its family: three stalwart rabbits, lolloping in cages, two black and white cows, three little puppy-dogs gambolling at their leads, and a small grey donkey smiling from his manger.

Many other peoples live with their animals under the same roof: none that I know treat their beasts with quite the same collusive intimacy. It is as though the rabbits themselves speak Basque. Yet other aspects of the Basque mystique are anything but gentle. It is Basques, for instance, who have given the festival of San Fermin at Pamplona, in Navarre, its brutal excitement. There the bullfight, elevated elsewhere in Spain to a tragic ritual, is played as black farce: for enthusiastic amateurs are let loose in the streets before the bulls, and the festivities open with a harum-scarum chase to the bullring, the animals goaded and irritated into bewildered frenzy, the humans posturing and showing off, sprinting for dear life, standing their ground for moments of spectacular bravado or shinning ignominiously up trees. It is a display of coarse-grained appeal, and other Basque pastimes, too, are notable less for grace or delicacy than for brute primitivism.

There is, for instance, the trapping of the pigeons at Echalar. Every autumn thousands of pigeons pass through the Pyrenees on their way to warmer roosts, and a large proportion of them choose the easiest crossing of all at Echalar, where the pass is low and narrow. It is the traditional custom of the Basques to lie in wait for them there, and to drive them into nets by blowing bugles, beating drums, shouting and throwing white wooden disks about. There is the appalling sport called the goose-game, now mercifully almost extinct, in which a live goose is hung by its legs from a wire above the water, and men in boats try to decapitate it with their bare hands. There are innumerable contests of strength or appetite – log-chopping, beer-swilling, stone-cutting, steak-eating.

Most famous of all, there is *pelota,* a game which for the world at large sums up the reputation of the Basques. The Basques call it *jai-alai* – 'the happy festival' – and this suggestively Japanesque title suits it, for it has a manner of violent sacrament not unlike karate. Everywhere in the Basque country, French or Spanish, the big pelota courts are prominent, like fives courts in every village: and wherever the Basques have gone they have taken the game with them, so that it has spread throughout Spain, is popular in Paris and thrives in Latin America. Nowhere can you see it more thrillingly played, or realize more vividly how close it lies to the roots of the Basque phenomenon, than in one of the great indoor courts of Bilbao, the metropolis of Basquerie.

There in the immense high-vaulted arena four young men in white bang a very hard ball against the three walls of the court. They do it with a queer hook-shaped basketwork glove, which gives them a sinister mutilated look, as though they have claws: and every time they hurl the ball out of this thing they do it with an immense physical exertion, a convulsion almost, straining every muscle, bent double with the effort, swinging the arm and its eerie hook with such momentum that when the ball leaves its socket at last – *whoosh*, it goes like a bullet, ricocheting madly here and there, off one wall, on to another, banging and bouncing and whistling and echoing – while the four young men hurl themselves, too, crazily across the court, with leaps and skids and tumbles, deftly catching the flying ball in their hooks and hurling it with paroxysms of determination back against the wall.

This is probably the most exhausting form of exercise man has ever devised. Even the spectators end a rally limp. Throughout the performance half-a-dozen bookmakers, lined up beside the court in smart blue blazers, are shouting the odds at the tops of their voices, and gesticulating to customers on the balconied seats. If somebody upstairs signals that he wishes to place a bet, the bookie throws up a rubber ball with a hole in it: the client pushes his cash inside it and chucks it back again. This activity provides an odd embroidery to the tournament, and it is conducted with an enigmatic panache that is very Basque. It is as though the four lunatics on the court, convulsed with their daemonic zest, are being watched by an audience of shrewd and genial trusties from some less ferocious ward of the institution.

In Bilbao there are public pelota tournaments twice a day – one in the afternoon, one starting at 11 p.m. It is one of the more peculiar experiences of European travel to find this unique game proceeding with such tremendous vigour in the middle of the night, played by the only people in the world who really know how to do it.

For it is the fact of Basque survival, more perhaps even than the nature of Basqueness itself, that gives this country its curious enchantment. It is like seeing nature defied. All the odds of history, of politics, of ethnic development seem to be stacked against this strange enclave, and the clash between logic and emotion, between new conformity and ancient individuality, is disturbing and sometimes strangely beautiful to see. Off the road between Vittoria and Pamplona, in the heart of the Spanish Basque country, I drove up a track one day to eat a picnic lunch: and spreading out my cheese, wine and bread-hunks on the tawny grass, I caught sight of five or six little cypress trees, planted in formal gravity upon a nearby mound. Nothing could look more quintessentially Spanish than such a group of funereal trees, all alone there in that magnificent expanse, speaking as they did of order, propriety and sacred purpose.

Taking my glass with me, I wandered across to see why they had been planted there, expecting to find some holy shrine or Civil War memorial, embellished with the official ornaments of Madrid: but when I climbed to the top of their little mound, I found something very different in the hollow at my feet. It was a stone cromlech, a prehistoric cell or burial chamber, erected there by the distant progenitors of the Basques in the days when States had not been invented, Spain had not been named and Madrid did not exist. It looked rather toad-like – greyish, speckled with lichens, squat. Authority had fenced it with those cypresses as if to reduce it to a more familiar level, like a cemetery or a commemorative slab: but the wind whistled superbly through its great boulders, and made the line of little trees seem a finicky irrelevance.

3

FANTASY OF GREATNESS

Bath, 1974

◈

*For some years in the 1970s I owned an apartment in Bath, then under
severe threat of spoliation by development. This essay was written as an
introduction to an architectural gazetteer (by Charles Robertson) which
did something, I like to think, to help stop the rot.*

There is one place in Bath, and one only, where I sometimes feel
that I am standing in a great centre of the European tradition. It
is on the south bank of the river Avon, and it is best reached by
walking up the river path beside the sports grounds. One passes
then beneath North Parade Bridge, and emerging from its
shadowy underside, fringed with ivy and ornamented by
enigmatic graffiti, one sees suddenly the heart of the city
gracefully disposed about its river.

The scene is dominated by the sound of it, for here the river
flows frothily over a weir, and its perpetual hiss always makes
me think of elaborate water-gardens in France or Austria, or the
rush of greater rivers through cities of nobler consequence. To
the left rises the square pinnacled tower of Bath Abbey, English
Perpendicular in fact, but looking from this vantage-point
squatter and stronger than it really is, and Romanesque in
posture. In front is the exquisite fancy of Pulteney Bridge, with
the windows of its shops opened over the water like a lesser
Ponte Vecchio, and the heads of a tourist or two eating cakes in
the Venetian Coffee Shop. On the left, above the wide belvedere
of Grand Parade, the bulk of the old Empire Hotel is an
unmistakable hint of Carlsbad or Baden-Baden. Gardens run
down to the water's edge, with a floral clock and deck-chairs in
them, and through the water-noise one can hear traffic on the
street above, and perhaps the thump of a brass band. There is a

steeple here, and a shallow dome there, and the brutal silhouette
of a new tourist hotel shows inevitably above the bridge: and
sometimes a man is fishing from a boat moored in the tumble of
the weir, and there are pleasure-launches or barges moored
beside the towpath. It is a scene that suggests grandeur and
decision – symphony orchestras, influential newspapers, stock
exchanges, parliaments perhaps. It feels as though up there
above the river stands one of the European fulcra, where art and
religion, history and economics combine to create a universal
artefact, common to us all.

This is an illusion. Bath has never been a great city at all, and
stands provincially aloof to the European mainstream. That
river, which suggests Seine or Volga, rises in the Cotswold
slopes twenty miles above, emerges into the Severn estuary
fifteen miles below, and Bath too is small, inconsequential, and
altogether English. It is true that the Romans, exploiting the hot
springs in this valley, made Aquae Sulis one of the best-known
of their colonial spas, and that the medieval Abbey, like all the
great English churches, grew up in close communion with its
peers across the Channel. But Bath itself, Bath of the Georgian
splendours, Bath of the golden stones and the Pump Room
minuet, the Bath that Jane Austen knew and loathed, that
Sheridan eloped from, that Gainsborough learnt his art in, that
Clive, Nelson, Pope and Mrs Thrale retreated to – Bath of the
Bath buns and the Bath chairs, Bath of the dowagers, Bath that
greets the visitor terraced and enticing as the train swings into
Spa Station down Brunel's line from Paddington – the Bath of
the persistent legend is a Somerset borough of the middle rank,
rather bigger than Annecy, say, about the size of Delft. Its
contacts with the greater world have been frequent, but tangen-
tial. A thousand years ago the first coronation of a King of all
England took place in Bath, but since then the monarchs, the
presidents and the premiers have come here only for pleasure,
escape or lesser company – an emperor in exile, a queen in
search of pregnancy, a prime minister electioneering, a king
comforting the victims of war.

Modern Bath is not, like those great archetypes, an organic
kind of city. Though it has existed on this site for nearly 2,000
years, the city we now know is more or less a fluke. For twelve
centuries after the departure of the Romans it was an ordinary
country town, distinguished from a thousand others only by the

presence of the springs, and it was a sudden flare of fashion and fortuitous genius that made it, in the eighteenth century, a city *sui generis*. For forty or fifty years, perhaps, Bath was the most fashionable resort in England, and almost everything unique about it was created then, for a particular local purpose, mostly by local men. The publicists call it Bath, the Georgian City, but Georgian Bath was hardly more than a flash-in-the-pan – a craze, a passing enthusiasm, which soon petered out as crazes do, leaving the city to potter on once more as a bourgeois West Country town, known to the world chiefly for its Roman past and its literary associations, and inhabited in the popular fancy almost entirely by retired valetudinarians.

Yet that transient flowering of fashion has left behind it one of the most handsome cities in Europe, ironically preserved by its loss of glory. This is not, like Venice or Vienna, the capital of a vanished empire, or the seat of a discredited dynasty. One cannot mourn here forgotten kings, ruined bankers, defeated marshals. Bath's function was never very significant. People came here first to cure their agues, and then to have fun. There is nothing to be sad about, as we survey Bath's towers and trees across the river. The view may be evocative, but it is not in the least disturbing, for it is only a suggestion anyway, just as the bright genius of Bath is hardly more than a beautiful display, the whim or flourish of an era.

Walk on a little further, past the new floodgate, up the winding stone staircase beside the bridge; and on the road above you will find no horseback monuments of Habsburg or Bernadotte, only agreeable little shops, and a closer view of the tourists in the coffee shop, on their second cream slice by now, and petunias in wire baskets, and the piano showroom of Messrs Duck, Son, & Pinker, and the gateway to the covered market behind the Guildhall, where Mr Bennett is licensed to sell woodcock, snipe and venison, and Mrs Reason offers her delectable and home-cooked pickled pork.

But if Power is not an attribute of Bath, Authority distinctly is – not the authority of political regimes, but the authority of manners. It is by no means a sanctimonious city: nineteenth-century Bath toughs were notorious, and Saturday night in Broad Street can still be a rumbustious celebration. It gives, though, an instant impression of order. Its very shape is logical.

Its true centre, the Abbey churchyard, stands on the site of the original Roman temple, above the hot springs themselves. Around it in a circle lies the medieval city, within the circuit of its mostly vanished walls, and spreading away in all directions, up the Lansdown slopes to the north, up Bathwick, Widcombe and Lyncombe Hills to the south, along the line of the river east and west, Georgian, Victorian and twentieth-century Bath extends itself in terraces, crescents and respectable estates. It is a compact and manageable place. It has few sprawling suburbs, and its patterns are straightforward and easy to grasp.

The Romans, of course, brought their own method here, and the plan of their Bath, now mostly buried under the city streets, seems to have been functional to a degree, with its oblong temple precinct and its systematic bathing establishment, elegantly disposed about the shrine to Sul-Minerva, patron goddess of the site. But it was the eighteenth century which, deliberately copying Roman precedents, made Bath synonymous with rational design and integrated manners. The fashionable world then adopted the spa as a gambling centre, and London society flocked to its tables, bringing their vices with them: but the enlightened if ludicrous major-domo Richard Nash, a fastidious Welsh opportunist, so disciplined them into more reasonable behaviour that his Bath set the style of an age, and permanently affected the English balance of life. Under his supervision society restrained itself, tamed its horse-squires, brought its duchesses down to earth, until the middle and upper classes actually danced with one another, and the old hierarchy was discredited for good.

'Beau' Nash's autocracy of deportment was to be miraculously translated into the stone serenity that is the architectural glory of Bath. The city's great builders of the eighteenth century were frankly speculators, spotting and satisfying a market – most of their houses were lodging houses, to be let to families visiting Bath for the season. But their progenitor, John Wood the elder, was an antiquarian too, and in building his squares and terraces he drew upon older inspirations – on the Roman example, on the Palladian disciplines, even some suggest upon ancient schemes of prehistory, with their astronomically exact circles of stone, and their arcane but determined intentions. Georgian Bath became a city of right angles or gentle curves, uniform heights, uniform materials, built into its hillsides with a classical assurance, and sometimes even managing to look, in its long unbroken expanses of column and window, Druidically reticent. Nothing could be at once more controlled and more allusive than Wood's celebrated Circus, a perfect circle with three exits, its thirty-three houses decorated with a frieze of artistic, scientific and occupational symbols, lyres, masonic tools, the Aesculapian staff: and from the air Georgian Bath looks, with its geometric patterning, the perfect diagram of civic system.

Even the florid Victorians were restrained by the reasonableness of Bath, and in their passage through the city expressed themselves classically. The Kennet and Avon Canal, duck-haunted and lily-floated now, once the highway of coal-barges and lumber-scows, passed with a calm resolution through the southern part of the city, with its fine stone locks and its truly Roman passage beneath the structure of its own headquarters, Cleveland House – where a trapdoor in the floor, we are told, allowed the administrators to pass their instructions directly into the grimy hands of the bargees sweating beneath. When I. K. Brunel drove his broad-gauge track so magnificently down the Thames Valley, coming to Bath he did as the Romans did, building his bridges and culverts and tunnels in a grandeur of fine-dressed stone, sweeping gloriously beside the river, and only pausing with the waywardness of genius to build his Bath Spa Station in a sort of castellated Tudor.

Today Bath's authority is of a weaker kind, and expresses itself chiefly in mock-Georgian buildings of a flaccid inoffensiveness. Occasionally, though, one sees in the city streets, or waiting in the station forecourt, big black limousines with flagstaffs on their bonnets, driven by chauffeurs of faintly military mien, and stepped into, when the train comes in or the luncheon is over, by men of unmistakable command. You may suppose them to be successors in some sort to the old Beau, supervisors of the city manners: but no, they are the senior bureaucrats and occasional admirals of the Navy Department, several of whose branches settled in Bath for safety's sake during the war, and have been here ever since. They do impose order of a kind on Bath, though, for they provide the city's biggest industry, and give to their scattered premises, from the Empire Hotel which is their headquarters to the massed huts and car parks of Foxhill, a recognizably tight-lipped air. What is more, they have actually brought to Bath, if only in ellipsis, a true element of power: for it is here in the Georgian city of reason that the Royal Navy designs its nuclear submarines, which prowl the oceans perpetually on our behalf, and can obliterate almost anyone almost anywhere.

But there, no city could be much less warlike than Bath, and the Vice-Admiral who generally heads the Bath naval establishment is always a popular figure at Bath civic functions, addressing Rotary Clubs or presenting prizes. Anyway Bath depends far less upon its achievements than its people. Nuclear submarines apart, Bath has discovered a new planet (Uranus), devised a new shorthand (Pitman's), invented a new biscuit (Bath Olivers), fostered a masterpiece (*Tom Jones*), given its name to a bun and an invalid chair; but in general the city prides itself much more upon its illustrious visitors. Most celebrated Britons come to Bath at one time or another, and many distinguished foreigners too, but they have seldom done much in Bath – they have simply been there. The houses of Bath burgeon with plaques recording the residence of writers and admirals, empire builders and politicians, but often they only spent a season there in rented lodgings, recuperating for another battle, or correcting proofs.

Never mind, each left his trace behind him, however shadowy, and added a little to the mystique. I see them often, those elusive shades, as I wander the city. Miss Austen looks a little disgruntled as she picks her way between the puddles towards the circulating library. Lord Nelson looks a little wan as he opens his window in Pierrepont Street to see how the wind blows. Livingstone is pursued by admirers when he returns to No. 13 Royal Crescent, from his lecture at the Mineral Water Hospital. The great Duchess of Queensbury gasps, bursts into laughter and apologizes when Beau Nash tears her point lace apron from her waist and throws it to the ladies' maids. Pope limps through the gardens of Prior Park with his host, the Bath entrepreneur Ralph Allen, whose quarries provided the stone of Bath, and whose mansion magnificently surveys it. Sir Isaac Pitman scrupulously supervises the lettering, in his own phonetic script, on his new 'PRINTIN OFIS'. Pepys taps his feet to the music of the peripatetic Bath fiddlers – 'as good as ever I heard in London almost, or anywhere: 5s'. Wolfe, at his lodgings in Trim Street, opens the letter from London which will send him to victory and death at Quebec. The exiled Emperor of Ethiopia, bolt upright in a silken cloak, disappears like a wraith on the morning train to Paddington.

They come and go to this day, celebrities of every category, still to be seen spooning the raspberry sillabub at Popjoy's, or nosing in hired Daimlers around the Lansdown terraces. Bath views them with pleasure, but with detachment. There will always be others, and anyway citizens of Bath, like retainers at some princely household, keep their own character, live their own lives, unaffected by the passing of the great. More than most of the world's cities, Bath is familiar with fame, but in a very English way it remains in its deepest essence an ordinary provincial town: and though I know of few cities less anthropomorphic in character, so that I am never tempted to call Bath 'she', or give the place human qualities of its own, still it depends for its true flavour not upon those commemorative plaques or imaginary shades, but upon its own inhabitants.

Though Bath is magnificent, you will soon find that it is more homely than proud, its personality being at odds with its appearance. This is because the Bathonian is essentially a countryman still. The Bath dialect is roundly Somerset. The Bath face is unmistakably West Country, plump, genial. Nearly everyone remarks upon the gentle Bath manners – not exactly graceful, but nearly always kind. Bath is well stocked with country things, in from the country that day, Mendip cheeses, Somerset butters, wholemeal breads from Priston Mill, rough ciders, Cotswold vegetables. Even in the central parts of the city kitchen gardens flourish, horses, cows and sometimes even sheep graze. It is only twelve miles down the road to Bristol, that gateway to the Americas, but Bath feels a thousand miles from the sea and its affairs, and is essentially a country town still, where the green hills show at the end of the street, and the country people buy their tights at Marks and Spencer's.

Bath looks so patrician that many visitors suppose it to be socially glittering still, as it was when, during the brief kingdom of Beau Nash, society preferred his court to that of the King of England. It looks, after all, like a city of great town houses, attended by cottage streets and council flats for the domestics. But again it is illusion. Grand people live in Bath, people with butlers, people with titles, people with Rolls-Royces – people with shoe factories, or useful speculative properties in South

London, or yachts in the Aegean. But they do not form a ruling caste, or even make one Bath address much better than another (though some of them would dearly like to). If you perambulate the city in the evening, peering through the half-drawn blinds and inspecting the names on doorbells, you will probably wonder what sort of people live in these parts: the answer must be – no sort. Bath still has its old-school tradespeople, kindly maiden ladies in haberdashery, or elderly white-coated grocers who ask if they may deliver the cheeses, Madam, and there is to the very courtesy of its populace a faint suggestion of old precedences: but in fact the city is a social *mélange*, all its classes jumbled, none of its addresses exclusive, hippy beside general, writer below property tycoon.

There are the officials of the Navy Department, of course, whose senior officials form perhaps the most tightly knit community of Bath, and who tend to live in the country outside, or in the villa-country of the southern slopes. There is the usual layer of provincial worthies, the solicitors, the doctors, the businessmen and their wives who provide the municipal conscience, and cover the municipal perquisites, in any such town. Retired people traditionally come to Bath: once they were likely to be rich West Indian planters, or East India merchants, and were buried beneath florid inscriptions in the Abbey, now they are usually pensioned and obscure, live among college crests or Ashanti shields in upstairs flats, and are interred in gloomy cemeteries.

There is an academic community, too, that emanates from Bath's technological university, and is inclined to inhabit bare rooms with Japanese lanterns and adjustable bookshelves – and a bearded and scrawny kind of hippy community which has made Bath a stopping place on the pilgrim routes to Glastonbury and St Ives – and a growing number of people who have come to paint, write, sculpt and meditate in Bath – and lots of teachers from Bath's innumerable schools – and all the shopkeepers, of course, and the artisans, and the workers in Bath's light industries, who provide the true constants of Bath, whose fathers and grandfathers lived in the street before them, and who feel as though they have remained totally unaffected, cheerfully grinning from their cranes, taking tea-breaks on the front stairs, or explaining why it can't be done, come rain or shine, climax or decay, since they took over the place from the Romans.

In 1974 squatters moved into an empty house in the Royal Crescent, the haughtiest of the Bath terraces, and settled there making mildly revolutionary gestures. Some of the neighbours thought this the beginning of the end, but in fact the revolution came to Bath long ago. Occasionally, it is true, I do imagine its crescents peeling and unkempt under a philistine dictatorship, or forcibly converted into workers' holiday homes, and I seem to see the last of the admirals' widows scrubbing the floors of ideological museums, and those dear old grocers' assistants surreptitiously delivering black-market butter to the back doors of lifelong customers. But I suspect it will never happen, for already the old structure is shattered, those aristocratic front doors are mostly no more than apartment block entrances, and the old styles linger on not as expressions of political form or social rigidity, but simply out of good country manners.

The hot springs of Bath, which gush from the ground at a temperature of 120°F, are the *raison d'être* of Bath. To understand what this means, one has only to go down to the Roman Baths, sunken among their perambulatories beside the Abbey, and enter the big bronze doors behind which the springs of Aquae Sulis still issue from the rock. By any standards of travel this is a profoundly moving experience, for men have been restoring themselves with these waters without a break for nearly two thousand years. 'THIS HOT SPRING USED BY THE ROMANS,' says an inscription above the door, 'HAS BEEN FROM TIME IMMEMORIAL THE PRINCIPAL SOURCE OF THE HEALTH-GIVING WATERS OF BATH'. The air is hot and clammy in there, the steam billows, but there is to that dark grotto a wonderful suggestion not merely of age, or continuity, but of solace.

Solace, in one form or another, is the truest purpose of Bath. Legend says that Prince Bladud, a hazy prince of the Britons, discovered the healing properties of the Bath springs when his leprous swine wallowed in the mud of this valley. Certainly the Romans soon discovered both the pleasures and the cures of the waters, and Aquae Sulis became a health resort well known throughout the western Empire. Though the baths themselves fell into ruin under the Saxons, and were not excavated until the nineteenth century, the springs were never forgotten: throughout the centuries of Bath's obscurity people drank and bathed in them – Charles II came in 1677, James II in 1687. One of Bath's most popular souvenirs is a print of the baths in 1675, a Hogarthian scene of squalor and vivacity, men, women and children all in the pool together, some naked, some ridiculously clothed, floating on their backs, splashing each other, diving off the conduit, while from the windows of the surrounding houses, from the balconies, all around the balustrade, the yokels of the city idly gawk. 'Methink,' wrote Pepys in 1668, 'it cannot be clean to go so many bodies together in the same water.'

Directly from the waters, too, sprang the eighteenth-century climax of Bath, though now the search for bodily health or vigour was diversified into a quest for pleasure. Bath was a place for gambling and dalliance, promenade and theatre, as well as a spa. Beau Nash was one of the sponsors of the Mineral Water Hospital, but he was far more concerned with the social life of Bath than its medical system, and so were most of his clients. Theirs was a solace of the spirit, and today too, though the Royal National Hospital for Rheumatic Diseases still pipes the waters to its treatment rooms, though Bath is full of prosperous doctors, and though most self-respecting visitors to the Pump Room take a dubious sip from the conduit ('wery strong flavour o' warm flat-irons,' Sam Weller thought), still the best purpose of the modern city is simply to give delight.

Like most pleasure-cities, Bath can be uncommonly displeasing, mostly by contrast. When the weather is wrong, or the mood jars, even the splendours of the place go sour. Then the honey-gold turns to grey, the hills look drab and lifeless, the young people seem to disappear from the streets, and Bath seems despondently sunk in its muggy valley – its sulphurous pit, as Pope called it. It can be a claustrophobic city: the hot springs underground, perhaps, give it a stifling feeling, and the orderly ranks of its terraces can look heartless and impersonal, standing there door by door in the drizzle.

But catch the right day, the right wind, and then Bath can be the very happiest city in England. The crescents and squares look no longer regimented, but benign and comradely. Then the grey deserts the stone, and the gold creeps back. The average age of the populace seems to drop by twenty years or so, the tables outside the pubs are full and lively, long skirts swish down Milsom Street, guitar music sounds from the upstairs pads of Park Street. Bath seems full of flowers then, and the little pedestrian alleys in the city centre are bright with fruit, trendy clothes and *Private Eye*, and on the green below the Royal Crescent the small boys of the Jamaican community set up their stumps and play deft and hilarious cricket in the sun.

Then the order of the place becomes not an imposition, but a liberation. As the black of a dinner-jacket sets off the bright colours of a dress, so the squares, crescents, quadrangles and circles of Bath provide a grand geometric stage for the flow of life that passes through it. Against such an imperturbable background, almost anything goes better: a military tattoo, a car rally, an outdoor performance of Molière, cricket, throwing frisbees, eating pork pies in pub gardens – Bath has the gift of heightening all activities, and giving an unexpected beauty to everyday affairs. If I am having trouble with a recalcitrant paragraph, I simply go outside and wander through the town for half an hour: and the proportions of the place, the green interventions, the honey-stone and the gentle faces soon put my adjectives in order, and calm my restless cadences.

This recuperative power resides partly in the manner of Bath – a smooth, bedside manner that is set by its Georgian dominants. It is a densely built city – no more than a couple of miles across, and rounded – and like many of the greatest architectural ensembles, like the cities of inner Spain, or the prairie clusters of the American West, its best parts have an oddly portable feel to them. So dexterously fitted are their sections to one another, so organically embedded in their setting, that one feels they could be prised *in toto* from their environment, and lifted for closer examination. All around the countryside shows, wherever you look, and this green frame accentuates the easy unity of Bath, too, as the sea undeniably gives extra point to an island.

Because of the narrow scale, the beauty of Georgian Bath depends heavily upon perspective. Depth and vista are essential to these buildings, and no city is more vulnerable to the distortion of the telephoto lens. Built on flat ground, Bath would lose half its fascination: its architectural emphasis is mostly horizontal, and the rolling hills around, the gradual slope towards the river valley, the rich green trees of park and garden, provide the necessary uprights. But there is no hint of *trompe-l'oeil* to the great buildings of Bath. They are rational, gentlemanly, straightforward buildings, thoroughly English, whose effects are achieved not by deceit, but by relationships.

One of the delights of Bath is the shift of its planes, building against building, street behind street, as though some master producer is juggling with his stage sets. Because it is not truly a great city, powerful of meaning or intent, the pace of this architectural parade can be light-hearted. One does not wish to hurry a Paris or an Edinburgh, solemn as they are with memories of faith and history, or even a New York, where humanity itself seems to have reached some kind of frenzied apotheosis. But Bath is only for fun, and anyway is so small that one can always come round a second time, so that for myself, though I love to walk about the city, I think it displays itself best of all from the windows of a slowly moving car. Then the surprises and entertainments of the place, which are essentially frivolous, move at the right cheerful pace. The smooth lines of the city masonry glide along unjogged, the crescents slide by with the proper sensuous motion, and the serendipities of Bath fall thick and fast.

Of these the most celebrated occurs at the end of Brock Street, on the lower slope of Lansdown. It is among the most famous of architectural surprises, and provides one of the happiest moments of European sightseeing. I experience it myself a couple of hundred times a year, but I never tire of it. This Bath moment especially is best observed by car, and I like to do it with the roof open and something blithe and brilliant on the tape – Mozart, Mendelssohn, or Astaire singing Cole Porter. Then I swing exuberantly around the Circus, beneath the marvellous centrepiece of planes (cocking a snook as I go at those grim purists who would chop them down for architecture's sake), and head down the short, straight link road called Brock Street. I pretend I have never been there before, and for visual reasons drive slap down the middle of the street. At the end there seems to be a vacancy – cloud, trees, a snatch of green, the corner of a large house protruding slightly in the middle distance, a transverse terrace beyond. Is it a park? Is it a football ground? Is it a demolition site? The plan gives nothing away; the vacancy remains vacant; only that sense of impending space grows as I approach the end of the road; and then, narrowly avoiding the Mini which, in a less exuberant condition, emerges aghast from Church Street, I top the barely perceptible rise, ease myself round the corner, and find before me one of the most splendid *tours de force* of European design, the Royal Crescent.

It lies there in a shallow arc, its wide lawns running away beyond the ha-ha down the hill below, and all is suddenly space, and green, and leisure. Though the Crescent is architecture on a truly palatial scale, and reminds many people of Versailles, to me it suggests far more pungently the seaside. It is like the grandest of all rows of seaside villas, standing on a promenade before a sea of grass: the children bathe on the green below, the householders walk their dogs along the beach, and the sign that enjoins No Organized Games is merely a delicate way of saying that if you are looking for What The Butler Saw, try the pier. I have seen visitors stopped in their tracks as, turning that same corner of Brock Street, they have discovered this glorious scene in front of them: and the look of astonished delight upon their faces is just the look the holiday-makers have when, tumbling from the train and walking down Beach Street from the station, they have reached the esplanade that is their destination, and see the sands, all balloons, whelks and motor-boat trips, there in the sun before them.

No *trompe-l'oeil*: but if the charm of Bath is not deceptive, it is unexpectedly intricate. It relies upon contrast, for all among those splendid set-pieces, wedged in here and there, corners of quirk or curiosity provide a filigree. Narrow steps and alleys lead the eye to greater spectacles; railings, brackets, details of stone and ironwork throw into grander relief the classical frontages behind; artisan cottages correct the scale of things; grace-notes relieve the splendour. Symmetries are broken. Incongruities occur. Much of this complicated sub-Bath, the civic undergrowth, has lately been destroyed, sometimes for good social reasons, more often because of planners' *naïveté*, developers' greed and architects' sterility. Just enough remains to preserve the flavour. There are enclaves of petty Georgian, like Beaufort Square, behind the Theatre Royal, which possesses a crooked, almost edible allure, as though all its little houses are made of pastry. There are follies, like Beckford's Tower on Lansdown Hill, or Allen's Sham Castle across the valley. There are streets like Walcot Street, beside the river, which begins with a bang in the jolly Hat and Feather, ends in a whimper with the hapless new Beaufort Hotel, but contains in its short length a heady jumble of chapels, terraces, junk shops, hippy hang-outs, derelict gardens, old steps, gates that go nowhere, cul-de-sacs, an arcaded corn market, a green graveyard – the whole made fragrant by the smell of new bread from the Red House Bakery and raw meat from the cold storage depot, and sneeringly overlooked by the immense curve of the Paragon above.

Take Lansdown Crescent, which stands regally on the upper Lansdown slopes, white-painted and festively illuminated by its own wrought-iron gate lamps. Lansdown has more panache than the Royal Crescent, with its undulating double curves and its rising and falling ground, but it is still very magnificent, and stylishly inhabited. Butlers and judges are to be found in these fine houses, rich manufacturers, bankers' widows, art historians. One house is furnished basement to attic entirely in the Georgian mode, and to the house once inhabited by the mystic Francis Younghusband a hardly less visionary American has brought a new kind of civilized living to Bath, part Japanese, part Manhattan, with a square sunken bath in the Roman kind, and a carpeted, sun-decked penthouse of delightful indulgence.

Yet this famous crescent is embedded in crinklier matter. Directly in front of those magnificent houses, an unkempt meadow tumbles steeply down the escarpment, infested by nettles and thistles, and grazed by horses, heifers, sometimes even sheep. Directly behind them, a gnome-like settlement flourishes. There are converted stables with creepers winding round their drain-pipes, and little cobbled yards with children's tricycles in them, and ivy-locked garden gates, and damp dead-end passages, and apple-trees, and motor-scooters in sheds, and summer-houses through whose windows, impenitently peering, one may discover half-completed water-colours, animal skulls, old pianos or book-presses. It is like another country back there, or a colony of churls and craftsmen in the purlieus of a princely court.

Or consider the piazzetta at the heart of Bath – the Abbey churchyard, site of the altar of Sul-Minerva, which one best enters under the colonnade from Stall Street. This lies in the middle of Bath's downtown circumstance, such as it it. One side of the little square is formed by the façade of the Pump Room, another consists of eighteenth-century shops, and the end is blocked by the imposing west front of the Abbey, with its huge carved door and its angels tumbling up and down their ladders to heaven.

It is quite a noble arrangement, but if the frame is monumental, the scene is miniature – like a toy piazza. On a summer day its benches are usually crowded with tourists, shoppers and idlers. A little bar is set up in the shadow of the colonnade, with sunshades and rows of bottles, and groups of very foreign visitors wander in and out of the Pump Room doors, in and out of the dark Abbey, gazing into the souvenir shops or wondering whether to commission a plaque to their family arms from Mr Howe on the corner. It is, though, fundamentally a domestic scene. The Abbey front towers above it all, but still there are prams about, and housewives gossiping over their coffee. You can have your hair done here, or order a pair of spectacles, and above the premises of Alfred Shore & Sons ('Distinction in Dress Shoes') one may sometimes see Mr Greenwood the dentist actually at his drill. Napoleon called St Mark's Square the finest drawing-room in Europe, but the Abbey churchyard is no more than the most agreeable parlour in England, a little place, an intimate place, a place to chat or sew in, or decide what to get for supper.

There is a poignancy to this diminutive side of Bath, or if not a poignancy, a wistfulness. Come inside the Pump Room, now. The Pump Room Trio is performing, as it does every weekday morning, and the handsome room is full of visitors, drinking fairly muddy coffee, sampling the spa water from the tap in the bay window, or looking down to the water of the King's Bath outside. Kindly waitresses bustle about, the tall Tompion clock ticks away against the wall, Beau Nash stares superciliously from his statue in its niche. The musicians play on stage behind a palisade of geraniums, potted palms on a balcony above their heads, and I often go down there to enjoy their company, correcting a manuscript over my coffee, or just observing the scene. It is not only that they play 'Rosemarie', 'Oklahoma' or 'Perchance to Dream' with a splendid enthusiasm: it is also because they seem to represent a culture that has almost died – a lost, innocent culture, fitfully and nostalgically surviving here. They must be almost the last café trio still performing in Great Britain; I take many visitors to hear them, and they often make a deeper impression than the Roman Baths.

This is a melancholy pleasure, but then some of Bath's fascination is melancholy. Before the Second World War it was a much sadder place than it is now, and old photographs show it drab, blackened and down-at-heel, even its prodigies looking sadly neglected, and its detail obscured with dirt and excrescences. But even today, though most of it is spick and span, it often has a sadness to it. People analyse this in different ways. Some think it is just nostalgia for the eighteenth century, which seems so close in Bath, but is really so far away. Some put it down to the climate, which can be horrid. Some again are depressed by the introspective feel of the place, or are enervated by the uniformity of its stone. Some dislike its museum feeling. Some are desolated by its changes, and one or two I have met are placed at a particular disadvantage by their distaste for Georgian architecture.

I myself attribute the sensation to an unfulfilment in Bath. Since the end of the eighteenth century, and the departure of the fashionable to newer and racier resorts, Bath has never recaptured its purpose – or rather, the particular purpose that the Georgians gave it, and for which their glories were designed. Bath is only a bourgeois Somerset town, dressed like a capital: a city built for art and pleasure, trying to be a Regional Shopping Centre. There are attempts to make it more – the Festival of the Arts, the Arts Workshop, the Bath Preservation Trust, the American Museum. Bath has many devoted amateurs, and several well-intentioned patrons. The City Fathers, though, are reluctant to accept its hedonist place in the world, so that it remains something of a façade. Its palaces are not palaces, only blocks of flats. Its Abbey is only a parish church. Its Festival happens once a year, and when it is over the performers and choreographers, arrangers and composers disperse again, leaving the city to the Pump Room Trio and the electronic organ in the Parade Gardens.

The backs of Bath buildings are very revealing. A few of the swankiest terraces are grand behind too, but for the most part Bath's builders did not much care about rear elevations, and successive improvers and developers have stuck their additions haphazardly on the back walls, giving half Bath a hodge-podge, job-lot look which I particularly like. The back of Marlborough Buildings offers one such spectacle. This is a large range of terrace houses, built speculatively in the late 1780s. From the front it looks decorous, especially No. 9 (where I live). From the back it looks an enthralling muddle. There are allotment gardens back there, and if you stroll among their beans and chrysanthemums, looking up to the massive wall of masonry above, the effect is troglodytic. It is as though a natural rock-face stands there, pitted with the thousand caves and burrows that are its windows. There are thirty-three houses in the row, and from the back all look different. Some have six floors, some five. Some are impeccably maintained, some look like slums. Their windows are splodged or hacked almost indeterminately across the cliff, and there are balconies stuck on here and there, and outhouses, and jutting alcoves like Turkish *mahrabiyas*, and sham windows here, and blocked doors there, and racks for flower-boxes, and washing-lines, and sometimes the curtains look richly velvet, and sometimes they appear to consist of a couple of discarded blankets strung up on cord.

In another city those little private havens would be full of purpose, and Marlborough Buildings does of course house its quota of business people, civil servants, students, even a writer or two. But Bath lacks the tautness of a truly functional city, a city that fits its own buildings, and when I stroll back there in the evening I often think what a melancholy diffusion of energy that cliff face represents. How many of those windows, I think, represent not a purpose, but a lack of it! Widows, childless divorcees, elderly unmarried ladies, dilettanti, pensioners, the retired – Bath is full of lonely people without occupations, counting the days until their grandchildren come to call, killing the evening with television, gin or marijuana, plotting another bridge party, waiting for bingo, or setting off down the hill for an hour with the Pump Room Trio. Every city has its share of the purposeless, but by the nature of things Bath has more than most, and the saddest of the bellpush names, I think, are those whose faded pride lives on in a polished but almost indecipherable brass plate, or a visiting card engraved in the deep copperplate of long ago.

This human emptiness has its physical counterpart too. If much of Bath is newly restored, much is hangdog still. There are houses never rebuilt since the blitz, or awaiting, year after year, planning permission or builders' cash. There are abandoned churches up for sale. Through the cracks of stately flagstone tufts of grass spring through, and sometimes the corner of a garden, the elbow of an alley, is choked with creeper and bramble, as though a civilization has retreated here, and the weeds are taking over. It is another illusion of course – Bath is in better shape than it has been for many decades: but still the *tristesse* is real, in this city that is too splendid for itself, and often it creeps through Bath in the late afternoon, or one awakes to find it hanging over the city like a cloud, deadening the repartee of the milkman, and sending many of the old ladies, I suspect, sensibly back to bed again.

I am thinking chiefly of public Bath, prodigy Bath, those districts of the city that were specifically built for its eighteenth-century climax. Elsewhere, of course, the older, more modest functions of the town survive as always, and all the structure of an English country borough has been handed down undisturbed from the Middle Ages. One pleasant way to sense this other Bath, I think, is to desert the Lansdown slopes and the city centre, where the tourists swarm, and cross the river, the railway and the canal to the hills of the southern side. Here is another city altogether, hardly less beautiful in its less showy way, and closer perhaps to the inner spirit of the place, which has resisted so many shifts of fortune, and remains essentially quiet and countrified.

There are terraces over there, and cottages, and new housing estates, and there used to be some fairly rugged slums, but it is above all villa country on the slopes of the southern hills. Scattered through the trees towards Claverton scores of half-Italianate, half-Regency villas stand among their gardens, some luxurious, some modest, all very private. They are lived in by families, most of them, not divided into flats, and they retain a sprightly and comfortable air. They are not show houses. They are real. Children play in their gardens, and the paterfamilias drives home from the office in his Rover. Here one realizes the true social condition of Bath: an unexceptional country town beneath it all, with its own private pedigree of burgher, tradesman and labourer, its own civic preoccupations, its own narrow coteries and rivalries, come legionary, come Beau.

Only the presence of lost genius makes it special, elevating it to a status far above itself, and the best place of all, I think, to enjoy this pungent and ironic state of affairs, where the ordinary meets the superb, the parochial touches the international, is at Widcombe, in the heart of the villa country. This is one of those ancient country hamlets which have been absorbed into the fabric of the city, and it is recognizably a village still, with its church, its manor house and its village war memorial. Widcombe feels immensely old, and stable in a rural way, as though it recognizes deep in its stones and roots that the business of life is living itself.

Beside the church a lane leads steeply up the hill. It meanders on for a couple of hundred yards, and then comes to a halt at an iron gate beside some cottages. To my mind this is the most Bathonian place in Bath, truer by far to the city's spirit than that metropolitan view beside the river, and more telling than any contrived delight of the Lansdown crescents. The cottages beside you are true country cottages, *rus in urbe*, with moss-grown steps and cherished vegetable gardens. Green fields rise all about, giving the dell a properly nooky feel, and through the gates one may see a gamekeeper's cottage, and a sedgy lake with swans, ducks and moorhens on it.

It is a gentle scene, part country, part town, and unpretentiously assured: but beyond the lake there stands something very different – the exquisite little Palladian bridge, roofed and pillared, built long ago for the delectation of Ralph Allen, when he walked with his guests in his mansion high above. It is a little golden structure, all by itself in the green, which stands there with an air of mock innocence, but which speaks of Rome and Vicenza, Pope and Goldsmith, minuets and royal visits, and all the heady ideas, idioms and experiences which have, down the centuries, brought to this modest English town a fantasy of greatness, and by fostering it with such grace, fun and harmony, made the illusion true.

4

THE IMPOSSIBLE CITY

Beirut, 1956

I make no apologies for this over-blown essay. It was written in true affection long ago, and for all its gush and hyperbole seems to me a fair portrait still of a city now made unrecognizable by catastrophe. In Memoriam . . .

Beirut is the impossible city, in several senses of the adjective. It is impossible in the enchantment of its setting, where the Lebanese mountains meet the Mediterranean. It is impossible in its headiness of character, its irresponsible gaiety, its humid prevarications. It is impossible economically, incorrigibly prospering under a system condemned by many serious theorists as utterly unworkable. Just as the bumble-bee is aerodynamically incapable of flying, so Beirut, by all the rules and precedents, has no right to exist.

Yet there it stands, with a toss of curls and a flounce of skirts, a Carmen among the cities. It is the last of the Middle Eastern fleshpots, and it lives its life with an intensity and a frivolity almost forgotten in our earnest generation. It has inherited some of the style of Alexandria, that queen of Mediterranean ports, now relegated by history to African provincialism, and nowadays it is to Beirut that all the divinities of this haunted seaboard, the fauns and dryads and money-gods, orgiastically descend. Beirut is a tireless pleasure-drome. It is a junction of intrigue and speculation. It is a university city of old distinction. It is a harbour, a brothel, an observatory on the edge of the Arab deserts. Its origins are ancient but it burgeons with brash modernity, and it lounges upon its delectable shore, half-way between the Israelis and the Syrians, in a posture that no such city, at such a latitude, in such a moment of history, has any reasonable excuse for assuming. To the stern student of affairs, Beirut is a phenomenon beguiling perhaps, but quite, quite impossible.

It is the capital of Lebanon, a small strip of hilly territory on the edge of Syria, between the sea and the deserts. It stands on no great river, commands no industrious hinterland, and all through the centuries it has been chiefly significant as a gateway and a conduit, the threshold of Damascus and the outlet of Syria. It has been a halting place or transit camp, through which successive civilizations have briefly tramped, leaving a stele here, a carving there, a legend in a library or a pill-box on a beach. Egyptians, Phoenicians, Assyrians, Hittites, Persians, Greeks, Romans, Arabs, Crusaders, Turks, Frenchmen, Britons, Americans – the armies or administrators of them all have passed this way, from the Pharaonic commissaries who bought their cedarwood in these parts to the United States marines who, in the 1950s, scrambled up the Beirut beaches from the ships of the Sixth Fleet. In its time Beirut has been a Giblite market, a Roman garrison town, a Phoenician metropolis, a Saracen fortress, a Crusader bishopric, an Egyptian outpost, a Turkish prefecture, a Syrian emirate, a French mandatory headquarters, a republican capital. It is a city of wide experience, but travels light.

A stele, a legend, a pill-box – nothing much more substantial has been left behind by the conquerors, for the texture of Beirut is flaky and unretentive. Earthquakes and fires have destroyed much of its heritage, but mostly it is the character of the place that makes this a city without a visible past. Beirut tastes, but seldom absorbs. It is always contemporary, shifting and tacking to the winds of circumstance. It is the capital of a state that is half Christian, half Muslim, and it remains poised between the Eastern way and the Western, between the Francophile and the Afro-Asian, between the suave hotels that line the waterfront and the tumbled Oriental villages spilled on the hillside above. It is not one of your schizophrenic cities: on the contrary, it has triumphantly exploited its own dichotomies, and become the smoothest and most seductive of entrepreneurs. Everything is grist to this mill: a crate of steel bolts, a letter of credit, a poem, a navigational system, a cocktail, a tone of voice, a power press, a soup – Beirut accepts them all, processes them if necessary, and passes them on at a profit.

It lives by standing in the middle, and by the itchiest of itchy palms. There is almost nothing the city will not undertake. It will pass your wheat inland to Damascus, or ship your oil westward to Hamburg. It will paint your upperworks, translate your thesis, introduce you to the Sheikh of Araby, accommodate you in pampered splendour in an air-conditioned suite beside the water. It will perform your atonal music at an open-air festival, or feed you with unreliable statistics about political controversies in Zagazig. It will, without a flicker of surprise, convert your Norwegian travellers' cheques into Indian rupees and Maria Theresa dollars. It has nothing of its own, no resources of iron or coal, no factories to speak of, no big battalions, but it will do almost anything you ask of it, providing you pay properly.

No, that's unfair – it is not all for cash. Beirut is also an entrepôt of ideas, linking the bazaars with Cambridge and the Sorbonne. From the hills above this city the poet Flecker used to watch his old ships sail, 'like swans asleep . . . for Famagusta and the hidden sun': and just as those dim vessels reminded him of Grecian glories, so the cool white ships that sail today for Venice and the Piraeus seem like couriers between the cultures. Every shift of Western thought is reflected in the conversations of Beirut (which lies well to the east of Cairo and Leningrad alike), every audacity from the Left Bank or Greenwich Village is rehashed here with relish. One of the great law schools of antiquity flourished in this place, and today Beirut is still host to two of the best universities in the Middle East. It is a mongrel city, but among mongrels it is a thoroughbred: under its influence many a pair of notions has gently fused, many opposites have been reconciled. Whether a man comes from Peking or Pittsburgh, he will soon find some corner of this liberal place where, lapped in eroticism or deep in the discussion of philosophic concepts, he is sure to feel at home. There is a tang in the Beirut air, bitter-sweet but easy-going, that survives nowhere else on earth: for it is compounded of an old alliance between East and West, washed in the humanism of the ancients and bathed in the incomparable Mediterranean sunshine. It is the spirit that created old Alexandria, and it makes Beirut, for

every lover of the classical mode, for every man of generous
instinct, a city of nostalgic regret.

Regret always, for Beirut is a prodigy of the second class – a
sideline city, never (as the literary critics like to say) very deeply
engagé. It stands on the rim of the Arab world, peering inside
with a wry and sceptical detachment, and its conscience is
rudimentary.

All this undeniably makes for fun. Glittering hotels form the
breastworks of Beirut, a clutter of banks is its keep, and sooner
or later every Middle Eastern bigwig strays this way, loud-
mouthed or surreptitiously. Here you may see the political
exiles, talking dark and interminable subterfuge, or the resplendent hawk-nosed sheikhs, in all the gilded refulgence of the
Arab patrimony, fingering their beads and indulging in flamboyant bickerings. Here are the silken ladies of Syria, svelte and
doe-eyed, Francophile to their last delicate gasp, and devoted to
Bernard Buffet; and here are the waterside harlots, curled but
smouldering, Semite with a touch of baroque. There are many
poets in Beirut, and artists of visionary tendencies, shaggy
existentialists in frayed sandals, dilettantes by the score, spies
by the portfolio. Sometimes you may see Druse tribesmen in the
city, out of the eastern hills, ferociously hirsute and gloriously
swaggering. Sometimes the fleet puts in (British, American,
French or Greek) and the waterfront bars are loud with ribaldry.
And when one of the perennial Middle Eastern crises erupts
into the headlines, then the imperturbable hotels of Beirut are
crammed again with foreign correspondents, the hall porters
brush up their jargon and sniff around for tittle-tattle, and the
whole city seems transformed into one sensitive, quivering
antenna.

But in Beirut you are seldom in the heart of things. The
firemen are always visiting, the crisis is usually somewhere else.
The oil comes from Mesopotamia, the machinery is going to
Syria, the dancing girls are supplied by an agent in Soho. Beirut
feels a transitory place, like an exceedingly corrupt and sophisticated girls' school. Such a way of life, you feel, cannot be
permanent: it is all too fickle, too fast, too make-believe and
never-never. It is Alexandria without the philosophers, without
the astronomers, without the Pharos, perhaps even without
Cleopatra (for age does distinctly wither the *grandes dames* of

Beirut, waddling with poodles and sun-glasses from salon to couturier). For all its age and history, for all its scholarly eminence, Beirut feels a rootless city – salacious but not earthy, virile but infertile. A breath of wind, it seems, a shift of fortune, and all this bright-painted fabric would be whisked away into oblivion, like the countless predecessor cities of this Phoenician shore.

Such is the nature of the place. Beirut itself would not have it otherwise, for the real purpose of this city is hedonism. The world comes here for pleasure: to live it up, to make money, to bump into friends and enemies, to water-ski or bask in moonlight ecstasies. The energies of the capital are geared to such aspirations, and even the ravishing climate conforms. No ascete could flourish in such a setting, no fervid demagogue can keep it up for long, and all the strident passions of our time, transmuted from violence or grandiloquence, are tamed here into sultry back-chat, boudoir rivalry and skulduggery. Beirut has none of the power of Cairo, and none of the defiant derring-do that gives to little Amman, away to the south-east, some of the dusty stimulation of a frontier town. When a political climax bursts upon Beirut, it is generally a climax of the parish pump. When a limousine speeds resplendently across the Place des Martyrs, it is not usually a dictator or a lordly general hastening into cabal, but only a playboy passing by. Beirut is the small capital of an infinitesimal republic, and its events do not often feel crucial. Give it time, Beirut always whispers, don't fuss, wait and see, have a drink. You can usually find a blind eye here, a hole in the corner, the back of a hand, the underneath of a counter. This is not an earnest city. Proper Victorians would have hated it. Harvard economists or British Civil Servants, examining its improbable methods, its flibberty-gibbet charm, its blatancy and its blarney – men of sombre purpose, deposited one scented evening in Beirut, would probably pronounce it irredeemable.

But who would redeem such a place, in a world of false redemptions? Club-women and bluestockings infest our age, but the frank and lovely libertine still makes the heart lift. Such a heedless delight, such a glint in a blithe eye, is the gift of Beirut. This is a city without much soul, but with allure immeasurable, and above all it is graced by a celestial beauty of setting: beauty of a classic and timeless kind, a blue and wine-dark kind, with bewitchment such as you dream about in long damp northern evenings, as you pine for a beaker of the warm south. The city of Beirut often feels second-rate, but the setting of Beirut is superlative. 'Dream-shadow-dim' is how Flecker described this shoreline:

> Where Kings of Tyre and Kings of Tyre did rule
> In ancient days in endless dynasty.
> And all around the snowy mountains swim
> Like mighty swans afloat in heaven's pool.

At this point on the Levantine coast the mountains of Lebanon stand in magnificent parallel beside the sea, so close that the citizens of Beirut may, if the wild whim takes them, ski in the morning and swim in the afternoon. It is the presence of these fine hills, all around the city, that elevates Beirut from the entertaining to the sublime, and provides, in its contrast between the ephemeral and the eternal, a marvellous foil to the bubbling frivolity of the metropolis.

Imagine a terrace table beside the sea in Beirut, during the brief moment of the Mediterranean twilight, when the shops are raising their shutters for the evening's business, and your restaurant rustles with the first silks and sibilances of the night. There are prawns on your table, perhaps, or red mullet from Sidon, fruit from the lush Bekaa valley, a gay white wine of Lebanon or some haughty vintage out of France. Around the bay the city rumbles, hoots and chatters: there is a clink of metal from some unseen smithy, a suggestion of spice and raw fish on the breeze, the echo of a blaring radio beyond the promenade, a distant clanging of trams – all the hot, heavy, breathless symptoms of an expiring Levantine day, like a sigh in the sunset. Below you the last of the water-skiers scuds home in a flurry of spray, showing off to the girls on the beach. Out at sea a tall elderly schooner loiters, like a ghost in the half-light, and beyond the breakwater, perhaps, a graceful Italian liner steals out for Greece, with a soft tread of her turbines and a flutter of her flags. Sometimes an airliner labours in from the sea, blinking its red lights as it lands beyond the cedar groves, and sometimes a razzle-dazzle sports car, top-heavy with blondes and young muscle-men, screams and skids along the corniche towards the night clubs. All along the shore the tall white buildings stand, concrete and rectilinear, with their parasols and their lighted balconies, their dim-lit bars and their muffled music. Away over the shopping street there flickers the radiance of the neon lights, orange and blue and scarlet, flashing through the city's glow.

Now, before the night comes, while the evening is still purple and hazy, while the velvet twilight lasts – now you may taste the impossible beauty of Beirut: for rising in strides above the capital, in serried terraces, above the skyscrapers, above the last suburbs, above the olive groves, above the foothill villages, above the winding Damascus road – there, lording it above sea and city, stand the mountains, 'afloat in heaven's pool'. A sheen of snow hovers about their high ridges, and their tawny slopes tumble away through scree and field and olive grove to the Mediterranean below. Beneath their serenity Beirut festers and celebrates: and even as you watch, sipping your wine or toying with your fish, the lights go on like star clusters in the villages of the hills, higher and higher up the slopes, until at last the dark falls, the end of the sunset fades, and away above Beirut only the snow of the summits remains like a dim corona in the night.

5

THE SCENE OF AN ACCIDENT

Berlin, 1957

✧

*Whether I came to Berlin out of the east (bringing caviare from Moscow)
or out of the west (in a lumbering DC3) the city never failed to chill me.
Divided though it was physically and ideologically, in the decade after
the Second World War it still seemed to possess an all too terrible unity.*

Berlin is the centre city of Europe – some might say of the world
– and Berlin's heart is the stark, scarred archway called the
Brandenburger Tor: not because it stands upon the last frontier
of the West, the very line where Ulbricht built his Wall, but
because, poised as it thus is between two overwhelming alien
philosophies, it remains quintessentially German. It is a harsh
and hated monument, but at least it feels real.

For though Berlin is an exciting and an ominous place,
divided as it is both by masonry and by method, yet for me it
feels chiefly like a queer façade. It is a stage-prop city. In the
east it reads its Communist lines, in the west its libertarian, to
a thump of dogmas or a tinkle of profit: but in neither rôle does
it feel quite natural. Not so long ago its subject territories
extended from the Atlantic to the Caucasus, and it had a brutal
ideology of its own. Today it has become a kind of nightmare
fair, where the two halves of the world meet to set up their
pavilions. There is an emptiness and a pretence to its spirit, as
though the meaning of the place was forcibly ripped out twenty
years ago, and replaced only by slogans and sealing-wax.

It is fashionable to say that Berlin is no longer neurotic, but I
cannot agree. This feels to me a terribly mixed-up metropolis,
tortured by old anxieties or inhibitions, and understandably
shot through with fear. That the Berliners have guts, diligence
and realism nobody can deny. They have an almost cockney

gaiety to them, an almost chirpy bonhomie, and they seem, on the face of things, undismayed by their ferocious ups and downs of fortune. But beneath their genial public veneer, I suspect, they cherish darker layers of emotion: cynicism, self-disgust, shattered pride, morbid resolution. Some people say the difference between East Berlin and West Berlin is the difference between light and shade. To me, though the transition from one to the other is shattering to endure, nevertheless they both feel at once dark and floodlit, like the scene of an accident.

Berlin is the capital of a lost empire, and its imperial past lies like a helmeted skeleton in a cupboard. The city forms on one side the capital of the Democratic Republic of East Germany, on the other a province of the Federal German Republic: but the Germanness of it survives by sufferance, by suggestion, by retrospection. In the eastern sector the placards and the exhortations, the State shops and the Khrushchev posters, the slit-eyed arrogance of Leninallee bring to the purlieus of the old Unter den Linden an oily whiff of Asia. In the west all the gallimaufry of the American world prances and preens itself: neon signs, juke boxes, *Time*, apartments by Corbusier, hotel rooms by Conrad Hilton, paperbacks, pony-tails, dry martinis and Brigitte Bardot. The old Germany lives on underground, surfacing sometimes in a splendid opera, a Schiller play, a melody or a neo-Nazi.

On the one side the East Berliners find themselves remoulded, month by month, year by year, crisis by crisis, into a new kind of people – brainwashed, as it were, *en masse* and by force of habit. On the other, the West Berliners have become walking symbols: inhabitants of a city that has no economic meaning, no geographical sense, no certainties and no security, but which is kept alive like some doomed and cadaverous magnate, just to spite the beneficiaries. Few Berliners seem to suppose that their city will ever again be the capital of a free united Germany. The East Berliners live for the hour, or the party meeting after work. The West Berliners accept what a paradoxical fortune offers them, and move blithely enough through life, like fish in a glittering goldfish bowl.

It remains, though, a single city, and there is no disguising its traumatic quality, its mingled sense of ignominy, defiance, futility and pathos. The horrible wall that bifurcates Berlin has not yet, not quite yet, destroyed its essential unity; every now and then somebody tunnels beneath the barrier, or vaults desperately over it, and another few years must pass before the last of the old ladies climbs her step-ladder to wave her white handkerchief forlornly to the other side. Bitterly mordant are the comments of the Berliners when they show you around their boulevards. Their jokes are coarse and often cruel, their allusions streaked with self-mockery. Caustically they tell you that each side of the Brandenburger Tor calls itself democratic – the East with a capital D, the West with a small one. Wryly they observe that the Perpetual Flame of Freedom uses an awful lot of gas. Almost apologetically they point to Tempelhof, still the most astonishing of the world's airports, as 'the one good job that Hitler did'. They sound resigned but secretly resentful. They know what you are thinking.

For in a way their city remains, to this day, a constant and terrible reproach against all that Germany has meant to the twentieth century – a reminder that in our times German values have been rotten values. Berlin, east and west, is a city built upon the ruins of Germany, watered with German tears, haunted by the shades of a million lost young men, a million lost illusions, the ghost of a dead and discredited patriotism. It is the most melancholy of cities, and for myself, I find its neuroses ever apparent: in the almost obsessive pride, for example, that Berliners have in their zoo, deposited in the very middle of the city, and famous for its shackled elephants; in the passion for flowers that blooms so eerily in this most warlike and fearful of capitals; in the flashy extravagance of the western sectors and the dullened apathy of the east; in the inevitable, ever-growing alienation of one side from the other; in the flushed contrast between Berlin's urban preoccupations and the impeccable park-like countryside that lies outside its gates; in the absolute stunned silence with which, when I was once in the city, the cinema audience filed out from the ghastly film *Mein Kampf*, an appalling laceration of German pride and self-respect.

So it is I say that Berlin's heart is the Brandenburger Tor, with the great Quadriga restored but hardly regnant upon the top of it. Around that symbol of old pomp the real Berlin still stands: the gaping Reichstag, the ruined Wilhelmstrasse, the shells of broken cathedrals and shattered palaces, Göring's offices and Hitler's bunker, the tumbled halls of the Third Reich, the grave of a lost empire. Anything may happen to Berlin in the second half of our century; but whoever rules it, until the shades of that dreadful capital are exorcized at last, until the very memory of it is dim, all the brilliance and bluster of the new city will be sham, and its spirit will never be easy.

6

SERENDIB

Ceylon (Sri Lanka), 1967

❦

They called it Ceylon then, and it was still recognizably a post-colonial island: although there were already signs of the racial schism which was later to debilitate it, I found it perfectly easy to ignore them, and thought it a very proper place to have given its name to the concept of serendipity.

At my window, a shiny-feathered crow; outside, an elderly steam locomotive sporadically snorting; palm trees in the yard, a glimpse of sea, the beginning of a heat haze, four or five distant swathed figures foraging upon the beach. The old electric fan above my head creaked protestingly every third time round. The servant who brought my breakfast shuffled comfortably about in sandals. There was a smell of eggs and bacon from below. I was awakening to a morning in Ceylon, from whose medieval name, Serendib, Horace Walpole derived the abstract noun *serendipity* – the faculty, as the *Oxford Dictionary* has it, 'of making happy and unexpected discoveries by accident'.

Not every Ceylonese discovery is happy, for this is an island that has seen better days, and has lately been depressed by addled politics and false finance. Unexpected, though, Ceylon certainly is – a fascinating anomaly of the Indian Ocean, a humped oval island not far north of the equator, with some of the most exquisite scenery in the world and a mountain so holy, to devotees of several religions, that even the agnostic butterflies hazily meander there, when they feel the death-urge coming on.

Northern Ceylon is actually joined to southern India by a chain of sandy reefs called Adam's Bridge, yet the two countries scarcely feel in the same continent. Ceylon is plump, genial, richly vegetated. Ceylon is small – two thirds the size of Ireland, with ten-and-a-half million people. Ceylon has always given pleasure: to the ancient Indians it was Lanka, the Resplendent Land, to the Moors the Isle of Delight, to the Chinese the Jewelled Island, to the Victorians the Pearl of the Indian Ocean, and even the sensible Dutch thought the shape of the place reminiscent of a dressed ham hanging from the rafters. Spices, rubies, beautiful slaves, aromatic teas have been staples of Ceylon down the centuries. A gently festive air seems to linger over the island, whatever the excesses of its politicians, and leaves in almost every visitor's mind an impression of balanced serenity.

In fact the island's history has been distinctly rumpled. The Hindu epics peopled Ceylon ferociously with demon-kings and monkey-armies, and in recorded times Indians, Portuguese, Dutchmen and Britons have all invaded the island, with varying degrees of penetration – until the British deposed it by force in 1815 there was still an independent dynasty of kings in the valleys of the interior. Hundreds of thousands of Indian Tamils have crossed the narrow strait to settle in Ceylon, and the island races have been so piquantly compounded that when I recently looked up the directors of a Ceylonese firm called Tuckers Ltd, I discovered that their names included Kotswala, Aloysius, Fernando and Mrs Mavis Tucker herself. Catholicism has been strong since the first European conquests, Hinduism thrives among the Tamils, and the clash and flare of the devil-dancers still enlivens the street corners of the island, and comforts its timorous villagers.

It is Buddhism, though, which sets the calm tone of Ceylon, and so differentiates it from the frenzied peninsula to the north. Buddhism came to the island from India in the third century BC, when the Ceylonese king, Tissa, was converted by a missionary from India. The sweet legends of the faith infuse the place now, its great ruined cities still meditate in the jungles, and its gentleness still makes the start of a Ceylonese day, whatever the newspaper headlines are screaming, a pleasant prod to one's serendipity. The waiter put down my breakfast that morning, and said he hoped I would have an enjoyable day. I told him I was going to make a pilgrimage to the grave of my father-in-law, a planter who had died in Ceylon during the war.

'By God,' he said at once, 'that's good, that's very good –

parents is a bigger thing than the Lord Buddha himself': and picking up my shoes, to clean them for the occasion, he bowed gracefully and withdrew.

On an artificial lake in the middle of the island, surrounded by soft wooded hills, stands the small city of Kandy, last capital of the Ceylonese kings, and still the home of all that is most deeply indigenous to Ceylon. The Dutch and the Portuguese never subdued this ancient place, and the British never much altered its character. It feels, like Kyoto in Japan, a repository of everything lasting and traditional, and it even has its own legal code, inherited from the Kandyan kingdom of old.

Its fulcrum is the Temple of the Tooth, one of the supremely sacred shrines of Buddhism, in whose inner sanctuary, layered in precious woods and metals, and surrounded by a moat full of turtles, there is preserved a tooth of the Lord Buddha. It is not really a tooth, and its temple, a high confectionery building that reminds me of the Victor Emmanuel memorial in Rome, is not really very beautiful: but the ancient sanctity of the relic gives an extra beauty to the little city, reclining most serenely about this holy place.

Cosy chalets of the British speckle the hillsides all around the lake like suburbs in Surrey, and echoing out of the valley you can often hear the ceaseless chanting of Buddhist priests in a seminary far below. On the edge of the city lies one of the loveliest gardens in the world, Peredeniya, and through the hills there wander delightful rural promenades, trodden out by dainty Victorian feet, and named for great ladies of the British Raj – Lady Horton's Walk, Lady Gregory's Road, Lady Longden's Drive. Kandy is the sort of place most of us would feel fairly happy to grow old in, and from its example you might suppose that the whole of Ceylon was a kind of half-pay paradise, trellised, embowered and sung in by priests.

It is not so. Outward from Kandy, more or less the centre of the island, the landscapes of Ceylon burst away in overpowering variety – landscapes cruel, seductive, grand or intimate in turn, so intricately jammed together that in a morning's journey you can pass from jungle to alp to classic tropical foreshore. The southern centre of the island is a massed jumble of mountains, with the holy Adam's Peak, where the butterflies go to die, standing there like a fang pre-eminent – visible, as a sacred mountain should be, not only to the buried thatched villages of the forest, but also to sailors out at sea. Tea gardens clothe these highlands, their big white factories facing this way and that across the valleys: and as you drive through the estates, whose big bobbing baskets above the shrubbery show where the tea-pickers are at work – as you travel through the brilliant atmosphere of mountain Ceylon, translucent blue and sudden green, the toasted smell of tea leaves follows you, factory to factory, as though an elderly but inexorable aunt were after you with the tea-caddy.

Out of the tea gardens into the rolling plains, with clumps of firs and eucalyptus and splendid trout streams. On the edge of this country stands Nuwara Eliya, an ineffable anachronism of a hill station. The Prime Minister of Ceylon has a house up there, surrounded by lovely lawns and rose-beds, along the road from the racecourse: and nearby the planters' Hill Club, dimly decorated with prints and stuffed fish, has changed so little with the Asian times that to this day no Ceylonese has been admitted to membership. Nurelya is another world from Kandy. It is like a slightly faded resort in the Scottish Highlands, even to the foliage – even indeed to the Scots, and I was not in the least surprised to notice one day, outside the half-timbered Grand Hotel, a car whose Ceylonese number plate flaunted the staunch appendage: 'Argyllshire'.

Away to the west stands Colombo, steamy and straggling around its harbour. In the south is Galle, once the great entrepot of Ceylon, where a big Dutch fort stands sentinel above the sea, and there are evocations still, in narrow street and rampart, of dhows, burghers and adventurers. On the east coast is Trincom-alee, one of the grandest of all harbours, a superb double-yoked bay that could, as the guidebooks like to say, shelter entire navies. In the north the scrub country peters out into lowland waste and coastal marsh: and all around the island the glorious beaches lie, fringed conventionally with coconut palms, backed by forests, with rickety fishing hamlets on the banks of creeks, and catamarans drawn up beyond the surf.

Bumpy pot-holed roads link these astonishingly disparate parts with one another. Slow rattly trains labour over impossible gradients. Doomed buses trundle from coast to coast. The package tour has scarcely reached Ceylon yet, the philosophies of tourism are not yet dominant, and the island still feels

properly organic. ('Bank Closed' said a chalked blackboard
notice when I went to cash a cheque one morning, 'On a/c Full
Moon Day'.)

Sometimes the transitions of Ceylon are so abrupt that the
colours clash, as though an interior decorator has botched the
job: and the emotions of the island, too, are often fierce. The
murder rate is among the highest on earth, though crime is
nearly always un-premeditated, and is often fired by love or
family feud. Even Kandy, that perpetual rest cure of a city, is
rich in bloody stories, and when I consulted a horoscope in a
magazine there one day, I was not surprised to be warned that
'bodily harm is not outside the orbit of your planetary possibilities today'. The clash of dry mountain air and equatorial
humidity seems to make for inner resentments. The original
Sinhalese resent the immigrant Tamils, the Buddhists resent the
Hindus, each wing of every political party conspiratorially
resents the other, and there are two Afro-Asian Solidarity
Leagues.

The primitive streak is strong, for all the cultured elite of
Ceylon (perhaps the most thoroughly westernized of any Asian
ruling class): drum beats on the night air, devil worship, queer
straggled bands of forest aborigines still eking out, in a few
hidden recesses of the island, their last years of the Dark Ages.
A recent Prime Minister of Ceylon was taken to task by the
Opposition for consulting an imported Indian magician. 'What's
your problem?' asked a recent advertisement in the Colombo
Press. 'Be it Love, Marriage, Employment, Domestic Unhappi-
ness, Subdue your enemy, Protection from others, Achieve
Promotions, Success at Examinations, Litigation, Delayed
Periods, Desertion – Meet or Write to Government Registered
CHARMIST (On Sundays, Arudha Hair Oil Office, Gampola)'.

In partnership, the hair oil and the charms. Ceylon is so dense
a country, so dovetailed, so ripe, that it will be generations
before the technical civilization of the west finally swamps the
place, and I know of nowhere comparably safe or comfortable
where you may still feel so close to the gnarled roots of nature.
If you have never seen monkeys outside a zoo, their presence
along the highways of Ceylon is one of the most delightful
experiences of modern travel: so exuberantly, divinely free do
they look, as they leap the main road in a couple of bounds, or

whisk their babies with merry elegance up a tree-trunk. If an elephant chiefly means to you only a sixpenny ride for the children, or a comic character in an animated cartoon, wait till you see one nobly manipulating logs in a Ceylonese teak forest, or best of all striding in wild grandeur, lordly and untamed, from one forest beat to another.

One can see such animals in greater numbers elsewhere, and in fiercer settings: the glory of Ceylon is that there they exist still in immediate neighbourhood to man himself, in an environment easily accessible and actually rather cramped. The fireflies that waver so haphazard through the shrubbery, as you drink your sundowner, are like friendly envoys from that other world beyond the suburbs, the world of the apes and the elephants: and I once drove five miles through a continuing wavering stream of yellow moths, whose antic progress across Ceylon was a reminder that a right of way is not the exclusive privilege of humans.

And proving this point majestically are the most celebrated of Ceylon's sights and surprises, the great ruined cities of her past – Anuradhapura, Polonnaruwa, Sigiriya – which are wonders on a par with the Pyramids or Machu Picchu, and are frequented now, in their abandonment, by the wild creatures of the bush.

Anuradhapura and Polonnaruwa are huge Buddhist cities of remote antiquity, the one succeeding the other as capital of Ceylon in AD 1017. They are astonishing complexes of temple, palace and ceremonial highway, with vast domed sanctuaries rising above the scrub, and dynasties of kings marching through their histories. Sigiriya, though, is something different in kind, and in its hushed purlieus, alone and bee-infested in a desolate landscape of the north-east, the drama of Ceylon is enacted most excitingly of all. Sigiriya, the Lion Rock, is a gaunt and immense column of granite, 400 feet high. It shows from many miles away, theatrically jutting out of a dun countryside, and at first sight seems only to be one of your geological freaks, like Ayers Rock in Australia, or the mushroom buttes of Arizona.

But it is a historical freak as well. Fifteen centuries ago the young prince Kasyapa, coveting the throne of Ceylon, buried his father the king alive in a wall in his capital at Anuradhapura: but terrified of the revenge of his brother, who was in India, he fled the city and set up his own usurping court on the rock at

Sigiriya – literally on the rock, for living as he did in perpetual fear of his life, he built a fortress-palace on the very summit, approached by precipitous staircases up the granite, with an audience chamber up there, luxurious apartments, military quarters, water storage tanks and even elephant stables. Around the base of the rock, within walls and a moat, an attendant city arose: but the parricide king, his courtiers and his courtesans, lived insulated high above in maniac asylum.

The rock may still be climbed, and in a gallery half-way are the celebrated Sigiriya frescoes, erotic portraits of half-nude women, full-bosomed and heavily jewelled, whom some authorities have assumed to be Buddhist vestals, and others women of royal pleasure. Up you go, clutching the iron railings erected in a less hell-for-leather age, and between the enormous sculpted lion's feet which have given the place its name, up staircase after staircase, through gallery upon gallery, until at last you emerge upon the flat surface of the rock. It is about an acre square, terraced still with the remains of the madman's palace, and at your feet the scrub-land of Ceylon lies empty and unchanged.

The hostile world feels impotent indeed, seen from such an eastern Berchtesgaden, and Kasyapa survived up there for eighteen years: but in the end his brother came, and he killed himself while the going was good.

Serendipity: not always happy, but never failing to surprise. You remember the waiter who brought my breakfast near the beginning of this essay? When he had left the room I hastened to fetch my notebook, to record his observations word for word: but while I was away from the breakfast table, that damned crow flapped in through the window, and stole a slice of toast.

7

'MY KIND OF TOWN'

Chicago, 1970

❧

Chicago, a place of astonishing beauty and force of character, seems to me the least known, to the world at large, of all the great cities. This is the only essay I have ever been invited to write about it.

Two remarkable sculptures embellish Chicago, Illinois. Both are by great masters from abroad, both stand grandiosely al fresco, and each represents, no doubt unintentionally, a Chicago attitude – a motive in the life of the city.

The first is by Picasso, and it stands unavoidably in the middle of Civic Center Plaza, itself the heart of downtown Chicago. This artefact is very tall, is made of steel, and looks like different things to different Chicagoans – to some a horse, to some a bird, to clots a load of old junk, to sophisticates *nothing*, just *nothing*, merely an expression of the creative act. To everybody, however, it represents one aspiration: cultured urbanity, a condition towards which Chicago has been assiduously striving throughout its brief but blistered history.

The second sculpture is by Henry Moore, and it stands less ostentatiously on the outskirts of the city, in the campus of the University of Chicago. This one is squat, bronze and burly. It is an alarming bulbous object like an egg, or a helmet, or a huge bald head, and it seems to heave itself out of the ground organically, beside a tennis court. It is called Nuclear Energy, and it stands near the spot where Enrico Fermi and his colleagues achieved the first atomic chain reaction: but in the Chicago context it stands for everything hefty, violent and swaggering in the traditions of the city, gunfight and cattle-yard, railroad king and ethnic fury.

The two great pieces have never stood face to face, but the

aspects of Chicago which they seem to symbolize are always clashing, mingling or standing aghast at each other: and it is the coexistence of two such persistent strains, each in some ways slightly comic, but each magnified by history or environment into an immense social force, which makes Chicago one of the most perpetually surprising cities in the world.

The lady who presides over the observation floor of the Board of Trade building generally prefers to look north, I think, in the general direction of the Picasso. She gives you a map, indeed, and offers a brief but telling statistic about railroad stations, but she talks most eloquently about the uptown view, where the glittering apartment blocks gaze superbly across Lake Michigan, like heirs-apparent to the brownstones at their feet.

From the start Chicagoans were eager to prove that they could be just as cultivated, just as sensitive, as any patriotic Easterner or European. They built their mansions, financed by the enormous profits of railroad and prairie, with an orgiastic flourish – château or mock-Tudor, oak-beamed or castellated, hung about with the most expensive pictures and draped in unobtainable tapestries. They did not want to appear hicks. Oscar Wilde, in his most preposterously aesthetic period, was kindly received by Chicago society, on account of his being a famous writer, and huge museums were presently crammed with loot from the older civilizations, enabling over-educated daughters to swell parental hearts by recognizing a Botticelli when they saw one.

This old snobbism was, of course, partly just social affectation. It survives even now, and still looks pretty silly. Nowhere in the world, I swear, will you hear the word 'Society', with a capital S, used so frequently: and nowhere is Society more fun to watch – eating an ineffably English tea, perhaps, in a carriage-trade Chicago restaurant, with Jasmine Tea and Toasted Muffins beside the indoor goldfish pool, overhung by chandeliers and baskets of artificial sweet peas, served by satiny capped-and-aproned waitresses.

It looks like a vanished Europe queerly mutated, as if by some malfunctioning time machine. It has a sprayed, clamped look. Its children behave with an almost fictional decorum. Its daughters wear pearls. Its young mums look as though they have come direct from committee meetings of charitable balls. Its husbands look as though they keep fit by riding hunters through parks before breakfast. Its grandmothers, best of all, talk in throaty turtle voices, as though the words are being squeezed out from beneath the carapace: and they are heavily loaded with inherited gewgaws, and are inclined to call the waitress 'Child', as though expecting pretty curtseys in return. 'Would you care for some more Jasmine Tea, Mrs Windlesham? Do you desire another Toasted English Muffin?' 'Why thank you, child – how pretty you are looking today!' 'Thank *you*, Mrs Windlesham, it's always a pleasure to serve you and the members of your family.'

But if Chicago's yearning for tradition and urbanity is some-times ridiculous, in other ways it is noble. It is not only a search for class, it is a hunger too for splendour. Thanks partly to the pretensions of the Mrs Windleshams, trying so hard to keep up with the Cabots or the Cecils, this is a city of majestic presence. Consider the view on a spring morning, for instance, from the shore of the Lake beside the Planetarium. A belt of green parkland fills the foreground, plonked about by tennis balls, splashed with tulips and cherry blossoms; then a moving strip of traffic, streaming relentlessly along the expressway; then, beyond the sunken railroad tracks, the tight-packed façade of Lake Shore Drive, which reminds me of Prince's Street in Edinburgh. Above and behind all this rises the skyline of downtown Chicago, and there it all comes true. It is one of the grandest of all silhouettes. It is a glorious jumble of styles and conceptions – here a cylinder, there a pyramid, Gothic bobbles and Victorian scrolls, bumps, domes, cubes, towers like the lattice masts of old battleships, gables, even a steeple – a tremendous congeries of buildings, without balance or sym-metry, which properly suggests a metropolis thrown together in an enormous hurry by a race of unappeasable giants.

Chicago fostered a famous literary school in the 1930s. Its wealth and earnestness have attracted men of talent and learning from all over the world. It seems to have a university, museum or art gallery in every other street, and even the *Encyclopaedia Britannica* emigrated here long ago (leaving the more determined Anglophiles and patriots, like me, still firmly consulting our Eleventh Edition, 1910). But its real splendour lies in its architecture. It is one of the great architectural showplaces of the world, and long since offered its own retort to the judgement passed by Oscar Wilde, wearing knee-breeches and a buffalo robe during a Press conference at the Grand Pacific Hotel: 'Your city looks positively too dreary to me.'

For whatever other criticisms may be thrown at Chicago, positively too dreary it does not look. It is full of masterpieces. The skyscraper was born in Chicago. Frank Lloyd Wright was a Chicago architect, and when Hitler closed the Bauhaus, Ludwig Mies van der Rohe made Chicago the world capital of architectural modernism. Mies, as every Chicago sophisticate likes to remember him, was the Michelangelo or Christopher Wren of this city. He lived here, in one of his own apartment blocks, and the city is stamped all over with his genius: a chill but towering genius of cube, glass and right angle, which preshadowed the age of the rockets and the computers, and will always make Chicago as symbolic of the 1950s and 1960s as Florence is emblematic of the Renaissance.

With Mies van der Rohe Chicago has finally made it. That great collection of buildings beyond the expressway, crowned by his dispassionate vision, vindicates all the old pretensions of this city – reaching as it did, for so many generations, so ludicrously but so poignantly for style.

Size, push and power come more easily to Chicago. 'Sir,' a nineteenth-century visitor was told by the conductor, as his train ran into Union Station, 'you are approaching the boss city of the universe!' Chicago still has a beefy reputation, and a boisterous penchant for superlatives – Biggest, Best, Richest, Heaviest. Brawn and blarney remain essential to the Chicago atmosphere, particularly well reflected I think in the menu of the Café Bohemia, which offers haunches of lion, beaver, moose, jaguar and many other fauna – 'Lion steaks are real good,' they told me there, 'tiger too, tiger's delicious when it's on.' 'I Will' is the unofficial slogan of Chicago: or 'I Will,' as the columnist Max Royko once suggested, 'If I Don't Get Caught.'

For that glorious waterfront is thin. It is like the front of some colossal folly. Immediately behind it sprawls the tumultuous Loop, the business district, still enclosed more or less by the clanking loop of the Elevated Railroad, and instinct with memories of burlesque, gangland and political machine. And behind the Loop again extend the neighbourhoods, the vast hinterland of this metropolis, the Negro quarters, the dingy tenements of the poor whites, half-cleared slum and railway track, steel mill and used car lot – Lawndale, Woodland, Oakland, Halsted Street and Blue Island, where the Ukrainians, the Lithuanians, the Mexicans, the Poles and the Sicilians fitfully preserve their tastes and customs, in the wasteland of their new world.

This is Capone's Chicago, beer-ringed, smoke-filled, whisky-breathed, a powerful, dangerous and notorious place. Almost nothing about it is small. Its area is vast. Its energy is tireless. Its problems are tremendous problems – Race, Poverty, Violence. Its solutions are grand solutions – immense slum-clearances, huge new roads, gigantic universities. It is full of crime and corruption, but it does not feel, like Manhattan, locked within its own anxieties, congested by traffic and exhausted by argument. This is the Windy City, and gusts of lake and prairie bluster incessantly down these streets, never scouring them indeed, but keeping all their rubbish helter-skelter on the move.

Chicago is never *tired*. Here one still senses the insatiable optimism of the Victorians. This remains a city of the railway age, with all its swollen faults and merits. 'Purr-fect Transport', proclaims a poster for the Baltimore and Ohio, and the railroad tracks still flood into this city like so many rivers, each to its towered or colonnaded terminus. Here in the birthplace of nuclear power you may still hear the mournful clang of the locomotive bell, as the freight train edges its way through the downtown streets, and here the old El, so long banished from most American cities, still sways merrily around the Loop, its cars jutting so perilously over the curves that it looks like a toy train in a nursery, approaching its inevitable derailment. Chicago has a Pullman braggadocio – swagger of brass and green liveries, swank of cheroot, wink of deal or shady profit.

It is an elemental sort of strength. One seems to feel the energies of America pouring into this heartland city, to be processed, refined or coagulated. The Chicago Stockyards are no longer the grisly spectacle they used to be, for nowadays most of the cattle are slaughtered at source, but among their maze of cattle-pens, all the same, you still know yourself to be in the capital of the beef country. The yards still smell strongly of manure and hot animal, and sometimes offer, obliquely perhaps through a cattle-pen gap, classic cameos of western life: the steers slithering frenzied by, breathing heavily, gasping, with a thud of hoofs in the mud and straw – and behind them out of sight the cowhands, cracking their whips and yippying – and then one glimpses their Stetsons, bobbing above the barricades, and one hears their swearing and spitting and coughing – and then for a moment they too appear in your gap, a couple of brown unshaven men, whose expressionless blue eyes look out at you with a haunting detachment, as though they have never emerged from those stockyards in all their lives, but will die inside there with their whips in their hands.

Chicago is a brutal city. It always has been, and used to be rather proud of the fact. Tourists were taken to see the site of the St Valentine's Day massacre, until a Canadian bought the celebrated garage wall for re-erection in his garden. Extortion and gang rivalry still happen in Chicago, but nowadays violence feeds upon different and deeper passions too – passions of race or ideology. One cannot spend long in Chicago today without sensing the undercurrents of fear and resentment which swirl beneath the great city. The Chicago police cars move about with weird and ominous bleeping noises: and it is as though they are keeping an electronic eye upon every emotion of the place, love or hate or nostalgia or avarice, for computer-stacking at head-quarters.

'Lucky you got me,' the cab-driver nearly always seems to say, if you want to visit the neighbourhoods. 'Not many guys would take you. I tell ya, I was a Marine four years, I fought in eight major battles, eight *major* battles, and believe me if any of these blacks gets in my way I'll just run 'em down, just like that. Lock your door now. Like I say, it's lucky you found me. Not many guys would come out this way.'

One such reassuring veteran took me to a street corner in Lawndale, a toughish Negro neighbourhood, which is almost a shrine of Chicago's unhappy preoccupations. It is called the Wall of Respect, and it is painted all over with frescoes commemorating the Negro struggle for power or self-respect: portraits of martyrs, emblems of epic sacrifice, symbolic scenes of hope or grievance, bitter jokes, exhortations, big Guernica-like pictures of tragedy. 'There's more inside,' a passing youth told me, and sure enough in the bar across the way, roped off inside its dark recess like a wall-painting in a cave, there faintly glowed a huge wall-collage of clippings, paintings and photographs, which reminded me of those side-chapels full of relics, ex-votos and discarded crutches that one sees in Spanish cathedrals.

It disturbed me, as though I had stumbled upon some secret consecration of the city, an inner dynamism. I felt I was intruding upon private quarrels. Outside in the street the cab-driver was pointedly reading a paperback: inside the bar the Negroes did not look at me, but leant at the bar laughing over private jokes, answering my diffident inquiries only in a kind of amused ellipse.

Sometimes the twin strains of Chicago, the colossal and the cultivated, are blended in a scene or an institution. This produces a flavour altogether unique to this city – which is, of course, a great capital without a nation, a Vienna that never had an Empire. It is, I think, essentially a saltless flavour – bland, fleshy perhaps. One misses intellectual Jews in this city, or sardonic Yankees. The wide pale lake, though it has its perilous gales, its ships direct from Europe, even its modest tides, is distinctly not the open sea, but looks as though its water would be soft and slithery to the touch. The blustering winds carry no tang, the waterfront spray leaves no tingle on the face. The posh apartment blocks on the Edgewater shore, complete with their marinas, striped umbrellas and private beaches, are like segments of Beirut deposited upon the edge of the Caspian. The conversation of Chicago mostly lacks edge, and tends towards the exhortatory monologue.

In the same way the uniquely Chicago phenomena are less stirring than stunning. They bowl you over by scale, or momentum. Take for instance the commodity market on the ground floor of the Board of Trade building. This is a peculiar spectacle. The setting is a large hall in which are sunk a number of pits like arenas for cockfights, or rings for Persian wrestling. Standing in these bowls are several hundred men behaving in a very eccentric way – holding up their forefingers in stylized gestures, suddenly jerked into activity by invisible alarms, shouting, lapsing into morose introspection, apparently bursting into song, and generally carrying on so incomprehensibly that the sensible females looking on from the public gallery are left in a state of distracted disbelief. Really, one seems to hear them say, grown men, behaving like a lot of clowns. This is Chicago, though, and behind the lunacy lies power, wealth and earthi-

ness. Look to your left, and there you will see upon the notice-
boards the names of the commodities handled in this internationally significant exchange: soybean, corn, oats, sorghum,
pork bellies – substances which bring you instantly back to
reality, place the antics below in a new and less comical
perspective, and remind you once more of Chicago's organic
kind of power.

Not far away is Playboy Mansion, the sybaritic palace-pad of
Hugh Hefner the publisher. I have never penetrated this building, which looks rather like a Soviet Embassy in one of the lesser
European capitals, and is similarly unenticing to gate-crashers:
but for my purposes it does not matter, for the point of Playboy
Mansion is not the fact but the legend. In this it honours a
tradition of the Chicago tycoons, who often grew celebrated
upon rumour – mouth-to-mouth statistics, tall tales of unimaginable opulence, whispers of enviable excess. Chicagoans, by
and large, seem very proud of Playboy Mansion, and willingly
take you to peer wanly, like displaced persons, through its high
railings. It is not merely that dozens of sexy girls are said to live
in there, or that the kitchen is staffed by twelve chefs around the
clock, or that you can swim out of the swimming-pool into a
subterranean grotto, or even that the whole building forms a
controlled environment, where Mr Hefner can decree the coming
of night and day, or the shift of the seasons. All this represents,
of course, the epitome of Chicago's instinct for scale and
technique, but there is more to the legend of Playboy Mansion
than mere tycoonery. There is the intoxicating knowledge that
real Poets, Writers, Actors and Artists frequent that house, that
even now Mr Hefner is probably hard at work upon his
Philosophy, attended by deft-shuffling library Bunnies – that
besides being terrifically rich, gaudy, vulgar, spectacular and
big, Playboy Mansion is genuinely and avant-gardely *cultured*!

For a last illustration of this particular Chicago sensation –
which strikes me as the feeling of Rubens, as against the feeling
of Rembrandt – let us stand after dinner on a wet, blustery,
overcast night upon the bridge that crosses the Chicago River
beside Tribune Tower. We shall see one of the great urban vistas
of the world, finer than anything in Manhattan, but our hearts
somehow will not soar. We shall merely be stopped in our tracks
with wonder. In the foreground, on the left, the ornate old
Wrigley Building stands savagely floodlit, a vast slab of white,

but beyond it in relative darkness the tree-lined North Michigan Avenue – 'The Magnificent Mile' – extends urbanely to the north. Thus through alternating dazzle and shadow we peer towards the other end, and there in a theatrical refulgence of lights stands a monumental group of structures, one against the other in deep projection.

Ironically in the centre of the group is the quaint old Chicago water-tower – Wilde's 'castellated monstrosity with pepper boxes stuck all over it' – brilliantly illuminated and looking from this distance like some kind of sacred totem. Behind, around and above it stand hotels and tall office blocks, plunged in darkness or ablaze with light, and loomed over tremendously by the black shape of the John Hancock Building, the second tallest in the world, a building clamped together with diagonal steel struts, like Prometheus chained. Up this vast tapering form one's eye rises, until the summit of the building is lost in swirling cloud: and somewhere up there through the drizzle a beacon searchlight plays, diffused mysteriously on the overcast sky, flashing off steel faces or slabs of glass. So low is the cloud, so tossed about by the winds, so dramatically illuminated by that restless beam, that once more the image seems to be of the steam age, and Chicago in its most formidably modern quarter harks back again to the flicker of furnaces in the night.

But salt, no, only limitless power: and when the daylight comes, and those immense structures fall back into their respective identities, out of the half-dream of their midnight ensemble, some of the magic fades, the water-tower is only a disused municipal facility after all, and most of the buildings turn out to be rather ordinary.

This is the most pungent surprise of Chicago – its underlying homeliness. I use the word in its English sense, to mean domesticity, unpretending kindliness, but even so I am aware it will infuriate Chicagoans. Almost any conclusion about their city infuriates Chicagoans. Theirs is one of the most perilous of all cities to write about, for they have a fatal gift of putting the most sympathetic visitor on the offensive. Whenever I go to the place it seems to be rumbling still with resentment against some recent essay: on my first visit it was a *New Yorker* piece by A. J. Liebling that the city was regurgitating, on my last a book by Norman Mailer. You cannot please Chicago.

But there we are: Chicago strikes me as essentially a nice, ordinary, middling, homely sort of town. People write affectionate songs about it – 'My kind of town, Chicago is' – 'Chicago, Chicago, that wonderful town' – not merely because of its euphonious Indian name, but also because it is somehow graspable and human. It never feels like megalopolis. For all its vicious reputation, for all its force and wealth, it still manages to feel like a provincial city in an older America. Every night the Negro migrants step off the midnight train from the South, as they have since the end of the Civil War, and in the streets of the Loop you may often see, dressed up in touching finery for a day in the big city, country corn-folk window-shopping, resisting Junior's demand for a complete circuit of the El, or sucking ice-creams beside the Picasso. On the lake shore one hot afternoon, passing through a bronzed Chicago family sporting themselves Americanly on the sward, with space-rays and Japanese cameras, I came across the patriarch of the group, an aged Lithuanian, ruminating behind white walrus moustaches in the tinted-glass recesses of the family car – a true image of the American idea.

People are polite in Chicago, when they are not rioting or expressing the darker prejudices. The pace is not quite so fast as it is in Los Angeles or New York, and the citizen is not so soured. He takes time to tell you the way, concludes with a pleasantry, very likely asks you where you are from or tells you about the eight major battles of his military career. 'Thank you,' said I to the waitress at Marshall Field's, when she brought me my English Muffins. 'Enjoy them,' she sweetly replied, as though she had made them herself from Grandma's recipe. 'All of CAR', says a sign at a parking lot in the Loop, in my favourite Chicago declaration, 'must be in off of sidewalk before getting Ticket'.

Of course this is Norman Rockwell's America. Chicago really is, in a newly significant sense, the All American capital. It remains relatively immune to the cosmopolitan forces, the last great stronghold of American Values. Here the charm of a lost America survives, in patriotic sentiments, family lakeshore groups, rhodomontade and nightly servings of what used to be called Showbiz. Parochial pride is endearingly intense: there is a mysterious channel on Chicago TV, never explained to me, which seems to transmit absolutely nothing except very slow-moving publicity films about the city itself. 'What are you,' asked the elevator man at the Merchandise Mart one day, eyeing my Chelsea haircut with an All-American eye, 'some kind of a singer?'

I can see that many young Americans must regard the place as Nadirville, a very sump of all they most detest about the American Way of Life: but I love it all, in a nostalgic, detached sort of way, knowing that I shall presently be taking the aircraft back to New York and dear old decadent London. Chicagoans, of course, will think me patronizing, but I do not mean it so. For me the persistent provincialism of Chicago makes perfect sense. Urbanity comes easy nowadays, power is painfully old hat, nobody wants to live in Megalopolis. The small nations are coming into their own, as the happiest environment for human existence, and so too are the provincial cities, where plainer human values can survive, where time is a little less compressed and there is space for a few extra prepositions, as you manoeuvre the CAR in off of the sidewalk.

And of these cities, Chicago is the boss.

8

VERY STRANGE FEELING

Chinese Cities, 1983

Sailing to China for the first time, after many years of wandering its perimeters, was one of the great experiences of my life. By then the cities I describe here were very well known in the West, and were visited by countless tourists, but to me they were still like places in another world. I felt as though I were starting all over again!

And in the distance, through the porthole, there stood China.

Of course wherever you are in the world, China stands *figuratively* there, a dim tremendous presence somewhere across the horizon, sending out its coded messages, exerting its ancient magnetism over the continents. I had been prowling and loitering around it for years, often touched on the shoulder by its long, long reach – watching the Chinese-Americans shadow-box in San Francisco, say, or being dragged screaming and kicking to the Chinese opera somewhere, or interviewing renegade patriots in Taiwan, or debating whether to go to the fish-and-chip shop or the Cantonese take-away in Dublin. It had seemed to me always the land of the grand simplicities, pursuing its own mighty way through history, impassive, impervious, where everything was more absolute than it was elsewhere, and the human condition majestically overrode all obstacles and reversions. I had wondered and marvelled at it for half a lifetime: and here I was at last on my way to meet it face to face, on a less than spanking Chinese steamship, rust-streaked, off-white, red flag at the stern, steaming steadily northward through the blue-green China Sea.

My fellow passengers assiduously prepared me for the encounter. They showed me how best to suck the goodness out of the smoked black carp at dinner. They taught me to count up

to ten in Mandarin. They drew my attention to an article in
China Pictorial about the propagation of stink-bugs in Gandong
Province. Mrs Wang, returning from a visit to her sister in
Taiwan, vividly evoked for me her hysterectomy by acupuncture
('when they slit me open, oh, it hurt very bad, but after it was
very *strange* feeling, very *strange* . . .'). The Bureaucrat, returning
from an official mission to Hong Kong, thoroughly explained to
me the Four Principles of Chinese Government policy.

Around us the sea was like a Chinese geography lesson, too.
It was never empty. Sometimes apparently abandoned sampans
wallowed in the swell, sometimes flotillas of trawlers threshed
about the place. Red-flagged buoys mysteriously bobbed, miles
from anywhere, grey tankers loomed by high in the water.
Islands appeared, islands like pimples in the sea, like long
knobbly snakes, islands with lighthouses on them, or radio
masts, or white villas. And always to the west stood the hills of
China, rolling sometimes, sheer sometimes, and once or twice
moulded into the conical dome-shapes that I had hitherto
supposed to be the invention of Chinese calligraphers. Ah, but
I must go far inland, the Bureaucrat told me on our third day at
sea, I must go to Guangxi in the south, to see such mountains
properly – mountains like no others, said he, the Peak of Solitary
Beauty, the Hill of the Scholar's Servant – 'but look' (he
interrupted himself) – 'you notice? – the water is turning yellow.
We are approaching the mouth of Yangtze!'

So we were. In the small hours that night, when I looked out
of my porthole again, I found we were sailing through an
endless parade of ships, gloomily illuminated in the darkness:
and when at crack of dawn I went on deck to a drizzly morning,
still we were passing them, up a scummy river now, lined with
ships, thick with ships, barges, and tugs, and container ships,
and a warship or two, and country craft of shambled wood so
fibrous and stringy-looking that it seemed to me the Chinese,
who eat anything, might well make a dish of them. Hooting all
the way we edged a passage up the Huangpu, narrowly avoiding
ferry-boats, sending sampans scurrying for safety, until after
thirty miles of ships, and docks, and grimy warehouses, and
factories, we saw before us a waterfront façade of high towers
and office buildings, red and shabby in the rain. It was my China
landfall: it was the city of Shanghai.

*

' "Moonlight Serenade"!' demanded the elderly American tourists in the bar of the Peace Hotel. 'Play it again!' The band obliged – half a dozen well-worn Chinese musicians, a lady at the piano, an aged violinist, an excellent trumpeter: Glenn Miller lived again in Shanghai, and the old thump and blare rose to a deafening climax and a smashing roll of drums. The Americans tapped their feet and shook their hands about, exclaiming things like 'Swing it!' The band's eyes, I noticed, wandered here and there, as though they had played the piece once too often.

They have been playing it, after all, since they and the song were young. Their musical memories, like their personal experiences, reached back through Cultural Revolution, and Great Leap Forward, and People's Revolution, and Kuomintang, and Japanese Co-Prosperity Zone, back through all the permutations of Chinese affairs to the days of cosmopolitan Shanghai – those terrible but glamorous times when European merchants lived like princes here, Chinese gangsters fought and thrived, the poor died in their hundreds on the sidewalks, and the Great World House of Pleasure offered not only singsong girls and gambling tables, but magicians, fireworks, strip shows, story-tellers, mah-jong schools, marriage brokers, freak shows, massage parlours, porn photographers, a dozen dance platforms and a bureau for the writing of love-letters.

No wonder the musicians looked world-weary. The Great World is the Shanghai Youth Palace now, the past of its former prostitutes being known only, we are primly told, to their Revolutionary Committee Leaders. The band plays on all the same, and in many other ways too I was taken aback to find Old Shanghai surviving despite it all. The Race Club building, it is true, has been transformed into the Shanghai Public Library, and the racetrack itself is partly the People's Square and partly the People's Park, but nearly everything else still stands. The pompous headquarters of the merchant houses still line the Bund, along the waterfront, surveying the tumultuous commerce that once made them rich. The Customs House still rings out the hours with a Westminster chime. The celebrated Long Bar of the Shanghai Club, which used to serve the best Martinis at the longest bar in Asia, is propped up now by eaters of noodles with lemonade at the Dongfeng Hotel. The Peace Hotel itself is only the transmogrified Cathay, where Noel Coward wrote *Private Lives*, with its old red carpets still in place, 135 different drinks still on its bar list, and the Big Band sound ringing nightly through the foyer.

Even the streets of Shanghai, where the poor die no longer, seemed unexpectedly like home. There are virtually no private cars in this city of eleven million people, but I scarcely noticed their absence, so vigorously jostled and tooted the taxis, the articulated buses and the myriad bicycles: if there were few bright flowered clothes to be seen along the boulevards, only open-neck shirts and workaday slacks, there were still fewer of the baggy trousers, blue jerkins and Mao caps that I had foreseen. The theme music from *Bonanza* sounded through Department Store No. 10; there were cream cakes at Xilailin, formerly Riesling's Tea Rooms; the Xinya Restaurant still ushered its foreigners, as it had for a hundred years, into the discreet curtained cubicles of its second floor. On my first morning in Shanghai I ate an ice-cream in the People's Park (admission two *feng*), and what with its shady trees and winding paths, the old men playing checkers at its concrete tables, the students at their books, the health buffs at their callisthenics, the miscellaneous meditators and the tall buildings looking through its leaves above, I thought it, but for an absence of muggers and barouches, remarkably like Central Park.

Mrs Wang had invited me to lunch at her apartment, and this was no culture shock, either. True, we ate eggs-in-aspic, a kind of pickled small turnip and strips of a glutinous substance which suggested to me jellified sea-water, but nevertheless hers was a home that would not seem unduly exotic in, say, Cleveland. It was the bourgeois home *par excellence*. It had the statutory upright piano, with music open on the stand, the 16-inch colour TV on the sideboard, a picture of two kittens playing with a ball of wool, a bookshelf of paperbacks and a daily help. It had a daughter who had come over to help cook lunch, and a husband away at the office who sent his regards. 'We are very lucky,' said kind Mrs Wang. 'We have a certain social status.'

So this was *China*? I had to pinch myself. The Dictatorship of the People (Principle of Government number three, I remembered) does not visibly discipline Shanghai. Occasionally be-spectacled soldiers of the People's Revolutionary Army trundle through town on rattly motor bikes with sidecars, and outside the Municipal Headquarters (*né* Hongkong and Shanghai Bank)

two fairly weedy-looking troopers stand on sheepish sentry-go.
Otherwise Authority is inconspicuous. The traffic flows in
cheerful dishevelment over the intersections, ineffectually chivvied along over loudspeakers by policemen smoking cigarettes
in their little white kiosks. Jay-walkers proliferate, and in the
crinkled back-streets of the old quarter there seems no ideological restraint upon the free-enterprise pedlars and stall-holders,
with their buckets of peaches, their plastic bags of orange juice,
eels squirming in their own froth and compounds of doomed
ducks.

Nobody seemed shy of me. Everyone wanted to talk. A factory
worker I met in the park took me off without a second thought
to his nearby apartment (two dark rooms almost entirely
occupied by cooking utensils and bicycles) and the only hazard
of the Shanghai street, I discovered, was the student who
wished to practise his English. Stand just for a moment on the
Bund, watching the ships go by, or counting the flitting sea-
bats in the evening, and you are hemmed in, pressed against
the balustrade, squeezed out of breath, by young men wanting
to know if the word 'intend' can legitimately be followed by a
gerund. Go and lick an ice-cream in the park, and like magic
there will materialize out of the trees Mr Lu and a troop of
elderly friends, all of whom remember with affection their
English lessons with Miss Metcalfe at the Mission School, but
none of whom has ever been *quite* sure about the propriety of
the split infinitive.

Well! So this was the policy of the Open Door, which is
bringing modernity to China, and has made foreigners and all
their ways respectable. It seemed remarkably liberating. I often
talked politics with people I met, and their answers sounded
uninhibited enough. The Cultural Revolution, that hideous
upheaval of the 1960s? A terrible mistake, a tragedy. The future
of China? Nobody knew for sure what kind of country this was
going to be. Communism versus Capitalism? There was good
and bad in both. Would they like to go to America? Of course,
but they would probably come home again. What a kind face
Chou En Lai had! Yes, he had a lovely face, he was a good kind
man, the father of his people. Did they like the face of Mao Tse-
tung?

Ah, but there was a hush when I asked this question. They
thought for a moment. Then – 'We don't know', was the

mumbled answer, and suddenly I realized that they had not been frank with me at all. Not a reply had they given, but was sanctioned by the political orthodoxy of the moment. Did they like the *face* of Chairman Mao? He was a great man they knew, he had fallen into error in his later years, it had been admitted, but nobody it seems had ever told them whether to like his *face*. My perceptions shifted there and then, and where I had fancied frankness, now I began to sense evasions, veils or obliquities everywhere. This was, I reminded myself, the very birthplace and hotbed of the Gang of Four, that clique of xenophobic zealots – it was from an agreeable half-timbered villa near the Zoo, Frenchified in a bowered garden, that their murderous frenzies were first let loose. A decade ago I might have had a very different greeting in Shanghai, and Mrs W. would probably have been banished to one of the remoter onion-growing communes for giving me lunch.

No, perhaps it was not so home-like after all. On the Bund one evening a man with the droopy shadow of a moustache pushed his way through the crowd and confronted me with a kind of dossier. Would I go through this examination paper for him, and correct his mistakes? But I had done my grammatical duty, I considered, for that afternoon, and I wanted to go and look at the silks in Department Store No. 10. 'No,' said I. 'I won't.'

At that a theatrical scowl crossed the student's face, screwing up his eyes and turning down the corners of his mouth. He looked, with that suggestion of whiskers round his chin, like a Chinese villain in a bad old movie, with a gong to clash him in. I circumvented him nevertheless, and ah yes, I thought in my new-found understanding, if the Gang of Four were still around you would have me up against a wall by now, with a placard around my neck, and a mob there to jeer me, not to consult me about participles!

As it was, I hasten to add, every single soul in Shanghai was kind to me, and as a matter of fact my conscience pricked me, and I went back and corrected his damned papers after all. The Open Door really is open in this city, and Foreign Guests are enthusiastically welcomed, from package tourists shepherded by guides in and out of Friendship Stores to bearded language students scooting about on bicycles. Back-packers labour through town in search of dormitories: peripatetic writers hang over the girders of Waibaidu Bridge watching the barges pass below.

Of these categories, the peripatetic writer seems the hardest for the Chinese mind to accommodate. 'What is your *field*?' Mr Lu asked me. I answered him with a quotation from the Psalms, to the effect that my business was simply to grin like a dog and run about the city. 'You are a veterinary writer?' he inquired. Other people urged me to contact the Writers' Association, or at least to visit the new quarters on the north-east of the city, 'where many intellectuals live', so that we could discuss common literary problems. Just running about the city did not satisfy them. It could not be productive.

One night I went to the acrobats, as every Shanghai visitor must, and realized with a jerk – I choose the word deliberately – what the sense of role means in China. There have been professional acrobats in this country for more than 2,000 years, and in Shanghai they have an air-conditioned circular theatre, elaborately equipped with trapdoors, pulleys and chromium trapezes, for their daily performances of the all-but-incredible. They were astonishing, of course. They leapt and bounced around like chunks of rubber, they hurled plates across the stage faster than the eye could see, they balanced vast pyramids of crockery on tops of poles while standing on one foot on each other's heads, they were yanked to appalling standstills after falling headlong out of the roof.

'It is interesting to think,' said my companion, 'that in the Old China acrobats were like gypsies, of very low status. Now they are honoured performers. They have their role in society.' They were slotted, in short, and as I watched them it seemed to me that they not only had acrobats' limbs, and muscles, and eyes, but acrobats' thoughts, too, acrobats' emotions, specifically acrobatic libidos, and I fancied that if you stripped away their masks of acrobat make-up, there would only be other masks below, left behind from previous performances.

And it dawned on me that all those homely shuffling Shanghai crowds could be slotted too, if you had the key, into their inescapable roles. They were not really, as I had thought at first, at all like crowds of Third Avenue or Oxford Street. Every single citizen out there had his allotted place in the order of things, immutable: not a layabout loitered on those sidewalks, not an

actor resting, not a busker, hardly a worker out of a job. What is
your field? I am a Housewife. I am a Retired Worker. I am a
Peasant. I am an Acrobat. I am a Student, and would be much
obliged, please, if you would explain to me in simple language
the meaning of the following English sentence . . .

I did see one beggar in Shanghai, on the pavement opposite
the former Park Hotel (famous once for its Sky Terrace, whose
roof rolled back above the dance floor). He seemed to have
broken his leg, and sat all bowed and bandaged, sobbing, while
an associate held up an X-ray of the fracture. I am a Beggar, it
seemed to say! The passers-by looked horrified, but whether by
the mendicant himself, or by the nature of his injuries, I was
unable to determine, the Shanghai dialect not being my field.

I went to the Yu Garden from a sense of duty – it is a National
Protected Treasure, even though it was built in pure self-
indulgence by an official of the Ming Dynasty, who caused its
Rockery Hill to be constructed out of boulders brought from
thousands of miles away and stuck together with rice-glue. I
was ensnared there however by the children. There must have
been a hundred of them outside the Hall for the Viewing of
Rockery Hill, all three or four years old, some of them tied
together with string to prevent them straying off into the Hall
for Watching Swimming Fish, and I wasted a good half hour
playing with them. What adorable merry faces! What speed of
mood and response, mock-terror, sham-apprehension, sheer
hilarity! I stayed with them until they were led off two by two,
a long crocodile of black-haired roly-poly imps, towards the Hall
of Jade Magnificence.

There is nowhere like Shanghai for infant-watching, but in
the end, among all the increasingly puzzling and deceptive
inhabitants of this city, it was the children who baffled me most.
They have a particular fondness for foreigners, and will pick
one out from miles away, across a crowded square, clean through
the Tower of Lasting Clearness, to wiggle an introductory finger.
They have no apparent vices. They never cry, they don't know
how to suck a thumb, and though their trousers are conveniently
supplied with open slits in their seats, I am sure they never
dirty themselves anyway.

How I wished I could get inside their little heads, and
experience the sensations of a People's Revolutionary childhood!

Do they never fret, these infants of the Middle Kingdom? Is that sweet equanimity of theirs force-fed or innate, ethnic or indoctrinated? Could it really be that this society is bringing into being a race that needs no diapers? The children in the Yu Garden waved and made funny faces at me as they stumped away, but they left me uneasy all the same.

So next day I went to one of the notorious Children's Palaces, after-school centres where children can either have fun, or be coached in particular aptitudes. I say notorious, because for years these places have been shown off to visiting foreigners, so that they long ago acquired the taint of propaganda. Certainly through my particular Palace a constant succession of tourist groups was passing, led by the hand by selected infants in somewhat sickly intimacy, and in the course of the afternoon the children presented a musical show, mostly of the Folk-Dance-from-Shanxi-Province kind, which did seem short on innocent spontaneity, and long on ingratiation.

But what disturbed me more than the stage-management was the utter oblivion of the children themselves to the peering, staring, bulb-flashing tourists led all among them, room by room, by those minuscule trusties (who have an unnerving habit, by the way, of calling their charges *Auntie*). With an uncanny disregard they continued their ping-pong or their video games, pedalled their stationary bicycles, made their model ships, practised their flutes, repeated once again that last crescendo in the Harvest-Song-of-the-Yugur-Minority, or sat glued to the pages of strip-cartoon books, turning their pages with what seemed to me an unnatural rapidity. Their eyes never once flickered in our direction. Their attention never wavered. They simply pursued their activities with an inexorable concentration, never idle, never squabbling, just turning those pages, batting those balls, pedalling those pedals, twanging those strings or piping those Chinese flutes.

I was bemused by them. Were they really reading at all? Were they even playing, in our sense of the verb? Search me! I can only report one odd little episode, which sent me away from the Children's Palace peculiarly uncomfortable, and came to colour my whole memory of Shanghai. Early in a performance of *Jingle Bells* by an orchestra of children under the age of five, the virtuoso lead xylophonist happened to get herself a full tone out of key. She never appeared to notice; nor did any of the other performers, all dimples, winsome smiles and bobbing heads up there on the stage. On they went in fearful discord, tinkle-tinkle, clang-clang, simpering smugly to the end.

The airline magazine on CAAC Flight 1502, Shanghai to Beijing, was six months old (and reported the self-criticism of a Chinese women's volleyball team defeated by Americans in 1982 – 'they were desperate with fiery eyes, whereas we were passive and vulnerable to attack'). It was like flying in a dentist's waiting-room, I thought. Also the seats in the 707 seemed to be a job lot from older, dismembered aircraft, some of them reclining, some of them rigid, while people smoked unrestrictedly in the non-smoking section, and our in-flight refreshment was a mug of luke-warm coffee brought by a less than winning stewardess. I was not surprised by all this. I was lucky, I knew, that there were no wicker chairs in the middle of the aisle, to take care of overbooking, and at least we were not called upon, as passengers on other flights have been, to advance *en masse* upon reactionary hijackers, bombarding them with lemonade bottles.

The enigmas were mounting. Why, I wondered, were the Chinese modernizing themselves with such remarkable ineptitude? Did they not invent the wheelbarrow a thousand years before the West? Had they not, for that matter, split the atom and sent rockets into space? Were they not brilliantly quick on the uptake, acute of observation, subtle of inference? The broad-minded Deng Xiaoping is boss man of China these days, and he is dedicated to technical progress of any derivation – as he once said in a famous phrase, what does it matter whether a cat is black or white, so long as it catches mice? China simmers all over with innovation and technology from the West: yet still the coffee's cold on Flight 1502.

The bricklaying of contemporary China would shame a back-yard amateur in Arkansas. The architecture is ghastly. In the newest and grandest buildings cement is cracked, taps don't work, escalators are out of order. 'Respect Hygiene', proclaim the street posters, but the public lavatories are vile, and they have to put spittoons in the tombs of the Ming Emperors. Western architects, I am told, often despair to find air-conditioning connected to heating ducts, or fire-escapes mounted upside-down, and though it is true that the Chinese-made elevators in my Shanghai hotel were the *politest* I have ever used, with buttons marked Please Open and Please Close, still I felt that all the courtesy in the world would not much avail us if we ever got stuck half-way.

Why? What happened to the skills and sensibilities that built the Great Wall, moulded the exquisite dragon-eaves, dug out the lovely lakes of chinoiserie? Feudalism stifled them, the official spokesmen say. Isolation atrophied them, the historians maintain. Maoism suppressed them, say the pragmatists. Communism killed them, that's what, say the tourists knowingly. But perhaps it goes deeper than that: perhaps the Chinese, deprived of their ancient magics, observing that nothing lasts, come Ming come Mao, have no faith in mere materialism, and put no trust in efficiency. *Feng shui*, the ancient Chinese geomancy which envisaged a mystic meaning to the form of everything, is banned from the People's Republic: and dear God, it shows, it shows.

Never mind: with an incomprehensible splutter over the public-address system, and a bit of a struggle among those who could not get their tables to click back into their sockets, we landed safely enough in Beijing.

The first thing that struck me about this prodigious capital, which commands the destinies of a quarter of the earth's inhabitants, was the nature of its light. It was a continental light, a light of steppes or prairies, and it seemed to be tinged with green. At first I thought of it as metallic, but later it seemed to me more like concrete: arched in a vast bowl over the capital, a sky of greenish concrete!

And concrete too was the dominant substance of the city down below: stacks of concrete, yards of concrete, parks paved with concrete, their trees ignominiously sunk in sockets of soil, vast highways like concrete glaciers across the city, and everywhere around the flat skyline the looming shapes of high-rise blocks, their grim squareness broken only by the outlines of cranes lifting final concrete slabs to their summits.

No need for rice-glue, I concluded, in Beijing.

I was staying on the outskirts of the city, almost in the country. There the concrete was interrupted often by fields of vegetables, and the traffic that passed in the morning was half-rural – mule-carts all among the buses, juddering tractors sometimes. Most of the drivers looked half-dead with fatigue, so early had they awoken in the communes, I suppose, and the traffic itself seemed to rumble by in monotonous exhaustion. I went one morning to the Lugou Bridge, which used to be the city limit for foreigners, and standing there amongst its 282 sculpted lions, all different, above its green-rushed river, watched those tired reinforcements labouring into the city: on the next bridge upstream, big black puffing freight trains, wailing their whistles and snorting; on the next bridge to the south, bumper to bumper an unbroken line of ugly brown trailer-trucks; across the old structure beside me, past the ancient stele eulogizing Morning Moonlight on Lugou Bridge, half a million bicyclists, half-awake, half-asleep, listless on their way to work.

Somewhere over there, I knew, was the source and fulcrum of the Chinese presence – the Inner City of Beijing, which used to be Peking, which used to be Peiping, which was Kubla Khan's Dadu – the home of Deng Xiaoping, the home of Chairman Mao, the home of The Manchu Emperors, and the Mings and the Hans before them. I approached it warily. Like the supplicants of old China, kept waiting for a year or two before granted audience with the Son of Heaven, I hung around the fringes of the place, waiting for a summons.

I grinned a lot, and ran (but not too energetically, for the temperature was around 95°F). If Shanghai felt at first unexpectedly familiar, Beijing seemed almost unimaginably abroad. Everything was different here. The faces were different, the eyes were different, the manners were colder and more aloof. Nobody wanted help with gerunds. Though as it happened people were more attractively dressed than they had been in Shanghai, far more girls in skirts and blouses, even a few young men in suits and ties, still they were infinitely more alien to me. The children, their heads often shaved or close-clipped, their cheek-bones high, did not respond so blithely. A sort of grave and massive contemplation greeted me wherever I went, as though through each pair of thoughtful eyes all the billion Chinese people, Jilin to Yunnan, were inspecting me as I passed.

Beneath that great green sky, treading those interminable concrete pavements, I felt awfully far from home: and when I followed the immemorial tourist route, and took a car to the Great Wall at Badaling, there on the sun-blazed masonry, looking out across those vast northern plains and purpled mountains, I felt I was breaking some strange and lifelong dream. The Wall has been reconstructed around Badaling Gate, and is overrun there by tourists of all nationalities, milling among the cars and buses below, having their pictures taken, riding the resident camel, eating little peaches and drinking Kekou Kele, 'Tasty and Happy' – Coke, that is. It is easy to escape them, though. You make the fearfully steep ascent away from the gate towards the watchtower to the west ('We certainly are thankful to you, Mr Kung,' I heard a sweating American businessman unconvincingly gasp, as he dragged himself, temples pulsing, up these formidable steps, 'for making this trip possible – isn't this a *great* trip, you guys?')

Once at the tower, you find that beyond it the wall is reconstructed no further, but degenerates instantly into crumbled stone and brickwork, rambling away over the undulating ridges with nobody there at all. I walked a long way along it, out into the empty countryside, all silent but for the wind, all lifeless but for the hairy caterpillars which crossed and re-crossed the uneven stonework beneath my feet. But lo, when in the middle of nowhere I sat down upon the parapet to think about my rather lonely situation, out of that wilderness four or five wispy figures emerged, and opening paper bags and wrappings of sackcloth, asked if I wished to buy some antique bells or backscratchers. Yet again, China had topsy-turvied me. I had fallen among old acquaintances, and when one by one they took turns to look through my binoculars, well, said I to myself, what's so strange about the Great Wall of China, anyway?

Looked at from the east, Peking is not remote at all – only 100 miles from the sea, only three hours or so by air from Tokyo. It is only when you come to it out of the west, or more pertinently out of the Western sensibility, that it remains so romantically distant. On a Monday afternoon I went down to the gigantic railway station, twin-towered and green-roofed (escalator out of order) to see the arrival of the Trans-Siberian Express from Moscow. This was a dramatic occasion. Hundreds of us had come to meet the train, for hours beforehand we waited in the cavernous International Travellers' Waiting Room, and when the bell rang, the great doors were opened and we burst on to the platform, an air of headiest expectancy prevailed. We stood on one leg, so to speak, we stood on the other – we looked at our watches again, we sat down, we got up – we gave the children another bottle of Kekou Kele to keep them quiet – and there, slowly round the curve into the station, very, very grandly appeared the Trans-Siberian.

With a triumphant blast of its whistle it came majestically to Beijing, the three engineers in their cab sitting there like a trio of admirals on a flagship bridge, and the waiting people clapped, and cheered, and waved newspapers, as the doors opened and from Mongolia or Siberia, Omsk or Moscow itself, their travel-worn loved ones fell home into China. One coach was full of a Western travel group: and these voyagers, as they emerged glazed and haggard on the platform, looking wonderingly around them, reminded me of the long-lost pilots returning to earth out of the space ship, in the closing sequences of *Close Encounters*.

There is not much left of Old Peking, except for Protected Treasures. The city walls have been torn down, most of the fortress gates have vanished, the clutter of medievalism which so entranced the old travellers has been swept away as though it never were. Across the face of the central city has been laid the cruel thoroughfare called Changan, down which the trolley-buses trundle and the bikes chaotically swarm. Here and there though, all the same, I felt a powerful tug of organic continuity, in this city of 2,000 years.

I felt it for instance at the Summer Palace of the last of the Manchu Empresses, which is now a public park, but is still everyone's idea of a Chinese imperial retreat, with its pagodas and its towering temples, its ornamental bridges among the water-lilies, its myriad boats upon the limpid lake, its covered way, decorated with a thousand scenes of Chinese legend, from which it is said no pair of lovers can emerge unbetrothed, and its ridiculous Marble Paddle-Steamer for ever moored beside the quay (the Empress built the place with money intended for the reconstruction of the Chinese Navy, and commissioned this nautical folly, they say, as a slap in the face of the outraged Fleet).

I sensed the constancy of things ominously when, lifting my head unawares as I walked up Qianmen Street, I saw the vast glowering shape of the Qianmen Gate blocking the thoroughfare in front, for all the world as though it were still the portentous

gateway, as it used to be, into the Inner City beyond. I sensed it
delectably beside the lonely neglected pagoda of Balizhuang,
twittered about by martens out on the western outskirts, at
whose feet the women of the local commune worked crouching
in their straw hats among the beanpoles, chitter-chattering half-
hidden like so many swallows themselves. I felt it pungently in
the traditional pharmacy called The Shared Benevolence Hall,
founded in 1669, which is a treasure-house of arcane specifics,
stack upon stack of mysterious powders, brown bottles of roots
and seeds, phials of restorative nuts, sea-horses, antlers, extract
of deer-tail, heart of monkey . . .

In the early mornings I used to go wandering through the
hutongs, the crooked quarters of small courtyard houses which
survive here and there off the huge new highways. A curious
hush pervades these parts. No motor-traffic goes along the
alleyways, high walls conceal the jumbled yards. Only by
peering through half-open gates can you glimpse the tangled,
crowded life within, meshed in laundry and potted plants, here
a man in no shirt eating porridge from a tin bowl, there an old
woman smoking her first cigarette of the day, or a girl in a
spotless white blouse extracting her bicycle from the rubble. A
faint haze of smoke hangs in the air, and from the public
lavatory, smelling violently of mingled excrement and disinfec-
tant, heavy breathing and a vigorous swishing of brooms shows
that some unprivileged comrade is fulfilling early-morning
labour norms. Nobody ever took much notice of me, wandering
these quiet lanes as the sun came up: only a fairly hooded eye
focused on me now and then, when a woman emerged to empty
her slops down a drain, or a bicycle bell chivvied me out of the
way.

And once very early I strayed over a bridge to a leafy path
beside a moat. I was led there by a curious cacophany of shouts,
singing and twanged instruments, and I found it to be the most
hauntingly timeless place of all. It was a place of self-fulfilment.
Resolutely facing a high stone rampart above the moat, like Jews
at the Wailing Wall, all along the path men and women were
rehearsing their own particular accomplishments privately in
the dawn. As we sing in the evening tub, so the people of
Beijing go to that wall. Here was a man, his face a few inches
from the masonry, declaiming some heroic soliloquy. Here a
woman was practising an astonishing range of arpeggios, shrill

soprano to resonant baritone. A splendid bass was singing a
romantic ballad, a poet seemed to be trying out a lyric, an old
man with a bicycle was plucking the strings of an antique lute.
I thought of joining in, so universal did these impulses seem,
sending To Be Or Not To Be reverberating down that wall, or
perhaps reciting some of my own purpler passages: but I
restrained myself, as a Foreign Guest, and just whistled my way
home to breakfast.

I must have walked a hundred miles! and gropingly I circled
towards the centre of things – to what the old Chinese would
have called the centre of *all* things. The measured and muffled
restraint of this city was like a fog in the sunshine. Gentle,
unpushing, polite, its people kept me always wondering, and I
missed the flash of under-life that gives most great cities their
clarity. I missed scamps, drunks, whores, hagglers, ticket touts
offering me seats (which Heaven forfend) for the Chinese opera.
I saw no Dostoevsky brooding over his minced shrimps, no
tragic rebel sticking up wall posters. All seemed in bland order.
I had been told to look out, in the dizzily westernized new
Jianguo Hotel, for Party officials in expensive suits taking
luncheon with their mistresses: but all I saw were security
guards from the American Embassy, eating Weight-Watchers'
Salad.

How bored this quarter of the earth must be! Even the
procreation of the urban Chinese is limited, if not by law, at
least by powerful persuasion. They must not gamble, there is
nowhere to dance, it is miles on a bike to a cinema, and if they
turn the TV on, what do they get but improving documentaries,
English lessons, historical dramas of suitable import or Chinese
opera. Their one emotional release seems to be eating, which
they do with a gusto in which all their passions are surely
sublimated. The grander restaurants of Beijing generally have
two sections, one for bigwigs and foreigners, the other for the
masses: but though the downstairs rooms are usually rough and
ready, with linoleum table-cloths and creaky old electric fans,
an equal riotous festivity attends them all.

No wonder the Chinese are such hypochondriacs. They live
so strangely, I was coming to feel, in a condition of such crossed
uncertainty and brainwash, that psychotic illness must be
rampant. I went to one restaurant devoted to the cult of

Dinetotherapy, sponsored by another 300-year-old herb store, and was not surprised to find it prospering mightily. When I told the waiter I was suffering from headaches and general debility, he prescribed Sautéed Chicken with Fruit of Chinese Wolfberry, followed by Giant Prawns Steamed in Ginger. They worked a treat: I walked out feeling terrific.

But not all the prawns in China can cure the stresses of history, and the real malaise of Beijing, I came to think, was its domination by an ideology so all-pervading, so arbitrary, in many ways so honourable, but apparently so inconstant, which can change the very way the nation thinks from one year to another. Today it is liberal and welcoming, Chinese tradition is honoured, people are free to wear what they like, consort with foreigners if they will, sell their ducks in a free market and even build themselves houses with the profits. Yesterday it was puritanically narrow, the revolutionary condition was permanent, aliens were devils, Mao caps and floppy trousers were *de rigueur*, angry activists with step-ladders and paint-brushes went all down that covered way at the Summer Palace, expunging pictures of unprogressive myth. And tomorrow, when another generation succeeds to domination, everything may be different again, and all the values so painstakingly absorbed into the public consciousness may have to be ripped out of mind once more.

There is a blankness to this despotism. What is it? Who is it? Is it the people we see on the TV news, smiling benevolently at visiting delegates, or is it scroundrels out of sight? Is it noble at heart, or rotten? Is it genial Deng Xiaoping, or some up-and-coming tyrant we have never heard of? If you climb to the top of Jingshan, Coal Hill, the ornamental mount on which the last of the Ming Emperors hanged himself from a locust tree, you may look down upon a string of pleasure-lakes. Their northern waters, within the Behai park, are alive always with pleasure-craft, and their lakeside walks are always crowded. The southern lakes look dead and sterile. No rowing-boats skim their surfaces. No lovers take each other's photographs. The buildings on their banks, contained within high walls, look rich but tightly shuttered, and only occasionally do you glimpse a big black car snaking its way down to Changan.

This is where that despotism resides. Behind those walls, beside those silent lakes, the condition of the Chinese is decided,

whether by cynical opportunists shacked up with girls and
Japanese electronics, or by sombre philosophers bent over their
calligraphy. The compound is called Zhongnanhai, and if it all
looks numb from Jingshan, it must really be full of gigantic
thrust and calculation. Its main entrance is to the south, with
tilted eaves and two great guardian lions. The red flag flies
bravely on a mast outside, and within the gate an inner wall –
the 'spirit wall' of old China – is inscribed with the cabalistic
text 'Serve The People'. You cannot see past it, though. Two
armed sentries stand there, with two more watchful over their
shoulders. They look distinctly unwelcoming, even to Foreign
Guests, as they stare motionless and expressionless into the
street: and sure enough, when I asked them if I could take a
stroll inside Zhongnanhai, they seemed to think not.

But anyway Zhongnanhai is only authority for the moment
– only a few years ago it was the private preserve of Mao's
widow Jiang Qing, chief witch of the Gang of Four, and now
locked up for ever. Power in Beijing runs much deeper than
that, is endemic to the very existence of the city: when the
summons came to me at last, I knew better where to go.
  From the top of Jingshan a dead straight axis runs from north
to south – or, as the Chinese always say, from south to north –
through the centre of the city. This is the line of Chinese power.
It is like one of those energy-leys the visionaries profess to find
in Europe, conveying the earth force century after century from
mountain to megalith. From the pavilion on the hill it runs
steeply down to the entrance of Jingshan Park (posters of
criminals, placards around their necks, stuck up for the public
example), and over a wide highway, and across that moat where
the singers sing at dawn, and through a great flowery gateway,
the Gate of Inspired Military Genius, into the Forbidden City of
the Emperors.
  This is only a museum now, but it retains the numen of
absolute command – a walled city in itself, a matchless assembly
of palaces, temples, gardens and gazebos for the exaltation of
one single man, the only Son of Heaven, the chieftain of China.
Marvellous objects litter our path through this fabulous enclave,
grimacing lions of gilded bronze, huge sculpted tortoises,
incense burners, ancient crinkled rocks. Now the way opens
into a noble courtyard, speckled with green grass, now it

narrows into a staircase, or passes through some tall gilded hall, or pauses upon a belvedere, or crosses a running stream. Here is the Palace of Heavenly Purity, and here the Palace of Earthly Tranquillity, and here the Hall of Supreme Harmony itself, where surrounded by gold and vermilion, seated on an immense carved throne amidst dimmed lights and incense, the Emperor looked down contemptuously upon the representatives of the rest of humanity, grovelling on the floor below.

But wait! The line goes on. Down the monumental steps – through the Meridian Gate, where the Emperor, reviewing parades of prisoners, decided there and then which should be decapitated – under that Gate of the Heavenly Peace, Tiananmen, which every good Chinese would wish to see before he dies – and suddenly the prospect opens into a plaza a hundred times, a thousand times as big as anything the Manchus knew. It is the forum of the new China, Tiananmen Square, the greatest square on earth, where an army could be massed, where all the kites in the world could fly, where a million people can gather to cheer their leaders upon the gateway balcony, and stare with curious awe at the 20,000 elders massed in their grandstands upon the northern side.

Nothing, not even in Beijing, is quite so utterly concrete as Tiananmen Square. Across it Changan runs mercilessly east and west, on each side of it are monstrous buildings in the Revolutionary Heroic manner, all columns and swollen symmetry – the Museum of History on the east, on the west the Great Hall of the People, which was built by 25,000 labourers in ten months, and is bigger than all the buildings of the Forbidden City put together. In the centre of the square towers the obelisk of the People's Heroes Monument; at the southern end, immense but squat, there stands the four-square Mausoleum of Mao Tse-tung, looking back in vindication past obelisk and Great Hall to the gate from which, on 1 October 1949, Mao himself, the Great Helmsman, proclaimed the new Heaven and the new Earth. Morose sentries stand guard at each corner of this tomb, wearing sandals or baseball shoes, there are gigantic sculpted panels of peasants resurgent, soldiers victorious, and inside, behind a towering effigy of himself, Mao lies in a crystal coffin embalmed, he hopes, for all the ages.

But wait again! The line ends not with Mao Tse-tung! Past the mausoleum, through the Qianmen Gate, straight as a die the power-force flows through the Outer City to the Temple of Heaven in the south. Three times a year, in old Peking, the Emperor journeyed to this holy place to communicate with his only superiors, the gods themselves. All windows were shuttered for his passing, and the city was plunged in silence: and though we ourselves can take the No. 116 bus down there (try not to hang on to the safety bars – they leave your hands all brown) still a mighty suggestion of celestial collusion awaits us there as it awaited him. After sundry rites and sacrifices in the Temple complex it was his duty to ascend the Circular Mound, built in arcane configurations of the number nine, there to seal the intimate association between this city and the ultimate source of all authority, Destiny itself.

We will do the same. Up those terraces we go, to the wide round platform at the top, and on the slab in the very centre we will stand like the Son of Heaven before us, and speak aloud to the gods. 'All Power is Illusion!' we may impertinently choose to cry: and instantly, by some eerie manipulation of the acoustics, we find ourselves surrounded by the sound of it – *Power, Power, Power, Illusion, Illusion!* – embracing us within the echo of our own thoughts, and making us feel that we really do stand at the bottom of a cylinder reaching directly, from that stone on the mound in Beijing, China, to the Emperor or Chairman of all things.

Dazzled, bewildered, profoundly affected, all at once, I retreated from the Chinese presence. Some of those caterpillars on the Great Wall, I had noticed, never make it to the other side, but settle in crannies among the paving: and from there if all goes well, I suppose, they turn themselves into butterflies, and flutter away into the empyrean from the very substance of China. I felt rather like them when the time came for me to leave, for I took the advice the Bureaucrat had given me, and floated my way out through those humped green mountains of Guangxi, away in the humid south.

My two cities of China had left me hazed with conflicting emotions and contradictory conclusions, and like a sleep-walker I wandered back towards the coast. I bicycled down dusty lanes through fecund communes, where labouring girls waved and laughed beneath their conical hats, as in propaganda posters. I clambered precipitous hillocks to take jasmine tea in faery huts.

I joined the great daily migration of the tourists down the Li river, stretched out flat in the front of the boat, eating lychees in the sun, drifting through a fantasy of bulbous mountains, and green, green paddy-fields, and dragon-flies, and ferry-men, and riverside villages clouded in the song of crickets, and cormorant fishermen squatting on bamboo rafts, and junks punted upstream by women bent agonizingly double at their poles, and geese in the shallows, and peasants high on rocky tracks, and water-buffalos snuffling, and old river steamers panting and thumping, while the lychees got steadily squashier in the heat, and the sad man beside me, erect in the prow, bared his chest in the breeze and sailed through those legendary landscapes singing the proud songs of his revolutionary youth.

And so I came out of the heart of China back to the sea once more. I had found no absolutes after all. I had found nothing immutable. I had met a people as confused as any other. I had seen marvellous things and miserable, I had eaten pickled turnip with Mrs Wang and been sent packing by the sentries of Zhongnanhai. I had been cured of headache by Chinese wolf-berry. I had successfully evaded the Chinese opera. I had bought a bamboo goat, and beaten Mr Lu at checkers in the park. I had visited the grand simplicities of my imagination, and found them grand indeed, but muddled. I had reached that mighty presence at last, and it was smiling nervously.

Out on the Pearl river, surrounded by black sampans, the ship lay waiting.

9

THE NAVEL CITY

Cuzco, 1961

❦

I had never been to Cuzco before, and I have never been there since, but few cities have left a more shining and sharp-edged impression in my mind. I remember vividly to this day the look in the eye of the baby to be glimpsed in the last sentence of this little cameo.

Out of a Peruvian mountain fifteen llamas sway down an ancient road, silently pursued by a man in a poncho and knee-breeches and a woman wearing a white straw hat, a blazing flurry of petticoats, and a baby-hammock on her back. The man is chewing an opiate wad of the coca leaf, the woman is planning to request the intercession of the Lord of the Earthquakes, whose miraculous figure in the town below is known to sweat in sympathy and weep real tears of compassion. To the north an elderly American locomotive, with a cow-catcher and an old wail of a whistle, is plunging zig-zag into the valley with a string of cattle-trucks. From the south a clanging of cracked bells rings out of a florid campanile. And as those travellers swing round the last dusty corner, with a soft shuffle of bare feet and padded cameloid hoofs, there below them they see, clear-cut in that alpine sunshine, the capital of the Land of the Four Quarters.

It could only be Cuzco, a little city of such supreme interest and historical symbolism, of such variety and punch, that in the South American context it combines the compulsions of a Stonehenge, a small Seville, and a Katmandu. It lies at 11,000 feet in the Peruvian altiplano, and to reach it from Lima you fly breathtakingly across the Andes in an unpressurized aircraft, nibbling an oxygen tube like a hookah: but its valley is green, the hills around it are as fresh and springy as English downland,

and only the testy pumping of your heart at night, and the celestial supervision of the snow peaks, remind you that on the other side of the world the ski-slopes of Saint-Moritz are 5,000 feet lower than your hotel.

Five centuries ago this remote and barricaded place, somewhere between Lake Titicaca and the dreadful Amazon jungle, was the capital of the Inca empire, a brilliant but baleful organism, part refulgent aristocracy, part deadening discipline, that extended its power over most of the Andean territories, commanding an area as large as France, Switzerland, Italy, Belgium, Holland and Luxemburg all reluctantly put together. Here the mummified Inca emperors, all entrails sucked out, sat flicked by fly-whisks down the decades in the glittering Temple of the Sun. Here the Chosen Women span their incomparable textiles in imperial virginity, here the ferocious Inca generals marshalled their armies, here the diviners interpreted the intestines of their guinea-pigs, the priests prepared their intoxicated victims for the sacrifice, the marvellous Inca surgeons performed their prodigies of trepanning, amputation and excision. In the fifteenth century, when we in Britain were just beginning to be ourselves, Cuzco was the heart of a civilization so strange, precise and rarefied that nothing remotely like it has ever been seen again.

Cuzco was the core of it all – the very name means 'navel' – and everywhere in the town you can still feel the presence of the Incas. Often it is vulgarized in tourism and profit, in Incaland souvenirs, costume jewellery of weird exoticism, schoolgirl vestals with lamps and improbable headdresses at folklore festivals. More essentially, though, it is perpetuated in the massive masonry that still forms, to this very day, the ground layer of Cuzco: vast and impeccably chiselled stonework, like the craft of meticulous giants, with queer unexpected angles and corners of daunting exactitude. The basis of the Temple of the Sun remains, marvellously rounded beneath a church, and so does the wall of the House of the Chosen Women. There are sacred Inca snakes still above a doorway, and sacred Inca sanctuaries still in a cloister, and brooding above the city, like a gargantuan Maiden Castle of limestone, stands the enigmatic fortress called Sacsahuaman, incorporating some of the largest chunks of stone ever raised into dubious utility by the ingenuity of man.

But all this terrifying structure Pizarro toppled, with few other weapons but guts, greed and a little gunpowder: and on the prostrate capital of the Incas, *sans* Emperor, *sans* Chosen Women, *sans* soothsayers and all, the Spaniards built themselves a second city, dedicated to a very different version of the Sun God. Gilded, ornate, candle-flickering, snobbish, radiant with Christian miracles and the titles of grandees, with arches and bell-towers and graceful plazas, with songs from Andalusia and Moorish doors and sizzling coquettes and silver tabernacles – there the Spaniards' Cuzco stands today, triumphant still above the Inca engineers. They called it 'The Very Noble and Great City of Cuzco, the Most Principal and Head of the Kingdoms of Peru': and deep among the canyons of the Peruvian Andes, it remains a paradoxical memorial to the virility of Europe.

Returned to its origins it might not be remarkable, but in this utterly alien setting, high on the continental divide, Spanish Cuzco really smacks, as its old divines would wish it, of the miraculous. Fretted, solemn and domineering are the churches that stand around the Plaza de Armas – the dark but glistening Cathedral, the arrogant Church of the Jesuits, the gloomy shrine of Jesus and Mary beside the hall of the Inquisition, the aloof Church of the Triumph from which, in 1536, Our Lady emerged with the Christ Child in her arms to disconcert an Indian rebellion. Elaborate and delectable are the mansions of the old magnificos, with their dazzling gardens glimpsed through crooked doorways, their dripping pitchers of flowers, their crests and carved balconies and suggestions of silken solace. Nearly every church has its specimen of the Cuzco School, a sickly but compelling seventeenth-century style of painting that specialized in the cherubic, the wide-eyed and the rosy-cheeked. Nearly every corner has its hint of Spanish pride: as one of the local guidebooks apostrophizes the city: 'We, your sons, who proudly bear you in our hearts alive with the fiery flood of your blood, do know well that the beating of your heart is still latent under the embers of the years.'

But the Spaniards do not dominate Cuzco today, for all the flourish of their architecture. Nor do the vanished Incas. Stonehenge and Seville it may represent, but for me it is, above all, a Peruvian Katmandu. Here you stand always among the mountains, and from here the ancient roads stride out to the trekking country of the Andes and the glorious snow summits. Cuzco today is mostly run by mestizos, half-castes of Spanish and Indian cross, but all its living colour and verve is provided by the fuller-blooded Quechua Indians of the countryside. Sometimes they look like gipsies; sometimes, in their trailing skirts, like Navajo Indians from Arizona; sometimes, with their tall white hats and shawls, like ladies out of Borrow's wilder Wales; but to me they usually seem, and sound, and smell, and move like Sherpas of the Himalayas – less carefree perhaps, less hearty certainly, but still instinct with dung-fires and potatoes, smoky dark interiors, sweat, untanned leather, back-breaking labour, poverty, superstition, resilience, and the viscous alcohol that is brewed in these parts by fermenting maize in women's saliva.

They are all over Cuzco, prostrate before the Lord of the Earthquakes like Tibetans in a tinkling temple, or hastening barefoot through the night, down the shadows of a cobbled alley, bent double with loads of straw. Away in the desolate expanses of the altiplano the Indians of Peru are usually demoralized, I am assured, often destitute, sometimes actually starving; but you would not know it in Cuzco. Their presence there is possibly a little wan, but still earthy. Their children are so adorable that I would happily adopt half a dozen myself. Their women, strolling thick-set through the tumbled market in their rakish hats and flounces, spinning their wool as they walk, look to me as though only an ounce of opportunity, only a dram of education, only a year of square meals, would release resources of wonderful strength and character. Their menfolk, half doped as they are by coca, malnutrition and the degradation of centuries, look as though nothing on earth, from a hostile omen to the most atrocious of hangovers, could deter them from the endless dull drudgery of their lives.

Undoubtedly the Indians win, in this Most Principal and Head of the Kingdoms of Peru. Beside them the half-castes look upstart, and the Lima gentry doomed. It will be a long, long time before they come into their own again – if indeed they ever do: but when I run my mind's eye back over the Cuzco scene, away from the snakes above the doorway, away from the smoke-darkened Lord of the Earthquakes, past the campaniles and the fortress on the hill and the puffing wailing train, in the end it rests again upon those distant figures of the Inca road, the fifteen lolloping llamas, the man with the plug of coca in his cheek, the barefoot woman in the bright but dusty petticoats, and the infinitesimal baby Quechua on her back, so swaddled in textiles that only one brown pondering eye shows through the muffles, jogging eternally out of the Andes.

10

HILL STATION

Darjeeling, 1970

I have mixed feelings about the Indian hill stations, some of which (Ootacamund for instance) are altogether too neo-British for my taste. The marvellous setting of Darjeeling, though, the most spectacular of them all, easily puts history in its proper place.

Darjeeling, the most celebrated of the Indian hill stations, is all smallness. It is small physically, of course – hard even to find upon the map of India, so tucked away is it like a trinket on the northern frontiers. But it is still smaller figuratively. It is the most deliberately diminutive town I know, as though it is always trying to make itself less substantial still. One crosses vast scorched plains to reach it from Calcutta, over colossally winding rivers, through a landscape that has no end: but at the foot of the hills Darjeeling sends a toy train to meet you – a gay little blue-painted trundle of a train, which takes you indefatigably puffing and chugging up through the forests and the tea-gardens to the town.

Little people greet you at the top. Little ponies canter about little streets. Hundreds and thousands of merry little children tumble all about you. The town is perched upon a narrow ridge, about 7,000 feet up, with deep gorges falling away on either side, and when I arrived there for the first time I found it swirled all around by cloud. It felt curiously private and self-contained – like a childish fancy, I thought, a folly, a town magically reduced in scale and shut off from the world by vapour: but then, as to a crash of drums in a *coup de théâtre*, a gap momentarily appeared in the ever-shifting clouds, and there standing tremendously in the background, their snows flushed pink with sunlight, attended by range upon range of foothills and serenely surveying the expanse of the world, stood the divine mass of the Himalayan mountains.

I saw Darjeeling's point, and cut myself down to size.

Some visitors never see the snow-peaks at all, for they are often invisible for days at a time. Anyway there is no need to go on about them. It is enough to say that to see Kanchenjunga and its peers from Darjeeling, in the cool of the morning, is one of the noblest experiences of travel. It is a kind of vision. It has moved generations of pilgrims to mysticism, and even more to over-writing.

Yet it is not the spectacle of the Himalayas that sets the style of Darjeeling. It is simply their presence. The town lives in the knowledge of them, and so acknowledges another scale of things. Its littleness is not inferiority complex, but self-awareness, and it gives the community a particular intensity and vivacity. Darjeeling is built in layers, neatly along its ridge like an exhibition town, from the posh hotels and the villas at the top to the jumbled bazaar quarter at the bottom: and all the way down this dense tiered mass of buildings life incessantly buzzes, hums and fizzes. Darjeeling's energies seem to burn the brighter for their smallness, and not a corner of the town is still, or empty, or dull.

It is a place of astonishing cheerfulness. Everybody seems to be feeling simply splendid. Perhaps they all are, for the air is magnificently brilliant, the heat is seldom too hot and the cold not often icy. The nineteenth-century Welshman who first put Darjeeling on the map saw it from the start as a sanatorium, and the Rajah of Sikkim kindly handed it over to the British Governor-General of India 'for the purpose of enabling the servants of his government suffering from sickness to avail themselves of its advantages'. Today Darjeeling's high spirits never seem to flag. The children never stop playing, the youths never end their horse-play, the tourists never tire of clattering hilariously about the town on hired ponies. The cicadas sing all day long in the gardens, and ever and again from down the hill come the hoots and puffs of the little trains (which prefer to travel gregariously, and come merrily up from Siliguri two or three at a time).

To the stranger it all seems intenser, more concentrated than real life, and especially after dark, when the braziers are aglow in the alleys of the bazaar, and the hotel lights comfortably shine above. Then half Darjeeling turns out for a stroll at Chaurasta, a triangular piazza half-way along the ridge, and on my own first evening in Darjeeling I went and sat on a bench there, and watched the town go by. Beyond the square the ridge fell away abruptly into the night, and there were only the dark foothills out there, and a suggestion of the snow-peaks, and the stars that now and then appeared in unnatural brilliance through the shifting clouds.

To and fro against this celestial backdrop the people of Darjeeling loitered, strolled and gossiped like Spaniards on their evening promenade, or more exotic Venetians at St Mark's. There were tall flashing girls in saris and nose-clips. There were brown gnome-like men in fur caps. There were slant-eyed children of astonishing beauty, and boys with wild eager faces like Gengis Khan. There were monks, and priests, and soldiers, and grand Indian gentlemen in tweeds, and giggly Indian girls in cotton party frocks. There were mountain porters hastening back from work, carrying rucksacks and tent-poles. There were ancient men with plaited pigtails. There were two hippies, and a nun, and four French tourists, and me watching it all, as in hallucination, from a corner bench beside the bandstand.

It was like a microcosm of the world, assembled up there from the plains and mountains, ushered into that little square, reduced to a neater and more manageable size, and given double shots of adrenalin.

'What is your country?' a man peremptorily demanded, as we met face to face and unavoidably on a narrow hill track, and when I told him Wales, to the west of England, he asked further: 'Is it a high pass to get there?'

Unimaginably high are the passes, indescribably remote the valleys, from which in the century since Captain Lloyd founded Darjeeling the population of the town has found its way to the ridge. This is a frontier settlement. Some of those snow-peaks are in India proper, some in Sikkim and Bhutan, some in the Kingdom of Nepal, some in the People's Republic of Tibet. The town stands on the edge of mysteries, and its people have migrated from many parts of the eastern Himalayas, and from the plains below. The old sanatorium of the memsahibs is far more nowadays: not merely a celebrated resort, but an important bazaar, a centre of local government and a kind of ethnic demonstration.

No small town in the world can show so many kinds, and types, and manners of people. The little Lepchas, the original inhabitants of the region, are seldom more than five feet high, but immensely strong and agile. The Sherpas from eastern Nepal, the high-altitude porters of Everest and Kanchenjunga, move with an inexorable striding impetus, as though they can't stop. The Tibetans often look immensely sophisticated, trendy almost, ready for any Chelsea discotheque with their flared pants and impeccable complexions. The Gurkhas look soldiers through and through, always marching, even off parade, with head high and chest out. One sees few sleepy or dullard faces among these Mongoloid peoples of the north: all seem eminently capable – straight square-set people, who look as though, deposited in a Brooklyn back-alley or one of the remoter villages of the southern Urals, they would instantly find their feet.

But they are only one element in the Darjeeling *mélange*. There are many other kinds of Nepalese, for instance – Gurungs, Magars, Tamangs, Newars. There are refugees from Tibet proper, and Indian Army soldiers from the Punjab and Rajasthan. Here comes a slim dark girl in blue pyjamas, who might be Annamese, or perhaps Malay. Here are four Rajput officers of the garrison, with their thin black Sandhurst moustaches and their suede boots. The Hindu holy man beside the lane is smeared mysteriously with yellow ochre. The Bengali family being hoisted on to its ponies is all guileless anticipation, proud young father holding the baby (who wears a pink peaked cap with yellow velvet ribbons), mother in gold and red sari assiduously combing the already immaculate hair of a small boy apparently dressed for an exceptionally extravagant wedding. The eyes that peer at you between bushy beard and bundled turban are, of course, the eyes of a Sikh: the shy porcelain smile from the lady at the next table is a smile from the palm trees and sands of Madras.

In the autumn they have races at Darjeeling, and then one may see this demographic jumble at its most cheerful. The racecourse is endearingly claimed to be the smallest in the world: at the end of a race the competitors run breakneck off the course into the approach road, an unnerving experience for newcomers. The meetings are not very formal. Young men play football in the middle of the track. Between races the horses graze casually on grassy spaces round about. A dribble of racegoers stumbles down the mountain track from the town above, carrying umbrellas and race cards, and a stream of jeeps and rattly taxis blasts its way along the motor-road.

Still, the traditional procedures are honoured. The races are run by the Gymkhana Club of Darjeeling, and in the official stand the Stewards and Judges, mostly Army officers, sit in well-cut elegance with immensely superior ladies. Sometimes the senior steward takes a stroll about the enclosure, moving with the lordly benevolence common to racing bigwigs from Longchamps to Kentucky Downs. The race card is printed with every refinement of the racegoer's jargon and the rules are, of course, severe ('Trainers and Jockeys are hereby notified that Riotous Behaviour, Intemperance, or other Improper Conduct, although not occurring on the Race Course, will be taken cognizance of by the Stewards'). It would take an iconoclast indeed, to defy the decrees of the Darjeeling Gymkhana Club.

But all around that grandstand, swarming about the bookies at their little wooden stands, picnicking up the grassy slopes behind, haggling with the sellers of nuts or the purveyors of infallible tips, is the infinite variety of Darjeeling, impervious to regulation. Such a conglomeration of bone structures, life-styles, tastes, gestures! Such a cacophony of voices, deep, cracked, sing-song or bell-like! Such a marvellous fugue of history performed there, in the intersections of history, religion, or ambition that have brought this pot-pourri of the human kind to place its bets on the fourth race!

The bell rings; the flap drops; hurtling around the track in billows of dust come three or four black Tibetan ponies, ridden at desperate speed and with savage concentration by fierce little high-cheeked jockeys – brilliantly liveried in scarlets and yellows, visors low over their eyes – rocketing around that mini-track, as the crowd rises tip-toe with excitement, until they shoot out of sight, with cheers, laughter and catcalls, behind the grandstand and off the course. It is as though the scouts of Attila have passed through. The stranger may feel a certain sense of shock, but the stewards do not seem disconcerted. 'Jolly good show,' they say to each other. 'Hell of a good race, what?'

For the most dogmatic progressive will not deny to little Darjeeling a tug of nostalgia. It is harmless. It is only a fragrance of earlier times, a Victorian bouquet still lingering up here along the ridge. Darjeeling is largely built in that gabled semi-chalet style so dear to Victorian pleasure-seekers, and imposed upon its gallimaufry of peoples is a decorous, poke-bonnet, tea-and-biscuits style. Nobody in their senses would wish it otherwise. It is an essential part of Darjeeling's minuscule mystique, and used to suggest to me a musical-box town, where pretty little melodies would tinkle in the sunshine, while clockwork figures in top-hats and bustles jerkily proceeded along the Mall. The very names of the place carry this old evocation – the Esplanade, Happy Valley, Step Aside: and the main road to the plains is still known in Darjeeling as the Cart Road.

Some of the hotels are deliciously Victorian. The porridge at the Windamere [sic] Hotel is, I am told by unimpeachable authorities, unsurpassed in Scotland, while the tea at the Mount Everest is tea, my dear, just like we used to have it. Shopping in Darjeeling, too, is agreeably old-school. Patiently attentive are the assistants, instantly to hand is the chair for memsahib, and one almost expects to find, winging it across the Kashmiri shawls and the Tibetan prayer-wheels, one of those wire-pulley change receptacles one used to see in provincial English drapers' long ago.

Most of Darjeeling's pleasure (I except the illicit joys of the bazaar quarter) would perfectly satisfy our grandparents. There is the classic pleasure, for instance, which I abstemiously denied myself, of getting up at three in the morning to see the sunrise and the top of Everest from Tiger Hill. There are the pleasures of Excursions to Places of Interest, like Ghoom Rock or Kaventer's Dairy Farm. There are the pleasures of identifying wild flowers and trees, or sketching, or looking at animals in the outdoor zoo (where the Llama and the Siberian Tiger, returning one's inspection morosely from their enclosures, look as though they wish the Victorian era had never dawned). There are pony-rides, of course, and there is miniature golf, and when I was there *Ruddigore* was being performed by the pupils of St Paul's School.

There is the pleasure of walking. In most of Darjeeling no cars are allowed, and this is one of the walkingest towns on earth. One may walk decorously around the town itself, or through the Botanical Gardens. One may walk into the foothills for a picnic. Or one may, stocking up with tinned pineapple and sleeping bags, engage a team of Sherpas and stride off into the distant mountains. Every year more and more people go trekking from Darjeeling, and a very healthy pastime it must be. 'No place like Darjeeling,' one stalwart matron reproachfully observed as, staggering beneath the weight of her accoutrements, she passed

me doing nothing in particular over a glass of lemonade –
'nowhere like Darjeeling for blowing the cobwebs away!'

As I say, our grandparents would have loved it: and sometimes
Darjeeling's scrapbook essence can be, to the sentimental visitor,
distinctly moving. On Jalapahar Hill, at the eastern end of the
ridge, there is a small military cantonment, complete with
parade ground, garrison church and shops for the soldiery. I
was once walking through this camp, enjoying its display of the
military aesthetic – polished brass, regimental signs in white-
washed pebbles, the clump of ammunition boots and the bristle
of sergeantly moustaches – when an unexpected sound reached
me from the parade ground behind. With a slow and melancholy
introductory wail, the Gurkha pipe band broke into the sad, sad
music of a Highland lament. I stopped dead in my dusty tracks,
and the tears came to my eyes: for what generations of my own
people, I thought, had stirred to that music in their exiles long
ago, and how strange and sweet and lonely it sounded in these
hills of the Indian frontier!

'Can I help you?' inquired a passer-by, seeing me standing
there. 'You are not ill?' Not ill, I assured him as I moved on up
the hill. Only susceptible!

Every morning before breakfast I used to walk up Observatory
Hill. This wooded hump, rising directly above the Chaurasta, is
holy to the Buddhists, who have a shrine upon its summit. All
along the steep and winding path to the top mendicants invite
the contributions of the pious – grave holy men who bow like
archbishops, jolly old crones, coveys of chirpy inquisitive
children. Two grinning stone lions guard the entrance to the
holy compound, the trees are hung all over with white prayer
flags, and mysteriously from the recesses of the shrine one may
hear the incessant murmur of prayers and tinkling of bells.
There are always people up there. Some are praying, some
meditating, some reading sacred scripts, and one I met each day
used to stand all alone among the bushes looking towards Tibet
and writing in a large black notebook.

If the weather is clear there is a glorious view of Kanchenjunga
and its peers, and while they were cooking my eggs in the hotel
down below I used to sit on the grass alone and marvel at the
immunity of Darjeeling. It has, it seemed to me, *escaped*. It knows
its own dimension, and is satisfied. Though its name is famous

everywhere, still it remains a small town of the Himalayan foothills, very close to the soil and the temple. There is material squalor enough, but seldom I think despair, still less degradation. The loads may be crippling, but still the porters find the energy to smile. The children and the chickens may be in and out of the kitchen, but the mothers never seem to get cross. The girls laugh as they laboriously chop firewood in the thickets, and the bundles of hay piled upon the backs of the labourers are speckled all over with flowers of pink and blue.

It is as though by an unconscious exertion of values Darjeeling has selected what it wants from the world below, and rejected all the rest. And such is the inner variety of the place, so lavish are its colours, so remote is it even now from the pressures of the industrialized society, that within its own limits it can afford to be tolerant. There is nothing censorious about the place. One may look, behave, dress, believe more or less as one pleases. During my stay in Darjeeling I often saw a young American dressed in the habit of a Buddhist monk. He was studying at a nearby seminary, I was told, and wore the brown cloak, the sandals and the hair-bun as to the manner born. Nobody appeared the least surprised by this anomalous figure, and even his father, who was paying him a visit from the States, seemed entirely at home with the phenomenon. 'I'm going to drink, Jimmy,' I heard him saying to his son one day, puffing at his cigar and raising his glass, 'I'm going to drink to all these wonderful, wonderful people of Darjeeling!' (And 'Say,' he tactfully added as he put his glass down, rather hastily I thought, 'is this Indian wine? *Delicious!*')

For there is an innocent merit to the place. One feels better and kinder for a visit to Darjeeling. Those stupendous mountains in the clouds have set the scale right, and adjusted the balance. It's no good fussing, they seem to say. It can't last. And this sententious thought, which occurred to me every morning after ten minutes or so upon the hill, used to remind me that my eggs were waiting for me down the lane – and down I would hurry, past that merry line of beggars, tagged by swarms of children and encouraged by avuncular sages, to where the waiter in his red turban and his polished brass badge, looking anxiously from the dining-room door, was waiting to whisk the cover off my porridge.

11

MRS GUPTA NEVER RANG

Delhi, 1975

❧

Indira Gandhi was in power in Delhi in 1975, but though she had clamped the country under a State of Emergency, harshly limiting the press and imprisoning much of the opposition, to the stranger the Indian capital felt much the same as ever. There is not much in this essay to reveal which particular regime governed India at the time of its writing: Delhi is one of those cities whose age, manner and disposition easily absorb the styles of its successive rulers.

'You see,' said the government spokesman, 'you may liken Delhi to the River Ganges, it twists and turns, many other streams join it, it divides into many parts, and it flows into the sea in so many channels that nobody may know which is the true river. You follow my train of thought? It is a metaphysical matter, perhaps. You will do best to burrow under the surface of things and discover what is not revealed to us ordinary mortals! In the meantime, you will take a cup of tea, I hope?' I took a cup of tea, milkless, very sweet, brought by a shuffling messenger in a high-buttoned jacket with a scarf around his neck, and between pleasantries I pondered the spokesman's advice. Indians, of course, love to reduce the prosaic to the mystic. It is part of their Timeless Wisdom. For several centuries the tendency has variously baffled, infuriated, amused and entranced travellers from the West, and India is full of pilgrims still, come from afar to worship at the shrines of insight. But *Delhi*? Delhi is not just a national capital, it is one of the political ultimates, one of the prime movers. It was born to power, war and glory. It rose to greatness not because holy men saw visions there but because it commanded the strategic routes from the North-west, where the conquerors came from, into the rich flatlands of the Ganges delta. Delhi is a soldiers' town, a politicians' town, a journalists', diplomats' town. It is Asia's Washington, though not so picturesque, and lives by ambition, rivalry and opportunism.

'Ah yes,' he said, 'what you are thinking is quite true, but that is the *surface* of Delhi. You are an artist, I know, you should look *beyond*! And if there is anything we can do to help your inquiries,' he added with an engaging waggle of his head, 'you have only to let us know. You may telephone us at any time and we will ring you back with the requisite information in a moment or two. We are here to help! That is why we are here! No, no, that is our duty!'

Certainly Delhi is unimaginably antique, and age is a metaphysic, I suppose. Illustrations of mortality are inescapable there, and do give the place a sort of nagging symbolism. Tombs of emperors stand beside traffic junctions, forgotten fortresses command suburbs, the titles of lost dynasties are woven into the vernacular, if only as street names.

One of the oldest and deadest places I know, for a start, is the crumbled fortress-capital of Tughluqabad in the city's southern outskirts. For a single decade it was a place of terrific consequence, for nearly seven centuries since it has been a grey wasteland of piled stones and ruined alleyways, a *memento mori* by any standard, inhabited only by the disagreeable monkeys which are the familiars of Delhi, and by a melancholy watchman who, recently transferred by the Archaeological Survey from some more frequented historical monument, now sees nobody but the apes from one day to the next.

Or consider, in another kind of allegory, the Lodi Gardens. These are popular promenades, but they are also the cemetery of the Lodi kings who thrived in the early sixteenth century. Here death and life consort on familiar terms, and especially in the early morning, when Delhi people go out for some fresh air before the sun comes up, they offer some piquant juxtapositions. All among the memorials the citizens besport themselves, pursuing their Yogic meditations in the tomb of Sikander Lodi, jogtrotting among the funerary domes, exercising their pampered dachshunds beside the Bara Gumbad Mosque or pissing, in the inescapable Delhi manner, behind the mausoleum of Mohammed Shah.

They used to say, to express the marvellous continuity of

Delhi, that seven successive capitals existed here, each super-imposed upon the last. Nowadays they are always finding new ones, and the latest tally seems to be fourteen. Few foreigners and still fewer Indians have ever heard of most of the dynasties represented, but here and there across the capital some of them have left not merely tombs or ruins but living remnants of themselves. Embedded, for instance, in one of Delhi's smarter quarters, almost within sight of the Oberoi Intercontinental, is the Moslem village shrine of Nizamuddin, built in the time of the fourteenth-century Sultan Ghiyasuddin Tughluq and still as holy as ever.

Through tortuous mucky lanes one approaches it from the busy highway, past the statutory Indian lines of beggars, crones and saddhus, through the spittle-stained portals where the old men stare, and into the intricate jumble of courts, tombs and arcades that surrounds the mosque of Nizamuddin and its sacred pool. Here mendicants lope around on knobbly staves, saintly scholars are at their books, sweet old ladies sit outside tombs (they are not allowed in, being female), and in the mosque there hustles and brushes the muezzin, an indefatigable goblin figure with white eyebrows and dainty tread. Nothing here is unpremeditated. All moves, though you might not guess it, to an immemorial schedule: the prayer call comes precisely to time, the rituals are meticulously ordered, even the whining beggars have their appointed place in the hierarchy, and when I left the precincts the imam gave me his visiting card – his name is Al Haj Hazrat Peer Qazi Syed Safdar Ali Nizami, and his cable address is HEADPRIEST DELHI.

Even more a living relic, so to speak, is the Begum Timur Jehan Shahzadi of Darya Ganj, in the old walled city of Delhi. This lady is a Moghul princess of the dynasty which made Delhi its capital in the seventeenth century and built the very city, Shahjehanabad, in whose labyrinthine recesses she lives now. Just go to the Old City, her son-in-law had assured me, and ask for the Begum Jehan's house: and though in the event this proved insufficient advice, and I spent half an afternoon stumbling through the high-walled maze of Shahjehanabad, vainly presenting the inquiry, still I relished the form of it, and thought it was rather like knocking on the door of the Great Pyramid, asking for Cheops.

I found her in the end anyway, ensconced in her front sitting-room between portraits of her imperial forebears: a short, decisive old lady with a brief mischievous smile and an air of totally liberated self-possession. There is no pretending that this princess lives much like a princess. Her old house, into which her family moved when they were ejected by later conquerors from their imperial palace, is a beguiling shambles in the old Islamic style: a couple of rooms in the Western manner for the convenience of visitors, the rest more or less medieval – a wide decrepit courtyard, a dusty trellised vine, thickly populated chambers all around. There are granddaughters and sons-in-law and undefined connections; there are skivvies and laundrymen and assorted sweepers; there are children and dogs and unexplained loiterers in doorways. Forty or fifty souls constitute the tumbled court of the Begum Timur Jehan, and through it she moves commandingly in green trousers, issuing instructions, reminiscing about emperors, traitors or ladies of the harem, and frequently consulting her highly organized notebook, all asterisks and cross-references, for addresses or reminders.

Like HEADPRIEST DELHI she lives very near the earth, close to the muck and the spittle, close to the mangy dogs and the deformed indigents in the street outside. Delhi is scarcely an innocent city, for on every layer it is riddled with graft and intrigue, but it is distinctly organic, to an atavistic degree. An apposite introduction to the city, I think, is provided by Map Eight of the *Delhi City Atlas*, which marks a substantial slab of the municipal area as being Dense Jungle: though this is now a city of a million inhabitants, it feels near the bush still. From many parts of it the open plain is in sight, and the country trees of India, the feathery tamarisks and ubiquitous acacias, invade every part of it – the animals too, for squirrels are everywhere and monkeys, buffalos, cows, goats and a million pye-dogs roam the city streets peremptorily.

There is simplicity everywhere, too, for rural people from all India flock into Delhi for jobs, for help, to see the sights. There are Sikhs and sleek Bengalis, Rajputs ablaze with jewellery, smart Gujaratis from the western coast, beautiful Tamils from the south, cloaked Tibetans smelling of untanned leather, clerks from Bombay smelling of aftershave, students, wandering sages, clumping soldiers in ammunition boots, black-veiled Moslem women, peasants in for the day from the scorched and desiccated Punjab plains. Endearingly they trail through their national

monuments, awe-struck, and the attendants intone their mono-
logues hoping for tips, and the tourist buses line up outside the
Presidential Palace, and the magicians prepare their levitations
and inexplicable disappearances in the dusty ditch below the
ramparts of the Red Fort.

This is the Gandhian truth of India, expressed in Delhi chiefly
by such reminders of an earthier world beyond the city limits.
Though I fear I might not give up my electric typewriter without
a struggle, still I am a Gandhian myself in principle, and respond
easily to this suggestion of a vast Indian *naïveté*, stretching away
from Delhi like a limitless reservoir, muddied perhaps but
deeply wholesome. The Gandhian ethic is rather outmoded in
India, in fact, and the Mahatma himself seems to be losing his
charismatic appeal, but still I liked the inscriptions in the
visitors' book at Birla House, where he died in 1948 (his body
was displayed to the public on the roof, illuminated by searchlight), and where many a country pilgrim reverently pauses.
'My heart heaving with emotion,' wrote P. H. Kalaskar. 'Moving
indeed,' thought A. K. Barat. Several people wrote 'Felt happy.'
One said 'Most worth seeing place in Delhi,' and when, quoting
from the master himself, I contributed 'Truth is God,' the
inevitable onlookers murmured, 'Very good, very good,' nodded
approvingly to each other and touched my hand in sympathy.

Delhi is a city of basic, spontaneous emotions: greed, hate,
revenge, love, pity, kindness, the murderous shot, the touch of
the hand. Its very subtleties are crude: even its poverty is black
and white. On the one side are the organized beggar children
who, taught to murmur a few evocative words of despair like
'hungry', 'baby' or 'mummy', succeed all too often in snaring
the susceptible stranger. On the other are the courtly thousands
of the jagghis, the shantytowns of matting, tentage and old
packing cases which cling like black growths to the presence of
Delhi.

There are beggars in Delhi who are comfortably off, and
people too proud to beg who possess nothing at all, not a pot or
a pan, not a pair of shoes. I saw one such man, almost naked,
shivering with the morning cold and obviously very ill, huddled
against a lamppost in Janpath early one morning. He asked for
nothing, but I felt so sorry for him, and for a moment so loved
him for his suffering, that I gave him a ten-rupee note, an
inconceivable amount by the standards of Indian indigence. He

looked at it first in disbelief, then in ecstasy and then in a wild gratitude, and I left him throwing his hands to heaven, singing, praying and crying, still clinging to his lamppost, and sending me away, slightly weeping myself, to coffee, toast and orange juice ('You'll be sure it's chilled, won't you?') at my hotel.

The voice of the people, Gandhi used to say, is the voice of God. I doubt it, but I do recognize a divine element to the Indian poverty, ennobled as it is by age and sacrifice. Indians rationalize it by the concept of reincarnation, and I see it too as a half-way condition, a station of the cross. 'In the next world,' I suggested to my driver after a long and exhausting journey into the country, 'I'll be driving and you'll be lying on the back seat,' but he answered me with a more elemental philosophy. 'In the next world,' he replied, 'we'll *both* be lying on the back seat!' For even the inegality of Delhi, even the pathos, often has something robust to it, a patient fatalism that infuriates many modernists but is a solace to people like me. It is disguised often in Eastern mumbo-jumbo, preached about in ashrams to gullible Californians and exploited by swamis from the divine to the absurd: but it is really no more than a kindly acceptance of things as they are, supported by the sensible thesis that things are not always what they appear to be.

But pathos, yes. Delhi is the capital of the losing streak. It is the metropolis of the crossed wire, the missed appointment, the puncture, the wrong number. Every day's paper in Delhi brings news of some new failure, in diplomacy, in economics, in sport: when India's women entered the world table-tennis tournament during my stay in Delhi, not only were they all beaten but one actually failed to turn up for the match. I was pursued in the city by a persistent and not unattractive Rajput businessman. I thought him rather suave as I fended him off, in his well-cut check suit and his trendy ties, confident of manner, worldly of discourse: but one day I caught sight of him *hors de combat*, so to speak, muffled in a threadbare overcoat and riding a battered motor scooter back to his suburban home – and suddenly saw him, far more endearingly if he did but know it, as he really was, smallish, poorish, struggling and true.

He dropped me in the end anyway, perhaps because I developed an unsightly boil in my nose – men seldom send roses to girls with red noses. The side of my face swelled up like a huge bunion, and I was half red and half white, and sniffly

and sad and sorry for myself. In this condition, self-consciously,
I continued my investigations, and at first I was touched by the
tact with which Indians in the streets pretended not to notice.
After a day or two, though, I realized that the truth was more
affecting still. They *really* did not notice. They thought my face
quite normal. For what is a passing grotesquerie, in a land of
deformities?

'Certainly,' said the government spokesman, perusing my list
of questions, 'by all means, these are all very simple matters. We
can attend to them for you at once. As I told you, it is our duty!
It is what we are paid for! I myself have to attend an important
meeting this afternoon – you will excuse me I hope? – but I will
leave all these little matters with our good Mrs Gupta and all
will be taken care of. I will telephone you with the answers
myself without fail – or if not I myself, then Mrs Gupta will be
sure to telephone you either today or tomorrow morning. Did
you sign our register? A duplicate signature here if you would
not mind, and the lady at the door will issue you with the
requisite application form for a pass – it will make everything
easier for you, you see. Have no fear, Mrs Gupta will take care
of everything. But mark my words, you will find the spiritual
aspects of our city the most rewarding. Remember the River
Ganges! As a student of history, you will find that I am right! Ha
ha! Another cup of tea? You have time?'

Even he would agree, though, that the spiritual aspect is
hardly predominant in New Delhi, the headquarters of the
Indian government and the seat of Indian sovereignty – the
newest and largest of Delhi's successive capitals. This was built
by the British, and despite one or two sententious symbolisms
and nauseating texts – 'Liberty Will Not Descend to a People, A
People Must Raise Themselves to Liberty' – it is a frank and
indeed noble memorial to their own imperial Raj. It is not
anomalous even now. For one thing it was built in a hybrid
style of East and West, to take care of all historical contingencies,
and for another, Britishness is far from dead in Delhi. Delhi
gentlemen, especially of the sporting classes, are stupendously
British still. Delhi social events can be infinitely more English
than Ascot or Lords. The following scrambled-names puzzle
appeared recently in a Delhi magazine: LIWL EFFEY (a

comedian); UALNIJ YHLXEU (a zoologist); ARMY SHES (a pianist); HIIPPLL LLEGAADU (a historian). Only two classes of people on earth could solve this riddle without reference books: Britons of a certain age, Indians of a certain class.

Besides, the grand ensemble of New Delhi, the Presidential Palace flanked by the two wings of the Secretariat, has adapted easily to the republican style. It was the greatest single artefact of the British Empire, perhaps its principal work of art, and there are men still alive in Delhi who spent all their working lives building it. I met one, a rich and venerable Sikh contractor, and he recalled the great work with immense pride, and spoke affectionately of its English architects, and said it never once occurred to him to suppose, during all the years he worked upon it, that an Indian would ever be sitting in the halls of the Viceroy's Lodge.

Seen early on a misty morning from far down the ceremonial mall, Rajpath, New Delhi is undeniably majestic – neither Roman, its architects said, nor British, nor Indian, but *imperial*. Then its self-consciousness (for its mixture of styles is very contrived) is blurred by haze and distance and by the stir of awakening Delhi – the civil servants with their bulging briefcases, the multitudinous peons, the pompous early-morning policemen, the women sweepers elegant in primary colours, the minister perhaps (if it is not *too* early) in his chauffeur-driven, Indian-built limousine, the stocky Gurkha sentries at the palace gates, the first eager tourists from the Oberoi Intercontinental, the entertainer with his dancing monkeys, the snake charmer with his acolyte children, the public barber on the pavement outside Parliament, the women preparing their washing beside the ornamental pools, the man in khaki who, approaching you fiercely across the formal gardens, asks if you would care for a cold drink.

Then the power of India, looming above these dusty complexities, is unmistakable: not only created but instinctive, sensed by its foreign rulers as by its indigenous, and aloof to history's permutations. Of all the world's countries, India is the most truly prodigious, and this quality of astonishment displays itself afresh every day as the sun comes up in Delhi. Five hundred and eighty million people, three hundred languages, provinces from the Himalayan to the equatorial, cities as vast as Bombay and Calcutta, villages so lost in time that no map marks them, nuclear scientists and aboriginal hillmen, industrialists of incalculable wealth and dying beggars sprawled on railway platforms, three or four great cultures, myriad religions, pilgrims from across the world, politicians sunk in graft, the Grand Trunk Road marching to Peshawar, the temples of Madras gleaming in the sun, an inexhaustible history, an incomprehensible social system, an unfathomable repository of human resource, misery, ambiguity, vitality and confusion – all this, the colossal corpus of India, invests, sprawls around, infuses, elevates, inspires and very nearly overwhelms New Delhi.

Searching for a corrective to such cosmic visions, I thought I would investigate the roots or guts of New Delhi, instead of contemplating its tremendous aura, so I inveigled my way not into the State Hallroom or the Durbar Hall but into the kitchens of the Presidential Palace, by way of an obliging aide-de-camp and a compliant housekeeper (for as dubious flunkies repeatedly murmured as I made my way downstairs, 'It is not allowed to visitors'). At first I thought I had succeeded in finding humanity among that majesty, for the way to the kitchens passed through a labyrinth of homely offices, workshops and storerooms and cupboards, supervised by smiling and apparently contented domestics. Here were the Pot Cleaners, scouring their big copper pans. Here were the Linen Keepers, standing guard on their pillowslips. Here were the Washing Up Men, ankle deep in suds themselves, and here the Bakers invited me to taste the morning's loaf. I felt I was passing through some living exhibition of Indian Crafts, diligent, chaste and obliging.

But even before I entered the kitchen proper, a clanking and grand aroma brought me back to the realities of New Delhi, for in the palace of Rashtrapati Bhavan, Downstairs is scarcely less consequential than Up. These kitchens are imperial institutions themselves, half Western, half Eastern, colossal in scale, lordly in pretension. Armies of cooks seemed to be labouring there. Foods of a dozen cuisines seemed to be in preparation. Batteries of aged electric ovens hummed and whirred. There were squadrons of deep freezers and battalions of chopping boards and armouries of steel choppers. The cooks and their underlings bowed to me as I passed, but not obsequiously. It was with condescension that they greeted me, one by one along the preparation tables, and when at last I reached the sizzling centre of that underworld, I felt myself to be more truly at a crossroad of the empires than anywhere else in Delhi – for there, just around the corner from the English ovens of the viceroys, they were smoking over charcoal braziers, scented with wheat grain, the aromatic yellow pomfrets that were a grand delicacy of the Moghuls.

So even in the kitchens power presides, in a traditional, ample sense. Delhi is full of it, for this republic, which came to office in a loincloth, rules in a gaudier uniform. Nehru said that modern Western civilization was ersatz, living by ersatz values, eating ersatz food: but the ruling classes of Delhi, the politicians, the businessmen, the military, have mostly adopted those values without shame. Gandhi said that his India would have 'the smallest possible army', but Delhi is one of the most military of all capitals: when I looked up some friends in the Delhi telephone book, I found that under the name Khanna there were four generals, an air commodore, twelve colonels, a group captain, twelve majors, three wing commanders, four captains, one commander, three lieutenant commanders and a lieutenant.

Nor is Delhi's display just a façade or a bluff. India often seems to outsiders a crippled country, emaciated by poverty and emasculated by philosophy, but it is only a half-truth. We are told that half India's population is undernourished and three quarters illiterate: that leaves nearly 180 million people who are well fed and literate. The Indian gross national product is the tenth largest on earth. The armies of India are very strong and are largely equipped from Indian factories. I went one day to the Delhi Industrial Fair, housed in a series of modernist ziggurats directly across the street from the gateway of the ruined city Purana Qila, and there I discovered that India makes not only warships, railway engines and aircraft, but Carbicle Grinders too, Lapping Machines and Micro-Fog Lubricators ('I'll take that one,' said I flippantly, pointing to an electric transformer as big as a cottage, 'please send it to my hotel' – and diligently the salesman took out his order form).

Power corrupts, of course, and in India it corrupts on a grand scale. At the top, the whisper of nepotism or opportunism repeatedly approaches Central Government itself. At the bottom, graft harasses the street hawkers of the city, who can scarcely afford the protection money demanded by the police. Even the stranger to Delhi feels the rot: in the arrogant petty official declining to look up from his newspaper, in the stifling addiction to red tape and precedent, in the affectations and snobberies which, as they thrive in Washington's Georgetown, flourish here too in the districts south of Rajpath.

As it happens, I am rather an addict of power. I do not much enjoy submitting to it or even exerting it, but I do like observing it. I like the aesthetics of it, coloured as they so often are by pageantry and history. I am everybody's patriot, and love to see the flags flying over palace or parliament, Westminster or Quai d'Orsay. I am very ready to be moved by the emanations of power in Delhi – the sun setting behind the Red Fort, the grand mass of New Delhi seen across the dun plateau or the ceremony of Beating Retreat on Vijay Chowk, when a dozen military bands pluck at the heart with the Last Post and 'Abide with Me'.

Nobody cries more easily than I do, when the bugle sounds or the flag comes down, but somehow I do not respond to the old magic in India. The British, rationalizing their own love of imperial pomp, used to claim that it was necessary to retain the respect of Asiatics. It availed them nothing, though, against the 'half-naked fakir', as Churchill called Gandhi, and now too the magnificence of Delhi seems paradoxically *detached* from India. How remote the great ensigns which, enormously billowing above their embassies in the diplomatic enclave, testify to the presence of the plenipotentiaries! How irrelevant the posturings of the grandees, hosts and guests alike, the Polish defence minister greeted by epauletted generals, the Prince of Wales inevitably winning his polo match, the resident Congress party spokesman puffed up at one press conference, the visiting minister of national reorientation condescending at the next.

And most detached of all seems the unimaginable bureaucracy of Delhi, battening upon the capital – a power sucker, feeding upon its own consequence or sustained intravenously by inter-departmental memoranda, triplicate applications, copies and comments and addenda and references to precedent – a monstrous behemoth of authority, slumped immovable among its files and tea-trays. Much of it is concerned not with practical reality at all but with hypotheses or dogma. Forty government editors are engaged in producing the collected works of Gandhi, down to the last *pensée* – they have got to volume fifty-four. Hundreds more are concerned with plans, for there was never a capital like Delhi for planners – the Multilevel Planning Section, the Plan Coordination Division, the Plan Information

Unit, the Social Planning Unit, the Project Appraisal Unit, the Socio-Economic Research Unit, the Programme Evaluation Organization, the National Sample Survey Organization, the National Survey Organization, the Central Statistical Organization. Big Brother is everywhere, with a slide rule, a clipboard and a warning in small print. 'This map', says one Delhi tourist publication severely, 'is published for tourists as a master guide and *not as legal tender'* – and there, in its mixture of the interfering, the pedantic, the unnecessary and the absurd, speaks the true voice of Indian officialdom.

But this is an essential part of the Indian mystery, always has been, probably always will be. Delhi is too old to care anyway, and takes the system as it comes. Which viceroy or president had he most enjoyed serving, I asked one antediluvian retainer at Rashtrapati Bhavan. He shrugged his shoulders with an almost perceptible creak. 'I serve the government,' he said. 'It is all the same to me.' With this indifference in mind I went that afternoon to a murder trial which, to much publicity, was proceeding then in the New District Court, a kind of permanent bad dream in concrete in the northern part of the city – filthy, cramped, dark and suffocatingly overcrowded. Here authority was at its most immediate and most awful. The case concerned the alleged murder of a well-known south-of-Rajpath lady by her husband, a fashionable eye surgeon, assisted by his mistress and an assortment of vagabond accomplices. It was a true *crime passionel* with thuggish overtones, and at least five people faced, there and then, the ultimate penalty. The judge was a grave and clever Sikh, turbaned and spectacled. The court was jammed with a festering, jostling audience, hungry for the salacious, the macabre and the terrible. The white-tabbed attorneys droned and argued, the watchmen barred the door with staves, the accused sat in chains along the side of the court, shackled to their guards.

Yet fearful though their predicament was, they did not seem awe-struck nor even alarmed. They were like sightseers themselves, of their own tragedy. They yawned occasionally. They exchanged comments. They laughed at the legal jokes. And sometimes, feeling the strain of the long day, they raised their manacled wrists to their warders' shoulders and, placing their cheeks upon their hands like sleepy children, dozed through destiny for a while.

*

'I will find that out for you, of course,' said the government spokesman. 'It will be no problem at all. You see, it is something I am not exactly sure of myself, but we have many sources of information. Do we have your telephone number? Ah yes. I have temporarily mislaid it. Would you give it to me again? Rest assured, dear lady, I shall find out this information, together with the answers to your earlier questions, and shall telephone you for certain, if not this afternoon, then tomorrow morning first thing.

'I don't know if you are familiar, you see, with the *Bhagavad-Gita*? As a student of the Gandhian philosophy you would find it very beautiful: and you would find it exceedingly relevant to your article about Delhi. It is self-awareness, you see, that is the key. Oh madam, you are laughing at me! You are very wicked! But never mind, you will see, you will see! And in the meantime you may be quite sure', he concluded with his usual charming smile and reassuring shake of the head, 'that I will be telephoning you with this information, or if not I myself, then our good Mrs Gupta is sure to. It is not very spiritual but we must do our duty!'

There is a species of telephone operators' English, often heard in Delhi, which is not exactly an articulated language at all, but a sort of elongated blur. Indian English proper, of course, is one of India's cruellest handicaps, for it is so often imperfect of nuance and makes for an unreal relationship between host and visitor, besides often making highly intelligent people look foolish ('CHINESE GENERALS FLY BACK TO FRONT', said a celebrated Indian headline long ago). But the elliptical, slithery kind is something else again, and has another effect on its hearers. It makes one feel oddly opaque or amorphous oneself, and seems to clothe the day's arrangements in a veil of uncertainty.

This is proper. One should not go fighting into Delhi, chin up and clear eyed. Here hopes are meant to wither and conceptions adjust. A single brush with a noseless beggar is enough to change your social values. Just one application for an import licence will alter your standards of efficiency. After a while graver mutations may occur, and you will find yourself questioning the Meaning of It All, the Reality of Time and other old Indian specialties. 'You will see, you will see!' Most disconcerting of all, you may well come to feel that the pomp and circumstance of Delhi, which struck you at first as illusory display, is in fact the only reality of the place! All the rest is mirage. Everything else in the Indian presence, north, east, south, west, across the Rajasthani deserts, down to the Coromandel beaches, far away to the frontiers of Tibet, everything else is suggestion, never to be substance.

I pick a Delhi newspaper at random. Crowd Loots Colliery. Police Kill Dacoits. Dacoits Loot Pilgrims. Students Raid Cinema. Farmers Arrested during Agitation. Teachers Boycott Examination. Police Fire on Crowd. Mizo Rebels Spotted. Peace Feelers for Naga Rebels. A State of Emergency exists in India, but one is hardly aware of it, for this is a country always in emergency, crossed perpetually by dim figures of faith and violence, prophets of revolution, priests of reaction, saints and spies and fanatics, moving here and there through a haze of hatred, idealism and despair. Experts Visit Bomb Blast Site. Police Charge Crowd. 600 Arrested. Government Minister Has Asthma.

Sometimes these shadows reach into Delhi itself, and chaos feels uncomfortably close. While I was there the hereditary Imam of the Jama Masjid, the greatest mosque in India, was engaged in a quarrel with the government. He was even heard inciting his congregation to political dissent over the loudspeakers of his minaret during a visit to the neighbourhood by Mrs Gandhi herself. His family have been incumbents of the Imamate since the mosque was founded by Shah Jehan in 1650, and are great figures in the Muslim community: nevertheless he was arrested, and in the ensuing riots at least six people were killed (always add a zero, an Indian acquaintance nonchalantly told me, if you want the true figure) and at least six hundred locked away for safety's sake.

It happened that I was wandering around the purlieus of the mosque on the day of the arrest, and bleak was the sensation of *déjà vu* with which I watched the riot police, brandishing their guns and batons, heavily clambering out of their trucks. But more ominous still, I thought, was the spectacle of the mosque itself a few days later. They slapped a curfew on the area, and when I next passed its outskirts, along the crammed and filthy pavements of Netaji Subhash Marg, where the beggar families crouch day and night beneath their sacking shelters and the teeming junk bazaars crowd around the Chadni Chowk – when I looked across to the Jama Masjid, I saw its great shape there

silent and eerily deserted – gone the milling figures of the
faithful on its steps, gone the stir of commerce and devotion
that habitually surrounds it, empty all the stalls and shops, the
kebab restaurants, the fortune-tellers, the silversmiths, the
tanners and the cobblers. All were empty, and the mosque
looked like some immense captive champion, brooding there in
solitary confinement.

Yet even this all-too-real reality seemed a deception upon the
composure of Delhi. I never feel insecure there, even when the
riot police are storming by. The only citizens who frighten me
are those damned monkeys, so beguiling of motion, so threatening of grimace. Delhi people treat these beasts with distinct
circumspection, crossing roads to avoid them or bribing them
with peanuts to go away, and in this, it seemed to me, poor
Indians behave towards monkeys much as Europeans behave
towards poor Indians – especially as, the monkey god Hanuman
being an important figure of the Hindu pantheon, some element
of conscience is presumably involved. This disconcerting parallel gave me an unexpected sense of membership, and every
time a monkey bared its teeth at me I felt like saying, 'Wait,
friend, wait – I'm the European, it's the poor Indian you want!'

For the Indian sense of hierarchy, which so contributes to the
bafflement of India, provides for each rank of society a kind of
comradeship; and in Delhi especially, which is like a shadow
play of India, one senses the hidden force of it. The Untouchables
of the capital – Harijans, Children of God, as Gandhi called them
– live in well-defined colonies on the edge of the city. Though
I knew better intellectually, emotionally I somehow expected,
when I drove out there one afternoon, to find them a people
made morose and hangdog by their status. In fact they turned
out to be a very jolly lot, welcoming and wreathed in smiles,
and looking at least as cheerful as the average member of the
Socio-Economic Research Unit, say. Why not? They might be
Harijans to the world outside, but they were doubtless Brahmins
to each other.

In the same way Delhi, preoccupied with its own diurnal
round of consequence and command, is paradoxically protected
against that dust storm of controversy, threat and misfortune
which hangs always, dark and ill-defined, over the Indian
horizons. That blur or slither of Delhi, which begins as a mystery
and develops into an irritation, becomes in the end a kind of

reassurance. After trying three times, you give up gratefully. After expostulating once or twice, it is a pleasure to accede. You think you can change the system? Try it, try it, and when the elaborations of Delhi have caught up with you, when you realize the tortuous significances of the old method, when it has been explained to you that only Mrs Gupta is qualified to take the money, that Mr Mukerjee is prevented by custom from working beside Mr Mukhtar Singh and that Mr Mohammed will not of course be at work on Fridays, when it dawns upon you gradually that it has been done more or less this way, come conqueror, come liberation, since the early Middle Ages, with a relieved and affectionate smile you will probably agree that perhaps it had better be left as it is.

As it is! India is always as it is! I never despair in Delhi, for I feel always all around me the fortification of a profound apathy. The capital is essentially apathetic to the nation: the nation is aloof to the capital. By the end of the century there will be, at the present rate of increase, nearly 1,000 million people in India, and I think it very likely that there will have been a revolution of one complexion or another. But the traveller who returns to Delhi then will find the city much the same, I swear, will respond to much the same emotions, indulge in just the same conjectures, bog down in just the same philosophical quagmires, and reach, if he is anything like me, about the same affectionate and inconclusive conclusions.

'You see? You see? Did I not say so? You are thinking metaphysically, as I foretold!' Well, perhaps. But the government spokesman proved his point better himself, for neither he nor Mrs Gupta ever did ring.

12

'DO YOU THINK SHOULD HE HAVE GONE OVER?'

Dublin, 1974

❧

1974 was a bad year for Anglo-Irish relations, and as I flew from London to Dublin to write this piece the Aer Lingus hostess said, 'Now you'll be sure to write something nice about the old place, won't you?' I did, and when the essay appeared the Irish Government offered me a free week's holiday in Connemara – 'down to the last Guinness' – to say thank you. I accepted without a qualm – the nearest I have ever got to corruption.

When I went to Dublin once, I found that the very next morning the fifth President of the Irish Republic, the *Uachtarán*, was to be installed in the Hall of St Patrick in Dublin Castle. Hastening out to buy myself a proper dress ('I congratulate you,' said the maid at my hotel in some surprise, 'you've got excellent taste'), and procuring an official pass (*Preas, Insealbhu an Uchtaráin*), promptly in the morning I presented myself at the Castle gates, made my way through the confusion of soldiery, officialdom and diplomacy that filled the old yard, and found my place beside the dais in the elegantly decorated hall ('No place for purple prose,' murmured my cicerone pointedly, 'more the Ionian white and gold').

It was a delightful occasion. All Eire was there, among the massed banners and crests of the ancient Irish provinces, beneath the stern gaze of the trumpeters poised for their fanfare in the minstrels' gallery. All the Ministers were there, with their invisible portfolios. All the Ambassadors were there, with their distinctly visible wives. *Both* Primates of All Ireland were there, side by side in parity. There were judges and surgeons, old revolutionaries and new politicians, clerics by the hundred, professors by the score. There was Conor Cruise O'Brien. There was John Lynch. There was Sean MacBride the Nobel Laureate. There was Cyril Cusack the actor. It was like seeing the Irish Republic encapsulated, dressed in its newest fineries, sworn to its best behaviour, and deposited in the building which, more than any other in Ireland, speaks of Irish history.

The new President, Cearbhall O'Dálaigh, seemed a dear man indeed, and gave us a gentle rambling speech much concerned with what the removal men said when they packed his possessions for the move. Some of it was in Gaelic, some in French, some in English, and I confess my mind did wander now and then, towards the Ruritanian Ambassadress's fur coat, towards the twin smiles of the Archbishops, towards the fierce survey of the bandmaster high above, who might easily have stepped from the ranks of the old Connaught Rangers. One phrase in particular, though, and not alas the President's own, caught my attention. It was a quotation from Thoreau, and it ran thus: 'If a man does not keep pace with his companions, perhaps it is because he hears a different drummer.'

A different drummer! What drummer beat in Dublin now, I wondered, where the best were always out of step? What pace would the bandmaster set today? Was the drumbeat different still, in this most defiantly different of capitals?

That evening, when the dignitaries, officials and soldiers had dispersed to their celebratory banquets (all except the poor military policeman who, vainly trying to kick his motor bike to life, was left forlorn in the Castle yard to a universal sigh of sympathy), I drove along the coast to Howth, and then the Joyceness of Dublin, the Yeatsness, the pubness, the tramness, the Liffeyness, the Behanness, in short the stock Dublinness of the place seemed to hang like a vapour over the distant city. It was one of those Irish evenings when the points of the compass seem to have been confused, and their climates with them. A bitter east wind swayed the palm trees along the promenade, a quick northern air sharpened that slightly Oriental languor, that Celtic *dolce far niente*, which habitually blurs the intentions of Dublin. Over the water the city lay brownish below the Wicklow Mountains, encrusted it seemed with some tangible patina of legend and literature, and fragrant of course with its own *vin du pays*, Guinness.

This is everyone's Dublin, right or wrong, and if it is partly myth, it is substance too. There is no such thing as a stage Dubliner: the characters of this city, even at their most theatrical, are true and earnest in their kind, and Dublin too, even today, lives up to itself without pretence. Are there any urchins like Dublin urchins, grubby as sin and bouncy as ping-pong balls? Are there any markets like Dublin markets, sprawling all over the city streets like gypsy jumble sales? Are there any buses so evocative as Dublin buses, lurching in dim-lit parade towards Glasnevin?

Certainly there are few more boisterous streets on earth than O'Connell Street on a Saturday night, when a salt wind gusts up from the sea, making the girls giggle and the young men clown about, driving the Dublin litter helter-skelter here and there, and eddying the smells of beer, chips and hot-dogs all among the back streets. And there is no café more tumultuous than Bewley's Oriental Café in Grafton Street, with its mountains of buns on every table, with its children draped over floors and chairs, with its harassed waitresses scribbling, its tea-urns hissing, its stained glass and its tiled floors, its old clock beside the door, the high babel of its Dublin chatter and its haughty Dublin ladies, all hats and arched eyebrows, smoking their cigarettes loftily through it all.

It is an all too familiar rhythm, but it beats unmistakably still, hilariously and pathetically, and makes of Dublin one of the most truly exotic cities in the world. One still finds shawled beggar women on the Liffey bridges at night, huddling their babies close, attended by wide-eyed small boys and holding cardboard boxes for contributions. One still hears the instant give-and-take in Dublin pubs and parlours. 'Ah, me rheumatism's cured,' says the old lady, quick as a flash when the landlord pats her kindly on the knee, 'you should advertise your healing powers.' 'Sure it was only my left hand too,' says the landlord. 'Well and it was only my left knee – try the other one, there's a good man.' I experienced the tail-end of a bank robbery in Dublin one day, and only in this city, I thought, could I observe the principal witness of a crime interviewed by the police in a butcher's shop – between whose ranks of hanging turkeys, from the pavement outside, I could glimpse his blood-streaked face enthusiastically recalling the horror of it all.

Dublin's gay but shabby recklessness, too, which so infuriated

its English overlords, brazenly survives. If there is a public clock
that works in Dublin, I have yet to find it, and I was not in the
least surprised when, calling at a restaurant at a quarter to five
to arrange a table for dinner, I found several jolly parties
concluding their lunch. The Irish honour their own priorities
still. 'It's not very satisfactory just to tell your customers,' I over-
heard a lady complaining at the GPO, 'that the mail's gone with
a bomb, it's not very satisfactory at all.' 'He'll make a fine
President,' somebody said to me of Cearbhall O'Dálaigh, 'nobody
knows what his name is.' 'Enjoy yourself now!' everybody says
in Dublin, and they mean enjoy yourself *notwithstanding*.

Dublin is very old – old in history, old in style. If there is no
such thing as a stage Dubliner, in a curious way there is no such
thing as a young one, either. The dry scepticism of the Dublin
manner, the elliptical nature of its conversations, the dingy air
of everything, the retrospection – all conspire to give this city a
sense of elderly collusion. Everyone seems to know everyone
else, and all about him too. Go into any Dublin company,
somebody suggested to me one day, and present the cryptic
inquiry: 'Do you think should he have gone over?' Instantly,
whatever the circumstances, there will be a cacophony of replies.
'Sure he should, but not without telling his wife' – 'And why
shouldn't he have, was he not the elected representative?' –
'Well it wasn't so far as it looked' – 'It didn't surprise me, his
father went too, remember.' Such is the accumulated familiarity
of the city that to any inquiry, about anybody, about anything,
every Dubliner – every true Dubberlin man, as the vernacular
has it – possesses an infallible response, usually wrong.

Such a sense of commonalty curdles easily into conspiracy,
and of course history has helped to fuse your Dubliners, making
them feel far more homogeneous than the people of most
Western capitals. This is not only a classless society, at least in
externals, it is an indigenous one too. Your Italian waiter, your
Chinese take-away *restaurateur*, your Jamaican bus conductor,
even your Nigerian student of computer technology are all rare
figures in Dublin still, and the consequent unity of method and
temper gives the city much of its exuberant punch.

It also gives a special pride, for this is not only the capital of a
nation, but the capital of an idea. The idea of Irishness is not
universally beloved. Some people mock it, some hate it, some fear
it. On the whole, though, I think it fair to say, the world interprets

it chiefly as a particular kind of happiness, a happiness sometimes boozy and violent, but essentially innocent: and this ineradicable spirit of merriment informs the Dublin genius to this day, and is alive and bubbling still, for all the miseries of the Irish Problem, in this jumbled brown capital across the water.

Sometimes I could hear other drummers, though. I rang up the *Dáil* one day and asked if there was anything interesting to observe that evening. 'There's always me,' said the usher, 'I'm interesting.' For if on one level Dublin is a world capital, to which subjects from Melbourne to the Bronx pay a vicarious or morganatic allegiance, on another it is the day-to-day capital of a little state. In this it is very modern. Ireland seems to me the right size for a country, the truly contemporary size, the size at which regionalism properly becomes nationhood, and the parliamentary usher answers the telephone himself. Small units within a large framework offer a sensible pattern for the world's future, and beneath the fustiness of the old Dublin, the world's Dublin, a much more contemporary entity exists.

Old Dublin is averse to change, but this smaller, inner Dublin welcomes it. 'If we know the Brits,' said a genial enthusiast at a Ballsbridge party, holding my hand and talking about London, 'they'll soon be having St Paul's down to make way for a new ghastly office block.' Well, the Micks are not much better when it comes to urban development. Visual taste is hardly their forte, and they have done little to improve the look of Dublin since the end of the Ascendancy. Wide areas of the Liberties are in that melancholy state of unexplained decay that generally precedes 'improvement', there are frightful plans for the Liffey quays, the Central Bank is building itself a structure which is not only grossly out of scale with the time and the city, but seems in its present state of completion to be made of Meccano – 'an awful thing in itself', as a bystander observed to me, 'and terrible by implication'.

More often the implications of change are merely sad. They imply a deliberate, functional rejection not perhaps of tradition or principle, but of habit. Gone is many an ancient pub, anomalous perhaps to a condition of progress, but beloved in itself. Crippled is many a Georgian square. Doomed and derelict is J. J. Byrne the fish shop ('This Is The Place'). Fearful ring roads threaten. No good looking in for Dublin Bay prawns at the old Red Bank: it was long ago converted into a Catholic chapel, where in the Dublin manner the local girls slip in for a moment's supplication before rejoining their boy friends on the pavement outside for a stout in the corner bar.

There are worse things to worry about, too. There are the Troubles, those endemic mysteries of Ireland, which are inescapable in Dublin if only by suggestion – *Beál Feirste*, as the road signs say, is only 100 miles to the north. A fairly muzzy security screen protects the offices of the Irish Government, and sends the unsuspecting visitor backwards and forwards between the guards – 'Did you not see this young lady when she came in?' 'I did not, she must have walked by like a ghost.' When I saw a big black car with two big men in it, standing outside my host's suburban house, I knew a Minister was calling, and I looked more than once over my shoulder before, in a spirit of pure inquiry, I entered the house in Parnell Square where they sell Christmas cards and *objets d'art* made by the internees of Ulster.

But far more immediate than the bomber is the rising price. In Britain inflation is merely another blow to the punch-drunk: in Ireland it is an unfair decision. For so many centuries a loser, in recent years Eire has found a winning streak, finding its feet at last, establishing its place in the world, evolving a mean between the practical and the ideal, forgiving and even half-forgetting the tragedies of the past. With change, it seemed, prosperity was coming. Many of the new buildings of Dublin might be unlovely, but at least they were earnests of success.

Now the poor Dubliners find themselves haunted once again by the prospect of failure. The Irish economy is less than hefty, and could not long resist a world recession. Then the brief holiday would be over, the cars would be sold, the colour televisions sold, the plump young Dublin executive would no longer be lunching at a quarter to five. You might not guess the possibility from the Grafton Street stores, which are among the most charming and fastidious in Europe, but your Dubberlin man sees it plain enough, and often speaks of it with cheerful foreboding, as he chooses a third sticky cake at Bewley's, or summons a second bottle of hock.

For luckily Dublin's rueful optimism survives, and pervades the Republic too. They said some fairly gloomy things in the *Dáil* that evening, and discussed some daunting prospects, but when they adjourned for a vote, and the deputies hung over the rail of the Chamber waiting for the tellers, with their rubicund laughing faces, their stocky country frames, their irrepressible chatter and their elbows on the rail, I thought they looked for all the world like convivial farmers at a cattle sale, looking down towards the Speaker's chair as towards the auctioneer, and waiting for the next Friesian to be led in from the robing chamber. 'Didja enjoy yourself now?' said the usher when I left, and the security man in his little lodge waggled his fingers at me as I passed.

I suppose there are terrorists plotting in Dublin, and bombers preparing their fuses, but it remains, all the same, pre-eminently the innocent capital of a star-crossed state – for the luck of the Irish is a wish more than a characteristic. One of its greatest charms is its intimate completeness. There are only three million people in Eire, scarcely more than there are in Wales, but Dublin has its diplomatic corps and its Government departments, its *Uachtarán*, in *Taoiseach* and all the trappings of a sovereign capital. Irish pictures, Irish plays, Irish artefacts, Irish heroes – Dublin is obsessed with itself and its hinterland, giving the little capital a character introspective perhaps but undeniably authoritative, for it is certainly the last word on itself.

Half its pleasure lies in its pride. Ten columns of the Dublin telephone book are needed to list the 660 institutions which boast the prefix 'Irish'. Like the Welsh and Scots, but unlike the hapless English, the Irish are still frankly affectionate towards their nationality, and this gives Dubliners an unexpected balance or serenity. I went one night to the Abbey Theatre, where Mr Cusack was playing the Vicar of Wakefield as to the manner born, and thought as I looked at the audience around me how enviably *natural* they looked. The burden of their history did not show, and they were not entangled by inhibitions of power or prestige. They had never been citizens of a Great Power, and never would be. They talked in no phoney accents, pined for no lost empires, and laughed at Goldsmith's gentle humour without much caring whether the world laughed too.

For if Dublin is parochial, it is not provincial exactly, for it remains original. British influences are ubiquitous, it is true, from the Aldershot drill of the Presidential guard to 'Coronation Street' on Monday evening, but there is no sense of copy-cat. Dubliners are their own men still. Even when a concern is foreign owned, as so many in Dublin are, it acquires a distinctively Irish flavour, so that even Trust House Fortes' Airport Hotel coffee-shop, physically a carbon of every airport coffee-

shop ever built anywhere, will give you eggs and bacon at lunch
time if you ask nicely, 'for sure the chef's a kindly man'.

And though it is small, still Dublin feels like a true capital.
Like Edinburgh, it deserves sovereignty. It is a fine thing to
walk through the Dublin streets on a Sunday morning, say,
when the sun is rising brilliantly out of the Bay, and to see the
monuments of Irish pride around you – the fire on Parnell's
column, O'Connell the Liberator on his plinth, the great columns
of the Customs House, the delicate dome of the Four Courts.
Over the great bridge you go, where the wind off the Bay
sweeps up-river to blow your hair about, and there is Trinity
before you, where Congreve and Swift and Burke were educated,
where Goldsmith stands on his pedestal and the *Book of Kells*
lies for ever open in its case. On your right is the old Irish
Parliament, on the left is the City Hall, and soon, turning the
cobbled corner at the top, you are –

Soon you are where? Why, back in the yard of Dublin Castle,
where Presidents of Eire are installed indeed, but where for 800
years, in a presence far more monstrous, far more stately, the
power of the English inexorably resided.

For like it or not, whatever your opinions, the drums of
tragedy sound still in Dublin, muffled but unavoidable, as they
sound nowhere else on earth. For eight centuries the Irish
struggled against the dominion of the English, and it takes more
than fifty uneasy years to silence the echoes.

The most compelling of all the figures at that Presidential
occasion was that of Eamon de Valera, who arrived in an aged
Rolls, and whose stiff blind figure, depending upon the arm of
a veteran officer, leaning slightly backward as the blind sometimes do, and tapping with his stick between the silent lines of
the diplomatic corps, cast a somewhat macabre hush upon the
assembly. 'The skeleton at the feast,' whispered an irreverent
observer somewhere near me, but I found the spectacle very
moving; and when with difficulty the old rebel climbed the dais
and sat ramrod-stiff on his chair a few feet away from me,
holding his stick between his knees and sometimes decorously
applauding, I envisaged all he had seen in the progress of the
little state, the Easter Rising, the war against the British, the
horrible Civil War, and so by way of plot and revolution,
obstinacy and courage, deviousness and boldness, to the instal-

lation of the fifth *Uachtarán* there on the bright blue carpets of St Patrick's Hall.

When I first knew Dublin, in the early 1960s, I thought the old fervours of revolution were fading, and that the memories of that sad struggle would die with its own generation. But the drum beats still, a drum to the treble of the Ulster fifes, and the presence there of Mr de Valera did not seem an anachronism to me, only a grave reminder. The terrible beauty lingers still, tainted perhaps but inescapable. That evening, after dinner, I wandered alone among the back streets behind the General Post Office, where little more than fifty years ago the fated visionaries of the Rising fought and died among the blazing ruins.

It is smart in Dublin to denigrate the Easter Rising now, and to say that it achieved nothing after all, but still those streets seemed haunted ground to me. The glow of the burning Post Office lit the night sky still, the Soldier's Song sounded above the traffic, and at the end of every street I could see the barricades of the British, and hear the clatter of their rifles and the clink of their tea-mugs. Sometimes machine-guns rattled, and the awful smell of war, of death and dirt and cordite, hung all about the buildings. I wept as I remembered that old tragedy, and thought of those brave men so soon to be shot at dawn, and of the ignorant homely English at their guns behind their sandbags, and I turned towards home in a sad despair, contemplating the deceits of glory.

But when I turned into O'Connell Street I looked up into the plane trees, swaying above me in the night wind, and dimly I discerned there the grey shapes of the pied wagtails, those miraculous familiars of Dublin. Every winter those loyal country birds come back to roost in the trees of O'Connell Street, settling down each day at dusk, fluttering away to mountain and moorland when the dawn breaks. They calmed and comforted me at once, and I saw in their silent presence a figure of my own gratitude – for the gaiety that takes me back to Dublin year after year, for the melody that sounds always above the drums and bombs of Ireland, and for the old comradeship of this city, which transcends all bitterness, ignores time, and is the truest of Dublin's contradictory truths.

13

A FREE CITY

Hamburg, 1958

❧

I visited most of the big West German cities in the 1950s, and the only one I did not find oppressive was Hamburg: partly I dare say because I have family connections with the place, but chiefly because it still seemed, even in the aftermath of a terrible defeat, bold, proud and independent.

On the top floor of the Hamburg Historical Museum there runs, four times daily through the year, the most elaborate model railway in Europe. Its locomotives are perfect replicas, its operations are marvellously complex, but for my money the most interesting part of it is the man who makes it go. He stands in a small glass cabin above the layout, earnestly fiddling with switches and delivering a running commentary into a microphone: and so solemn does he look up there, so dedicated in his attitudes, so conscientiously does he abandon his own voice, now and then, to impersonate the station announcer on a platform beneath – so *respectful* is his manner of controlling that prodigious toy, that you might think its trains were performing some symbolic ritual, and that he was only acolyte to its mysteries.

Hamburg is not a gullible town. It mostly escapes the dread innocence that gives Munich and Berlin their undertones of wide-eyed menace. As German cities go today, it is argumentative, even sceptical – '*Hei lucht!* – He's a liar!' Hamburgers sometimes like to shout, when the tourist guide has reached some pinnacle of hyperbole, and they have a little grog inside them. It nevertheless possesses, beneath its dazzlingly affluent new veneer, an old-fashioned air of wonder, as though the world is still worth gaping at. The marvels of technique, so casually accepted in Frankfurt or Düsseldorf, here still provoke gasps of admiration, as the talking doll talks, the shipyard crane hoists, or the jet takes off for Idlewild. The economic miracle of Germany, elsewhere a little tarnished by time, still seems divine and pristine to the Hamburgers. A little of the magic of foreign places has rubbed off on to Hamburg, a seaport for a thousand years, and this is a city whose character has not yet been smoothed out, deprived of its bumps and wrinkles, and tight-laced in superhighways. Most of Hamburg's legendary gabled houses were destroyed in the war, but somehow it does not seem to matter: it is an ancient port, gilded by centuries of foreign trade, and that is still exactly what it feels like. It takes more than a war or two, the collapse of a civilization and the reshaping of a continent to expunge the signature of the merchant venturers.

For this is a dyed-in-the-wool merchant city, sabled and aldermanic, like Bristol in England, or Genoa in the south. It is also, in tradition and in political fact, a Free City – one of the eleven constituent *Länder* of the German Federal Republic. Hamburg, so the official guidebooks like to say, 'is one of the larger among the small States of Europe' – larger than Andorra, Liechtenstein, San Marino or Monaco, and big enough to contain several thousand Vatican Cities. For several centuries Hamburg, champion of the Hanseatic League, was one of the Powers of the world, and though Germany has progressed from chaos to confederation, from Empire to Federal Republic, from Zollverein to The Six, still Hamburg thinks of itself as a State apart, bigger than Liechtenstein, the place where the great ships are built and the traders come home from the east – the gateway, the dockyard, the dour open end of Germany.

It is one of those cities, devastated though it has been by fire and war, whose personality assaults you the moment you arrive. The five great spires of Hamburg stand above the twin lakes of the Alster in almost stylized comity, like a foreshortened old engraving, embellished with curly horsemen, or a poster whose landmarks are scrunched together for impact. The tremendous port of Hamburg, surveyed by towering shipyards, patrolled by fleets of tugs and ferries, with the ceaseless flash of its welders and the high white shapes of its liners in dry dock – the port of Hamburg looks for all the world like one wide animated

Kokoschka, so bold but smudged are its effects, so muscular and functional its patterns. The *Fleets* of Hamburg, the meshwork of narrow old canals that link the Alster lakes with the Elbe, still seem at once secretive and diligent, though most of their old warehouses have vanished and the fur-bales are no longer piled along their crumbled quays. Hamburg is a city of the Baltic north, sister to Lübeck, Visby and Novgorod, tempered by the long gloom of the northern winter – a city of furs and scarves and fattening cakes and pudgy, buttoned, hurrying, humourless people. It feels spacious but also money-grubbing, cosmopolitan but also mean. It is the greatest city of West Germany, Berlin apart, but it feels far from the centre of things: though it has its fine opera house and its celebrated newspapers, its millionaires and its shipyards, it is still unmistakably provincial. Germany is a country without a convincing capital, and Hamburg, for all its two million people, never feels properly metropolitan.

In some ways it is cramped and crabbed. Its aristocracy, a caste of cultivated merchant princes, is notoriously snooty and clannish. Its manners are often brusque, its attitudes often curmudgeonly – it speaks the Low German dialect, *Plattdeutsch*, which, mumbled testily under the breath, has fine powers of petulant invective. It displays towards the rest of Germany, not altogether in fun, a lofty and sometimes contemptuous façade. It is obsessively, even comically, self-engrossed, buttressed by its own history and fortified always by favourable statistics: that historical museum, train and all, is really one enormous monument of civic conceit, beautifully arranged, meticulously planned, and instinct in its every showcase with the assurance that everything about Hamburg is biggest, best and unbeatable. To the world at large the reputation of Hamburg is essentially genial: but Germans from the regions often loathe it, and find it too pleased with itself by half.

This may partly be because Hamburg, though self-satisfied, has never been violently nationalist, and has seldom shared the inner passions of Germany. The hunger for *Lebensraum* has never meant so much to Hamburg, with the world's expanse beyond its breakwaters, as it has to the inland German cities, circumscribed by fears and frontiers. Hamburg has always looked outwards, down the Elbe to the North Sea and the Atlantic, Africa and the Americas. The tall boat-prowed Chile-haus is a symbol of Hamburg's foreign enterprise, and so is the

Hamburg-America Line, whose ships not only sail from this port, but were often built here, too. Hamburg is a city of the sea, and around its core of parochial complacency there are encrusted rich layers of experience, like geological evidence. Its streets are laced with salt and spice. If you wander down to one of its stuffy little waterfront restaurants, their windows steamed up with fug and black tobacco, you may eat one of the great seamen's dishes of Europe – eel soup, flavoured with prunes, herbs and onions and washed down with beer-and-schnapps. If you walk up the Reeperbahn after dark you may inspect one of the most raucous of all sailors' pleasure quarters, the stews and cabarets of St Pauli, where the show-girls ride their bare-backed camels, the female wrestlers grunt in the small hours, and through the eerie silence of the prostitutes' alley, sealed off from the streets by high wooden walls, the harlots gaze from their windows pink-lit and grotesquely painted.

Hamburg is full of foreigners, wandering Levantines and African students, shashlik in the all-night cafés, Persian mosques and Scandinavian churches and Japanese ships and English bankers (successors to those who, in the prime of the British Empire, acted as intermediaries between German industry and the vast markets of the Raj). Two Englishmen built the first Hamburg waterworks, many French refugees contributed to the skills of the Free City, the Church of St Nicolai was once restored by Giles Gilbert Scott, and half the Swiss merchant fleet is based on this port. There are fifty-three consulates in Hamburg, more than anywhere else except New York, and at the marine gateway of Schulau ships of all nationalities are played into port with their own national anthems, boomed over loudspeakers from the shore. Hamburg knows far more about the world than most of Germany does: within its narrow limits are concentrated the maritime and mercantile skills of a vast, mostly land-locked, and endlessly ingenious nation.

Hamburgers like to think that all this has made them more broad-minded than most Germans. They often voted against the Nazis, they have often had a Socialist government, and they seem less guilt-ridden by memories of war than the Bavarians, say, or the sinister Berliners. They may not be a very *soigné* citizenry, but at least they do not resent independence of view. They have never cringed to the central government in Bonn: Ministers of the Hamburg *Land* Government are even forbidden to accept Federal honours. The English, old friends of the Hamburgers, are apparently well liked still, and several English wives lived unmolested in Hamburg while the Royal Air Force was bashing the city into rubble. Some of Germany's most liberal newspapers and magazines are published in Hamburg, and some of Germany's liveliest young artists work there. Hamburg was never a viciously militarist city, by German standards. It is scarcely open-hearted, let alone open-fisted, but it was never one of the screaming jackboot communities, neurotic with grievance.

But if it is hard to conjure up the shades of the Nazis in Hamburg, or to imagine the Jews dragged from their beds in this plump *bourgeois* seaport, it is scarcely less difficult to envisage the city fitting comfortably into the new Europe – so steely, so hard, so uniform. Already, as this new entity develops, Hamburg feels a little ill at ease. As the growing power and responsibility of the United States of America has whittled away the blithe sparkle of San Francisco, so the emergence of a United States of Europe is likely to leave Hamburg high and half dry. Its great days, one senses, are passing. It is one of the greatest of European cities still, the most productive place in Germany, the fourth port of the world: but the times, one feels, are catching up with it.

What will its function be, when Europe coalesces at last, and the frontiers of Germany dissolve? The German Customs Union made it rich, but the union of Europe may well enervate it. Soon the ports of Germany will range from Venice on the Adriatic to Antwerp and Rotterdam on the North Sea, and the German industrialists will have the choice of a hundred efficient outlets. Then Hamburg's principal *raison d'être* will fade. This is a northern port, built for the cold-water routes, designed to handle the trade of a Germany that looked, willy-nilly, northwards: but today the impetus of Europe is moving southwards, and the centre of German gravity is shifting towards friendlier climes and warmer seas. Like Trieste, Hamburg is losing its hinterland. Like London, it is suffering from a shrinkage of geography.

But it will be a long, slow, stubborn decline, caused not by the end of an Empire, or even the devastation of a war, but only by more ponderously organic processes of history. Hamburg is a very substantial sort of pageant, not easily faded, and many a

big tanker must yet slide down its slipways, many a breathy
assignation emanate from the table-telephones of its night clubs,
many a clickety-click of wheels vibrate the layout of the most
elaborate model railway in Europe. It is not exactly bland, nor
even urbane, but it has something heavily imperturbable about
it – the stolid, simple, almost fatalistic spirit, I suppose, that
sustained it so resolutely through the nightmares of war. I was
once standing at the entrance of that whores' alley, beneath the
flickering neon-sky of the Reeperbahn, when an unexpected
figure passed through its portals, weaving a bustling, purposeful, businesslike way among the pallid lechers loitering inside.
It was a waiter from a neighbouring café, nattily dressed in
white, and carrying a cup of coffee neatly on his polished tray,
with two lumps of sugar hygienically wrapped. He made his
way dexterously to one of the brothel windows, and peering
into the gloom to pick his customer from the row of ghoul-like
prostitutes inside – dim, apparently phosphorescent images of
flesh, paint and pink nylon – he handed her the tray with a
polite little bow, and returned to the world outside.

14

DOING WHAT YOU LIKE

Helsinki, 1961

I have very ambivalent feelings about Russia, and they show in this little composition about the pleasures of arriving in Helsinki through what used to be called the Iron Curtain.

Liberal though you may be, and broad-minded, and looking for the best in everybody, nevertheless leaving the grey purlieus of Communism constitutes a festivity: an airy, lacy celebration, like having your first swim of the season, or falling in love. They check your baggage very carefully in Leningrad, and thumb laboriously through your manuscripts, and visibly brighten when they come across a chart of the Seven-Year Plan, and send you off to your aircraft feeling obscurely chastened, as though the headmaster is not precisely angry with you, only just a little disappointed. But a brief hour in a bumbling Ilyushin, alone with the wistful stewardess (wearing her brown fur-collared coat over her uniform), and at Helsinki you tumble into the other half of the world. The man at the desk merely says 'Passport, please': but bells ring, birds sing, and somewhere a bottle pops.

Here are the things that overjoyed me most, when that kindly man, with a barely perceptible examination of my passport, sent me whistling into Finland, guided by an exquisite airline hostess: Finnish airline hostesses first, for their reviving breath of elegance; clean, glistening architecture second, for its whisper of liberty; nice little houses in a row; Esso and International Harvester, for their welcoming gleam of profit; cars of all nations, driven at a proper pace (in Russia they never seem to exceed thirty, even in the howling spaces); the rosy cheeks of plump burghers, and children playing in their own gardens; shop

windows gracefully dressed, well-cut suits, a quayside that
anyone can walk along, a jolly polished steam train beside the
docks, Simplicity patterns, *My Fair Lady* in Swedish, coffee-pots
whose lids, you may be confident, will not fall off with a dismal
splash into the coffee-cup.

Even after Leningrad, that loveliest wraith among cities,
Helsinki feels marvellously free, easy, and undaunted, and
down its comfortable streets all the breezes of the West sweep
like a cocktail of elixirs. A visit to the city's most famous
bookshop, which claims to be the largest in Europe and is
bursting with the books of a dozen languages, is like a shot in
the arm and a sniff of salts after the drab, dutiful, brownish
bookshelves of the Soviet Union. A stroll beside the harbour,
where the patient ice-breakers (when they are not on strike)
potter stolidly backwards and forwards down the shipping
lanes, is wonderfully exhilarating: the wind off a Russian sea
feels like a death in the family, but when it blows out of the Gulf
of Finland it is only a tingle in the cheek. An hour in a sauna,
the Finnish steam bath, where you are slapped periodically with
birch twigs and plunged deliciously from agonizingly hot to
shivering cold, is enough to scour the very miasma of Russia
from your person and leave you as clean, brisk, and spanking as
a magazine advertisement.

After the stocky, buttoned Russians, the people of Helsinki
seem marvellously lithe and light-footed, big but agile, jovial at
smorgasbords or loping and sloping across their snow-fields like
Tibetan holy men. Their children, slithering about with ice-
hockey sticks, give the heartening impression that they came
into the world on skis, and have not just put them on in the
interests of some ideological demonstration. Their wives are as
neat as pins, and gossip sharply in expensive coffee-shops.
Their hotels are either delectably modern, all pale wood and
sliding glass, or fragrantly Edwardian, with murals and cigar-
smoked panelling. Their suburbs are posh with provincial
snobbery, and they are a people that nobody in the world could
possibly feel sorry for. They are as tough as nails, and twice as
spiky.

In Helsinki, only an hour from the Winter Palace, you can do
exactly what you like. You can take a ride in a sleigh across the
frozen harbour, unimpeded by suspicious policemen and pulled
by a bleary kind of pony. You can build yourself a little hut on

the ice and fish for your dinner through a hole. You can drink
mystical liqueurs from the forests, made of berries, pine cones
and arctic brambles. You can eat, stifling a sentimental tear,
smoked reindeer tongue with salad, or guzzle your way through
a fish cock – pork stuffed with fresh-water herring, and baked
peculiarly into a loaf. You can go to a French film or an American
play, and read the English papers with a flourish outside the
Presidential Palace (a pleasant minor mansion of the kind
described by estate agents as being 'suitable for conversion').

All these many pleasures and stimulants greet you as your
taxi skids genially into Helsinki; and all the fun and freedom of
the West welcomes you, and all the vitamins and calories are
there to bolster your wasted stamina. Most people, when they
leave the potato world behind the Curtain, seem to pine for
some fresh or virile victual – a lettuce or a pineapple, a cucumber
or a pickled egg. My own craving, when I flew into Finland out
of eastern Europe, was for raw carrots, and when I arrived in
Helsinki I went straight to a grocer, ordered half a pound,
washed them in my hotel bathroom, and ate them luxuriously
with a glass of schnapps.

But here is an odd and provoking fact: I ate those rich red
vegetables with delight, and I wallowed like an emperor in all
the milky pleasure of capitalism; but when, later that day, I
wanted something to read with my dinner some unexpected
instinct guided my choice, a kind of reluctant nostalgia, a
niggling trace of respect and affection, and when I sat down to
my pig's trotters I found myself dining with Turgenev. (And all
that well-dressed little capital, I felt, all that brave and courteous
citizenry, could not offer me quite such company.)

15

ANGLO-CHINA

Hong Kong, 1974

It hardly seemed to occur to the businessmen of Hong Kong, in the 1970s, that before long the colony would pass into the hands of Communist China, then still ruled by the enigmatic Mao Tse-tung: but by the end of the decade the truth began to dawn, and the city was never to feel quite like this again.

A foreign devil of my acquaintance, on my first morning in Hong Kong, took me to the top of an exceedingly high mountain, by funicular from Garden Road, and invited me to worship.

The kingdoms of the world lay before us. The skyscrapers of Victoria, jam-packed at the foot of the hill, seemed to vibrate with pride, greed, energy and success, and all among them the traffic swirled, and the crowds milled, and the shops glittered, and the money rang. Beyond lay the ships in their hundreds, like a vast fleet anchored in the roadsteads from Chai Wan to Stonecutter's Island, here a supertanker, here a cruise ship, there a warship all a'bristle, with their attendant sampans busy beside them, and the junks and tugs and pilot boats hurrying everywhere, and the hydrofoil foaming off to Macao, and the ceaseless passage of the Star ferries backwards and forwards across the harbour. Across the water lay Kowloon on the mainland: deep among its structures ran the great gash of Nathan Road, violent with advertising, and off to the east the airport protruded brutally into the harbour, and sometimes a jet threw itself screaming and smoking into the sky.

Beyond it all again lay the hills of China, but these my guide ignored. His eyes were focused, intense, almost fanatical, upon that brilliant pulsation at our feet, moving from ship to bank building, harbour-front to hotel, like the most diligent of landowners surveying his inherited estate. 'You may not like it,' he said. 'We don't ask you to like it. We don't *expect* you to like it. But you must admit it *works*.'

He meant that it worked in a Victorian, ideological sense, like a steam-pump as an agency of Progress, or some unarguable theory of the Manchester School. It is certainly true that Hong Kong has a greased, thumping feel to it, suggestive of well-turned brass pistons, or persuasive statistics. In the reference books, or on the map, it seems a weird political and economic anomaly: on the spot it feels, if not exactly organic, at least habitual. It has been there a long time. There is a mystic saying in Hong Kong that one must not express an opinion about the place until one has been there for nineteen years: but the corporate experience of the place has now lasted for four or five generations, since that fateful 26 January 1841, when the Royal Navy raised the flag on the foreshore at Possession Point – just along the road, that is, from the Macao hydrofoil station. 'There can be neither safety nor honour for either the British or the Chinese,' Captain Charles Elliot, RN, had declared, 'until Her Majesty's flag flies on these coasts in a secure position': and since then no British Government, and perhaps no Chinese either, has seriously considered lowering the Union Jack again, and returning Hong Kong to its hinterland.

It may look precarious in *The Statesman's Year Book*, but it is an Oriental fact of life. Poised minutely, all 400 square miles of it, upon the skin of China, it is a sort of permanent parasite. It is divided into two constitutional parts. Hong Kong Island, with the mainland peninsula of Kowloon, is British by right of possession, ceded in perpetuity by the Chinese: the New Territories, 365 square miles of the adjacent mainland, are British by virtue of a ninety-nine-year lease, expiring in 1998. But though to outsiders there sounds a crucial difference between these two categories, the one organically British, the other British by licence, so to speak, when you are there they both seem much the same. The present Chinese Government, as it happens, does not recognize the New Territories lease anyway, so that the date of its expiry is more than usually hypothetical even by diplomatic standards, and the British would probably put it out of their minds were it not for the fact that land tenure in the Territories is inevitably linked with the expiry date, so that a reminder of 1998 appears on every deed of estate. No frontier divides the one part from the other, and though to gentlemen abed in England there may seem something risky to an investment that theoretically collapses in twenty-five years, capitalists in Hong Kong seldom seem to give the matter a thought, and behave as though the whole place will be true-blue British for ever.

And if the parasite is well established, it is also full of the life-force – bile, venom, adrenalin, according to your diagnosis. More than four million people live in Hong Kong. Its port handles 7,000 ocean-going ships a year. It is a great producer of textiles, toys, plastics, electronics, and one of the most brilliant and bullish of the world's entrepôts. If you consider it as part of the almost vanished British Empire, then it is more populous than all the rest of the Empire put together. If you think of it as part of China, it is the third biggest Chinese city, and easily the richest. On the one hand it is a dazzling showcase of Western capitalism, on the other a microcosm of China herself, within whose cramped and isolated confines there live emigrants from every Chinese province, class and philosophy.

It ticks, wriggles and itches there, on the edge of Kwangtung Province – sometimes an irritant to the People's Republic, perhaps, but a safety valve too, and perhaps even a comfort. Whatever else I felt about Hong Kong, when my friend on the Peak invited me to admire it, I did not think it in the least temporary. It is always rash to prophesy political longevity, as Voltaire realized when, waking up in Paradise one day in 1798, he remembered his forecast that the Venetian Republic would last for ever: but this I will take the risk of saying, that like many another anomaly, Hong Kong may well outlive the norm. It reminds me of those quirks of English society, wrinkled customs, immemorial exceptions, which linger on through change and election all the more tenaciously because they stand outside the rules.

'What an anachronism!' people exclaim. 'A British colonial Government, totally unrepresentative, like something out of Victoria's day, lording it over four million Chinese! How do the Chinese stand for it?' They stand for it, I think, largely because they *are* Chinese. They know a useful compromise when they see one, and so well does the device of Hong Kong suit their needs and genius that for all I know they invented the arrangement themselves, like everything else, 10,000 years ago in Soochow.

*

The Chineseness of Hong Kong, unlike the tempered Chinese-ness of Singapore, is so terrific, so furious, so complex in texture that I have always despaired of capturing its sensations in words, and on my first visit to the colony, in 1958, I was reduced to a symbolic description of the clumps of edible frogs, tied together around the waist and still vigorously alive, which are the piquant prodigies of the Central Market. I cannot do much better now. The noise, the push, the sheer physical mass of the Chinese in Hong Kong overwhelms the senses, and reduces the most grandiloquent writer to vignette.

Take, for instance, for a start, one's arrival at one of the second-class hotels with grand names which cluster, gaudy with neon lights, around the waterfront end of Nathan Road. This is a daunt-ingly Chinese experience. The doorman indeed is probably a turbaned Sikh, offering old imperialists a poignant reminder of better times, but inside the lobby everything is garishly Chinese. Tasteless, loud and faintly suggestive of humdrum varieties of sin, it is nevertheless exceedingly efficient. The receptionist throws you a steely gold-toothed smile, but has your reservation at her fingertips. The porter's greeting is perfunctory, but you can be sure he has the right key. The room itself is clean, and has plenty of towels, and lots of hot water, and a list of Girlie Clubs prepared for your comfort by the Tourist Association.

But ah, when the porter closes your door, and you are left in that small cubby-hole of Hong Kong, how more than impersonal, how dehumanized the place turns out to be! You look out through the metal-framed windows, and across the great filthy pit of the hotel, littered with old sacks and piles of discarded masonry, a huge slab of building confronts you. All its windows are brilliantly lit, and in each a little Chinese cameo, separate from all its neighbours, is joylessly displayed. Here four girls sit tense over their sewing-machines, silent and unsmiling, motionless but for the quick twist and tug of their fingers. There a solitary shirt-sleeved man is hunched over his files and calculators, beneath the dazzling light of his naked bulb, dead to all else and perhaps to himself. Along the way eight or nine families seem to be packed into one room, and one sees only flashes of infant limbs, waves of drapery, buckets, black loose hair, bedclothes and grinning mop faces, as though some perpetual and appalling farce is being played inside.

Every room is ablaze, every room full, and across the inter-

vening gloom one hears radios, clicking machines, shouts and
children's screams. In another city all that life over there might
be a comfort, a reminder that if you happen to be alone that
night, all around you is the warmth of community. In Hong
Kong it is different. Nobody out there seems to take the slightest
notice of anyone else – let alone of you as, peering through the
orange fabric curtains, your wan Western face gazes aghast
across the chasm.

At another Chinese extreme, take the walled village of Kam
Tin, which stands antique and morose in the heart of the New
Territories. This is Chineseness of a very different sort. It is not
a very large walled village, but it is one of the tourist sights of
the colony, for better than any other local monument, perhaps,
it evokes the continuity of the Chinese presence – antedating as
it does by four centuries the arrival of Her Majesty's frigates
upon the foreshore. Kam Tin is Chinese in a tortoisean way, a
carapacial, scaly way. Modernity has long besieged it, and just
across the way there is a garage, and a small supermarket: but
the village lies hot and secretive still within its towered walls,
and the Teng clan, who built it in the first place, live in it
exclusively still. Wrinkled crones in black pyjamas and coolie
hats guard it, half-heartedly offering a selection of spurious
antiques, and an aged man in black directs you to the slot in the
wall in which you are invited to place your charitable offering.
Then through the wrought-iron gate you pass, and into the
brown brick labyrinth beyond.

It is the very opposite of picturesque. Rectangular, dowdy,
brown, it reminded me of old Swindon, down by the locomotive
works. Everybody seems immensely old in Kam Tin. Old dogs
lie about. Old ladies look at you through unglazed windows.
Old flies buzz. There is no sound of traffic, for no wheeled
vehicles can enter, except for a few old bicycles: so a hush hangs
over the place, a very old Chinese hush, pursuing you down the
narrow alleyways, between the drab mud-brick houses, like a
venerable reproach, or a dictum. I found it all rather unnerving,
and seemed to feel the oldness of Kam Tin clinging to me when
I left, impregnating my clothes and my thoughts, until at last I
overpowered it with peeled shrimps and fried rice in the floating
restaurant at Sha Tin Hoi.

*

But for a last, blither cameo of Hong Kong's Chinadom, let me take you to the small island which stands, linked by a causeway to the shore, on the edge of Tolo Harbour, north of Kowloon. There is a house upon the island, but we will circumvent it, and scramble around the bluff below until we reach the little point at the end, where the grass is prickly and sun bleached, and small bright flowers have gone feral from the garden above. Behind us now we may hear a radio from the kitchen, or children's laughter from an upstairs room, but before us lies classic China. The bay extends blue and limpid towards the China Sea, and beyond it lie low tawny hills, speckled here and there with villages, hot, dusty, arid: and in the still basin below us ten or twelve junks lie, tied close together in twos and threes, like painted ships.

Their awkward but elegant forms, high-prowed, top-heavy, are reflected romantically in the water, and sometimes there are signs of life upon them: men moving ropes about, women emerging with pots or laundry, children scrambling among the rigging. Generally, though, they seem to lie there motionless, as if for show. It is a scene of infinite calm and balance, a posed scene. It is as though those painted vessels never move from their moorings, but lie there for ever as upon a china plate, lovingly etched and baked in the glaze, and traditionally coloured.

They are not there for artistic reasons. They are there to make money. Making money is the purpose of Hong Kong, and it was the prospect of profit that induced the British to found the colony in the first place. The great British merchants of Hong Kong, the *taipans* who first made their fortunes in opium and tea, have never relaxed their grip upon the opportunities of the place, and have survived war, depression and the end of Empire to remain great men of the China coast. 'Look, there goes the *taipan*,' Chinese people sometimes say, when they see one of the moguls of Jardine Matheson sweep by in his limousine: and though they say it partly in fun (the commonest kind of *taipan* is a chief pimp), and partly by force of habit, they also speak out of an empathetic esteem. The British and the Chinese may spring from utterly alien cultures, from opposite ends of the world, but they are fused in the furnace of Hong Kong, and made colleagues by the hope of profit.

The rich British still live very grandly. They appear with visiting earls in gossip columns, and form a well-known element in the entrepreneurial jet set that swishes about between Beirut, London, New York, Tokyo and Sydney. 'I'm so sorry,' I was told when I inquired after a friend of a friend, 'but Mrs W— is away in Japan, launching a ship.' They have country houses on the delectable eastern shore of Hong Kong Island, they have closed-circuit colour television in the boxes at Happy Valley racetrack, and so long have they been on the China coast, if not in person then at least by the proxy of their forebears, that the quirks of Hong Kong life have become their orthodoxies. Peking holds no mystery for them: they have maintained their contacts with China through the Kuomintang and Cultural Revolution, and they regard the aspirations of Chiang and Chou alike with an urbane indulgence. *Plus ça change*, they seem to shrug, and ringing for a specially bound copy of the company's annual report, with their compliments, they draw your attention to last year's highly satisfactory trading account.

Hong Kong nowadays is only their base, and their activities extend, in shipping and trading, banking and insurance, speculation and agency, all over the Far East. Even so their stake in the colony is staggering. Wherever you look there stand the artefacts and enterprises of Jardine Matheson, Butterfield & Swire, and the other old houses of the British connection: mammoth new office blocks, enormous shopping complexes, a tunnel under the harbour, the China Motor Bus Company, swank hotels, graving docks, television services. They have their fingers in innumerable pies, and they are still distinctly British. When Jardine built their vast new headquarters building, the tallest structure in Asia unless you count television towers, the architects were Palmer & Turner, the consultant engineers were Mitchell McFarlane, the air-conditioning was by Jardine Engineering Company, the tiling was by Marley, and only the hinges, so I discovered from the board at the construction site, were by Shun Fung.

If the Chinese acquire an alarming new bite and dominance when they leave their homeland, so do the overseas British, and British capitalism in Hong Kong retains an edge and confidence it has long lost at home. There is no sentimentality to the *taipans*. They are pushing men in a men's world, and their wives, I am told, sometimes get bored with their perpetual enrichment,

handed down from father to son, and pine for more modest
indulgences, like a concert now and then, or a visiting poet.

There are poorer Britons too, of course. You often see them on
the Star ferry, open-necked or cotton-frocked, browned by the
China sun, and bearing themselves like what they are – almost
the last of the workaday British colonialists.

Some are sailors, and are on their way to the China Fleet
Club, that almost legendary institution, familiar to a million
matelots, which stands on the edge of the Suzy Wong country
beside the waterfront of Wanchai. Some are soldiers – stationed
in Hong Kong not to keep the Chinese Communists out, but,
as official handouts discreetly say, 'to assist the Government in
maintaining security and stability', the classic role of British
imperial forces. Many more are accountants, clerks, or housewives, who speak in Londonish or more probably Surreyish
accents, and tend to grumble about the servant problem. Some
are technical advisers, or journalists, or airline pilots, or university teachers. Nearly all are unmistakably British. There are
Europeans of many sorts in Hong Kong and more than 6,000
Americans, too: but the British vastly predominate – there are
nearly 30,000 of them – and in some indefinable way they
remain different from all the others, too, and even now carry
themselves apart.

I loved to sit on the ferry and contemplate these people. They
were trapped for me there, like historical specimens, deep in
their tabloids or compiling their shopping lists. What a line they
represented, I used to think! What generations of exiles culminated in their persons, listlessly looking out across the passing
harbour, or doing the crossword puzzle! Their fathers blazed a
way across the world, veld to outback, pioneering in shacks,
beachcombing on reefs, disciplining recalcitrant Sioux or
bayoneting fuzzy-wuzzies: and here they were beside me, the
last of the long parade, indifferent to their origins, unconscious
of them perhaps, unexcited on the slat-seated ferry-boat between
Kowloon and Victoria!

The boat shudders: the gangplanks clatter down, top and
lower deck; the blue-jerseyed Chinese seamen swing open the
iron gates; in a trice, as the crowd streams off the vessel and
hastens beneath the subway into town, those unobtrusive
imperialists are overwhelmed by their Chinese fellow subjects,

four million to 30,000, and you would hardly guess from the look of things that there was a Briton left in the crown colony at all.

Yet Britons still rule it, directly and absolutely. The Governor and Commander-in-Chief of Hong Kong is still guarded by Gurkha sentries in his white palace below the Botanical Gardens, and unglamorously installed in rambling Indianified offices, or making do in temporary shacks, the Hong Kong Government is modestly at work. Most of its senior members are British, some of them Chinese-speaking, most of them staunch believers in the rightness of their own methods. They do not merely rule Hong Kong, indeed; they rule it absolutely. Subject only to the distant distracted authority of Queen, Parliament and Whitehall, the Governor and his officials are as all-powerful now as their colleagues were a century ago in India or Bermuda. No local legislature restrains them. The only elected representatives in Hong Kong are members of the Urban Council, and even they are in a minority, and represent only a minute proportion of the population. Both the Executive and the Legislative Councils of the Colony are entirely *ex officio* or nominated by Government, and both are presided over by the Governor. The Empire lives in Hong Kong. With names like Luddington, Haddon-Cave or Lightbody, with duck suits and straw hats, with a formidable expertise and a truly dedicated zeal, the gentlemen of the Hong Kong administration direct the affairs of the last of the great Crown colonies superbly in the tradition of the later Raj.

'Hong Kong subscribes,' one distinguished public official observed to me, 'to Victorian economic principles: these are the only economic principles that have ever actually *succeeded*.' *Taipans* may complain of too much official interference: officials believe themselves to be operating the last of the *laissez-faire* administrations. Hong Kong is a free port; it is charged by the energies of free enterprise; even the great civic works, the public transport, the harbour tunnel, are financed largely by private money. Government in Hong Kong is unobtrusive partly because it cannot afford flamboyance, but partly because it believes its function to be supplementary. 'Our job is to do the things private enterprise cannot or will not do, and to keep the whole caboodle on the rails.'

It suggests to me a conscientious vicar in a particularly well-heeled parish, pagan, rather condescending but not by and large unfriendly. Until the 1950s the British Government regarded Hong Kong more or less as any other colony, and schemes were prepared for constitutional reform: today there is no pretence to liberalism, but the colony's officials are essentially philanthropic in their approach. No taint of jingo vulgarizes their attitudes, and they are rightly hurt when visitors suspect them of snobbery or racialism. They are the very opposite of your stock imperialists, and are proud of Hong Kong chiefly as a haven, which has welcomed so many millions of refugees, over many generations, and has done its best to support them fairly. Nor are they in the least chauvinist. It did not seem to me, I innocently observed to one of them, that Hong Kong *felt* British at all – look at the way the traffic moved! 'I agree with you there,' he replied. 'Good road manners are dead in Britain.'

They say that pragmatism was always an imperial quality, and in Hong Kong it is certainly evident. The British rulers of the place have been obliged to live not for the ideal, not even for the principle, but for the situation. Other colonies may have had leisure for introspection, for historical awareness and cultural ambitions; Hong Kong has no museum, a public library smaller than Fiji's and an archive only established in the past couple of years. Some British colonies were always fortresses; some were settlements; some were transit stations on the imperial routes. Hong Kong was always a place of profit, and when Captain Elliot spoke of safety and honour all those years ago, he was really thinking of capital and dividends. To this overriding purpose the Hong Kong Government has always adapted its attitudes, and very successfully too. It has had few rebels within its ranks, demanding emancipation or self-government; it has recognized itself primarily as a law-and-order government, perpetually holding a ring, and with works of goodwill thrown in as a sideline; and to every criticism it offers, like my friend on the Peak, that last rationalization of imperial pragmatism: 'It *works*!'

In some ways it is an ugly mechanism. Hong Kong is a very beautiful place, full of colour and of splendour, but it is charmless. It is hard and humourless. It ought to lift the spirits, with its marvellous vistas, its perpetual surge of energy, its contrasts and its anomalies: in fact it somehow falls flat. Hong Kong is generally popularly coupled with Rio, Sydney and San

Francisco as one of the loveliest harbour cities in the world: of the four it is the biggest, liveliest and perhaps even the richest, but to my tastes it is also the least invigorating.

I think this is partly because, for reasons I cannot analyse, the confrontation between Chinese and British lacks piquancy, or even style. It is rather an *ordinary* meeting. I went one day to visit an acquaintance in one of the big apartment blocks that have lately been built beside the Kowloon waterfront. These are inhabited almost entirely by Chinese, but they look rather like a corner of Sheffield, say, and offer a peculiarly dispiriting combination of life-styles. Into those moulds of concrete, by Greater London Council out of Radiant City, have been squeezed all the dourest qualities of the Chinese. The buildings are indistinguishable from each other, there seem to be a million more or less identical tenants on every floor, and nobody appears to know anybody else. It is as though they are all in immediate competition with one another, for air or living space, so that the *bonhomie* is removed from Yorkshire, the comradeship from Canton, and one is left with a formidable but unlovely hybrid.

Formidable, because there is no breath of the haphazard to this life-style: the Hong Kong Chinese is a man of relentless logic, and rational foresight is his forte. I even sense it in the tumbled picturesque market streets of Victoria, which straggle higgledy-piggledy up the lower slopes of the Peak, and are fragrant with soups when the sun goes down, but in which, I suspect, absolutely nothing is left to chance: and there is a bleak sense of order, too, to the industrial centres of the New Territories, where the powerful new factories, set in green gardens but towered over by chimneys, derricks, and elevators, look like model factories in an exhibition. I am reminded sometimes of Rhodesia: not just in the newness, and the determination, but in a certain bland distortion of culture – as though Hong Kong is not quite true to itself, and lacks fizz accordingly.

I felt it on other levels, too. I went to a very grand dinner party one evening, and sensed it strongly there. The food was sumptuous, the service soft-footed, the conversation civilized. About half the guests were British, the other half Chinese, all rich, all widely travelled, all equally Hong Kong: and after a while, I found, it was difficult to distinguish one from the other. They all spoke more or less the same upper-class English. They mostly shared the same kind of humour. They dressed alike, with slight cultural variations like split skirts or OE ties. It is true that one elegant young Chinese of indeterminate profession ('Well, I call myself a merchant on my passport – it sounds romantic, don't you think?') did admit to me that he sometimes felt isolated between the two cultures, but for the most part everyone seemed suavely at home on the cross-benches.

Yet I hope my host will not think me ungrateful if I say that the evening lacked fire. Perhaps they were all too alike? There was none of the mordant fun of a similar evening in India, say, where East and West parry each other with a wary and exhilarating love-hate. In Hong Kong the profit motive paradoxically defuses life, and makes nearly everyone brothers beneath the skin.

Yet I have a reservation at the back of my mind. It occurred to me that evening, as I contemplated my fellow guests, that the Chinese knew far more about the British than the British knew about the Chinese. The British had been on that coastline for 150 years, and had created Hong Kong: but in a deeper sense the Chinese had been there always. The British would mostly go home in the end, to Scotland or to Sevenoaks: the Chinese were there to stay. Few of the British spoke a Chinese language: all the Chinese spoke English. My merchant friend could doubtless have given me a fairly succinct account of, say, the difference between Presbyterian and Anglican: but no Briton there could have told me much about Taoism, or ventured to explain the nature of Chinese loyalty. The British of Hong Kong know a great deal about China as a trading opportunity, but when it comes to the profounder complexities of Chinese life, they are generally not much less ignorant than you or me.

Why should they be? They stick to their last, and this limited range of British vision suits the Chinese too. One feels in Hong Kong a sense of compromise. You mind your business, it seems to say, and I'll mind mine. The British seldom pry into the privacies of Chineseness: the Chinese do not often agitate for change. Almost everywhere in the old Empire foreign government came to be considered, rightly or wrongly, the worst sort of government there was. Not in Hong Kong. Government is a chore there. Let the barbarians do it.

*

They do it well, but not of course perfectly. After a few days in Nathan Road I moved over to Hong Kong Island and put up at the Hilton. From my window there I looked down upon the Supreme Court, and often I observed there, in a space largely and freshly painted 'NO PARKING', the large black Daimler of the Chief Justice. The *South China Morning Post* noticed the car there too, while I was there, and photographed it in this self-incriminating station, but there was no response from His Honour, and the Daimler still stood there when I left.

It has not been suggested, I think, that in any larger way the judiciary of Hong Kong is corrupt. Its distinction is more doubtful. I went to court one day to watch the judges in action, and through all the usual flummery of English law, the wiggery and the pedantry, the royal ciphers and the stained mahogany, thought I detected up there on the bench no more than a provincial adequacy – unremarkable men, lucky (like most judges) to be elevated to such dramatic dignities, and living perhaps (like many expatriates) rather more loftily than they might at home. One does not, of course, expect brilliance from a colonial bench – a schoolmasterly fairness and honesty are all one can reasonably demand. In Hong Kong, though, a place full of brilliance, this judicial plod strikes one the more flaccidly, like a dollop of pastry in a rhubarb pie: and when I asked lawyers about it they ascribed it to a lack of incentive or opportunity among local Chinese to become judges themselves.

The reasons they gave were unimpeachable, and were concerned with salaries and legal education, but I could not help wondering if another cause might not be Hong Kong's infinite prospects of profitable mayhem, far more easily tapped by astute advocates than by honourable judges. Hong Kong is fearfully corrupt, and always has been. Before the last war the Government itself was involved in an intricate scandal – many a Hong Kong cupboard has its skeleton – and ever since the foundation of the colony the natural instincts of the place have bred skulduggery and intrigue. Hong Kong is one of the great drug entrepôts of the world; its protection rackets are ubiquitous; much of its daily life is based, in one degree or another, tacitly or explicitly, upon squeeze.

Hong Kong is touchy on the subject. The colony has had some bad publicity lately, and the wise visitor, if she wishes to be invited to dinner next time, treads carefully around the subject of graft. 'You don't understand!' they say. 'This is Asia. Standards are different here. Compared with Saigon or Djakarta Hong Kong is lily-white!' The truth must be, though, now as ever, that Empire cannot have it all ways. If law and order is the speciality of the Raj, then it must honour its own standards. Old China hands may justifiably claim that Hong Kong, for all its myriad rackets, for all its 100 murders a year, for all its crooked policemen and opium entrepreneurs, is a more law-abiding city than most of its peers: admirers of the British tradition still expect higher standards of the last and greatest of the crown colonies.

Yet even as I write, I hear within my own mind charges of hypocrisy. I have always relished the freebooting side of Empire, the swashbuckle, the fur traders, the nabobs, the merchant adventurers. Yet what was that dashing enterprise but romanticized graft? I prefer to think of it as an eye for the main chance, but all too often it obeyed just the same principles as west African dash or Hong Kong tea money, and dealt often enough in the same commodities – 'chasing the dragon' as the Hong Kong underworld still calls the pursuit of narcotics. Hong Kong is no more than a microcosm of imperial enterprise – good and bad in collusion, as they were in the old Empire itself.

I would guess that the vast majority of Hong Kong government officials are there simply to do their best, while the vast majority of everybody else are there to get what they can. Opportunism is the *raison d'être* of Hong Kong, and virtually every private citizen of this colony is a speculator and a capitalist, from the richest developer to the poorest labourer.

I have observed some striking social contrasts in my time, *barriada* beside Lima penthouses, Rollses in Calcutta, oil sheikh and Bedu scavenger, but few have struck me as more curiously disturbing than the contrasts between Chinese rich and poor in Hong Kong. I am not sure why this is. It is not exactly a moral shock, for as I say virtually all Hong Kong people are animated by the same impulses, and the poor beggar would certainly be the swell investor if he could. It is certainly no post-imperialist shame: I am of the opinion that the British Empire has done well by Hong Kong, on the whole. Perhaps it is because the apparent homogeneity of the Chinese, their compact sense of racial power and superiority, somehow make disparities among them seem out of character. 'I believe the Chinese,' wrote the British General Lord Wolseley in 1903, 'to be the most remarkable people in the world, and destined to be one of the master races.' The Chinese have some such effect upon most of us, and it is disconcerting to realize that they too have their winners and losers, their ups and their downs.

I felt this irrational shock most forcibly when I returned to Kowloon one afternoon after a visit to one of the settlement areas in the New Territories, where refugees from China proper are helped and housed. Out there a sense of barely escaped disaster informed the scene. The place was partly a housing area, partly a huddle of shacks, and it possessed all the trappings of twentieth-century calamity: the bundles of poor possessions, the ramshackle shelters of wood and canvas, the cluttered strings of washing in the tenement buildings, emaciated old people, pot-bellied young, hunger, bewilderment, good works, smells of dirt and open-air cookery, makeshift markets, bicycles, noise, congestion, runny noses – all the standard paraphernalia, in fact, of modern misery, translated this time into the Chinese idiom, and deposited upon the foreshore of Hong Kong. It was perfectly familiar to me. I had grown up with it, like any wanderer of my age, and it did not look out of place against the harsh rocky hillsides of Hong Kong.

But when I drove back to Kowloon I dropped into the Peninsula Hotel for tea, and there I discovered a Chinese contrast I had not experienced before. I was familiar enough, of course, with rich Chinese of the old kind, with collections of ivory carvings, and curly stone lions in their gardens: they offered no real contrast to the poor of the resettlement areas, but seemed to me of the same tradition, only temporarily more successful – exchangeable perhaps in the last resort, so that the beldams of the tenement could, given a damask dress and a pair of golden slippers, quite easily preside over the dinner table of the Victorian connoisseur. Now, however, ordering their cream cakes and India tea to the strains of Gershwin from the promenade orchestra, I observed an altogether new kind of Chinese upon display, so alien to those people of misery that for the first time I realized how fissiparous the Chinese civilization might be after all.

They frightened me rather, these new Chinese of the Peninsula. They had achieved some new synthesis of their own, freed from their own traditions but by no means subservient to ours. They were all young, and evidently rich, and they had to them a kind of stylized menace, suggestive of Kabuki more than Kung Fu. They were taller than Chinese used to be, and slinkier, and they were heavily made up, and wore fur fabric coats and many rings, and they dyed their hair in streaks, and sat slouched and disdainful in their chairs, reading *Time* magazine. The expression that our grandfathers used to call enigmatic seemed to have curdled, upon their faces, into an elegant sneer – for they *were* elegant, and handsome too, the girls languid and *svelte*, the men perhaps the first truly beautiful Chinese I had ever seen.

I encountered their kind often afterwards, making films, eating ice-creams, booking tickets to Zurich or sweeping in perfumed cars to floodlit race meetings. They came to dramatize for me the extreme nature of life in the colony, the violent range of the phenomenon. I sometimes went for my supper, if I had nothing better to do, to the open-air market beside the Macao ferry station, which springs up at sunset and provides a lively spectacle and an excellent cuisine – a bright hissing congeries of stalls, offering everything from monkey wrenches to Thai silks, and spilling hugger-mugger over the car park and across the road into the pavement of Connaught Road. I was always kindly welcomed there, and I generally ate a bowl of aromatic soup, piping hot, exquisitely spiced, nourishingly mucous of texture and compounded chiefly of clams, crabs and bamboo.

One night, though, I decided to eat in my room, and consulting the Chinese menu always available at the Hilton Hotel, ordered a bowl of crab, clam and bamboo fungus soup. It arrived aromatic, mucous and exquisitely spiced: but when I compared the price of it with the price of the soup at the market stall, identical in merit and if anything more generous in quantity, I found that the Hilton version cost just twenty-eight times as much.

Yet the balance holds, and I sometimes fancied in Hong Kong a sense of reconciliation – Asia and Europe come to terms. Thirty years ago, when Japan's Greater Prosperity Sphere reached across to Hong Kong, it seemed that Europe's day was ended on the China coast, and that Hong Kong would soon go the way of Weihaiwei, Shanghai and the other old footholds of the West. Even the Americans assumed, at the end of the Second World War, that Hong Kong would be returned to Chiang Kai-

shek's China, and to many Britons too that seemed the natural
course of events.

The loss of Singapore, in 1941, affected the British traumati-
cally. It was the end of an age. The fall of Hong Kong, six weeks
earlier, hardly seems to have affected them at all. By now the
years of Japanese occupation seem almost forgotten even within
the colony: the story is muffled, the tragedy muted, as though
people wish not to be reminded of it. I drove out one day to the
site of the Stanley prison camp, where most of the British
population was confined for nearly four years, and where many
died. The prison building is a prison still, and there are some
sad tombstones in the graveyard along the road, crudely carved
by the prisoners themselves in the midst of their misery: 'Skull
of Unknown, December 1941', 'After Life's Fitful Fever She
Sleeps Well', or 'K. S. Morrison, Chieftain, St. Andrew's Society'.

Even in Stanley itself, though, people responded vaguely,
even evasively, to my questions: and when I called at the British
Army camp which is still there, the soldiers at the guardroom
seemed to think of the past as mere legend or superstition –
'She's got hold of some information,' they told the orderly
officer, 'about this being where they interned people during the
war' – and offered me only macabre and inaccurate anecdotes.
I expected to experience some hush or charisma over a place
that had seen so much suffering: but now the sun shone genially
over the old compound, the air was fresh, the junks loitered
prettily offshore, and even the spot where, thirty-five years ago,
twelve Britons were beheaded for having a radio set, seemed to
possess no air of elegy.

The Japanese left scarcely a mark behind them, except for the
ugly tower they superimposed upon the Governor's palace, and
they scarcely interrupted the progress of Hong Kong – which, in
the resilient way of capitalism, resumed its affairs when they
had gone almost as though nothing had happened. But the
occupation did permanently affect relations between the British
and the Chinese – between Britain and Asia, in fact. There lives
in Kowloon an Irishman, a former member of the Hong Kong
government, who was exempted from internment by the Japanese because of his Irish nationality, and who advised the
occupation authorities about the disposal of sewage, on which
he was an expert. After the war, I am told, the British community,
released from the torments of Stanley, reacted fiercely against

this man, and he was forced out of the government service, and ostracized by his colleagues. Today he is spoken of without resentment. His actions have fallen into a gentler perspective; the affront has been tempered by time; what once seemed treason to a cause, even a civilization, now seems little more than quixotry, or even common sense. The British in Hong Kong no longer seem to themselves to represent some other, superior order, some uncompromisingly separate set of values: if they have lost the imperial conviction, they have lost the delusions too.

Before the war their racial chauvinism was notorious. It survives still, of course, though chiefly in what British sociologists might call the lower-middle-class expatriates, among whom, here as everywhere, a wog is still occasionally a wog. ('They're no good,' one of those soldiers assured me, 'they don't *want* to understand, and they smell.') On more sophisticated levels I found no trace of it, unless you count bafflement as prejudice; on the contrary, I thought the British rather overdid their admiration of Chinese qualities, and could not help feeling, when inefficiently cheated by a kiosk girl, or unconvincingly blarneyed by a taxi-driver, that the Chinese sometimes underestimate us.

Certainly the community is full of Sinophiles. Some are scholars, devoted to the Chinese arts and sciences. Some just admire the industriousness of the race. Some, like me, respond to the almost Scottish mixture of kindliness and reserve so often to be discovered behind the Chinese mask. One well-known Hong Kong Englishwoman takes her bicycle to Peking for an annual holiday, and potters about the Celestial City sketching. An earlier generation of Britons was able to despise China, and to speak of Hong Kong as a notch cut by a woodsman on the trunk of China, to mark the spot for a later felling. Nobody can despise China now, and so one source of bigotry has been eliminated, to be replaced, if not yet by universal trust or affection, at least by a cautious respect.

Some Britons, following an old imperial tradition, have transferred their loyalties to Asia itself, and will live out their lives in Hong Kong. If anything, indeed, I found less resentment against Peking than against London. Like many another colony, Hong Kong is often at loggerheads with its distant Whitehall masters, especially perhaps when they are socialists, and what

used to be called 'the imperial factor' irritates people as much
on the Peak as it once riled Rhodes at Kimberley. In particular
the issue of convertibility raises local tempers: London insists
that Hong Kong's tremendous balances in London should
remain in sterling, while the Hong Kong Government, like the
Hong Kong banks, would like to diversify them into other,
stabler currencies – to the detriment perhaps of sterling itself,
but to the advantage of Hong Kong and its four million Chinese.
I was reminded again of Rhodesia, at the time of UDI, and
wondered if Hong Kong, too, was ever tempted to break away
and constitute itself another city-state, like Singapore: but no, I
was told, while Peking was prepared to tolerate a British Hong
Kong, it would not stomach an independent Anglo-Chinese
republic there on its very doorstep, like a nearer and still more
equivocal Singapore.

   Well, then, I used to ask, as a supplementary, was there no
danger that the Chinese might, in one of their cyclic periods of
aggression, simply march into Hong Kong anyway? 'Oh, I don't
think so,' was the general tenor of the replies I got. 'That
wouldn't be very civilized, would it?' This is the tenor of
reconciliation: and those Britons who have elected to make
Hong Kong their home for ever, and who have retired to villages
on Repulse Bay, or are living out their years cherished by soft-
footed familiars in tapestried apartments of the Peak – those
who, by settling for ever in the colony, have become the first
properly Hong Kong British, are staying there not because the
island flies the British flag still, but because it is truly and
irrevocably a corner of China.

   A corner of China! Behind the relentless push of Hong Kong
I often sense something gentler and more haunting: a yearning
for China. It is not, obviously, a political yearning, nor even
exactly a cultural urge, but only perhaps an instinctive impulse
towards that mighty presence over the hills. China! If the name
rings marvellously in London or New York, in Hong Kong,
where the islands of the Kwangtung shore run away magically
into the evening, where the junks chug in each morning from
the Pearl river, where the acupuncture doctors practise their
mysteries and the Chinese Merchandise Emporium offers you
crystallized plums from Hunan – in Hong Kong the name of
China is like the word of truth. China! It is the reality that

underlies every illusion of Hong Kong, and even the Peak itself, that high place of Western complacency, is really no more than an outcrop of the Kwangtung hills.

Before I left Hong Kong I drove out to Lok Ma Chau, on the frontier. This has become a famous tourist spot. The casual visitor is not allowed at the frontier post itself, beside the Sham Chun river, but a little way behind it there is an observation post upon a hill. There the Hong Kong Chinese have set up souvenir stalls and a café, and all day long a stream of visitors, mostly Japanese, steps out of its cars to wander up the winding path and gaze out to the north. The stalls offer a curious variety of wares, mostly from China proper: dingy postcards of Shanghai, table mats with Chinese horses on them, cheap jade bracelets, plaster figurines of ping-pong players, ideological tracts: but in the Chinese way the salesmen do not pester you as you pass on your way to the viewpoint. They know they can catch you on the way back.

It was a lovely day when I was there, and the view seemed almost complementary to the prospect my friend had offered me, two weeks before, looking over Hong Kong harbour from the top of the funicular. If that view was all punch, this was all pull. There across the river lay a silent country, green, blue and mauve – green for the paddy-fields that stained the wide plain, blue for the sheets of water that lay mirror-like beneath the sky, mauve for the hills of the horizon. China! It struck me not so much as peaceful or serene, as *simple* – innocent, perhaps. It looked like a world stripped of its pretensions and complexities, and as I stood there in the sunshine thinking about it for the first time I felt a stir of that yearning within myself, and found myself looking towards China as though that silent landscape were calling me home.

Home to where? Home to what? As I wandered down the track towards my car, one of the stall-sellers spoke to me quietly, without urgency, across his wares. 'Why don't you buy,' he inquired, as though he genuinely, if mildly, wanted to know the answer, 'the thoughts of Chairman Mao?' – and he held up a small red book, bound in plastic.

'Get thee behind me,' I said.

16

BOOMTOWN!

Houston, 1982

There were not many boom towns in the Western world of the 1980s, but Houston was unquestionably one of them: even by Texan standards, even at a time of general economic distress, it was big, brash and successful. I wrote the essay for Texas Monthly, *but it was reprinted in several other regional magazines of the USA — enviously I suspect, few of them having such prodigies of their own to celebrate.*

I have seen *another* future, and for five full days I watched it work! Houston, Texas, is hardly my own idea of a new heaven or a new earth, deposited as it is amorphous and distended up from the sweltering Gulf, but like Lenin's St Petersburg or Victoria's London, like New York and Chicago in their time, to a large proportion of the human race this improbable metropolis represents the best hope the times can offer.

The world converges upon Houston, Texas. The unemployed pour into town in their hopeful thousands, clutching the Want Ads; the migrants illicit and respectable swell in like a rising tide, talking in unknown tongues; the Icelanders, the Equadorians, the Haitians beaver away in their consulates, the Irish solicit investors to their Industrial Development Authority; the passengers of Andes Airlines, Cayman Island Airways or Sahsa Honduras fly in all agog; the myriad ships tread up the Ship Channel, the scientists beyond number swarm to NASA; hour by hour the freeways get fuller, the downtown towers taller, the River Oaks residents richer, the suburbs gnaw their way deeper into the countryside, and what was just a blob on the map a couple of decades ago becomes more than just a city, but an idea, a vision, the Future Here and Now!

Civic usages elsewhere obsolescent are still in their prime in

Houston – boom, burgeon, destiny, dream – and some new words are appositely applied to the city too: *metastasizing*, for instance, which means to spread cancerously and uncontrollably, from cell to cell, from district to district, yesterday the Heights or Tall Timbers, tomorrow desirable addresses or country clubs unborn, far down the freeway where the swamp resumes.

But whether the phraseology is toxic or tonic, Houston is one of the few places in the Western world today whose vocabulary is habitually in the future tense, and the positive mood: I will, not I used to, yes rather than sorry, we're out of it. 'If you think it's a dump now,' a Houstonian said to me with pride, 'Wait till you see it in ten years' time . . .'

It is a bit of a dump, I suppose, but of a paradoxical kind. It is the fourth city of the United States, and is changing more spectacularly than any, but still no great city of my experience seems closer to its own roots. So my first day in Houston I spent contemplating the origins of the place.

From the air most of it looks even now like some spasmodic settlement in the scrub, so ubiquitous is its sub-tropical foliage still, and even on the ground the city has decidedly exotic strains. The viscous puddles that lie here and there make me think of mangroves, crocodiles, tsetse flies and things like that, and outside the zoo that first morning, indeed, as I smelt the hot oily breeze off the Gulf, and walked beneath the dark and tangly oaks, and heard the squawks, yaps and wheezes of the creatures inside, I felt myself almost physically transported to a very different city far away – Calcutta of all places, as though the dead men might be lying on the sidewalks of Westheimer, and scabrous lepers haunt Hermann Park.

The solidest layer of the Houston palimpsest, it seemed to me, must be the bottom layer, a sediment of pure southernness, y'all-ness, bayou-ness, sluggishly defying all the onslaughts of change. The grateful dogwoods, magnolias and loblollys of the suburban streets, the rough buffalo-grass of the parks, the raucous grackles, the humid embrace of the air even in early summer, the dark meandering creeks to be encountered half-buried among the concrete, all made me feel that I was standing in a clearing among the woods. Coyotes, racoons, armadillos naturally, even red wolves I am assured, are still at large within these city limits; egrets, great blue herons, spoonbills are there for the spotting; the hognose snake quite likes the urban life, and even the Houston toad, described to me in the local manner as The Most Unique Creature in the City, still I was delighted to hear occasionally flops and grunts through Harris County.

The temper of the South is inescapable in Houston. You can see the swagger of it, for example, in the postures of the cattle-people come into town for dinner or convention: hulking rich men in Stetsons and silver belt buckles, paunchy with their generations of beer and prime steaks, lacquered observant women in bangles, talking rather too loud as Texans are apt to, the wives greeting each other with dainty particularities ('Why, hi Cindy, my you're looking pretty!'), the husbands with spacious generics ('Well, boy, what's things like in East Texas?').

You can see the poignant charm of it in the faded white clapboard houses of the Fifth Ward, stilted above the dust of their unpaved streets, and conveniently loomed over by the downtown skyscrapers for the benefit of allegorically minded photographers. There the black folk still idle away the warm evenings on their splintered porches, as in the old story books – there the vibrant hymns still rise from the pews of the Rose of Sharon Tabernacle Church – there the garbage still blows about the garden lots, and you may still be asked, as I was, if, say, ain't you Miss Mary's daughter from the old store? 'Bless your heart, I used to be one of Miss Mary's best, best customers . . .'

Sometimes too you can taste the old spite and coarseness of the South. Macho rednecks ride ostentatiously around with guns hanging in their pickup cabs; Ku Klux Klansmen threaten the livelihoods of Vietnamese refugees; harsh stories of old Southern justice seep in from local jails – chainings, beatings, 148-year sentences, Death Row interviews; just now and then, I fancy, you may detect even in the 1980s a faint spasm of distaste on the faces of the more elderly bellboys in the posh hotels, as they accept the gratuities of their blacker clientele.

But most tellingly of all the Southernness of Houston shows in the very place where it all began – Allen's Landing on Buffalo Bayou, where for no very good reason in 1836 the Allen brothers of New York disembarked, pitched their tents in a glade beneath the Spanish moss, and founded the city of Houston. There is no pretending that this historic spot is greatly cherished by Houstonians, most of whom have undoubtedly never set foot there, but lying as it does bang in the middle of town, hardly a stone's throw from the tallest skyscraper west of the Mississippi, just around the corner from the Albert Thomas Convention Center and National Space Hall of Fame, it does startlingly demonstrate how abruptly Houston's future has arrived.

Lord, how it takes one back! Above our heads passes the Main Street viaduct, its pillars scrawled with illiterate graffiti and leant against in the shadows by miscellaneous layabouts. To the west stands the melancholy off-white façade of the Houston Terminal Warehouse Cold Storage. The road behind us forlornly sprouts with grass, like the old roads behind the levees. The trains clank and shunt, as shunt they must in all such Southern cameos. And half-hidden down there by its gloomy foliage, tentacled trees and impenetrable brambles, there in the womb of the city slowly swirls the old brown bayou. A ponderous kind of dragon-fly frequents this ancient hollow; spin-drift floats about; and when the water momentarily eddies, with a gas bubble perhaps or a Houston toad, really it might almost be the surfacing of one of those Texan alligators which, in prints of the first steamboat's arrival at this shore, the crew are shown shooting right and left as they churn their passage into history.

But, no, the alligators have probably backed away by now, like the steamboat *Laura M.* itself, which found the Buffalo Bayou too narrow for comfort, and was obliged to retreat from Houston ignominiously stern-first towards the sea. Beside that bayou, upon that swamp, in the succeeding 150 years the Houstonians have built what is in many ways the very model of a modern megapolis, and I spent my second day in the city thinking about *that*. A generation ago this was hick-town, today it possesses all the essentials of American municipal sophistication: to wit, a civically commissioned bronze by Henry Moore, a manic Hyatt Hotel with external elevators, a Gay Quarter (Gay Week in June), a branch of Sotheby's the auctioneers, two or three buildings by Philip Johnson, a symphony orchestra with a Rumanian conductor, a $2 million Picasso in a Fine Arts Museum, restaurants where waiters will sneer at you if you don't want garlic on your shrimps and sidewalk cafés where you may eat health-food omelettes cooked in bean oil and stuffed with Afghan artichokes.

Houstonians, it dawned upon me that second day, are under

the impression that their city is in all respects remarkable. This is because they have seen it grow so explosively from Rice Hotel to Hyatt, visiting stock to City Opera, catfish and hominy grits, I dare say, to *coq au vin* or Afghan artichokes. In fact in most ways it is, to the stranger, rather an unsurprising city. It is much what you expect. The crime rates, police brutalities, traffic congestions and Adult Book Shoppes that Houstonians so deplore are sufficiently familiar to us all; the Hobbit Hole sandwich place has its equivalents, God knows, elsewhere on this planet; the Alley Theatre they never stop talking about is not much different from your repertory company, or mine.

Look at the place as I did, through the traveller's eye. There lies the grid of the old downtown, as it lies everywhere else in America, towered over now of course by the conventional clump of skyscrapers, some plain and ugly by Hankmore, Scribbles, Fujiyama and Olsenjohn Architectural Associates, some slant-wise and beautiful by Philip Johnson, all sheathed in those mirrors and tinted windows which make them look, as modern skyscrapers must, utterly unfrequented by sentient beings. There are the usual frenzied ring roads, upon which citizens here, like citizens everywhere else, earnestly advise you not to venture – Houston's rather bumpier than most, I think, and less intelligently planned than some, but all in all much as you will find them in L A, Chattanooga, or for that matter Paris, France. There to the west extend the standard interminable suburbs, the rich here, the poor there, the academics in the middle, interrupted occasionally by incipient lesser downtowns and institutions medical, sportive or touristical. Houston is perhaps more *splurgy* than its peers because it has done without zoning laws, and it is certainly greener because of that irrepressible foliage; but in its domestic and commercial shape, style and pace it is nothing very special. Astonish me! I like to challenge the cities I visit, but I collected only six items in suburban and downtown Houston, bourgeois Houston that is, which really raised my eyebrows, and here one by one they are:

The labyrinthine downtown tunnel system, so cool, elegant and incomprehensible, which by spewing you calmly into the foyers of totally unexpected office buildings, or the lobbies of hitherto unheard-of hotels, seems to bind the whole place into a mysterious unity.

Jamail's the grocer on Kirby, surely one of the world's supreme supermarkets, where they offer six kinds of English orange marmalade, and where when I went to buy half a pound of cheese to nibble during my explorations it took me a quarter of an hour to narrow my choice down to Irish Blarney or imported Turkish.

The concentrated opulence of River Oaks, even by American standards an unusually well-heeled enclave, but almost comically out of scale with itself – mansion upon mansion, mock-Tudor to Spanish Mission, grand enough to command estates in Virginia or deer-forests in Scotland, but so crammed all together in their poky green yards that there seems hardly space for your five-car garage or your Mexican servants' quarters, let alone room to swing an Abyssinian cat.

The Astrodome in the evening, approached along the South Loop Freeway, when its huge humped dome, set all ablaze by the evening sun, really does look as though it has landed there and then incandescent among its empty parking lot.

The macabre and thrilling mock-up, upstairs in the Albert Thomas Convention Center, of Congressman Thomas's office on Capitol Hill in Washington: nose against the glass I peered with an awful enthralment into this little chamber, and the dim images within, the signed photographs on the walls, the paper knife upon the desk, the foundation-stone hammer, the presentation pens and scrolls, the vaguely perceived portrait of the late Congressman himself upon the wall, made me feel as though I was looking into some unopened dynastic grave, whose treasures would, if I were to shatter the glass in a moment of madness, crumble into dust.

And what else? Surely, you are saying, the famous Galleria? Well, yes, but not its architecture especially, nor the predictably obscene profusion of its merchandise, but something I saw happening upon the ice-rink there, as I sat drinking my coffee on the terrace above. Suddenly the strains of 'Yellow Rose of Texas' were gigantically blasted into the glass roof of the arcade; and looking down below me I saw a group of Houston ladies preparing to practise an ice-chorus routine. They struck me, to be frank, as a mature class of chorine, but they swung wonderfully robustly into the gliding steps of their performance – *swing right, one two, swing left, one two, cross over, cross back, into circle one two three* – while all the while the 'Yellow Rose' went thump thump from Neiman-Marcus to Lord and Taylor. It was evidently an early stage of their preparations, and just occasionally somebody fell over: but with what dauntless diligence they kept at it, how resolutely they repeated themselves, how indefatigably their leader shrilled her instructions, how untiringly the record player returned, ever and again, to the opening drumbeats of their anthem!

They were your archetypal *doers*: and the true astonishment of Houston, the allure that draws the migrants and fuels the imagination of the nations, is not what it is, still less what it looks like, but what it does.

To grasp what it chiefly does, on my third day I went and sat upon a grassy bank beside the Houston Ship Channel, with my back to the old battleship *Texas*, the last of all the world's dreadnoughts, now berthed for ever in its dock at San Jacinto Park, and my front to the waterway itself. It is not at all a straightforward waterway, like the Suez Canal, say, since it is really only the same old Buffalo Bayou in disguise, and it winds its way sinuously up from the sea by way of Black Duck Bay and Goat Island, and spills frequently into side-basins and creeks, and is gouged away at the edges into mooring berths. But up and down it night and day the sea-traffic of Houston inexorably proceeds, and I sat in the sunshine there and watched it pass: tankers from Arabia, peculiar Japanese container ships, long strings of blackened barges, queer truncated tugs, ferries, speedboats, sometimes heavy old freighters – ships from sixty nations in 1980, ships from the whole world heading up the old bayou for Houston, Tex.

And the minute they pass the battleship there, with a formal hoot of their sirens sometimes, they enter a stupendous kind of ceremonial avenue, Houston's truest Mall or Champs Elysées: for all up the banks on either side, jagged and interminable stand the oil, chemical and steel plants that have brought Houston into its future – plants with the magical raw names of capitalism, Rohm and Hass, Paktank, Diamond Shamrock, Bethlehem, plants with towers of steel and ominous chimneys, with twisted assemblies of pipes or conduits, with domes, and tanks, and contrapuntal retorts – hissed about here and there by plumes of steam, hung over by vapours, one after the other far away into the haze of the city centre, as far as the eye can see towards the distant blurred shape of the skyscrapers.

The Ship Channel takes its vessels almost into the heart of the city, well within the freeway loop. On the western side of town, the suburban side, you would hardly know this staggering complex existed: but it seemed to me down there beside the water as though some irresistible magnetism was impelling those ships willy-nilly upstream into town. Houston is now the first international port of the Western Hemisphere, the place where America's ocean lifeline, as the editorialists like to say, comes ashore at last: that spectacle before me, those ships, that channel, those eerie tanks and towers, really is one of the most significant of all the sights of modern travel.

The power that created Houston also redeems this otherwise banal metropolis. Power must stand in the middle of any Houston essay, for it is power in its most elemental form, the power of physical energy, that has turned this once provincial seaport into a prime force among the Powers. Houston's publicists like to speak of it as the Giant City, but the truth is far greater than the image, a reversal I think of the Texan norm, and from the indomitable skating ladies of the Galleria to the metallic splendour of the Ship Channel, it was the mighty resolve of the place that moved me most in Houston.

Power pursues power, too, and so the ambition, the opportunity, the greed and the enterprise – the banks and the laboratories, the refiners and the constructors – all coalesce in this city. When the world thinks of Houston, it thinks of bold, brawny, urgent things. If your oil-rig is ablaze in the North Sea or Venezuela, you ring up Red Adair's Oil Well Fires and Blowouts Control Company, out on the Katy Freeway. If your Prime Minister inconveniently collapses in the middle of an election, you send for Dr Cooley of the Texas Medical Center. If you need a survey of the Hormuz Strait, you get in touch with Western Geophysical Company, 10001 Richmond. And if you want to convey a load of scientific equipment into space, where else to book space on the shuttle but Houston, Tex.?

Actually the most obvious energy down at the NASA Memorial Space Center, when I drove on there that day, seemed to be the enthusiasm of the children who, erupting from endless convoys of buses, burbled, screamed and skidded about the public exhibits preparing class projects, evading the eye of Mrs Hawkins Sixth Grade, or perhaps dreaming up the infant poems and aphorisms displayed upon the auditorium walls –

> It won't be the life I really knew,
> It will be the life of the final frontier

or

> There once was a ship called Skylab
> Skylab was its name
> It was launched from Cape Kennedy
> And got itself some fame.

The power of the Space Center itself, though, seemed to me of an altogether more steely and calculated kind. It is a distinctly patient power. Some of the astronauts trained here have waited a whole decade before actually going up on a rocket, and now the imagination of the place seems to be groping far, far into the future, far beyond the space shuttles into infinitely distant dreams of the empyrean, with whole cities floating about up there in the dark, and colonies cocooned among the planets, and artificial brightnesses, as they picturesquely say, of A Sun and a Half. The flight control centre was empty of people when I was there, but its lights were winking all the same, its digits were faithfully counting down, its great map stood illuminated still between the television screens: it was as though some genius organism was lying low there, counting, thinking, working out the equations before the next colossal effusion of its force.

It is only proper that the very first word ever uttered by a man on the moon should be the name of this city: 'HOUSTON', radioed Armstrong as soon as he got there, 'TRANQUILLITY BASE HERE. THE EAGLE HAS LANDED.' As the Mayor of the day was inspired to write, in a composition engraved indelibly on the wall of Tranquillity Park (there are literary advantages to Mayoralty), 'the moon has long been humanity's treasure trove . . . so close it could only beckon . . . so far that it could only dare . . .' As it happens my guide at NASA told me her uncle down at Clear Lake City flatly denies that they ever got to the moon at all, believing it all to be a monumental hoax; but there are many people in Africa, she told me too, who assuming that Houston's association with the heavens has necessarily brought it closer to God himself, write very particularly to this city to order their Bibles.

This is undeniably the Big Time. No other city on earth can match this junction of dynamics: no other town is closer to the Almighty! Houstonians at large, though, scarcely seem to notice it. They are hardly modest people, but they are not megapolitan braggers: they do not realize, perhaps, how towering is the reputation of their city – I heard far more about that damned Alley Theatre than ever I did about the ship canal, the petrochemical industry or manned space flight, and when, pointing out a full moon one night, I ventured to say, 'Look, there's Houston's moon up there,' my companion failed to notice the allusion, and turned the conversation to a forthcoming performance by the unavoidable Baryshnikov.

On my fourth day in Houston I considered these anomalies. Though newcomers in their hundreds of thousands are invading Houston nowadays, though it is so full of Mexicans already that I sometimes wondered if it could really be called an English-speaking city, though it is in such a state of cosmopolitan flux that my Sierra Leone taxi-driver, when I arrived at the airport, invited me to map-read him into town, still your average white middle-class Houstonian seems to honour his city in a distinctly parochial frame of mind. There are strong intimations of the homely in this momentous city. Judge Don E. Walton smokes his pipe as he presides over the 178th District Court down at the County Courthouse, and at one moment I even thought he might put his feet on the table: when I inadvertently found myself included in jury selection, I was touched how elementary, how childlike almost, was the exposition of the Common Law thought necessary for the miscellaneous housewives, wispy pensioners, sagging businessmen and bewildered Hispanics about to decide the fate of the poor devil under trial. Wow! is the habitual response of Houstonians, I discovered by hanging around his cage, to the Binturog who is a prime exhibit of their zoo: and on the whole Wow!, no less, no more, seems to enunciate their response to their city's new-found greatness.

Three million strong already, the energy capital of the Western world, Moon-City, The Giant, still Houston looks back affectionately to its homegrown heroes and backyard epics. This is an agreeable trait, but it makes for myths and iconographies baffling to the uninstructed visitor. The eponymous Sam Houston, a hero otherwise unsung in the larger world, rides still, cloak a-flying, through Houston's civic consciousness. The glories of San Jacinto, the tragic memories of Goliad, recur all too obscurely in municipal pamphlets. What was this Rice, for whom an entire university is named? Who were these Hobbys, immortalized in an airport? What knight of the bayous, what swashbuckler of the swamp, gave his name to Blodgett Street?

Houston is a tight town, I think. It has its raffish parts of course, its fair share of the contemporary violence, its streak of the insensitivity which is part of the Southern heritage. But its general posture strikes me as respectable and conventional. Even Montrose, the quarter of town most hospitable to quirks and exceptions, is remarkably genteel of mien; even at Butera's, a hang-out frequented by writers, artists and the like, hard though I tried I could find no outrageous exhibitionists. The 1960s were so long ago by Houston's calendar that they seem never to have happened in this city at all, and I find it hard indeed to imagine draft cards burnt upon the trim Rice campus, or hear the rhythms of Baez or Dylan dirge-like over Memorial Park. Jews tell me they sometimes sense loveless vibes in Houston, and for myself, as an anti-nuclear neutralist, animal liberationist, Welsh nationalist and aspirant anarchist, I am seldom altogether at ease with the stern Free World exhortations of the Houston *Post* or *Chronicle*.

It feels a city, too, of strong and close alliances, bonds of neighbourhood, profession or background, whose direct loyalties are to Bellaire, say, the Symphony League, the principle of vascular stimulation in cardiac therapy, or most of all perhaps to your own resilient family. There are five columns of Rices in the Houston telephone book, three of Houstons, and fourteen lines of Blodgetts: and when I went to a gallery party one evening in town, I found that not only did all the other guests seem to be related to the well-known local artist we were honouring, but the shop itself belonged to his mother-in-law – 'you must be from out of town,' said one eminent old body indulgently when I expressed surprise at these happy arrangements.

I missed some element of salt or spice to flavour this somewhat steak-like city. I pined for fantasy in Houston, Texas! I was sitting that same evening in a house in – well, in Sherwood Acres let us say, for I do not wish to be discourteous, engaged in a characteristically Sherwood Acres conversation, not altogether unrelated to the Alley Theatre and the Rumanian conductor, when I looked through the window and saw a dream-like figure pass sauntering by. He had a sack over his arm, and a stick over his shoulder, and he wore a high-crowned hat and a cloak I think, and his face was black and bearded, and he strolled past easy, insolent and amused. On my fourth day in Houston, my heart leapt to see him. 'Who was that?' I cried, rushing to the window, 'that man with the stick, and the high-crowned hat, and the sack on his arm?' But there was no one there, and my hostess returned me a little reprovingly to our discussion. 'I saw nobody,' she sweetly and carefully said. 'But tell me, have you had time to see our new Picasso in the Fine Arts Museum? And will you have an opportunity to meet with Mrs Oveta Culp Hobby?'

And so on my fifth day in Houston I tried to imagine the future of this future. Actually I went to have my palm read by Mrs Williams, on Holcombe Boulevard – you know, just around the corner from the Tot Haven Progressive Child Day Center. She charged me five bucks, shoo'd away the children and prophesied that with God's help I would presently overcome my jealous enemies and move to Houston myself. 'You will not like it at first,' said Mrs Williams, eyeing me rather shrewdly I thought, 'but with God's help you will get used to it.'

Well, maybe. The centripetal quality of Houston is undeniable, and nobody can be altogether immune to the blazing promise of the place. Who in an impoverished world can look unmoved upon forty Sunday pages of Help Wanted, for architects as for rig drillers, blasting supervisors and dental ceramists, restaurant managers for Burger King or polygraph examiners for Image Research Inc.? And who in a jaded world, sapped by nostalgia, disheartened by experience, can be left unexcited by a city that looks so confidently and ruthlessly ahead? In seventy-five years, they say, Houston may well achieve the grandest and brashest of all its ambitions, to be the ultimate city of them all, the greatest conglomeration of energies and artefacts ever known to history. Now who can sneer at *that*?

But then the future never lasts. 'Sir,' said the train conductor to Charles Dickens the novelist, as they ran into Chicago a century ago. 'Sir, you are entering the Boss City of the Universe.' Today it is Houston that greets its settlers and visitors with such grand hyperbole, but its particular future is doubtless just as ephemeral as any other. Look at Leningrad! Look at London! Look at knocked-about New York! In fact I felt to this city something especially transient and impermanent: I could not see it getting old – it doesn't feel built to last – and on my last day in town a dark and fateful fancy overcame me, and I seemed to see the City of Destiny abandoning itself after all, the whole grand circus of it moving out again, and in an exodus as terrific as its influx, pouring away once more down the waterways and freeways.

I saw in my mind's eye the Mexicans streaming for the border, their cars hung all about with beds, baskets and bundles – I saw the oil men hastening out from Hobby in their Gulfstreams and helicopters – the smoke of burning documents from the roofs of consulates – the Amtrak for the North bursting with fugitives, wistfully looking through its sealed windows for a last glimpse of dear old Sherwood Acres – the last ship swinging in the turning basin, to sail away past the deserted *Texas* to the open sea – the final flight of Cayman Island Airways announcing its departure to the East – the terminal patients at the Texas Medical Center passed tenderly, entangled with tubes and drippers, into their waiting ambulances – the last pipe closed, the last tank emptied, the last furnace dampened at Exxon or Armco Steel – the last shuttle controllers switching off, with a sigh, those blinking lights and digitals down at the Space Center.

And then, gleaming but sterile in the sunshine, crinkle-reflected still in each other's mirror-glass, I saw the empty downtown skyscrapers left like tombs, all elevators stilled, as memorials to the future past: while the cottonwood, the hickory and the Spanish moss, creeping up again from the bayou, entangled parks and gardens once again, choked the downtown tunnels, and wormed a way into all the fancy plazas.

17

ON THE FRINGE

Iceland, 1970

I have always felt at home in Iceland, perhaps because in some ways it is rather like my own country, Wales, and I am sorry that the economic well-being recorded in this essay was not to last: never mind, I flatter myself that its analysis of the national character will not so soon be out of date.

They get up unexpectedly late in Iceland, and there were few people about when I left my hotel and walked through the streets of Heimaey, in the Westmann Islands. One or two trucks clattered down to the harbour, a few early workers hurried preoccupied towards the fish meal factory, but the little grey houses were mostly silent and lifeless, their lace curtains decorously drawn.

Past the graveyard I walked, where stunted conifers were encased in protective stockades against the wind, and the children's graves blazed with artificial roses: and across the meadows above the town, stopping to greet the sheep entombed in their winter bunker of turf, stone and corrugated iron – the dim interior of the shack thick with their breath, their wide wondering eyes staring back at me through the crack in the door. The snow was quite deep up there on the hillside, and the world lay white and crisp around me, the wide pale vault of the Arctic sky above, away to the north the glacial immensities of the mainland. Birds sang twitchily, a hooter sounded from the factory below, and presently, reaching a ridge that opened to my view to the south, I saw in the distance the sea on fire.

Not smouldering, nor even sparking, but furiously ablaze – smoke streaming from the sea, flashes of red flame, a plume of black bent by the wind until it lay almost parallel with the water.

The sea in those parts is littered with squarish lumps of island, dressed in the winter with a crust of snow, and disposed at artistic intervals, as though a Zen seascape master has arranged them there: among them, like a phoenix in that water-garden, the island volcano of Sturtsey raged day and night. Fire and ice and a cold blue ocean. A steam-hammer was thumping now, somewhere in the town, a morning stir was filling the streets, and turning my back upon that prodigy I presently sat down to an Icelandic breakfast – rye bread, cheese and marmalade, served by a ravishingly lovely girl on a preternaturally clean table-cloth to the sound of radio music.

The weirdness of Sturtsey is nothing new. Fire and ice and fierce seas have always been the staples of Icelandic legend, and old representations of the island invariably show it dominated by the violent glow of Hekla, the great volcano of the southern mainland. There is something allegorical about the very fact of Iceland, something that puts most visitors in mind of still remoter grandeurs – Dantean visions of heaven or hell, or classical conceptions of Elysium, improbably transplanted to these icy realms with asphodels among the glaciers. This is an island of absolutes, where nothing is blurred, and sometimes it feels less like a country than a prophecy, a mystery play, or a topsy-turvy sort of Utopia.

Iceland is a large island almost in the middle of the North Atlantic, poised equivocally between Europe and America, and so near Greenland that in the summer they run day excursions there. It is rather larger than Portugal, and looks rather like a chunk of the moon sliced off and dropped in the ocean – so like it that early American astronauts were taken there to give them a foretaste of moonfall. The island is not so cold as it looks or sounds. The Arctic Circle passes just to the north of the Icelandic mainland, and the Gulf Stream warms its shores. It is, though, a violent country. A thousand volcanoes have pitted its landscapes with craters, jagged lava lumps, wildernesses of grey basalt. The ferocious winds of the north have kept it almost treeless, only a few scraggy thickets or cosseted garden rowans pathetically surviving the blast. About an eighth of the island is one vast snowfield, the Vatnajökull, which is itself about the size of Corsica, and sweeps away in grand sterile silence from the peak of Hekla.

In summer this colossal landscape is clothed in a fragile green, speckled with wild flowers and charmed by the song of one of Europe's richest bird populations – salmon leaping in its glacial streams, the glorious little ponies of Iceland gliding Pegasian through a crystal sunlight. In the winter the snow falls like a clamp upon the island, closing the rough roads of the interior and filling, like saucepans, the shallow craters of extinct volcanoes. Summer or winter the weather is startlingly changeable. One moment the sky is an incomparable northern blue, and the girls are tanning themselves on the park benches: the next a mad wind is driving sleet and mist wildly through the streets, and one reads in the morning that the farmers have been feeding their animals on all fours themselves, unable to stand upright for the blizzard. Through it all, heat-wave or snowstorm, the geysers and hot springs of Iceland bubble and fume away – some in the middle of Reykjavik itself, the capital, so that citizens bathe in open-air pools all the year round, and heat their homes with subterranean steam, some away in the desolations of the interior, their clouds of vapour billowing from the bare mountainside, or hissing malignantly out of thick sulphurous pools.

Most of Iceland is uninhabited desert, and the people nearly all live along the coast, around the narrow fjords and river estuaries. In most countries the sea is only an accessory. In Iceland it is a living presence, more vital than the landscape. The Icelanders depend upon it utterly, for their income comes almost entirely from fishing. The Atlantic is inescapable, and the smell of fish hangs everywhere – from the trawlers in every harbour, from the racks of drying cod, head-down in their thousands on the outskirts of every town, from the pickled whale and dried shark on the restaurant menus, from the terrible fish meal factories, malodorous steam issuing from their every crack and manhole, where ghastly things go on with bangs and clanks of machinery.

Even Reykjavik, where more than a third of the Icelanders live, is recognizably a fish-port still. It has its parliament, its Lutheran cathedral of corrugated iron, its university and its national museum, its villas spreading into the stark countryside around: but look down the main street of the city from the main square, only a stone's throw from the Cabinet offices or the National Library, and there blocking the vista stand the ships, an essential part of the city scene. The trawlers chug in and out

of town as familiar as suburban buses, the trucks bounce out of
the docks loaded deep with herring, and the stink of the fish
factory at the end of the quay hovers perpetually over that end
of town – 'Mm,' say the Icelanders appreciatively, 'the *money-
smell* . . .'

They are a people hard-headed but fey, and love to boast of
their Celtic blood. The Icelanders are an odd mixture of the
urbane and the primitive, or for that matter ugliness and allure.
Beauty and the Beast is one of the Icelandic allegories. Everybody
who goes to the island is struck by the splendour of the girls.
Pick a choice example now – the shopgirl, say, who is packing
up your stuffed puffin in the souvenir shop, or pricing your
lava-stone powder-box. What a gorgeous strapping girl she is,
what a terrific golden girl, with her wide-apart eyes, her hair
bleached in Arctic sunshine, her exquisite complexion mixed
out of snow and pink blossom! Take your eye off her for a
moment, though, and observe the young man now shambling
down the street outside – towards his trawler, perhaps, or off to
his fearful shift at the fish factory. He is the original Viking, I
suppose. He looks like a very determined specimen of Neander-
thal man: his forehead and his chin symmetrically recede, his
cheeks are wolfishly sunken, his eyes blaze, and there is to his
loping walk a suggestion of immense loose-limbed power, as
though a tap on his shoulder would unleash his two-headed
battle-axe, and send him instantly off to Greenland with horns
on his head.
    From these disparate strains the Icelander has emerged. He is
part Norseman, part Celt, and is very conscious of everything
appertaining to race – pedigrees, national characteristics, cross-
strains, inherited aptitudes. The very first Icelanders were
hermits, who came to these inconceivably inhospitable shores
from Ireland, and settled in caves to cogitate. They were
succeeded, in the ninth and tenth centuries, by Viking adventurers, Norwegian by stock but often accompanied by wives and
slaves from Ireland and the Scottish isles. The Danes became
rulers of Iceland in the fourteenth century, and since then almost
no alien blood has joined the Icelandic stream (except when the
allied soldiery was here in the Second World War). Ethnically
the Icelanders are all on their own, and not much like anybody
else. Many people suppose themselves extraordinary – the

English, the Americans, the French, the Swedes, they all like to
think that the rest of the world considers them eccentric. Of the
peoples I know the only ones who really seem to me a little mad,
in the engaging sense of easy-going dottiness, are the Icelanders.
They are full of surprise – very quiet at first acquaintance, so
that you may wonder if you have displeased them in some way,
by talking too loud or wearing the wrong colour, but unpredict-
ably bursting into uninhibited *bonhomie*, with gargantuan toasts
and awful hangovers.

Perhaps the long northern winters are the cause, and that cage
of the winds above one's head. It is as though the Icelanders feel
a physical need, every now and then, to break into carnival or
even bacchanal. They are great drinkers, and even greater lovers.
Love is approved of in Iceland. In the old days, when the
fisherman's life was short and dangerous, there were always
more men than women, and free love was a social necessity.
Today it is a respected tradition. Illegitimacy is no disgrace, and
most young people live together before marriage – 'Rooms
wanted', runs a familiar small ad in the Icelandic newspapers,
'by engaged couple with baby'.

In so small a country, so intricately intermarried, paternity is
hard to deny, and most Engaged Couples with Baby seem to
live happily ever after: all Iceland knew the facts, some years
ago, when the daughter of one eminent politician was made
pregnant by the son of another (though in this particular case,
I was told, the girl's mother was so distressed that she 'went to
bed' – the standard Icelandic solution to problems). Iceland is a
very sexy country – a young country, with the highest birth-rate
in Europe, and a high-spirited one, where the dances are fast
and frequent, and far into the night in Austurvöllur Square, at
once the Piccadilly and the Red Square of Reykjavik, the young
people linger when the last dance is over – tooting their car
horns in the small hours, dancing on the sidewalk outside
Parliament, singing what one assumes to be bawdy songs and
laughing so boisterously that the foreign visitor to the Borg
Hotel, peering from his darkened window on that lusty dalliance
below, either pulls his pillow over his head with a pang of lost
youth, or hastily gets dressed again.

This streak of excitement, this Celtic ore to the Nordic mass,
runs through the life of Iceland. There sit the Parliamentarians
at their morning coffee (they drink gallons of coffee in Iceland),

and they look senatorial enough. They are big-built, heavy-jawed men in sombre suits, their eyes cold and blue as ice, hunched over their cups and talking, one imagines, about caucuses and constituencies: but if you venture to intrude upon them, announcing yourself a foreigner, you will find a dizzy variety to their conversation. This well-known politician plays the flute, this one is an enthusiastic follower of English football, this one recently translated one of Goldoni's comedies into Icelandic – and presently others will join you, a businessman with a taste for oratorio, a journalist turned art dealer, or one of those folk-heroes of modern Iceland, a trawler-skipper, who is likely to look much the most suave of them all, and cherish a particular interest in kinetic abstractionism.

Most sensible foreigners stay at the Borg, if they can spare the money. It is no longer the grandest or dearest hotel in Reykjavik, but it is an institution. It is like a Russian hotel of the old school, very plush, with caryatids to support the wall-lights in the restaurant, and portraits of anonymous Icelandic worthies in the bedrooms. When I stayed there last I often noticed in the foyer an elderly Icelander of appearance at once benign and distracted. He was tall, a little stooped and exceedingly craggy, with a well-worn cravat around his neck, hair flying like snow about his head, and clothes of an Edwardian gypsy elegance. This was Johannes Kjerval, the most famous artist in Iceland, if not in Scandinavia – the greatest painter of the North, Icelanders say. 'He is not like other men,' somebody warned me. 'He is very strange in Icelandic, and will be stranger still in English.' I introduced myself none the less, and so it proved to be. A strange, marvellous man! He had moved into the hotel from his own house, he told me, because 'I have lost my sleeping there, and can't catch it'. Sometimes his conversation struck mysteriously off into Italian, a muffled sort of French, and English doggerel of his own composition; sometimes he fell into a smiling silence, or produced a vast wad of papers from an inside pocket to show me a reproduction of a painting. Whatever he did there was an immense power to his presence – an unpredictable force, which seemed to me, like his art and his old-fashioned cravat, disconcertingly but movingly Icelandic.

Patriotism burns fiercely in the island. This is distinctly their own, their native land, and they are born last-ditchers and never-say-diers. It is only a generation since they gained their full independence from the Danes – the Germans had occupied Denmark, the British had occupied Iceland, and the Republic was proclaimed after a national referendum. Until the 1850s Danish control had been so absolute, in this then poverty-stricken island, that there was actually a Crown monopoly of trade, and virtually every shopkeeper in Iceland was a Dane from Denmark. The Icelanders themselves were so little regarded, and their attachment to their homeland seemed to the Danes so unlikely, that at one time there was talk of shipping them all off to Denmark, and leaving the island to the elements once more, or the hermits.

Now there is little hard feeling against the Danes, and a faintly Danish patina is still apparent. A stone crown of Denmark still ornaments the Parliament building, and the sense of humour which distinguishes the Danes from their fellow-Scandinavians still echoes in this spirited little state. The national pride of the Icelanders is far older than mere politics. It revolves around the Icelandic language. Through many centuries it was the ancient literature of Iceland, cherished by word of mouth, which kept the Icelandic nationality alive, and enabled the distinctive Icelandic culture to survive. Above all the sagas, the great prose narratives of medieval Iceland, embody the spirit of this people: those high-flown tales, half fact, half fiction, which commemorate the families and heroes of Viking Iceland, and form a priceless repository of history, mythology and romance. The language of the sagas has survived intact, and is still the everyday speech of the people. If an Icelander can read today's paper, he can read the Njalasaga, a tragedy of Icelandic life at least six centuries old. There are no dialects in Icelandic, and no accents of class: to the foreigner it looks like some kind of Esperanto, the sort of language in which one can often bluff or worry one's way to comprehension – if *'kalfahryggjarvodvi, skeinka og egg'*, may defeat one, at least *'vinstukan er opin daglega'* fairly obviously announces that one can get a drink any day of the week.

A mystic exaltation, not without comedy, surrounds this hallowed tongue. Committees of dedicated sages devise new words, when the vocabulary proves inadequate to the times: a military tank is a *skidreki* – 'creeping dragon'. Bards abound, people launch themselves without warning into poetic decla-

mation, the tales of Nils the Law Man or Grettir the noble robber
are as familiar to Icelandic children today as they were to the
Icelanders of the Middle Ages, crouched enthralled over their
peat-fires as the story-tellers postured on. The Icelandic language
and its literature links every era of island history with the next,
and enables almost every islander to trace his origins gloriously
back to the poets, kings and navigators of antiquity.

This makes for an extraordinary sense of continuity. Iceland
is one of the very few European countries where elderly women
still wear national costume as a matter of course – a dress of
shiny black and gold embroidery, a bodice laced over a coloured
blouse, worn with braided hair and a tasselled velvet cap to give a
dauntingly Wagnerian effect. The ages are truncated in Iceland.
People speak to you of Grimur Goatbeard or Leif the Lucky as
though they are neighbours up the road, or first cousins once
removed. I first went to Thingvellir, the site of the ancient
Icelandic Parliament, on a lovely summer day in the company of
an elderly Icelandic businessman. He looked an ordinarily
respectable citizen, and seemed indeed rather too prosaic a
companion for the occasion, when we drove through the
scowling declivity in the rocks that gives access to the place: but
once we stood on the edge of Thingvellir, and looked across that
wide lava plain, flecked with green and shining with reflected
sunlight from its lake, my companion seemed to be lyrically
transformed, and in lofty terms and a rather booming voice
peopled the scene before me with the heroes and poets of old,
Eilif the Eagle and Audun the Bald, the wandering bards, the
explorers home from the west, the young athletes in the
sunshine. I viewed him with a new respect, but on the way
home all he talked about was the national balance of payments.
Every Icelander seems to know every other Icelander, even if
a century separates them. It is like a family of intense internal
loyalty, welded together by generations of hard times. There are
virtually no surnames proper in Iceland, only patronymics – you
merely add your own to your father's christian name, and
become Stefan Jónsson, for example, or Sigrid Jonsdóttir. This
means that an immense number of people have the same name,
like Joneses in Wales; and like the Welsh, the Icelanders identify
themselves by their trade – 'I'm Kjarval the Painter,' they will
say, and the telephone directory too adds a calling to the

subscriber's name, to differentiate Olaf Stefansson the Dentist from Olaf Stefansson the Ships' Chandler. Class differences scarcely exist, in an island where everybody seems to claim descent from Ornold Fish-Driver or Sigurd Snake-Eye, and there is little sense of gulf between young and old. All are, so to speak, members. The only Icelandic titles are bestowed upon bishops and priests – a clergyman is Sir Priest, like Shakespeare's clerics – and children are admitted to responsibility at astonishingly early ages. Nothing is more surprising in Iceland than to hand over one's fare in a country bus and find it accepted by a character apparently not much more than four years old, who deposits it solemnly in an enormous satchel, peels off a ticket and grumbles with absolute adult authenticity if you haven't got the right change. Privacy is not much in demand, in so egalitarian a society. Even private funerals are broadcast on the State radio, for a fee, enabling the entire nation to share the family grief.

Iceland has no army, no air force and only a vestigial navy, but there are few countries of more militant outlook. The Icelanders have never fought a war in their history, at least since Viking times, but they seem ready to take on allcomers any day, in defence of the cod and the sagas. Their island has a fortress air, and there is a touch of regimental discipline to their society. It is forbidden to adopt surnames other than patronymics. It is forbidden to keep dogs, except on farms. The absolute equality of life gives the place a paradoxical uniformity – there are no stately homes and no hovels, no millionaires and nobody on the dole. This little nation has a manner of faintly fanatic conviction, like a proselyte to some new and urgent faith. One evening in Akureyri, on the northern coast, I heard the sound of solemn singing emerging from a restaurant, and peering through the door I saw that a large party was in progress. Akureyri has a reputation for particular reserve, and I felt as I looked in as though I were physically separate from those rituals, on the other side of the goldfish glass. There the Icelanders sat in ordered ranks, their arms linked around the long tables, and as they sang what seemed to be some kind of sacramental anthem, or Viking marching song perhaps, they swayed heavily from side to side in a rhythmic motion. It gave me a queer impression of secret solidarity. Everybody knew the words of the song, and the whole assembly seemed to be in arcane collusion: I noticed that if ever I caught an eye, as the celebrants sang and swayed there at the table, after a moment's puzzled focusing it abruptly switched away from me, as if to dismiss an illusion.

I like a robust national spirit, though, especially in little nations that can do no harm with it. I enjoy the Icelanders' jealous insularity, and am not in the least offended when they seem to think I must be some mistake. Sometimes indeed the closeted intimacy of Iceland possesses great beauty. The President of the Republic lives in a farmhouse built by the Danes on a spit of land outside the capital, and a visit to this official residence, especially in winter, hauntingly illustrates the aloof self-sufficiency of Iceland. No head of state could live more simply. The house is a pleasant gentleman-farmer's sort of establishment, with a conservatory against one wall, a pair of antlers above the garage door, and a clutter of impeccable farm buildings behind. There is a little white steepled church in which the President will one day be buried, and the swallow-tailed flag of Government, red and white on dark blue, flies from a flagpole on a terrace. Neat little paths have been cleared in the snow around the property, to keep the Presidential spats dry.

All around this modest homestead the white flat shore, melting into the sea, is speckled with farms not quite so big as the First Citizen's house, but not much different in kind – neighbourly looking houses, whose families, one feels, might easily pop over to His Excellency's for a schnapps or a game of bridge in the evenings. To the south, superb glacial mountains heave along the horizon; pinks and icy blues and dazzling morning whites. To the north, beneath the rampart of Mount Esja, Reykjavik stands upon its bay like an Arctic Alexandria. Before long, very likely, the fickle Icelandic weather will change, and the view will be obliterated by fierce driving mist or stinging hail: but a glimpse is enough, of that silent prospect from the Presidential farm, to show what Iceland's independence means.

Iceland stands on the fringe of European civilization, but not beyond it. In some ways it is less insular than Britain, and is rather like a Baltic State without the Russian or German influence. It is an outrider of Europe. I went to church one Sunday in the Lutheran Cathedral at Reykjavik, and sat in the gallery beside the choir. The music was exceptionally beautiful. The pastor in his white ruff sang the prayers with a tragic

richness of tone, like a fair-skinned rabbi, and the organist
suggested to me a figure from some Baroque music-school, or
the Kapellmeister of a princely court in old Germany. He was
young, grave, long-faced, with a high forehead and wavy
gingerish hair falling over his collar at the back. I could not take
my eyes off him, as he strode with splendid assurance into the
Bach fugue that ended the service, so paradoxically did he
remind me of greater cities and other traditions far away: and
sure enough, when I mentioned him to a friend later I learnt
that he stood in direct professional descent, by way of successive
masters and pupils, to an organist of Bach's own church in
Leipzig.

The Icelanders are not cultural chauvinists. Haldar Laxness,
the most celebrated modern Icelandic writer, told a story of an
Icelandic singer whose supposed fame in the world at large,
which made him a national hero at home, was in fact altogether
spurious – a satire on provincial values set in the Iceland of fifty
years ago. In those days Reykjavik was a tiny town that knew
no better. Today, Iceland, like one of those fervent literary and
debating societies one comes across in lumber camps or polar
settlements, is earnestly in touch with every-intellectual movement, and pressing always on the heels of the avant-garde. The
Icelanders buy, and publish, more books per head than anyone
else in Europe, and no bestseller, in any Western language, long
escapes translation into Icelandic.

They are very musical, too – part of their Celtic heritage, no
doubt. There is a national symphony orchestra, with musicians
imported from Britain or the Continent to augment the local
talent, and choral societies, string orchestras or at least gramophone clubs spring into existence in the most improbable fishing
hamlets. Professional musicians are much respected. At the
airport one day I noticed among my fellow-passengers a well
known Icelandic opera singer whom I had heard in a concert the
day before, and who was now off to sing in Germany. He had
looked imposing enough on the platform, but in the flesh and
the camel-hair coat, with his admirers clustered around him,
the airline officials solicitous and the general public awe-struck,
he seemed a very Napoleon: when I thanked him for the beauty
of his performance he bowed with superb condescension, as
though to compliment me upon my finesse in first removing my
gloves.

On the other hand most Icelanders appear to have no sense of visual fitness, and Iceland is perhaps the most unpicturesque country in Europe. Its people have never had the gift of blending their buildings organically to the environment. Even the old gabled farmhouses seem to sit awkwardly upon the surface of the land, in no way integrated to its folds and colours, and the small towns and villages are almost uniformly plain. No tottering merchants' mansions, timbered and aromatic, stand upon the quayside at Reykjavik, as they do across the water in Bergen: no quaint pubs or thatched seafarers' cottages give character to the fishing towns of the east. Concrete is the Icelander's building material now, and his favourite style might be described as Bourgeois Functional – square, that is, with picture windows. The hot springs and geysers of Iceland are so abundant that at one village, Hveragerdi, they grow grapes, bananas and passion flowers under glass: yet very few Reykjavik householders bother to have greenhouses of their own, to soften the angular greyness of their city – 'we would do it for business,' they say, 'but we have no time for hobbies.'

For the Icelanders like money. A century ago life here was as hard as it could be anywhere, and the comforts of Copenhagen or London must have seemed utterly unattainable. Now the Icelandic standard of living is among the highest in Europe. The fabulous earnings of the herring fishermen, with their new electronic aids, have forced up the standards of everybody else. To the visitor, Iceland seems cripplingly expensive, but hardly any Icelanders are poor. They are a generous people, and self-indulgent too: a classic sight of Icelandic life is that of a party of fishermen at the Naust restaurant, the most famous on the island – pale, plump young men they generally are, after their weeks at sea, but buoyantly high-spirited, swilling away the schnapps with gusto, eating gargantuan meals of steaks or lobster-tails, and looking as though they have simultaneously survived a war of decimation and come into a fortune.

Iceland is *nouveau riche* in an agreeable sense. It has suddenly come into its own. It has leapt from miserable poverty into wealth, from provincial ignorance into cosmopolitan awareness. This gives it an air of tingling opportunity, and has its effect on almost everything. Fifty years ago there were no painters in Iceland, and precious few paintings: now scarcely a living-room in the Republic is without its water-colour Hekla, its fluffy kittens in baskets or its multi-coloured visions of piety. Fifty years ago most Icelanders lived, like the Westmann Island sheep, in cabins of basalt and turf: now they have nearly all moved into houses so excessively decorous, so frilled about with lace and potted plants, so ineradicably tidy, that one wonders where the children ever go, to spill their paints or distribute their space-helmets. There has never been a public railway in Iceland, but from horses and sledges the Icelanders have leapt so exuberantly into cars and aeroplanes that hardly anybody walks anywhere, and the visiting Briton is chaffed for his dogged pedestrianism, when he decides to take a turn around the square.

It has all gone delightfully to the Icelanders' heads. They blow their car horns more guilelessly than anyone, they listen to music more intently, they load their walls with more pictures, they read more books, have more babies, eat more food. They seem to laugh more than most people – and sleep more. Their lovely little ponies, a generation ago the only means of country locomotion, are now creatures of pleasure, trotting about on Sunday mornings with gum-booted young Icelanders on their backs. Their snow-slopes, once unvisited from one year to the next, are now littered with little trolls on skis. One can almost feel the new ideas arriving, the latest skirt lengths and the most experimental dramas, as the aircraft from London and New York sweep in low over Reykjavik to land. 'If we must be vulgarized,' say the more liberal of the old hands, 'let us at least be *internationally* vulgar!'

Fortunately the touch of innocence remains. This is too small a community for cynicism, and the extraordinary nature of the terrain means that Iceland can never be quite like other nations, however congested the traffic crossing of Reykjavik, or thronged with group tours the distant glaciers. A proper corrective to the glittering new affluence is a visit to the Althing, which claims the oldest pedigree of any Parliament, and sits in its nice little grey assembly house next door to the Cathedral. No pomp and little circumstance attends the deliberations of the Althing. If it is winter the members' goloshes are parked neatly outside the chamber door, and in the public gallery loungers cheerfully read the morning newspapers or climb over the wooden benches to chat with friends nearer the front. Icelandic politics can be vicious enough, but the Parliamentarians rarely burst into invective, perhaps because they are nearly all each other's cousins, and often in armchairs at the side of the chamber men may be comfortably smoking their pipes, for all the world as though they have dropped by for a family discussion. Occasionally a page hastens in, with a quotation for the Foreign Minister, perhaps, or a statistic for the Minister of Finance; but he is likely to be wearing a check shirt, a green jersey and corduroy trousers, and as often as not he interrupts the flow of debate by banging the door behind him. Nobody minds. Drat the boy, one seems to hear them murmuring. His father was just the same.

18

CITY OF *YOK*

Istanbul, 1978

❧

In the late 1970s traditional Islam was enduring a period of violent discontent, powerfully affecting all the countries of the Middle East. Turkey, still largely Muslim, was no exception, and this portrait of Istanbul is coloured by the sensations of unrest and uncertainty which dogged my explorations of old Byzantium.

The favourite epithet of Istanbul seems to be *yok*. I don't speak Turkish, but *yok* appears to be a sort of general-purpose discouragement, to imply that (for instance) it can't be done, she isn't home, the shop's shut, the train's left, take it or leave it, you can't come this way or there's no good making a fuss about it, that's the way it is. *Yok* (at least in my interpretation) is like *nyet* in Moscow, 'Sorry luv' in London or 'Have a good day' in New York. It expresses at once the good and the bad of Istanbul civic philosophy: the bad, a certain prohibitive attitude to life, a lack of fizz or obvious hopefulness, a forbidding fatalism and an underlying sense of menace; the good, an immense latent strength, an accumulated toughness and stubbornness, which has enabled Istanbul to keep its personality intact, if not its fabric, through 1,600 years of viciously variable fortune.

Istanbul is a traumatic kind of city. Standing as it does on the frontier between Europe and Asia, it is like a man with a squint, looking east and west at the same time; it is also a northern and a southern city, for immediately above it is the Black Sea, a cold Soviet lake, while almost in sight to the south are the warm waters of the Mediterranean, waters of Homeric myth and yearning.

Contemplating all this one evening, wondering about the meaning of *yok* and looking at the famous view from a high

vantage on Galata hill, I found myself peculiarly disturbed by
my thoughts. Morbid fancies assailed me, and wherever I looked
I seemed to see threatening images. Up the Bosporus towards
Russia, a mass of water traffic steamed or loitered between the
green, villa-lined shores of the strait, but the ships did not have
a cheerful air – they seemed balefully assembled, I thought, like
a ragtag invasion fleet. To the south, the Sea of Marmara, which
ought to have looked wine-dark and heroic, seemed instead
bland, pallid, almost accusatory. Across the inlet of the Golden
Horn the ridge of Stamboul, the original core of the city, was
crowned in sunset with a splendid nimbus of domes, towers
and minarets, but its flanks of hills below seemed to be festering
in the shadows, like a maggot heap beneath a throne.

I shook myself free of the obsession, and hurried down the
hill for a late tea; but *yok, yok, yok*, the birds seemed to be
squawking, as they whirled beady-eyed above my head.

Istanbul leaves many of its visitors similarly unsettled, for it
is not an easy place. It is one of the most obsessively fascinating
of all cities, but indefinably deadening too; a gorgeous city, but
unlovely; courteous, but chill. If you came to it by sea from the
south, the classic way to come, you may sense these paradoxes
almost from the start. The view from the Marmara is an
unforgettable first prospect of a city, but its beauty is somehow
unwelcoming. The tremendous skyline stands there, high above
the sea, like a covey of watchtowers: one after another along the
high Stamboul ridge, the pinnacles seem to be eyeing your
approach suspiciously.

For Istanbul does possess, as you can feel from the deck of
your ship, the arrogance of the very old: like the rudeness of an
aged actor whose prime was long ago, whose powers have failed
him but who struts about still in cloak and carnationed button-
hole, snubbing his inferiors. Seen from the sea, Istanbul seems
to be sneering from across the confluence of waters, the junction
of the Marmara, Bosporus and Golden Horn, which is its *raison
d'être*, and all the caiques and motorboats and ferries seem to
scuttle past it as though afraid of wounding comments.

It is only when you get closer that you realize the illusion of
it, just as you observe, if he leans too close to you on the sofa,
the creases of despair around the actor's mouth. Then that proud
mass above the water dissolves into something crumblier and

shabbier; the watchtowers lose some of their haughty command, the great sea wall of Stamboul is no more than a ruin, and it turns out that the passing boats are taking no notice of the city at all, but are simply impelled to and fro across the waterways, up and down the Golden Horn, zigzagging across the Bosporus, like so many mindless water insects.

For half the civilized world this was once *the* City, the ultimate – Byzantium, Constantinople, the stronghold and repository of all that civilization had retrieved from the wreck of Rome. For the Turks it still is. It is no longer the political capital of Turkey, but it is much the greatest Turkish city: the place where the money is made, the books are written, the place, above all, where the Turks see their own national character most faithfully mirrored or fulfilled. When I put myself into Istanbul's shoes that evening, I felt only some inkling of schizophrenia: when Turks do so, I am told, by immersing their imaginations in the history and spirit of the place, they feel most completely themselves.

I know of no other city that is so impregnated with a sense of fatefulness, and this is partly because few cities have been so important for so long. Constantine founded his capital, the New Rome, in AD 330, and there has not been a moment since when Istanbul was not conscious of its own mighty meaning. The successive dynasties that ruled the place competed with each other to proclaim its consequence. The Romans built their showy Hippodrome, adorning it with captured trophies and staging terrific chariot races beneath the golden horses of its tribune. The Greeks of Byzantium raised their marvellous cathedral, decorating it with precious frescoes and genuflecting in dazzling ritual before its jewelled reliquaries. The conquering Muslims of the Middle Ages commemorated themselves with mosques, schools and caravanserais across the city, each larger, more pious and more philanthropic than the last. The Ottomans built their vast Topkapi Palace, crammed with vulgar jewellery, where the ladies and eunuchs of the Seraglio gossiped life away in marble chambers, and the Sultans eyed their odalisques in exquisite pleasure kiosks above the sea. The mound of old Stamboul, the original Byzantium, is studded all over with monuments, so that every alleyway seems to lead to the courtyard of a stately mosque, a blackened obelisk or a triumphal column, a casket church of Byzantium or at least a magnificent city wall.

But in between them all, under the walls, behind the churches, like a hideous carpet spreads the squalor of the centuries. It is as though these famous buildings were built upon a foundation of undisturbed muck – as though every scrap of rubbish, every gob of spittle, every bucket-load of ordure, has been stamped into the very substance of the place, never to be cleaned or scraped. When it rains, which it often does, the lanes are soon mucky: but it is not just mud that cakes your shoes, not plain earth liquefied, but actually a glaucous composition of immemorial city excreta. The market streets of Istanbul are not exactly picturesque, if only because the citizenry is so drably dressed, in browns, greys and grubby blacks, but they are vividly suggestive of unbroken continuity. The dark cluttered mass of the covered bazaars – the clamour of the market men – the agonizing jams of trucks, cars, horses and carts in the backstreets – the clatter of looms in half-derelict tenements – scuttling dogs and scavenging cats – bent-backed porters carrying beds or crates or carcasses – the click-clack of the man selling plastic clothes pegs, the toot-toot of the man selling wooden whistles, the ting-ting of the water seller with his tin cups – listless detachment of coffee-shop men, oblivious over their cups and dominoes – stern attention of policemen strutting through the shops – the shouts of itinerant greengrocers – the blare of pop music from the record stores – the glowering stone walls, the high towers above – the tumultuous odours of spice, coffee, raw meat, gasoline, sweat, mud – the sheer swell and flow and muddle of humanity there, seething through that urban labyrinth, makes one feel that nobody has ever left Istanbul, that nothing has ever been discarded, that every century has simply added its shambled quota to the uncountable whole, and made these streets a perpetual exhibition of what Istanbul was, is and always will be.

Just as decomposing matter makes for fertile vegetation, so from the compost of Istanbul a timeless vigour emanates. Few cities move with such an intensity of effort, such straining virility. The generations of the dead are risen, to prod the living into life.

For yes, this is a vigour of the grave. These are bones rustling, and the restless ferry-boats of Istanbul are so many funeral craft, carrying their complements of dead men to and fro between the railway stations. Though Istanbul is home to some three million souls, though its suburbs stretch far along the Marmara shore, deep into Thrace, up the Bosporus almost to the Black Sea, though there are few towns on earth so agitated and congested, still it sometimes feels like a tomb-city.

Of all the great Turkish despots, only Kemal Ataturk, the latest, rejected Constantinople as his capital. It was Ataturk who renamed the city Istanbul, and he had no sympathy, it seems, for its sedimented pride – he visited the city reluctantly during his years in office, though he died there in 1938. He was a futurist, a reformer, a secularist, and old Byzantium must have seemed the very negation of his aspirations. To this day Istanbul has never really absorbed his visionary ideas, or become a natural part of the Turkey he created.

Of course it has lost much of the Oriental quaintness that the great man so resented. No longer do the gaily skirted peasants swirl into the covered markets: gone are the tumbled wooden houses of tradition, and only a few of the old Ottoman love nests along the Bosporus, those tottering clapboard mansions that the romantic travellers used to relish, still stand frail and reproachful among the apartment blocks. Ring roads and fly-overs have cut their statutory swaths through the slums and city ramparts. The obligatory international hotels ornament the best sites. Here and there one sees blighted enclaves of contemporary planning, blown by litter, stuck all over with peeling posters, invested with car parks and sad gardens.

But it is not really a modern city at all, not modern by taste or instinct, and it seems to reject transplants from our century. In the Municipal Museum (housed in a former mosque in the shadow of the Emperor Valens' great aqueduct) there is dimly displayed an American plan for a new bridge over the Golden Horn, with ceremonial approaches at either end. It is a lavish conception of spotless plazas and gigantic avenues, but it was doomed from the start, and survives only in an old brown frame upon a musty wall; even if it had been built, I do not doubt, long ago the mould of old Stamboul would have encroached upon its symmetries and rotted its high pretensions.

There can never be a fresh start in Istanbul. It is too late. Its successive pasts are ineradicable and inescapable. I always stay at the Pera Palas Hotel on the Galata hill, almost the last of the old-school grand hotels to survive the invasion of the multi-

nationals – a haven of potted plants, iron-cage elevators, ample
baths with eagle feet. It has been halfheartedly modernized once
or twice, but like Istanbul itself, it really ignores improvements
and is settled complacently into its own florid heritage. My
bedroom this time was Number 205, overlooking the Golden
Horn. It was clean, fresh and very comfortable – I love the hotel
– but when, on my first morning, I lay flat on the floor to do my
yoga, lo, from the deep recess beneath my double bed an
authentic fragrance of the Ottomans reached me, dismissing the
years and the vacuum cleaners alike: an antique smell of omelets
and cigars, slightly sweetened with what I took to be attar of
roses.

Something fibrous and stringy, like the inherited characteristics of a patrician clan, links the ages of Istanbul, and is as
recognizable in its people today as a six-toed foot or albinism.
For all its distracted air, in small matters at least Istanbul is a
surprisingly reliable city. I never feel vulnerable to assault or
robbery here, I seldom feel the need to check the bill, and even
the most pestiferous of the local bravoes generally prove, if
approached with sufficient firmness, dependable guides and
advisers. *Yok* stands for rigidity, but for staunchness, too.

Istanbul has had to be staunch, to withstand the corrosions of
time and retain its stature in the world. It has outlasted most of
its rivals, after all, and generally wins its battles in the end.
Scattered around Pera, the old foreigners' quarter of the city, are
the former embassies of the powers, the nations of Europe that
have periodically foreclosed Turkey as the bankrupt invalid of
the Golden Horn. Nowadays, with the government in Ankara,
they are mere consulates, but in their very postures you can still
recognize the contempt with which their envoys and ambassadors, not so long ago, surveyed the pretensions of the Sublime
Porte: the Russian embassy, like Tolstoy's estate behind its
forecourt; the British a huge classical villa by the architect of the
Houses of Parliament; the French with its private chapel in the
garden; the Italian (once the Venetian) like a stately retreat upon
the Brenta. They are still functioning, but they are half buried all
the same in the debris of history, forlorn down messy cobbled
alleyways or peering hangdog through their railings across the
turmoil of the old Grand Rue.

Or take the Greek quarter across the Golden Horn. Here there stands the Patriarchate of the Greek Orthodox Church, the Vatican of Orthodox Christianity. Once it was an organization of immense power, attended by pilgrims and plenipotentiaries, surrounded by acolyte institutions, defying even the dominion of the Muslim caliphs down the road. Now it is pitifully diminished, an unobtrusive little enclave in a semi-slum, its ceremonial gateway symbolically painted black and welded shut forever: while on the hill behind it the huge Greek *lycée*, once aswarm with aspirants, now stands empty, shuttered and despised.

Istanbul outlives all its challengers, reduced of course in worldly influence since the days of the Ottoman Empire, but hardly at all in self-esteem. Those powers and principalities have risen and fallen, some humiliated, some exalted, but the matter of Istanbul outlasts them all. This is a survivor city, essentially aloof to victory or defeat. The nearest a foreign enemy has come to assaulting Istanbul in our century was in 1915, when the armies of the Western alliance in the Great War, landing on the Gallipoli Peninsula some 150 miles to the south, tried to march north to the city. Supported by the guns of the most powerful battle fleet ever seen in the Mediterranean, they threw half a million of the world's finest infantry ashore on Turkish soil and expected to be at the Golden Horn within the month.

Though Istanbul was rigidly blockaded, though British and Australian submarines roamed the Marmara and bombarded the roads to the city, though a warship was torpedoed within sight of the sultan's palace, though the rumble of the battle shivered the minarets on the heights of Stamboul – still the enemy armies never advanced more than five miles from their beachheads.

Istanbul had said *yok*.

In theory this is a secular city, just as Turkey is a secular state. Ataturk decreed it so. In practice the voice of the muezzin rings out across the city, electronically amplified nowadays, almost as insistently as it did in the days of the caliphs, when this was the formal capital of all Islam. Like everything else in Istanbul, the faith proves irrepressible, and it remains the most potent single element, I suppose, in the personality of the place. I went one day to the Blue Mosque at the time of Friday prayers and positioned myself inside its great doorway – discreetly I hoped – to watch the faithful at their devotions. Not for long. A young man of distinctly unecumenical aspect rose from the back row of worshippers and approached me darkly. 'Beat it,' he said, and without a moment's hesitation, beat it I did.

The muezzin voices are voices from the glorious past, never silenced, calling Istanbul always back again, home again to itself – back to the great days of the caliphs, the noble Ahmets and the munificent Mehmets, back to the times when the princes of this city could build incomparable monuments of belief and generosity, high on their seven hills above the sea. Nobody has built in Istanbul like that since the end of the caliphate and its empire, just as nobody has given Istanbul a faith or a pride to call its own. Even the name of the place has lost its majesty. 'Why did Constantinople get the works?' a popular song used to ask. 'That's nobody's business but the Turks' ': but the new name lacks the grand hubris of the old, and sends a *frisson*, I am afraid, down almost nobody's spine.

So many a patriot of this city looks back to Islam. The mosques are busy, the fanatics are aflame, regressive religion is one of the fiercest political movements in Istanbul. Though it used to be postulated that Turkish Islam, like capitalism, would wither away in time, the average age of that Blue Mosque congregation looked strikingly young to me. And though the veil has been officially forbidden for half a century now, women are going to the university these days with black scarves drawn pointedly around their faces. The activist Muslims of Istanbul look outside their own country for inspiration – to Iran, to Pakistan, to the Arab states, where militant Islam is on the march or already in power: and when they take to the streets, as they recently did, or engage in student skirmishes, or burn cars, or break windows, the newspapers are unable to define this heady amalgam of nostalgia and zealotry, and cautiously describe them as Idealists.

On the other side, now as always, are the leftists, by which the press means the heterogeneous mass of liberals, anarchists, hooligans and real Communists, which roughly stands for change in an opposite direction. The longest graffito in the world is surely the one that somebody has painted along the whole expanse of the mole at the Kadiköy ferry station, containing in its message almost the entire idiom of the international Left, and leaving those with strong feelings about neo-Fascist hyenas with nothing much more to add. The leftists think of themselves as progressives, modernists, but they are really

honouring a tradition older even than Islam: for long before the
caliphate was invented, the city crowd was a force in Byzantium.
In those days the rival factions of the Blues and the Greens,
originally supporters of competing charioteers in the Hippodrome, were infinitely more riotous than any soccer crowd
today, and the great circuit of the racetrack, around whose
purlieus the back-pack nomads now drink their mint tea in The
Pub or the Pudding Shop, was the supreme arena of anarchy,
the place where the frustration of the people found its ferocious
release in bloodshed and insurrection.

Even now, I think, the quality of mercy is fairly strained in
Istanbul, and the threat of public violence is always present. It
is not so long since the mob, in its inherited and ineradicable
suspicion of Greece, burned down half the covered bazaars of
the city and destroyed everything Greek they could find. Step
even now from a bus in Beyazit Square, on the Stamboul ridge,
and you may find yourself looking straight down the gun barrel
of a military patrol. Hang around long enough in Eminönü, by
the waterfront, and you are sure to see somebody frog-marched
off the scene by plainclothes toughs or clapped into handcuffs
by the implacable military police.

But you feel these antagonisms, this touch of the sinister, only
so to speak by osmosis. The Turks are a courteous people, very
kind to harmless strangers, and the ruthless side of their nature
is generally masked. For that matter, nearly everything in
Istanbul is blurred by its own congealment and decay. Cairo,
Calcutta, Istanbul – these are the three great cities of the world
where you may observe the prophecies of the doomwatch
specialists apparently coming true. Chaos has not arrived yet,
but it feels imminent enough. The ferry steamers seem to swirl
around in a perpetual state of near collision. There is hardly
room on the sidewalks for the press of people. Ever and again
the city traffic, balked by some unseen mishap far away along
the system, comes helplessly to a halt. The festering rubbish
dumps of Stamboul seem to heave with incipient disease.

It has not happened yet. The ferry-boats generally evade each
other in the end. The traffic does move again. The plague rats
have not yet emerged from their garbage. But the suggestion is
always there, the shadow of breakdown and anarchy: incubat-
ing, one feels, in the day-to-day confusion.

*

The sense of foreboding that characterizes Istanbul has a half-illusory quality, and seems to bewilder its citizens as it does its visitors. This is a city of theatrical hazards. Fires and earthquakes have periodically ravaged it. Empires have risen and fallen within its boundaries. There is a humped island called Yassiada, ten or so miles from Istanbul in the Marmara, which was pointed out to me one day as the place where Prime Minister Menderes was imprisoned after a military coup in 1960. It looked a nice enough place to me: a companionable little island, not at all remote, which looked as though it might have some agreeable bathing beaches. And what became of Menderes? I ignorantly asked my companion as our ship sailed by. 'They killed him,' he replied.

Now *that* hardly seemed real, on a blue and sunny day, on the deck of a pleasure-steamer, on a trip around the islands. Half fictional, half fact, a nebulous sense of menace informs the conversations of Istanbul. The foreign businessman has chill presentiments as he leans with his gin and tonic over his balcony by the Bosporus, watching a Russian cruise-ship sliding by, cabin lights ablaze and hammer-and-sickle floodlit, towards Odessa and the Motherland. 'Something's going to happen. Something's going to crack...' The Turkish bank official, pausing didactically with your traveller's cheques beneath his thumb, attributes the malaise to strategy. 'Strategy is the curse of Istanbul – it's where we live; we can never be left in peace.' The army colonel, over a drink at the Hilton, talks apocalyptically through his moustache of conspiracies and conflicts. 'I'll tell you quite frankly – and the Americans know this well enough – the Greeks don't simply want Cyprus for themselves, they don't simply want to make the Aegean a Greek lake – *they want Istanbul itself*! They want to restore Byzantium!'

It is easy to feel perturbed in Istanbul. Every evening at the Pera Palas a string trio plays, attentively listened to by the German package tourists at their communal tables, and gives the place a comfortable, palm-court air. Two elderly gentlemen in gypsy outfits are on piano and accordion, and they are led by a romantic fiddler, adept at waltzes and polkas.

I was sitting there one evening when suddenly there burst into the room, driving the trio from its podium and severely disconcerting the *Hausfraus*, a team of ferocious Anatolian folk dancers, accompanied by a young man with a reedy trumpet and an apparently half-crazed drummer. The dancers were fairly crazed themselves. Apparently welded together into a multicoloured phalanx, they shrieked, they roared with laughter, they leaped, they whirled, they waved handkerchiefs – a performance of furious bravura, leaving us all breathless and aghast. They were like so many houris, come to dance over the corpses on a battlefield.

They withdrew as abruptly as they had arrived, and in the stunned hush that ensued I turned to the Americans at the next table. 'My God,' I said, 'I'm glad they're on our side!' But a knowing look crossed the man's face. 'Ah, but *are* they?' he replied.

You can never be quite sure, with the Turks. They are nobody's satellites, and they habitually leave the world guessing. This does not make for serenity, and Istanbul is not a blithe city. For foreigners it is a city, all too often, of homesickness and bafflement, for Turks a city where life gets tougher every day. I saw a protest demonstration one day clambering its way up the hill towards the Hippodrome, on the Stamboul ridge, and never did I see a demonstration so lacking in the fire of indignation. The hill is very steep there, and the cheerleaders, men and women in antiphony, found it hard to raise a response among their panting protégés: while flanking the procession on either side, guns across their bellies, helmets low over their foreheads, an escort of soldiers did their chesty best to keep up. An armoured car brought up the rear, flashing blue and white lights, but even it found the progress heavy going.

More telling still perhaps, one day I walked up a hill on the Pera side (every walk in Istanbul is up or down a hill) in the wake of a big brown bear, chained to the staff of a lanky man in black. It was a distinguished-looking bear, lean and handsome, but it walked through Istanbul in movements of infinite melancholy and weariness, as though the day, the walk up the hill, life itself would never end. I overtook it presently, and prodded by its master it stood on its hind legs for a moment to salute me as I passed: but it did so disdainfully, I thought, and somewhat *grandly*.

Istanbul indeed is nothing if not grand. It may not be exuberant, it is seldom funny, its humour running characteristically to not very prurient posters and bawdy badinage. It is hardly uplifting: sometimes, when I take the old funicular from

Galata hill to the Golden Horn, I feel that its carriages, sliding
into their narrow black tunnels, are plunging me into perpetual
night. It is never optimistic: one feels that dire things may
happen at any moment, and all too often they do, arrests,
accidents, collapses, unidentified gunshots and screaming sirens
in the night being commonplaces of the city.

But grand, unquestionably. For all my unease in Istanbul, I
greatly admire the place, and it is the grandeur that does it: not
the grandeur of history or monument, but the grandeur of *yok*,
the ornery strength and vigour that gives a living dignity to its
affairs. There is one incomparable vantage from which to
observe this ironic vitality – the deck of one of the restaurant
boats which are moored beside the Galata Bridge; and there at
a typical Istanbul lunchtime – greyish, that is, with a warm
breeze off the Bosporus to flutter the canvases – I will end my
essay.

The setting down there is terrific. The bulk of Stamboul rises
magnificently behind our backs, the iron-brown Galata hill is
stacked across the Golden Horn, and to the east the ships pass
to and fro along the wide expanse of the Bosporus. Everything
is a little hazed, though: not merely by the cloud of spiced smoke
in which the restaurateur is cooking our fish, on the open
quayside by the boat, but by a kind of permanent opacity of life
and light along the Golden Horn, through which everything
moves powerfully but inexactly.

Those inescapable ferry-boats, for instance, twist and scuttle
in a dream-like frenzy, and across the bridge the traffic seems to
lurch without pattern or priority. Peddlers, defying the massed
tide of pedestrians like Californians wading into the surf, offer
balloons, cutlery, incomprehensible household gadgets and
sizzling corn on the cob. Military policemen saunter watchfully
by, eyes darting right and left for deserters or unsoldierly
conduct. From their boats below the quay smoke-shrouded
fishermen hand up chunks of grilled fish to their customers
above, who sprinkle rough salt upon them from pots tied to the
railings and wander off munching into the crowd. Lines of
indistinguishable youths hang over their fishing rods beneath
the bridge, and sometimes clouds of pigeons, suddenly emerging from their roosts in the dusty façade of the mosque at the
end of the bridge, swoop across the scene like huge grey
raindrops.

It is a wonderfully animated scene, but animated it seems by habit: numbly animated, passively animated, like a huge mechanical theatre worked by the engines of history. Presently our food comes, with a chopped tomato salad on the side, a glass of beer and some fine rough Turkish bread. 'Oh,' we may perhaps murmur, in our foreign way, 'excuse me, but I wonder if we could possibly have some butter?' The waiter smiles, faintly but not unkindly. '*Yok*,' he says, and leaves us to our victuals.

19

A FOURTH DIMENSION

Kashmir, 1970

This rather dream-like piece says as much about my own state of mind, I fear, as it does about the vale of Kashmir. I was having doubts about the nature of reality, and for that matter the reality of nature, and Kashmir seemed the perfect medium for their expression. From that year to this the man who said he loved his life so much has never failed to send me a Christmas card.

It was in Kashmir, late in travel and half-way through life, that I first went transcendental. Reality seems distinctly relative in that high and timeless vale, truth bends, distance is imprecise, and even the calendar seems to swing indeterminately by, week blurred into week and Friday arriving unannounced upon the heels of Sunday night.

For my first few days I stuck to the facts, but ever less tenaciously. Nobody else seemed to find it necessary. No decision seemed sacrosanct there, and life was apparently suspended in some limbo between events. I lived myself on a lake of no particular shape or exact location, linked by meandering reedy waterways to a fifteenth-century city down the valley. It took me an hour to get to town, reclining full-length in the cushioned recesses of a boat, while the paddle-man behind me sang high-pitched melodies to himself, took occasional gurgles at a water-pipe, and drank green tea with salt in it. Sometimes I stopped to make an improbable purchase – a jade bangle, a duck for dinner, a chunk of honey off the comb. Sometimes perfect strangers asked me how old my watch was, or told me about their forthcoming examinations in elementary economics. Sometimes, having spent the whole day maundering about the city, I returned to my lake late in the evening with not the slightest recollection of anything specific having happened to me at all.

So in the end I emancipated myself, and soared unimpeded beyond actuality, seldom quite sure where I was, or when, or even sometimes who – answering all questions with abandoned fancy, never seeking a reason or providing a cause. I felt myself disembodied between the green-blue lake and the snow mountains all around, in a gentle Nirvana of my own: nowhere existed, it seemed to me, beyond the celestial vale of Kashmir, and whether the vale existed itself was a matter of individual perception.

I was not the first to enter this airy plane of sensibility. Kashmir has been having such an effect upon its visitors for at least 400 years. The Moghul emperors, who conquered it in the sixteenth century, responded to the vale with a sensual passion, embellishing it with seductive gardens and honouring it with royal dalliances. The British, who became its suzerains in the 1840s, thought it the ultimate retreat from the burdens of empire, and took its magic home with them to the strains of 'Pale Hands I Loved, Beside the Shalimar'. Today's wandering hippies find themselves rootlessly at ease there, and Middle Americans who spend a couple of Kashmir days between Treetops and Hong Kong often feel the interlude to have been an insubstantial dream.

Kashmir has always been more than a mere place. It has the quality of an experience, or a state of mind, or perhaps an ideal. The Muslim sectarians called the Ahmadiya believe that Christ did not die upon the Cross, but was spirited away to Kashmir, the last haven of perfection: and the Moghul emperor Jehangir expressed the wish on his deathbed that Kashmir and Paradise would turn out to be, as he had always thought, one and the same place.

In my more lucid moments, I must here interject, I did not *altogether* agree with the Emperor. Looked at hard and realistically, Kashmir falls short of Elysium. Situated as it is high in central Asia, north of Tibet, squeezed between Russia, China and Afghanistan, it can hardly escape the world's contagion. Beside the golf course at Srinagar, Kashmir's capital, one often sees the waiting white cars of the United Nations, chauffeurs patient at the wheel: and there are soldiers about always, and angry politicians, and students with grievances, and unpersuadable men of religion. Kashmir is one of the world's perennial trouble-spots. Though its people are mostly Muslims, it was ruled until 1947, under the aegis of the British, by a Hindu dynasty of Maharajahs: since then it has been disputed by India and Pakistan. The whole of the vale of Kashmir falls within Indian territory, but sizeable chunks of the outer state are governed by Pakistan, and legal sovereignty of the whole has never been decided. Kashmir is one of those places, deposited here and there in awkward corners of the earth, that never seem quite settled: a bazaar rumour kind of place, a UN resolution place, a place that nags the lesser headlines down the years, like a family argument never finally resolved.

Besides, in my Paradise nobody will be poor: most of the inhabitants of Kashmir are very poor indeed. My Paradise will always be merry: Kashmir is infused with a haunting melancholy. In my Paradise there will be no tourist touts, sharks or hawkers: Kashmir, for more than a century one of the great tourist destinations of the earth, boasts the most charmless touts and indefatigable hagglers in Asia. In my Paradise burgundy will flow like water: in Kashmir all but the most extravagant of Moghuls must make do with Indian Golconda, sixteen rupees a half-bottle from the vineyards of Hyderabad.

Where was I? Drifting, that's right, all but motionless across a Kashmiri lake, preferably in a shikara. A shikara is a distant relative of the gondola, canopied, low in the water, looking rather stern-heavy and propelled by that boatman with the water-pipe, squatting at the stern. From *outside* a shikara looks like a fairground novelty, brightly coloured and curtained, and generally full of gregarious Indian youths waving and crying 'Hi!', wrongly supposing you to be a research student in comparative ethnology from the University of South Utah. *Inside* the shikara feels a very different vehicle – like a floating capsule or divan, exquisitely cushioned, moving unguently through the water-lilies towards pleasure-gardens and picnics.

Though the vale of Kashmir is 800 miles from the sea, and surrounded on all sides by immense mountains, still its prime and symbolic element is water. The Kashmir thing is essentially a rippling, liquid kind of happening. Geologists say the whole valley was once a lake, and a string of lesser lakes ornaments it still. Srinagar stands in the middle of four, and is criss-crossed too by ancient canals, and intersected by the great river Jhelum. Boats are inescapable in the capital: boats grand or squalid, spanking or derelict; boats thatched, shingled, poled, engined; boats deep with fruit, nuts, timbers, furs, livestock; barges, and punts, and canoes, and skiffs, and elderly motor-boat taxis; above all those floating figures of the Kashmir scene, those vessels of fragrant legend, houseboats.

Kashmiris have always used houseboats of a kind – straw-thatched craft like arks, chock-a-block with cooking-pots, washing-lines and chicken-coops, leaking wood-smoke from their every crack and often ominously clamped together with iron struts. It was the British, though, in the heyday of Empire, who devised the standard Kashmiri houseboat of the love lyrics and the tourist brochures – what one might call the Pale Hands Houseboat. Sensibly denied the right to acquire land in the valley, they took to the water instead, and evolved their own kind of pleasure-craft. I suspect they based it upon the barges which used to form the clubhouses of Oxford rowing clubs – themselves developed from the ceremonial guild barges that once conveyed London aldermen up and down the Thames from board meeting to turtle soup.

The Kashmir version has come to be a sort of chalet-boat, or water-villa. It is often gabled, and shingle-roofed. There is a sun-deck on top, with an awning, and the poop is comfortably cushioned, and has steps down to the water. The boat is generally fitted in a Victorian mode: heavy dark furniture, baths with claw feet, antimacassars very likely, hot-water bottles for sure. Each houseboat has its own kitchen-boat moored astern, and its attendant shikara alongside, and its staff of resident servants, and its own special smell of cedar-wood, curry, roses and ingrained cigar-smoke: and living upon such a vessel, moored beside the orchard-bank of Nagin Lake, or lying all among the willows of a Srinagar canal, very soon one finds reality fading. The lap of the water takes over, the quacking of the ducks in the dawn, the hazed blue smoke loitering from the cook-boat, the soft water-light, the glitter of the dewdrop in the water-lily leaf, the flick of the little fish in the clear blue water, the dim purplish presence of the mountain beyond the lake, fringed with a line of distant snow.

Time expands in such a setting, and loses its compulsion. The hours dawdle by, as the bearer brings you your coffee on the sun-deck, and the shikara man lies on his own cushions awaiting your instructions, and the peripatetic trading boats sidle into your line of vision – 'You like to see my jewellery, madam? Any chocolates, cigarettes, shampoo? You want a very nice suede coat, sir, half the price of Savile Row? Flowers, memsahib? Haircut? Fur hat? Laundry?' Nothing very particular occurs. A meal comes when you want it. The shikara is always there. The ducks quack. If one considers the matter carefully one finds that the sun rises and sets, and some time between tea and sundowner it does begin to get dark.

Scale, on the other hand, contracts. The focus narrows, within the frame of the Kashmir water-life. The picture gets clearer, more exact, and one finds oneself concentrating upon minutiae, like the number of leaves upon the plucked waterweed, or the twitchy movements of the kingfishers. I took Jane Austen's novels with me to the vale of Kashmir, and perfectly with this delicate awareness of the place did her quill dramas and porcelain comedies correspond.

Sometimes, as I say, I was swishily paddled into town. Then through lily-thick channels we proceeded, willows above us, green fields and apple orchards all around, and as we approached the city the texture of life thickened about us. Barge-loads of cattle glided by to market. Infants sploshed about in half-submerged canoes. Women in trailing kerchiefs, neatly folded about the head, cooked in shanty-boats or washed their clothes at water-steps. Solitary fishermen cast their nets in the shallows: sometimes a man paddled an empty punt along, sitting cross-legged and gnomish in the prow. We passed beneath medieval bridges trembling with traffic, and beside tall houses latticed and mysterious, and past open-fronted waterside stores where merchants sat grandly upon divans, smoking hubble-bubbles and bowing condescendingly in one's direction. We paddled our way, like an admiral's yacht at a review, through flotillas of houseboats – *Young Good Luck*, *Winston*, *Kashmir Fun* – all apparently De Luxe With Sanitation, some with tourists jolly on the poop, some all dank and deserted, like funeral boats between rituals.

And presently we found ourselves upon the muddy water of the Jhelum itself, with its parade of old bridges (Zero Bridge to Eighth Bridge) and the brown jumble of Srinagar all around:

distractedly I would disembark to loiter through the labyrinth of
the bazaars – pursued by suggestions proper and profane, and
seldom knowing where I was going. Though Srinagar is only
seventy minutes from Delhi by daily jet, yet it is a frontier town
of Central Asia. Here since the start of history the caravans from
Sinkiang or Kazakhstan rested on their way to India, and these
tangled suks are more like Turkestan than Bengal. Here one feels
close to the Uzbegs, the Kurds, the Mongols, the merchants of
Tashkent or Bokhara: and often one sees exotic figures from the
remotest north swinging through the bazaars, in goat-skin
cloaks and fur hats, to remind one of the grand mysteries, Pamir
and Hindu Kush, which stand at the head of the valley.

Srinagar has its westernized quarters, of course. It has a golf
course, and a grand hotel that was once the Maharaja's palace,
and a slightly less grand hotel that the British used to frequent,
and a bank with a genuine Scottish manager in an Edwardian
villa above the river, and a pleasant waterside esplanade called
the Bund, and a Club, and heaps of tourist shops, and a
Government Emporium of Kashmiri Crafts – carpets, woodwork,
papier mâché, jewellery. There are a couple of cinemas in town,
and there is a brand-new Anglican church, the old one having
been burnt down in 1967 in a fairly obscure protest, it seems to
me, against the Six Day War.

But downstream from this enclave, strewn around and within
the bends of the Jhelum, medieval Srinagar magnificently survives. No addict of the mouldering picturesque could complain
about these bazaars. They possess all the classic prerequisites of
oriental allure – spiced smells, impenetrable alleys, veiled women,
goldsmiths, mosques, sages, dwarfs. The air of old Srinagar is
heavy with suggestion, not too closely to be analysed; and its lanes
are so crowded with shrouded and turbanned personages, so
opaque with dust and smoke and vegetable particles, that invariably I lost my bearings in them, and wandering fruitlessly among
the temples and the cloth merchants, over the Third Bridge and
back past the tomb of Zain-el-Abdin, at last I used to clamber into
a tonga, and went clip-clop back, to the flick of the whip and the
smell of horse-sweat, to my patiently waiting shikara at the Dal
Gate. 'Houseboat now?' the shikara man would murmur; and back
to the lake I would be unnoticeably propelled, eating walnuts all
the way.

*

Yet it has not been an exhilarating progress. The eye of
Kashmir is a brooding, almost a baleful, eye – the eye of the
shopkeeper, calculating above his wares, the eye of the military
policeman on his traffic-stand, the eye of the floating trader,
peering ever and again through the houseboat window in search
of victims within. The movement of Kashmir is grave and
measured, and even the humour of the valley has an enigmatic
heaviness, revealingly expressed in shops that call themselves
The Worst, or Holy Moses.

The Kashmiris are a hospitable people, but not inspiriting.
They seem to be considering always the possibilities of misfortune. In the autumn especially, a lovely season in the valley, the
fall of the leaf seems a personal affliction to them, and the
passing of the year depresses them like a fading of their own
powers. Then in the chill evenings the women disappear to
private quarters behind, and the men light their little baskets of
charcoal, tuck them under their fustian cloaks and squat
morosely in the twilight, their unshaven faces displaying a faint
but telling disquiet. 'Come in, come in,' they murmur, 'come
and join us, you are welcome, sit down, sit down!' – but for
myself I generally evaded their sad hospitality, preferring Miss
Austen's gaiety on the poop.

Yet I was half-ashamed as I did so, for their kindness is very
real, and all the truer for its reticence – a flick of the head to
disclaim gratitude, a discreetly forgotten bill, an unexpected
appearance at the airport just when you most need someone to
hold the typewriter while you fumble for the porter's tip. There
was a touching pathos, I thought, to the Kashmiri style. 'How
do you like your life?' I asked one new acquaintance there, when
we had progressed into intimacy. 'Excellent,' he replied with a
look of inexpressible regret, 'I love every minute of it' – and he
withdrew a cold hand from the recesses of his cloak, and waved
it listlessly in the air to illustrate his enjoyment.

The vale of Kashmir is like a fourth dimension – outside the
ordinary shape of things. About 100 miles long by twenty miles
wide, it is entirely enclosed by mountains of great height and
splendour – a green scoop in the Himalayan massif, hidden
away among the snow-ranges, desperately inaccessible until the
coming of aircraft, and still magically remote in sensation. The
Moghuls, on their holiday progressions to Srinagar, used to

climb with convoys of camels and elephants over the southern
ridges from Delhi. The British generally came on horseback or
in coolie litters over the hill-tracks from the west. Even today, as
you fly effortlessly in from the south, the impact of the valley is
strangely exciting, as you cross the ramparts of the mountains
and see its lakes, its orchards, its great plane trees richly
unfolded there below. It is not exactly an escape – one does not
escape into an enclave. It is a mood of transference or even
apotheosis: a trip without drugs, a pot-less ecstasy.

Kashmir does bear some paradoxical resemblances to other
places far away. The country villages with their thatched tall
farmsteads, their coveys of plump ducks, geese and chickens,
their grain-stores and their woodpiles, look like villages of
eastern Europe. The side-valleys of the mountains, down whose
lanes cloaked herdsmen drive their sheep, goats and ponies in
scrambled majesty to the lowlands, remind me very much of
Persia. The waterways of Srinagar suggest to every visitor some
less gilded Venice; the evening cry of the muezzin, echoing
across the lake at dusk, is an echo of Arabia; for four or five
generations every Oxford heart has responded to the willow-
meadows of Kashmir, so like the banks of Isis that one can
almost hear the cricket-balls and transistor radios of *alma mater*.

But these details of the familiar only intensify the oddity of
the whole. There is really nowhere like Kashmir. There are no
gardens so voluptuous as the great Moghul gardens around Dal
Lake – Shalimar and Nishat, Cashma Shaki and Nazim Bagh –
intoxicating blends of the formal and the unassuming, grand
with terraces and cool with fountains and sweet with roses,
with splendid pavilions at the water's edge, and glorious
towering trees. There are no ruins so unexpected as the ancient
temples of Kashmir, dotted around the valley in astonishing
neo-classical elegance – Greek in their grace, Egyptian in their
grandeur, uniquely Kashmiri in their flavour. I know of no crop
so startling as the saffron crop of Kashmir – acres of purple
crocus-like flowers lavishly splashed like mad paintwork across
the valley. I know no holy place more disconcerting than the
Hindu shrine of Mattan, where hundreds of thousands of sacred
carp thresh their lives away in horribly congested pools, jammed
tight together in a seething fishy mass. And I shall never forget
the wayside stall, north of Srinagar, where I stopped one day
to buy something for my supper: it was piled high with the

weirdest variety of game-birds I ever saw – ducks of all colours, huge wild geese, black straggly moorhens, and most authentically Kashmiri of all, I thought, a solitary grey heron all folded inside itself, its neck tucked beneath its belly, its legs crumpled below its rump. (No rooks? I asked. No rooks: the Koran forbade it.)

For the ultimate aloofness of Kashmir the traveller must climb to the rim of the valley, to the high alpine meadows of Gulmarg or Pahalgam. There the separateness of the place achieves a disembodied quality, and the whole valley seems to be resting in some high cradle among the clouds, supported by the snow-peaks all around. You have to walk to attain this mystic detachment – away from the little chalet-hotels and bazaars of the resorts, up through the silent pine woods, along the banks of slate-grey trout streams, up through the last crude huts of the highland shepherds, beyond the tree line, over the granite scree until you stand among the snows themselves, on the rampart ridge.

Often the vale below is half-veiled by cloud, and one sees only a green patch here and there, or a suggestion of water: but all around the white mountains stand, holding Kashmir on their hips – peak after peak, ridge after ridge, with Nangar Parbat supreme on the northern flank to set the scale of them all. Kashmir is, as I say, a place like no other: yet even from such a vantage point, high up there in the snow and the sun, its character is curiously negative. It could not possibly be anywhere else: but it might, so it often seemed to me in the hush of those high places, be nowhere at all.

One can judge it only by itself. The fascination of Kashmir is essentially introspective, a mirror-pleasure in which the visitor may see his own self picturesquely reflected, adrift in his shikara among the blossoms and the kingfishers. It is no place for comparisons. Paradise, here as everywhere, is in the mind.

20

CAPITAL CITY

Kyoto, 1957

◈

I did not terribly like Kyoto, when I went there in 1957 to write about it for an American magazine: but that may well have been, it occurs to me now on re-reading this essay, because I totally failed to understand it. In Japan, of all countries, it is dangerous to be ignorant.

Kyoto means Capital City. For a thousand years this famous place, encouched in mountains upon the Kamo River, was the capital of Japan and the emblem of Japanese civilization: and even today it remains to the Japanese something special among their cities, far more than just an elderly provincial metropolis in the central hills. It reigns still as the supreme repository of their ancient traditions, their culture and their custom, their religion and their high-flown patriotism, their golden heritage and their resilient pride.

To the foreigner, though, bouncing in by bus from Osaka, it seems at first sight something less than lovely: for though its setting is magnificent and its pose perennially imperial, yet the face it shows to the world is sadly coarsened. The frenzy of the new Japan has fallen upon Kyoto, too, cramming its streets with wild-driven traffic, tainting its old wisdom with doubt and disillusion. Kyoto was spared the worst tragedies of war, but it shares with the rest of Japan a sense of causes lost and ideals soured, of warped emotions and passions suppressed. The shape of this town was decreed by the Emperor Kammu eleven centuries ago, when he laid out his capital in the classical Chinese manner, four-square and impeccable: but though you can still recognize this grand design, nevertheless Kyoto has long since lost its symmetry and pattern, and seems to lie there, as your bus lurches through the faceless streets, floundering and inelegant, a city of lost style.

Both views are right: the impassioned Japanese, the disappointed alien. Kyoto as a whole is a plain place, shabby and shanty-like: but like others of the world's great cities – like Oxford, like Florence – it is a place of reticent enchantment, a private place, a place behind walls, a place whose beauties you must search out, and whose meanings, like the exquisite subtleties of the Japanese tea ceremony, are hidden beneath layers of innuendo. Kyoto is the most conservative of Japanese cities, still half living in its gilded heyday, when its monarchs and shoguns luxuriated in cultivated splendour, and the four great sects of Japanese Buddhism settled beneath its hills in ritual and meditation. The patricians of Kyoto are aloof and lofty still. The ultimate treasures of the place are jealously guarded. The tourists may click their shutters, the traffic may rage, the radios deafen: but away beyond the tawdry façade, even beyond the temples and the incomparable gardens, the spirit of this deep city lies inviolate and unruffled, like a carp in a sacred pool.

Temporal consequence abandoned Kyoto a century ago, when the emperors left it. Today it is poorer than Nagoya, smaller than Osaka, quieter than Yokohama, infinitely less virile than the *parvenu* Tokyo. No pounding steel mills give it force or energy, no ferocious chimneys belch away among its suburbs, no cameras, cars, radios or computers stream from its assembly lines: all it makes is silk, porcelain, lacquer ware, adorable dolls and nice little novelties for the tourists. Even its writers scuttle away to Tokyo, where the publishers live, and its old universities, distinguished though they are, lack the fire and sparkle of their contemporaries in the capital. Economically Kyoto is dominated by its gigantic seaport neighbours, Osaka and Kobe. Intellectually it is revered but fuddy-duddy. In all too many ways it is not much more than a museum, or a memory.

Yet for all its faded majesty, it feels unmistakably a great city still, a city of lingering power and paramountcy, and sometimes even of menace. All that is most deep-rooted in the Japanese character persists in this introvert community: some of it delightful, some of it hideous, some of it alarming, some of it delicate and fastidious beyond compare, some of it (to Western minds) perfectly inexplicable. In Kyoto you may observe, still extant and vigorous, an advanced and elaborate form of society that has no real contact with the ways of the West. It has its department stores and its television studios, its airline offices and its air-conditioned hotels; yet it remains at heart among the most Oriental of cities, looking at the world slant-eyed and cross-legged, like some heavy-lidded potentate peering across the fun-fairs from a high window of his castle.

A myriad shrines, temples and mansions powerfully fortify this sense of hidden strength and exclusivity. They are scattered across the city like gems in mud, unexpectedly at the ends of culs-de-sac, magnificently among pine groves on hillocks, splendidly in flamboyant courtyards. In Kyoto there are nearly two thousand Buddhist temples, Shinto shrines and palaces of importance, giving to every corner of the metropolis oblique suggestions of sanctity, delicacy and wisdom. Some are vast and portentous, their steep cypress-bark roofs rising high in grandeur above the houses, their ceremonial gongs gigantic beneath their wooden shelters, their passages meandering interminably through gilded screens, painted anterooms, gardens of infinite sophistication, tea-houses of faultless proportion. Some are no bigger than garden chalets, flickering small shrines of contemplation, reclining in rotting silence beneath high garden walls, or balanced beside rushing rivulets. Some are the empty palaces of the emperors and the shoguns, soaked in grandeur and symbolism: their wonderful gardens representative of the ocean, or the Inland Sea, or peace, or Paradise, or a fleet of treasure-ships, or the cosmos, their chambers rich with painted tigers, bamboo groves, sea birds, turtles. Some are the great prayer-houses of monks and holy men, mysterious with candles and slow movement, the tinkle of bells, the fragrance of incense, the murmured incantations that will bring the Jodo brethren, in their after-life, infallibly to the Western Paradise.

Some are the storehouses of mighty treasures, like the thousand images of the goddess Kannon in the Temple of Sanju-sangendo – a fabulous phalanx of glistening golden figures, silent, many-armed, sad-eyed, accusatory, each one stuffed with Buddhist scripts, rank upon rank, eye upon eye, attended by the Gods of Thunder and Wind, the Spirit of Merciful Maternity, the Spirit of Devotion, the Spirit of Exorcism. Some are airy gems of lucidity,

like the little golden pavilion called Kinkakuji, which was once
burnt down by a mad monk, but now stands again in feather-
weight lucidity above its lake, with one room reserved for poetry-
reading and incense parties, and a rustle of conifers all around.
Some are shrines of awful solemnity, poised upon high places,
with pagodas lonely among the larches and mountain streams
rushing by below. The great buildings of Kyoto are inexhaustible
and inescapable. It would take weeks only to glimpse them all,
and because they are distributed through every ward and every
suburb, they give the city dignity in depth, and clamp its drab
sprawling fabric powerfully together.

Kyoto is a city of whimsical grace-notes. Jammed beneath the
eaves of one great temple you may see an old umbrella, dropped
there aeons ago by a divine personage, and preserved there for
ever as a sign of holy favour. In another you may admire a
painting of Fujiyama whose perspective falls into accuracy only
if you kneel before the canvas. In a third you may hear the
floorboards, squeaking beneath your tread, 'emitting a sound'
(as the guidebook says) 'resembling the song of a Japanese
bush warbler'. You may walk the soft paths of a garden clothed
entirely in moss, a padded shadowy retreat for contemplatives;
or you may hear the hollow rhythmic clatter of a deer-scarer, a
hinged wooden tube animated by the passing water of a stream;
you may wonder at the great chains hanging down the rooftops
of the Imperial Palace – placed there for the convenience of fire-
fighters, but 'also forming', says the guide hopefully, 'a kind of
ornament'; or you may have your fortune tactfully told and
beguilingly translated ('Lucky Spring comes with happiness on
a mountain and field . . . Your wants would be able to accom-
plish . . . You would have many treasures of child'). If you are
specially privileged you may even catch sight of the slightly
improper medieval picture which, wrapped in innumerable
silks and stored in impenetrable caskets, is regarded as so
precious a possession that only twenty people are allowed to
view it each year.

The rice-paper windows of the Kyoto palaces are often
pierced, by children's fingers or the beaks of inquisitive birds,
but they are mended characteristically: over each hole a small
piece of paper is meticulously glued, cut by eager fingers into
entrancing flower patterns, every petal of perfect symmetry.

*

Everyday life in Kyoto is patched with similar fastidious grace. Of all the big Japanese cities, this remains nearest to the water-colour Japan, the Japan of the print-makers and the flower-makers. The main streets are dreadfully banal, but beyond them are alleys of seduction. Here the butterfly kimono, the white stocking, the cloven boot and the flowered kerchief may be seen down any back street, and the fringes of the city are full of brawny country folk, brown as goblins and wreathed in grins. The fishermen of Kyoto grapple with the river torrent with marvellous sinewy skill, like images from a Hokusai print, and the sages you sometimes meet in rambling temple court-yards look like archaic hermits or astrologers. Often you will hear, as you pass beneath some towering wall, the shrill whistling of strange flutes, or the pad of a Japanese drum. Possibly you will encounter, on the grassy sunlit verge of the river, a wandering monk in a grey robe and a bulbous basket-work hat, begging his way to immortality. You may go to a Noh or a Kabuki play in Kyoto, and sit chilled or stimulated by the formalities of those immemorial arts, or you may watch them dipping the dyed silks into the waters of the Kamo as they have in this valley for a millennium and more. All around the city, on the high mountain skyline, the pine trees stand in willow-pattern silhouette, and sometimes you may catch the local students, in their peaked caps and drab serge uniforms, entreat-ing a Shinto shrine for good marks in their examinations.

Kyoto is *par excellence* the home of the geishas, where those talented performers (part artists, part courtesans) are trained to an apogee of perfection, to perform their elaborate dances deliciously in many a lacquered *salon*, and bring contentment to many a paunchy protector. Half close your eyes one evening among the narrow streets of the geisha quarter, and you might almost be back in feudal Kyoto, before the razzle-dazzle West arrived. The lanes are bright with tea-houses and restaurants, dainty screens masking their entrances, soft slippers paraded invitingly at their doors. Hundreds of globular lanterns light the district, bathing it in orange radiance, and high above your head there floats an advertiser's balloon, flaunting illuminated letters on its tail. Now and then between the houses you may glimpse the Kamo River, wide and gurgling, with a glitter of light and gaiety on the opposite bank, and the dim moonlit hump of the hills beyond. From the terraces beside the water you may hear

the clink of cups, the murmur of liquid, the whisper of evening
ecstasies. A blind beggar stands mumbling among the shadows;
an old crone looks testily out of a doorway, a platter of fish in
her hand; two or three young men go rolling noisily pleasure-
bound; and suddenly there emerges from some unexpected alley
a vision of the legendary Japan – a geisha in all her plastered
glory, moving fast and purposeful towards an assignation.
Immensely tall is her mound of hair, jet black and shiny; her
face is vivid with white and scarlet; her costume is gorgeous
with silks, sashes, the gaudiest of clashing colours and the
floridest of patterns; and as she hastens awkwardly down the
street, embellished from head to foot with paint and brocade,
she feels less like a living woman than some fabulous toy, some
last masterpiece by Fabergé, enamelled like a queenly trinket,
animated by the ultimate refinements of clockwork.

Everything delicate thrives in the soil of Kyoto. A divine
simplicity informs the shop displays of the city. A sort of ascetic
chic graces the little gardens, with their ineffable arrangements
of stones and shrubs, and their air of mischievous meaning.
When they serve you a dish in a famous Kyoto restaurant,
poised above the river rapids, perhaps, with fish-pools in the
garden outside and the feathery branches tickling the veranda –
when they bring you your prawns, your quails' eggs, your lily
bulbs, your eels or your red seaweed, you will find each small
victual arranged with bewitching artistry upon your plate, like
an abstract miniature of marvellous sensibility. Kyoto is a city
of cool calm interiors, gossamer screens, rooms of geometrical
precision, women of porcelain fragility. It is a place of cherished
animals: little white Spitz dogs and affectionately collared cats,
the neat oxen that pull its country carts, the cranes, pheasants,
ducks, geese, squirrels that bask among its decorations. Away
from the motor-cycle thoroughfares, its air is full of crickets,
frogs, bells, birds, the sliding of fingertip doors, the clip-clop of
clogs, the slither of slippers. It is a city of a million souls, yet you
never feel far from the countryside: all around are the woodlands,
sliding down towards the town, and the whole place seems
inlaid with beautiful timber, aromatic planks, woods of lovely
grain and dedicated workmanship.

All this is true, and it is the continuity of Kyoto life that gives
this place its sense of power. No less real, though, are those

corroded aspects of modern Kyoto that affront the foreign
visitor like a juke-box in an abbey; and it is the harsh juxta-
position of the near-sublime and the almost unbearable that
gives the city its pungency and piquancy of character, its sting
and its bitter after-taste. Kyoto does not leave every visitor
soothed or elevated: there is something disturbing to its quality,
some hint of the morbid or the unhealthy. In some ways it is a
dead city, rotting among its mementoes, but in others it is, like
the rest of Japan, pulsing and proliferating with hybrid life, part
ordered familiar past, part groping present. It is not serene, no
longer Heian-kyo – the City of Peace.

Hardly anywhere in Kyoto is ever empty, except the cloistered
family gardens or the remoter forest glades. Down every street
the citizenry pushes with a babel of horns and a gallimaufry of
styles, from the immaculate *obi* to the jeans and sweaters of rip-
roaring adolescence. Through every brooding temple the Japanese tourists noisily pour – schoolchildren by the multitude,
festooned in satchels and luncheon bags, honeymooners cease-
lessly photographing each other, businessmen gravely bowing
one another out of the sightseeing bus. At every holy portal the
souvenir-sellers raucously greet you, brandishing their postcards or dangling their toy birds, and the mendicant ex-soldiers,
in parade-ground travesty, salute you with a hook hand or stand
their wooden legs to attention. The trains, those unavoidable
essentials of the Japanese scene, rumble through the night
beside the river, and the taxis career maniacally among the
rattling trams. Sometimes you may see a bride in kimono, but
just as often you will see her in a hired Paris copy, with her
bridegroom pin-striped and wing-collared, and her father displaying the unmistakable satisfaction of a man who is going to
charge it all on his expense account. They play baseball in the
shadow of Kyoto's shrines. They practise athletics around the
wall of the Imperial Palace. In Kyoto today you can never be
quite sure whether some picturesque bauble is an object of
Shinto veneration or an advertising notion. It is a two-faced
city: one head a phoenix, one a jackdaw.

Is it a ferocious city, too? Do there linger yet, among these
symbols and sanctities, some old savageries of the Japanese
spirit? Does a sword glint sometimes, up on the hill? Perhaps.
Kyoto, for all its enclaves of perfection, feels a troubled place.
Even the most fulsome of tourists may sometimes sense, as she

passes from temple calm to highway frenzy, some buried malaise in the flavour of this great city. Kyoto is the soul of Japan, a microcosm of the inner nation. You may taste all the fascination of this astonishing country as you wander among Kyoto's marvels – the Sparrow Chamber or the Wild Geese Chamber, the Silver Pavilion or the Hall of a Thousand Mats, the paintings of the Thirty-Six Famous Poets, the effigy lacquered with the ashes of the sage Shinran, the Veranda of the Archery Contest, the immortal garden of Ryuanji: but you may feel obscurely ill at ease in the Hall of the Imperial Visits, and all too likely the blare of a loudspeaker or the vicious hooting of a taxi horn will drown the sound resembling the song of a Japanese bush warbler.

21

THE WINTER QUEEN

Leningrad, 1957

❧

This little essay records my first visit to Leningrad. I have never even tried to write about it again.

I first flew into Leningrad out of the wintry womb of Russia, and it seemed to me that morning like a city of light.

Peter the Great called it his 'window on the West', and it remains a look-out still, watchfully Western in style and manner, a magnificent artefact of Europe at the gateway to Asia. They have tamed Leningrad and harnessed it, driven away its emperors, turned its palaces into museums and its academies for young ladies into political offices – coarsened its exquisite restaurants, exiled its fan-makers and its riding-masters, swamped its bookshops with dialectical materialism, deconsecrated its cathedrals, humbled its hierarchies, stifled its frivolities, left its great avenues peeling and pining. Yet it rides above its fate like the queen it is, and seemed to me that day, as I flew out of the horny Ukraine, still a Cleopatra among cities.

Leningrad is more than just a geometrical, but actually an astronomical metropolis: for Moskovsky Prospekt, the southern entry to the place, is not only six miles long and dead straight, but runs along the meridian from the Pulkovo Observatory on the southern heights. Calm, precise, and elegant seemed the city that morning as I drove along this celestial boulevard: a thoroughbred still, balanced and proportioned, with no uncanny Mongolesque skyscrapers to mar the skyline, only a serenity of classical colonnades, baroque mansions, domes and gilded steeples. Sea-light and snow-light filtered perpetually through the structures and shone icily from the broad frozen stream of the Neva, scattered with islands, lined with impeccable archi-

tecture, and running away between the quaysides to the Gulf of
Finland and points west.

Dazzled, the scales of the Ukraine still in my eyes, I wandered
through all this lucidity. Across the river the sunshine gleamed
miraculously upon the golden finger-spire of St Peter and St
Paul, slim as a stiletto above its ramparts. In the upstairs galleries
of the Hermitage, flooded in sunshine and surveying a brilliant
landscape of white, gold and baroque, the great Renoirs, Gau-
guins, Monets and blue Matisses stood there in gorgeous
vivacity, to be inhaled like a fragrance or gulped like a draught
of some exalting wine. Russia in winter is a dread and dreary
country, clogged alike with sludge and dogma; but fly into
Leningrad as I did, and your very glands will be rejuvenated.

For all its shrines of materialist revolution, its thumping
industrial fringe, the atomic submarines upon its shipyards – for
all these signs of the times Leningrad retains, like an ageless
courtesan, many an inessential charm. I bought a batter-wrapped
sausage that morning from a solemn woman in a white overall
at a street-corner stand. I found a 1905 Baedeker Russia in the
jumble of an old-school bookshop, inscribed in a spindly
German hand in the ink of long ago. I strolled among the hidden
statues of the Summer Garden, each one locked away for the
winter, like a wayward nymph in a rock, inside its own little
wooden house. I wondered at the profusion of fresh flowers on
the tomb of Peter the Great, and I gazed from the balcony of St
Isaac's Cathedral upon the glinting steeple of the Admiralty,
like a Buddhist stupa above the ice, and the fabulous immensities of the Winter Palace, where the Tsars lived in immeasurable
splendour and the revolutionaries stormed their way into
history. In Moscow it is difficult not to feel a kind of snob; in
Leningrad you are a serf in untanned thigh-boots, gaping at the
carriages and climaxes of the past.

For this is a city with the gift of timelessness. Elsewhere most
Russians seem so unalluring that it is a mystery to me how the
reproduction of the species is maintained. Here there are still
girls of a haunting and nostalgic beauty, such as you meet in the
pages of the immortal novelists, and men of a natural elegance
beyond class or era. Forgotten Western echoes, too, linger
suggestively on. I observed two young diplomatists in my hotel,
wearing heavy coats and high fur hats, whose immemorial
English faces and languid long-limbed attitudes at the reception

desk made them look like thrusting fur traders from Eastcheap, awaiting a concession from the Empress. I drank my morning coffee in a shop that might have sprung from Imperial Vienna, and I listened to jazz so brassily honky-tonk that I might have been in some forgotten burlesque of the Loop, thirty years ago in Chicago.

Leningrad is a humorous city. The cloak-room attendant puts your hat on your head with a delightful parody of courtly excess. Even the official guides are slyly amused by the presence in the Anti-God Museum (the museum, that is, of the History of Religion and Atheism) of a section reverently devoted to the adulation of Lenin. The young people of Leningrad, often rakishly and sometimes brazenly dressed, preserve a sense of bubbly fun: traces of taste, style and delicacy have survived the convulsion, and there are still a few citizens whose clothes fit and whose eyes are lit with a glint of gaiety.

There are modernistic trams in Leningrad – devices I had hitherto regarded as a contradiction in terms. There are polite and mercifully unobtrusive policemen. There is a mosque like something out of Isfahan, a square in which practically every building is a theatre, a house once inhabited by the inventor of the aeroplane (twenty years, I need hardly say, before the Wrights), a Wedding Palace for the white weddings now officially encouraged in Russia, a mammoth in a museum, a vase weighing nineteen tons and twenty-five Rembrandts. Even the snow-ploughs do their work with a special kind of symmetry, moving around Palace Square in lumpish ever-decreasing circles, like old-fashioned reapers, until at last they can revolve no more, and a squad of cheerful women with brooms and shovels leaps through their clouds of exhaust to remove the last central pile of snow, where the hare should be.

I went to a children's puppet theatre in the afternoon and watched its entrancing fooleries among an audience so enthusiastically disorganized that it made the end-of-term play at an English village school feel like Order in opposition to Chaos. And in the evening I saw *Die Fledermaus*, staged with a genuine rollicking panache, and so instinct with the magic of the waltz, the whirl of white skirts and the flick of tail-coats, that when I inspected the faces of the women about me, Soviet proletarians every one, I found them glazed with a true suburban enchantment.

They gave me champagne at dinner, placing a neatly folded napkin like a white cone over the bottle-top, and very late that night, with the fizz still in me, I slithered down the river bank beside the Admiralty, and crunched a path across the frozen Neva. The sky above me was a deep cold blue. The lights of the city shone dimly off the ice, like phosphorescence. The golden steeple of the Admiralty was floodlit and resplendent, an archangel's wand in the night, and beneath the bridge I could just make out the three tall funnels of the old cruiser *Aurora*, and the speckled lights of her portholes. Leningrad lay lucent still, even at midnight, and seemed to me like an exemplar, a paradigm, an obituary of the European ideal.

Next morning a fog fell upon the city, and you could not see across the river from one side to the other.

22

PIZARRO'S PLACE

Lima, 1963

⬱

I ignored the political situation of Peru, in writing this essay — at that particular moment, as it happens, Peruvian democracy was functioning quite well: I could not however evade the social truths of a country where 2 per cent of the population controlled all the wealth, and a quarter of the capital's inhabitants were living in slums of unspeakable squalor.

Four and a quarter centuries ago Francisco Pizarro the conquistador founded the city of Lima, and to this day he dominates it.

He was an illiterate adventurer, a swashbuckler whose savage but indomitable energies had contemptuously toppled the Incas from their golden thrones, and it was against all the augurs that he chose this place for the Spanish capital of Peru. The site was suggested to him, so tradition says, by resentful Indians convinced that its rotting vapours and humidity would soon kill all the Spaniards off. To north and south stretched a desiccated wasteland, to the west lay the unknown Pacific, from the east the dry Andean foothills slouched down to the sea. Beyond the mountains brooded the wildest of hinterlands, tangled with steaming forests, patrolled by weird tribes, frequented by tapirs, anacondas and creatures of unsuspected fantasy. Earthquakes repeatedly ravaged the area, rain scarcely fell there, and throughout the winter a damp, dank vapour hung low over the place, blanketing the narrow plain like smoke in a saucer. Yet Pizarro's city flourished, flaunted itself, and grew prodigiously in consequence. Lima became the headquarters of a Spanish viceroy, the seat of a powerful bishopric, and eventually the capital of the Peruvian Republic. For several generations it was the greatest city in South America, and legends of perfumed allure sur-

rounded its name. In culture, in elegance, in wealth, in reputation it stood alone among the cities of the New World – 'the
fairest gem', as the historian Prescott wrote, 'on the shores of
the Pacific'. It was called the City of the Kings, because its site
was selected upon the Feast of the Epiphany: but it was really
Pizarro's place.

Even now, four centuries later, the spirit of that old freebooter
dominates the Peruvian capital. His lofty splendour glimmers
down its boulevards, his opulence fructifies its suburbs, his
cruelty still corrupts its attitudes. Like man, like city. Pizarro
was a character of fascinating bestiality, and Lima is a metropolis
of heartless charm. Beside the Plaza de Armas, the heart of the
place, an equestrian statue of the conquistador stands in lordly
sentinel: his sword is fiercely and permanently drawn, and this
is both apposite and inevitable, for by a quirk very characteristic
of his great city, the sculptor has neglected to give him a
scabbard.

Lima is the city aristocratic, to the manner born. It lies only
twelve degrees south of the equator, on a line with Angola and
Madagascar, but beside its coastline there flows the cool stream
of the Humboldt Current, where the Antarctic whales court and
whelp, and beneath its bridges there leaps out of the mountains
the boulder-strewn River Rimac (which has given its name,
clumsily mispronounced by the conquerors, to the city itself).
Lima is no sweaty equatorial market-place, as the map might
suggest. On the contrary, it has a quality icy, aloof and self-
possessed, like a grandee in a Velázquez canvas, or a high-bred
filly in the ring. Even its neighbouring deserts feel like chap-
erons, sheltering a sensitive charge against vulgarity. Even the
winter smog seems to veil the city in a gentlemanly indolence,
and indeed the fond citizens of Lima prefer to call it their *niebla
perlada* – 'pearly haze'. It is true that Lima is no longer a
conventionally beautiful city. Generations of philistines have
done their worst to it, demolishing old treasures willy-nilly and
swamping it in mediocrity. Its distinction, though, is not
physical, nor even animal, but pre-eminently atmospheric, a
matter of suggestions and evocations, the shifting shadow of a
tree on a rococo façade, the squeak of an elderly tram beneath
your window, clattering hoofs and trumpet calls at breakfast,
sweet shrill street cries, the smell of incense and laundered

surplices, legends of courtesans and magnificos, repercussions of old arrogance.

The heart of Lima is the Plaza de Armas, the finest square in South America. Pizarro laid it out himself, and here more than anywhere you may sense how powerfully his imperial hauteur still colours the capital. Through this place the whole of Peruvian history has marched, in endless parade of triumph and blood-shed – shootings, and garrottings, feuds and reconciliations, the last ignominies of condemned revolutionaries, the ultimate glories of patriots. Look around you, and you may feel the very air heavy with the past. There stands the superb Cathedral, whose first beam, so legend says, was carried across the threshold on Pizarro's own hefty shoulders: a frowning, echoing, twilit edifice, haunted by pilgrims and high memories, with the Captain-General's mummified corpse, strangely shrunken with the centuries, displayed in a glass case in a corner chapel. There beside it is the Archbishop's Palace, elaborate with balconies, sculptured scrolls, lions' heads and obelisks, from which gen-erations of crimson divines exerted their authority – mighty men with flamboyant names, like Santo Toribo de Mogrejezo or Jeronimo de Loayza, sometimes gifted with such powers of command that they were not only archbishops, but Viceroys of Peru at the same time. There is the City Hall, grandly arcaded, with the ensign of the Republic nobly billowing above its roofs, built upon the very spot where, until the Spaniards stormed this way, a local satrap of the Incas held his feathered court. And there on the north side, gay but grandiose, stands the big white Presidential Palace, among its palms and courtyards: in that same place Pizarro lived and ruled, and there his enemies fell upon him at last, leaving him to trace the sign of the cross in his own dying blood upon the floor.

Around the great fountain in the centre of the Plaza sixteen stubby bronze monsters, crouching grotesquely pick-a-back, have been spouting water without a pause for three and a half centuries. Outside the Palace gates a squad of Peruvian dragoons stands in perpetual sentry-go, squat hunched men with Indian faces, wearing plumed brass helmets, spurs, boots, huge epau-lettes, swords and white gloves, and looking at once elegant, suspicious and formidable. Across the way a tramways man diligently shifts the streetcar points with an iron poker. Nearby, on an alley corner, a public weighing-machine stands like a severe confessor, for night and day, year after year, its mechanisms nag and prod the passer-by, with flashings and winkings and clicking noises, and out of its recesses there oscillates a placard with the searching challenge '*YA se pesó HOY?*' – as if to demand of every transient Christian if he has weighed his sins that day in the balance.

All around this famous centre-piece sprawls the City of the Kings, and though the rich Limenians have long moved out to the palatial suburbs, and a certain blight of tourism and neglect has settled upon the city centre, nevertheless it is still the crowded, antique streets around the Cathedral that set the character of Lima, and sustain its pungency. Sometimes they are spacious enough, sometimes they are so awkward that a tram with a list to port and a bus inclining starboard can pose insoluble problems of navigation: but whatever their design, they have a crooked flavour. This is a subtle sort of city, alive with quibbles, fancies, private jokes and nicknames – Avenida Nicolas de Pierola is the proper name of the street that runs across the Plaza San Martín, but for donkey's years everyone in Lima has called it *La Colmena*, The Beehive. It is a metropolis with an Eastern sense of the picaresque, and a crab-apple astringency.

Innumerable small churches, set in minute *piazuelas* among the hurly-burly, give to this part of the city an inescapable twinkle of surprise. Each has some curious marvel of its own: in one a miraculous image, in another the relic of some gentle saint, in a third the tomb of Don Ambrosio O'Higgins, Irishman, Marquis of Osorno, Captain-General of Chile and Grand Marshal of Peru. In the Church of San Agustín there stands a figure of Death, armed and skeletonic, so horrific that its own sculptor, chancing to enter the vestry one evening, is said to have died of fright when he saw it grinning at him through the shadows. On a wall of the Church of Las Nazarenas is the holy image called the Lord of the Miracles, found among the debris of an earthquake in 1687, and now the talisman of a fervent processional cult. In the cloisters of Santo Domingo the canaries of the monastic aviary nibble their corn-cob among the mosaics. Beneath the floor of San Francisco lie, in a musty labyrinth of catacombs, the tumbled skulls and skeletons of a thousand dead monks, tied together like asparagus in anatomical bundles, displayed in ornamental arrangements of ribs, or still seated in cowls and cassocks in rickety kitchen chairs. In the Sanctuary of Santa Rosa, the patron saint of the Americas, you may see the garden in which bloomed the first of all American rose-bushes, and the well into which the virgin threw the keys of the chains she had locked round her own waist (the garden is open to everyone once a year, but Santa Rosa's chapel may be visited only by the President of Peru himself). The Convent of La Merced was founded by Fray Miguel de Orens, 'an enthusiastic monk', so the guidebook says, 'who arrived in Peru at the age of 110'. The mosaics of San Francisco were made by a man who took refuge in those cloisters after committing a *crime passionnel*. Everywhere you trip over such details of piquancy, sometimes refulgent with sanctity, sometimes dark with intolerance, always rich in a kind of easy eccentricity, a liberty of style that sprang from a society very sure of itself, its privileges, its opportunities and its God.

Indolent individualism infuses, too, the old palaces of Lima, now mostly decayed into commercialism or crumbled into disuse. Sometimes news-stands or trinket stalls occupy their pompous portals, and their courtyards are stacked with bales of cloth or ironmongery, like Syrian caravanserais. Sometimes they have been divided among a dozen poor families, and are bursting with washing, animals and cheerful children, like the Tsarist town houses of Odessa. But usually they bear themselves like great mansions still, for all the erosions of time. Tall and gaunt are their peeling walls, austere but condescending their staircases, florid but melancholy their patios, wonderfully cool their *salons*, and high above the streets there still project, like harem peepholes above the traffic lights, the shuttered wooden balconies, the famous *miradors* of Lima, from which the ladies of the household used to spy upon the lusty world below.

The Peruvian Foreign Office occupies one such house, a former Prime Minister owns another, but the best-loved of them all is linked only with the name of a woman of fortune – La Perricholi, 'The Half-Caste Bitch', who turned the head of every Peruvian grandee as lesser ladies twist the handle of a corkscrew. It lies on the northern outskirts of the city, almost on the desert's edge, and it is supremely evocative of Lima's languorous heyday. Its gardens are soft and exotically scented, its bowers are deliciously secluded, its gazebos are delicately light-hearted, fresh little streams run through its flower-beds, and even the fact that it is now partly occupied by a school of military music, so that in any dainty summer-house you may find a trumpeter earnestly practising his fanfares, or a trombonist exercising his wrists – even the queer thumpings and *glissandi* of Peruvian Sousa cannot dispel its shades of old flirtation, or drown the ghostly rustle of its silks.

Most of all the essence of this old Lima is crystallized in Union Street, one of the great urban thoroughfares of the Americas, which strides lively but peremptory through the centre of the colonial city. This is a street of idiosyncrasies, with an air of tight self-sufficiency, like Bond Street in London fifty years ago, the sedater parts of the Kalverstraat in Amsterdam, or the once-glittering Sharia Sharif Pasha in Alexandria. Some of its shops have polished brass rails affixed to their façades, for the support of tottering window-shoppers, and they boast a baroque variety of names – Pinky, Oxford, Casa Persia, Le Chic Parisien, René, Grand Bon Marché de Lima, Sears, Roebuck of Chicago. One bookshop is frequented by a little tame ape, one cinema claims to be the only anonymous movie-house on earth – they removed its name during a renovation, and never bothered to put it back.

A wild range of Peruviana stares out from the shop-fronts of this street, from Inca jugs and aboriginal masks to stuffed llamas, vicuña wools, turkeys in beaten silver, alpaca slippers and decorative gourds. A splendid cross-section of Lima's citizenry saunters or staggers along its pavements: policemen in white tropical topees, looming quixotically through the pearly haze; stooped Indian women, in felt hats and tousled blouses, with babies shrouded upon their backs, and festoons of bags and bundles attached to their persons; newspaper-boys no bigger than monkeys themselves, and pavement vendors with poly-chromatic arrays of combs and toothbrushes laid out with infinite precision upon the sidewalk; flighty girls arm in arm, each with an ornamental hair-clip at the side of her head, as though she has inadvertently left a curler in; soldiers, too, in coarse high-buttoned tunics or elaborate gold braid, and bawling lottery-sellers, and nuns in huge white waving coifs, like the wings of early flying machines, and eager tourists disguised in ponchos, and beldames in black crossing themselves outside La Merced, and pomaded bigwigs bowing to each other with smiling formality, like old-school Japanese, outside the Aereo

Club, and many a poor blistered beggar, palms uppermost and eyes downcast, slinking from door to door or statuesque beside an intersection. Union Street is traditional Lima in microcosm. Its jumbled and fretted beguilement, tarnished by a tinsel commercialism, exactly expresses the rather faded, slightly seedy, elderly fund of style bequeathed to this metropolis by its fiery progenitors, and never quite exhausted.

They were men of greed, Pizarro and his men-at-arms, who made incalculable fortunes in Peru, and demanded as ransom from one poor Inca emperor enough gold to fill his cell of captivity from floor to ceiling. Lima remains an ostentatious city, instinct with ingots and goblets, with a gourmet's palate and a playboy's gaiety. Nowhere on the Pacific coast of the Americas, not even in San Francisco, can the rich man of taste enjoy himself more, feed himself better, house himself more luxuriously, surround himself with lovelier women or more exquisite possessions. Some of the finest private art collections on earth are locked away behind the garden walls and man-servants of Lima, and one or two of the city's clubs are reputed to be the most expensive in all South America.

A swathe of affluence rings the gnarled core of inner Lima. Away to the south spread the golden suburbs, flowered and air-conditioned, running away through olive groves and gardens to the heavenly Pacific shore, where the penguins meditate off-shore and the speedboats scud from one delight to another. Mellow but impeccable are these fortunate quarters, and mar-vellously rich in foliage – bougainvillaea spilling down its trellises, jasmines and jacaranda, yellow frangipani and flaming poinsettias, plumbago and hibiscus, and one mysterious shrub whose blossoms change colour as the sun goes down, the blue dying as the white unfolds its petals. This is the world of little black dresses and starched nursemaids, Chanel and country club, diffused in the misty sunshine elegantly, like the haughtier purlieus of Los Angeles. It has its racecourses and its night clubs, its golf courses and its polo field. It even has, tucked away improbably between the Avenida Antonio M. Quesada and the Avenida del Ejercito, its own imperturbable cricket club. Here the Ambassadors live, and the Peruvian millionaires. One house contains a collection of forty-five thousand pieces of ancient pottery, every single one dug up within the area of the owner's own country estate. Another houses the richest private assembly of arms in the world. A third is so excessively seignorial, so magnificent in porticoes, terraces and colonnades, that a simple Indian is said to have rung the doorbell one day and asked for a confessor, assuming it to be the Cathedral. These are suburbs in the grand manner, boudoirs and pleasure-houses for a City of Kings.

Sybaritic, too, are the pleasures this capital offers its visitors, high in new skyscraper eyries, or discreetly dim-lit among the courtyards and sculpted cherubs of old mansions. You may drink Pisco sour, most delicately biting of cocktails, made of Peruvian grape brandy, sugar syrup, lime, bitters and egg-white. You may eat succulent sea things out of the Humboldt Current, or noble meats from the *haciendas* of the interior, or fabulous rainbow trout from Titicaca, where they grow to thirty pounds in waters 12,500 feet above the sea, or spiced creole dishes out of the Peruvian past – beef chunks soused in vinegar and chili sauce, doughnuts made of yuccas, eggs and syrup of molasses. You may roister away the night hours at Ed's Bar, the Bagatelle, the Black Out or the Rancho. You may struggle with chopsticks and abalone in Chinatown, or dance till dawn beside the Pacific breakers. Lima is a city of luscious escapism, where the oil-men of the deserts come to wash it off and live it up, where the befurred, doll-like, neat-ankled women of the city eat gargantuan quantities of cream cakes among the potted palms of the Bolívar Hotel, and where many a rip-roaring adventurer, jumping ship at Callao or bumming down from California, can still throw his money away with carefree and uncensured extravagance.

It is not a very cultured city nowadays. Its theatre is vestigial, its newspapers are unremarkable, its poets, writers and thinkers not often distinguished. But it is a city that knows to a nicety how to please itself, a sensual city, a city where money counts and the window table nearly always has, so the waiter informs you with a sniff, already been reserved.

From all this fun and privilege, cruelty springs. Cruelty haunts this moneyed city, as it distorted the energies of the conquering gold-hunters, and makes the last taste of Lima acrid in the mouth. The best vantage point in the capital is the hill of San Cristobal, which rises steep and pyramidical within sight of the

Presidential Palace, covered with ash-like dust and crowned with a cross of pilgrimage (first placed there, as it happens, by Pizarro himself, in gratitude for the humiliating failure of an Indian revolt). From here you may survey the whole panorama of the City of the Kings, from the drab wilderness of its attendant deserts to the ineffable blue sheen of the Pacific. The pale prosperous suburbs lie in a splurge of gardens. The brave new office blocks tower above the business streets. Lima of the Viceroys lies there intricate and higgledy-piggledy, a meshwork of greys, browns and duns. It is a splendid prospect, a famous one, with the Andes behind you and the ocean horizon in front.

Look below your feet, though, over the crest of the hill, and there lies misery: for straggling up towards the summit, clinging to San Cristobal like some nightmare belvedere, squats a slum so bestial, so filthy, so congested, so empty of light, fun, colour, health or comfort, so littered with excrement and garbage, so swarming with barefoot children, so reeking with pitiful squalor that just the breath of it, borne on the fresh sea wind, makes you retch into your handkerchief. From these unspeakable hovels and rubbish-piles a stench of degradation rises: it veils the City of the Kings in a kind of haze, and it even eddies around Pizarro's cross of thanksgiving, high on the top of the hill. Lima is a pleasure-drome indeed, but only for the few. When once you have climbed San Cristobal, you will never quite enjoy its Pisco sours again.

For all around lie these dreadful slums, the notorious *barriaras* of Peru, in which 250,000 people live like gutter-creatures in the dirt, and they give to Lima the reproach of a guilty conscience. Wherever you go among its pleasures, the stink of the *barriaras* hangs over your shoulder, and already their presence intrudes uncomfortably, like the nagging insistence of the weighing-machine, into the equanimity of the city. Already the beggars shuffle through Union Street like scouts of Barbary, scarecrow mothers with pinched babies, shifty unshaven vagrants, an epileptic lop-sidedly staggering from door to door, a hunchback in the alley shadows. Already, when the comfortable citizens roll past this pitiable motley, on their way to clubs, fitting-rooms or mahogany desks, you may feel history rolling up its sleeves: and when the window of a car slides down, and some passing burgher tosses out a bank-note to the whimpering mendicants on the sidewalk – when such a man's limousine sweeps by, it does not need second sight to imagine tragedy crouching there in the back seat.

This is a city virtually without a middle class. There is almost nobody between the very rich and the cruelly poor. In Lima you can never forget that of every hundred baby Indians born alive in Peru, seventy die in infancy. There are few nice little, trim little houses in this city. You do not often hear the tidy hum of second-hand lawn-mowers on Sunday afternoons, or see the proudly polished family cars setting off for the seaside with pop and picnic baskets. This is, to a classic degree of symbolism, a revolutionary capital. It is run by a polished, cultivated oligarchy, but it is invested by the grievances of the poor. Injustice stalks its streets, and through its affairs runs constantly an undertone of apprehension, a shiver of expiring time. The ancient University of San Marcos, the oldest in the New World, is addled with the protests of young discontent, and the city is littered with the offices of the politicians, always plotting and arguing, always at each other's throats, with their strong-arm minions and their high-flown manifestos, their banners and their big drums. Lima is not essentially an energetic city – its attitudes are languid, easy-going, often a little foppish: but into its froward politics, fed by unfairness and debasement, many a burning passion is poured. You cannot ignore the selfishness and rising anger of Lima, or evade its ghastly desolations, just as, when you read with admiring wonder about Pizarro's rumbustious courage, you cannot skip the bigotry and arrogance that scarred his record with evil.

(And if you are a hedonist born, and think you can easily stomach it all, try revisiting the *barriara* of San Cristobal in the early evening: for then, in the mist of the Peruvian dusk, you may sometimes descry the shapes of small children and brown pigs, side by side, snuffling about together in the garbage.)

So Lima is not a happy city. 'Woe and desolation', says Prescott, were brought by Pizarro and his followers to the devoted land of the Incas: and even now the pleasures of his capital soon turn sour. You can blur the truth with alcohol, perhaps, drug yourself with bullfights and cloisters, swamp your sensibilities with seashore orgies or Titicaca trout. The most effective way to get the slum-taste off your tongue, though, if only for an afternoon, is to take a car to the archaeological museum, among the villas of San Isidro: for there you may retreat to the Peru that thrived before the Spaniards came, the dim legendary Peru of the Incas. You may marvel at the incomparable textiles of Cuzco, wonder at many a gorgeous mask and trinket, sense the unearthly majesty of the Sacsahuaman masonry, stumble dream-like through a menagerie of *huacos* – pots like llamas, pots like dragons, pots like old men, pots like spotted dogs, pots like fish, like cats, like skeletons, like pumas, like monkeys, like drooping but inscrutable owls.

Only there in that long-lost world, among the eerie Inca echoes, can you escape, till tea-time anyway, the sneer of Pizarro.

23

THE KNOW-HOW CITY

Los Angeles, 1976

❦

Los Angeles was a surprise to me when I went there in 1976. Though I had often visited the city, and written about it once or twice, I had never stayed so long before, and I found my responses greatly changed. Like most people, I had thought of it before as vulgar, un-beautiful and above all formless. Now I discovered it to be . . . well, read on if you please!

Los Angeles is the city of Know-How. Remember 'know-how'? It was one of the vogue words of the forties and fifties, now rather out of fashion. It reflected a whole climate and tone of American thought in the years of supreme American optimism. It stood for skill and experience indeed, but it also expressed the certainty that America's particular genius, the genius for applied logic, for systems, for devices, was inexorably the herald of progress. As the English had thought in the 1840s, so the Americans thought a century later. They held the future in their hands and brains, and this time it *would* work. Their methods and inventions would usher not only America herself but all mankind into another golden age. Know-how would be America's great gift to history: know-how to rescue the poor from their poverty, to snatch the coloured peoples from their ignominy, to convince the nations that the American way of free enterprise was the best and happiest way of all. Nothing was beyond know-how. Know-how was, if not actually the substance of God, at least a direct derivative.

One city in America, above all others, came to represent this enviable conviction. There has never been another town, and now there never will be, quite like El Pueblo de Nuestra Señora la Reina de Los Angeles de Porciúncula, Southern California,

where the lost American faith in machines and materialism
built its own astonishing monument.

Los Angeles, in the generic sense, was a long time coming. It
is not a young city. Spaniards were here before the United
States was founded, and I never get the feeling, as I wander
around LA's vast, amorphous mass, that it lies thinly on the
ground. It is not like Johannesburg, for instance, where almost
within living memory there was nothing whatsoever. Nor does
it feel transient or flimsy, like some of those towns of the Middle
West, which seem to have no foundations at all, but await the
next tornado to sweep them away in a tumble of matchwood. In
Los Angeles there are reminders of a long tradition. There is the
very name of the city, and of its euphonious streets and suburbs
– Alvarado, El Segundo, Pasadena, Cahuenga Boulevard. There
is the pattern of its real estate, still recognizably descended from
the Spanish and Mexican ranches of long ago. There is its exotic
taste in architecture, its patios and its deep eaves, its arcades, its
courtyards. There are even a few actual buildings, heavily
reconstructed but still authentic, which survive from the first
Spanish pueblo – swarmed over by tourists now, but fitfully
frequented too, I like to think, by the swaggering ghosts of their
original caballeros.

A sense of age informs the very setting of LA. From the air
the city looks like some enormously exaggerated pueblo itself:
flat, sprawling, rectilinearly intersected, dun coloured, built of
mud brick by some inconceivable race of primitives, and behind
it the tawny mountains run away in a particularly primeval way,
a lizardy, spiny way, their dry expanses relieved only by the
flicker of white on a snow-peak here and there, or the distant
glimmer of a lake. In a huge amphitheatre the city lies, accessible
only by passes through the surrounding ridges, rather like a
gigantic mining camp: and through the veil of its own artificial
mist, suggestively whirled about and blended with the California sunshine, it looks across its golden beaches toward the most
enigmatic of the oceans, the Pacific (never called the sea in Los
Angeles, always 'the ocean').

There is nothing Johnny-come-quick to this scene. Los Angeles is a complex merger of separate settlements, containing
within its scrambled presence eighty different municipalities,
and sprawling district by district, decade by decade, over its

central plain and into its foothills. The witty Mr David Clark, when he named his book *L.A. on Foot: A Free Afternoon*, was ironically emphasizing the amoebic immensity of the place, territorially among the largest urban settlements in the world, and psychologically one of the most involved. Though I would guess that nine tenths of its buildings were erected in the twentieth century, still Los Angeles is, like some incurable disease, a balefully organic phenomenon. Its streets are forever nibbling and probing further into its perimeter hills, twisting like rising water ever higher, ever deeper into their canyons, and sometimes bursting through to the deserts beyond. If the city could be pried out of its setting, one feels, it would be like a dried mat of some bacterial mould, every bump, every corner exactly shaped to its landscape.

This is partly because the landscape itself is so individual, so that unlike Chicago, say, or Paris, Los Angeles is inconceivable anywhere else. But it is also, I think, because this city genuinely springs out of its own soil, possesses a true *genius loci* and forms a kind of irreplaceable flashpoint: the point on the map where the intellectual, the physical and the historical forces of American history met to produce – well, combustion, what else? Whatever happens to LA, it will always be the city of the automobile and the radio, showbiz and the Brown Derby restaurant, the city where the American ideal of happiness by technique found its folk art in the ebullience of Hollywood. It is essentially of the forties and the fifties, and especially perhaps of the Second World War years, when the American conviction acquired the force of a crusade, and sent its jeeps, its technicians and its Betty Grables almost as sacred pledges across the world. Los Angeles then was everyone's vision of the New World: and so it must always remain, however it develops, a memorial to those particular times, as Florence means for everyone the spirit of Renaissance, and Vienna speaks always of *fin de siècle*.

Across the car park from the remains of the original Spanish pueblo, where the Mexican souvenir shops now huddle profitably along Olvera Street, there stands Union Station. This was the last great railway depot to be built in the United States, completed in 1939, and one of the most handsome. Cool, tall, elegant, and nowadays restfully unfrequented by trains, it has patios green with flowers and trees, shaded colonial-style arcades, and is rather the sort of railway station a multibillionaire might devise, if he wanted one at the bottom of the garden. In this it is very proper, for while paying graceful respect to LA's origins and pretensions, it honours too the first and fundamental quality of this city: organized, stylized movement.

It was not liberty that Los Angeles cherished in its prime, or at least not absolute liberty. A spiritual culture can be anarchical, a material culture must be disciplined. Implicit to the promise of technological fulfilment was the necessity of *system*, and LA soon became a firmly ordered place. The original Los Angeles public transport system, the electric trains and streetcars of the early twentieth century, drew together the scattered settlements of the time, bringing them all into cityness.

When the car arrived the mesh was tightened, and LA built its incomparable freeways. These remain the city's grandest and most exciting artefacts. Snaky, sinuous, undulating, high on stilts or sunk in cuttings, they are like so many concrete tentacles, winding themselves around each block, each district, burrowing, evading, clambering, clasping every corner of the metropolis as if they are squeezing it all together to make the parts stick. They are inescapable, not just visually, but emotionally. They are always there, generally a few blocks away; they enter everyone's lives, and seem to dominate all arrangements.

To most strangers they suggest chaos, or at least purgatory, and there can certainly be more soothing notices than the one on the Santa Ana Freeway which announces 'MERGING BUSES AHEAD'. There comes a moment, though, when something clicks in one's own mechanism, and suddenly one grasps the rhythm of the freeway system, masters its tribal or ritual forms, and discovers it to be not a disruptive element at all, but a kind of computer key to the use of Los Angeles. One is processed by the freeways. Elevated as they generally are above the flat and centreless expanse of the city, they provide a navigational aid, into which one locks oneself for guidance. Everything is clearer then. There are the mountains, to the north and east. There is the glimmering ocean. The civic landmarks of LA, such as they are, display themselves conveniently for you, the pattern of the place unfolds until, properly briefed by the experience, the time comes for you to unlock from the system, undo your safety belt, and take the right-hand lane into the everyday life below.

The moment this first happened to me, Los Angeles happened

too, and I glimpsed the real meaning of the city, and realized how firmly it had been disciplined by the rules of its own conviction.

Confusing, nevertheless, the Santa Ana with the San Diego Freeway, missing the exit at Bristol, mistaking Newport Avenue for Newport Boulevard, getting in the wrong lane at Victoria, miscounting the traffic lights on 22nd Street, an hour late exactly I arrived for lunch with the world's greatest authority on European naval history in the early twentieth century.

Through apparent chaos to unmistakable authority. This was a not uncharacteristic Los Angeles experience. Expertise is the stock in trade of this metropolis, and behind the flash and the braggadocio, solid skills and scholarship prosper. There are craftsmen everywhere in L A, craftsmen in electronics, in film-making, in literature, in social science, in advertising, in fashion. They say that in San Francisco there is less than meets the eye: in Los Angeles there is far more, for the reputation of the place makes no allowance for this corporate diligence and dexterity. Here Lockheed makes its aircraft. Here NASA makes its space shuttle orbiter. Here is UCLA, one of the most fertile universities in the Western world. Here the McCulloch Corporation has patented a device to pop the golf ball *out* of the hole, to save its owner stooping. This is no place for dilettantes. Even sport is assiduously, sometimes grimly, pursued: the tennis players of Beverly Hills joylessly strain towards perfection, the Malibu surfers seldom lark about, but take their pleasures with a showy dedication.

I went one morning to Burbank Studios to see them filming Neil Simon's macabre comedy, *Murder by Death*. This is one of those movies in which everyone is a star, and the set was cluttered with familiar figures. There was Truman Capote, described in the studio publicity as 'acclaimed author and international celebrity', huddled with a young friend in a corner and wearing a wide-brimmed hat. There was Peter Falk, charmingly chatting with Elsa Lanchester. Alec Guinness looked truly gentlemanly, David Niven looked almost too elegant. Ray Stark the producer looked preternaturally successful, Robert Moore the director looked alarmingly gifted.

I am antipathetic to the famous, though, and I found that my eyes kept straying from these luminaries to the two sound technicians who, just off the set, sat nonchalantly over their equipment wearing headsets and reading the trade papers. One was called Jerry Jost, the other Bill Manooth, and they had both been in the business twenty years and more. How calm they looked, I thought, how sure of themselves, how easily aware of the fact that nobody in the whole world could do their job better than they could! They had seen the stars come and go, they had helped to make flops and winners, they had suffered every temperament, they had seen the film industry itself in boom and decline. Sometimes they looked up to exchange a pleasantry with a passer-by, sometimes they turned a page of the *Hollywood Reporter*: but they were always alert when the moment came, always watching their quivering instruments, always ready to mouth the magic word 'Speed!' – which, with its assurance that they had got things right, gave the signal to that whole assembly, director, cameraman, actors, Capote and all, to proceed with their flamboyances.

For somewhere near the heart of the LA ethos there lies, unexpectedly, a layer of solid, old-fashioned, plain hard work. This is a city of hard workers. Out on the hills at Santa Monica, overlooking the Pacific Ocean, the writer Christopher Isherwood and the painter Don Bachardy share a house, sunlit and easygoing, with a view over the rooftops and shrubberies of the canyon. In such a place, with such occupants, in such warm and soothing sun, with the beach down the road and Hollywood up the freeway, it might seem a house for cultivated indolence, interminable wit around a swimming pool, long cool drinks with worldly neighbours before lunch. Not at all. 'We are *working* people,' Isherwood says, and so they literally are: each at his own end of the house, each with his art, the one surrounded by his books, the other by his brushes and pictures, carefully and skilfully they work through the day, friends and fellow labourers.

I very much like all this. It suggests to me, unexpectedly, the guild spirit of some medieval town, where the workers in iron or lace, the clockmakers and the armourers, competed to give their city the glory of their trades. All the mechanisms of Los Angeles are like apprentices to these matters: the robot lights and the TV cameras, the scudding helicopters, the labouring oil pumps bowed like slaves across the city, or the great telescopes of Mount Wilson, brooding among their conifers high above the city, which in the years before the Second World War more than doubled man's total knowledge of the physical universe.

It is true that this expertise is sometimes rather dated, but then LA is essentially a survivor of earlier times, and one is constantly plucked back to that simpler world of the forties, when values were surer than they are now, and the attainment of wealth or fame seemed the true gauge of contentment.

One citizen who honours those values still, in life as in principle, is Ed Davis, the celebrated police chief of Los Angeles. He is an inescapable figure there. I doubt if there is another police chief in the world better known among his citizenry. Powerful, controversial, dogmatic, his name entered almost every conversation I had about the city, and aroused powerful reactions everywhere. He was a pseudofascist reactionary. He was a great police chief. He was bigoted, unbalanced, hysterical. He was a staunch upholder of right and decency. He was a brute. He was a father figure. He ought to be shot. He ought to be President.

So I arranged to meet him, and arriving one sunny morning at police headquarters, familiar to everybody in Western civilization from a thousand prime times on TV – arriving in those hallowed halls, trodden before me by Sergeant Friday – arriving there reverent and docile ('Say,' they told me, 'there was a cop here from England only the other day – he was *dazzled* by the level of crime we have here') – dazzled then, by the historic ambience, I proceeded to the *piano nòbile*, where Davis was attended by his faithful middle-aged secretary Helen and by sundry lesser acolytes.

He was on the whole the most impressive man I met in LA, but impressive in a faintly forlorn way. It is not that he really believes, as he once claimed, that hijackers should be publicly hanged at LA airport, or that he really harbours malice when he speaks of 'raving faggots' or inveighs against illegitimate massage parlours: what dates him, and gives him a paradoxical poignancy, is his apparent belief that Order can somehow *cure* society's ills. He talked to me of crime in intellectual terms – 'situation ethics', 'symbionic relationships', 'the new morality', and he argued that even victimless crimes are like cancers on the body public: but he is really animated, I think, by an old-school, traditional faith in the redemptive power of discipline.

He is a man of unchallenged technique, but like the technique of the automobile which has made LA what it is, it is the technique of an older America. It is not yet discredited – Ed Davis really has kept organized crime to a minimum in his city – but it is distinctly outmoded.

I thought him, for all his force and brilliance, rather a nostalgic figure, pining for the days of faith and family: and nostalgia too blurs the realities of Hollywood, the Versailles of Los Angeles, and peoples it forever with the royalty of another era, the Astaires, the Tracys, the Garbos, and nobles of even earlier vintage. Now as always the tourist buses circumnavigate the homes of the Stars, and the touts peddle their street plans on Sunset Strip. Now as always Hollywood feeds upon narcissism, cosseted in sycophancy and sustained by snobbery. Scattered over the Hollywood Hills, and over the Santa Monica Mountains into the San Fernando Valley, the houses of the movie people stand sealed and suspicious in the morning, the only sounds the swishing of their sprinkers, the snarling of their guard dogs, or perhaps the laboured breathing of their gardeners: and in their garages the cars are profligately stacked, Jag beside Merc, Rolls upstaging BMW. Hollywood prefers its own world to ours, loving and living, generation after generation, its own fairly tawdry legend.

I stayed in the middle of it all, and soon came to feel how period a piece it was. My hotel was the Chateau Marmont, a monument in itself, built in the French manner half a century ago, and directly overlooking Sunset Boulevard. Everyone in Hollywood knows the place. That's where Bogart proposed to Bacall, they say, that's where Garbo used to stay, Howard Hughes had a suite there, Boris Karloff loved it, Valentino preferred the penthouse. It is impregnated with showbiz, from the gigantic antiques in the downstairs lounge to the strains of the electronic organ from the pop group practising in the garden bungalow: but what seems to the aficionado amusingly evocative seemed to me only a little threadbare, the ghostly thread of stars did not make up for the lack of a dial telephone, and I often found myself pining for an honest downtown motel, where never a Gable raised his eyebrow, or a Garland threw a tantrum.

Every morning, too, I walked across the boulevard to have my breakfast at Schwab's, 'The World's Most Famous Drugstore'. Everyone knows Schwab's, too. Schwab's is where Lana Turner was discovered, sitting on a barstool. Hardly a Hollywood memoir is complete without a reference to Schwab's, and it is heavy with the old mystique. Elderly widows of émigré directors reminisce about Prague over their cornflakes. Young men in jerkins and expensive shoes ostentatiously read *Variety*, or greet each other with stagey endearments and expletives. Ever and again one hears across the hubbub, in the whining intonations peculiar to not very successful actors offstage, an exchange of critiques – 'I love her, she's a fine, fine actress, but it just wasn't *her*' – 'Well, but what can you expect with Philip directing, she needs *definite* direction' – 'True, but shit, it just made me *puke*, the way she did that last scene . . .' Nearly everyone seems to know nearly everyone else at Schwab's: I used to drink my coffee at the counter, until I found this instinct for intimacy too cloying for comfort, and took to sitting at a table with the divorced wife of a Mexican set designer who shared my enthusiasm for Abyssinian cats.

If fetish and nostalgia often make for vulgarity in LA, they often make also for homeliness, in the English sense of the word – a community feeling, a domesticity. Even Hollywood is far less repulsive in its private aspects than in its public goings-on. This is largely because Los Angeles is a haven, to whose doors people have come from all over the world. It is a fraternity of refugees. Isherwood, showing me the view from his window one day, remembered the days when Stravinsky, Schönberg, Brecht and Aldous Huxley had all lived in the city out there. Hardly a day goes by without the death of some celebrated European resident, driven here long ago by war, ambition or persecution, and the British consul general told me that within his area there live more than 50,000 British subjects, some of whom fly Union Jacks from their roofs. San Francisco, up the coast, has an intimacy of a totally different kind, a hereditary or environmental closeness, bound up with the beauty of the place and the allure of its traditions. There is no such grace to the brotherhood of LA. This is a charmless city really, humourless, often reactionary, a city without a gentry. Its comradeship lies only in a common sense of release or opportunity, tinged with a spice of holiday.

I used to buy my bread at Farmer's Market, a rambling enclave of stalls and tables off Wilshire Boulevard, and sitting over an orange juice afterwards, nibbling bits off the end of my loaf, loved to watch the Angelenos go by. Often, of course, they were not Angelenos at all, but Japanese businessmen being shown around by bored local agents, or package tourists in wild sunglasses and kerchiefs, or bookish Europeans from UCLA deep in *Sociological Ratios in Southern California*. But there were always plenty of indigenes too, and they were instantly recognizable, not so much by their looks as by their posture, for they displayed all the somewhat impatient complacency of people who have discovered a Promised Land, and don't want to miss a minute of it. Though there are obviously lots of unhappy people in LA, lots of dispossessed blacks, unemployed layabouts, junkies and nuts and winos and miscellaneous *bêtes noires* of Mr Davis's department, still by and large this strikes me as a happy population – determinedly happy, perhaps. Nobody I met wanted to go back to New York or Detroit. With its Middle West squareness, its Manhattan bitterness, its imported touch of the European and its glorious Pacific sun, LA seems to please most people in the end – or for the moment.

In particular it provides a cheerful refuge for the jollier kind of American widow or divorcée, and many of these belatedly liberated souls frequent Farmer's Market. I often talked to them. There was a certain sameness to their appearance: in their bright blouses, leather jerkins, rather too tight slacks and rather too rakish sailor caps, bowed often by arthritis but resolutely vigorous of step, most of them looked more or less like Mr Capote except, of course, for the layered make-up ineffectually disguising their cod-skin complexions. To their attitudes though there was a sprightly element of freedom. Briskly, gaily, talkatively they walked around the stalls, a pumpernickel loaf here, a bag of cashews there, and often they exchanged rather throaty comments with acquaintances about last night's movie or tomorrow's meetings of the Democratic Party.

For such citizens LA offers an unexpected security, for its hard efficiency provides a bedrock, so to speak, upon which they can safely reconstruct their lives. It is nourished by the certainties they were weaned upon, like the pre-eminence of gadgetry or the goodness of capitalism. For all its cosmopolitan excitement, to a far greater degree than Chicago or San Francisco, let alone New York, it is still a provincial American town. 'Did you know,' one Farmer's Market lady asked me, supposing me, I imagine, to be a bit lost for social satisfactions, 'did you know that the telephone company offers a free tour every day? My, that's a rewarding way of spending an afternoon!'

More exotic refugees share an intenser camaraderie. Members of the alternative society, for instance, seem to live rather in phalanx, perhaps because Mr Davis sees no moral necessity for them. Southern California indeed has a long tradition of religious tolerance, sprouting cults, sects and rites like vivid fungi, and LA itself welcomes eccentrics if they are rich and famous enough. Your honest dropout, though, your simple hash man, often finds the atmosphere inhospitable, and among the more poignant corners of the metropolis is Venice, a struggling enclave of unorthodoxy on the ocean of Santa Monica. It is a forlorn kind of suburb anyway, for it is the remains of a *fin-de-siècle* attempt to recreate the original Venice, 'Venice, Italy', upon the Pacific coast. A few Renaissance arcades remain, a Ruskinian window here and there, and there is a hangdog system of canals which, with their low-built bridges, their loitering ducks, their dog-messed paths, their smells of silt and dust and their air of stagnant hush, really do contrive to preserve a truly Venetian suggestion of decay. Here we seem to see a philosophy with its back to the wall. It is like a caricature of itself, squeezed into this ocean beachhead by the colossal pressures of Los Angeles, and the society that frequents the place, too, suggests to me a culture on the verge of dissolution.

On the other hand, aliens in the older sense, foreigners that is, stand amazed still at the munificence of LA. In some immigrant cities – in Toronto, for example, perhaps the archetypal melting pot of our time – your newcomer from Turkey or Sweden generally views his new home cynically, simply as a place to make money. I do not get this feeling with LA's immigrants. They seem to see it still as a place of hope and blessing. I went one night to one of those Hollywood parades one used to see on newsreels long ago. Nothing much had changed. The long motorcade crawled down Hollywood Boulevard in a welter of self-esteem, with drum majorettes and elephants and Scottish pipers and US Marines and belly-dancers and coveys of movie personalities in antique cars who stopped now and then to be interviewed by TV men – 'Hey Bob, great to see you! How's everything? Isn't this a great parade?' 'Sure is, Jim, fantastic, just great, and I wantya to meet my family, Jim,

my wife Margie, this is my son Jason, my daughter Laureen!'
'Great, fantastic, great to meet all you folks, nice talking with
you, Bill.' 'Sure thing, Jim, sure is a great parade, fantastic . . .'
The echoes of the bands trumpeted across town, the belly-
dancers spangled their way past Grauman's Chinese Theater,
and overhead the helicopters clanked and circled, playing their
searchlights upon the junketings below.

I was touched by the crowd that watched this display, for I
felt in it a truly innocent wonder. Its people came from
everywhere. There were a few of my Market friends ('I forgot to
mention this morning, dear, that the Municipal Cleansing
Department offers a very interesting lecture tour Tuesday
mornings'); but there were Mexicans, too, in bright ponchos
with babies on their backs, and lots of Italians, and Hindus
talking impeccable English, and Greeks talking Greek, and there
was a Scotsman in a kilt looking maudlin when the pipers went
by, and a man who looked like a Zulu chief, and a voluble family
who seemed to be talking Finnish, or perhaps Basque, and there
were thousands of that particular new-American blend, of no
particular colour, no specific race, no exact dialect, the *Homo
californii*; and though the cops strode up and down fiercely
slapping their nightsticks against their thighs, still everybody
seemed genuinely, guilelessly delighted to be participants in
such an unmistakable Angeleno spectacle.

I stayed till the very end, and the last I saw of the parade were
the winking red lights of the police cars which brought up the
rear, blinking away slowly down the boulevard as the crowds
flooded off the sidewalks to follow them.

Much of LA's expertise is devoted to such display. The
Goodyear dirigible loiters effortlessly over town. The freeways
often seem to me to be as much showmanship as engineering.
Sunset Strip, 'The Billboard Center of the Western World', is
one and a half miles of unremitting posters, seventy-eight when
I was there in the sixteen blocks between Crescent Heights and
Doheny Drive: every day most of them seem to be changed, as
one might replenish the drawing-room flowers, and marvellous
is the professionalism by which the billboard men, with their
slender cranes and their hefty trucks, bisect the torsos of rock
singers, demolish romantic countrysides, split rodomontades or
separate superlatives to hoist those tremendous announcements

down in their several sections and trundle them away to oblivion
or Las Vegas.

Yet Hollywood itself, its fact and its reputation, its studios
and its publicity machine, is a family of sorts, not always very
loving indeed, and frequently incestuous, but still bound by a
common loyalty to its own legend. Its members often speak of
it with true affection, especially if they are old. As the glamour
of success fades, as the meaning of money blurs, so Hollywood
memories acquire a mellower force, and elderly directors,
dowager stars, speak of old Hollywood as others might remember happy schooldays, or Edwardian society. Age is paradoxically venerated in Hollywood, and one is told without pejoration
that So-and-So is living in a home for aged actors, or assured
with respect that Miss Estelle Winwood really *is* in her ninety-
third year. The new breed of entertainer often seems awkwardly
anomalous, almost alienated, in this hierarchical community:
which is why the Hyatt hotel on Sunset Boulevard, where the
rock bravos tend to congregate, was long ago nicknamed the
Continental Riot House.

Sometimes the camaraderie is oddly attractive. I went one
day to a taping of the *Carol Burnett Show*, itself approaching
institutional status after so many years on the screen, and found
it an endearingly domestic occasion. Miss Burnett the star was
married to Mr Hamilton the executive producer, Miss Lawrence
the *ingénue* brought her baby along. Everyone had known
everyone else for years, and easily broke into a sort of family
badinage: so that when somebody playfully pretended to sock
somebody else on the jaw, even the sound effects man, somewhere out of sight, instantly contributed an impromptu *thunk*.
Though it is currently the longest running show on television,
and one of the most consistently successful, it suggested to me
a rehearsal for some unusually polished but still folksy high-
school show, so that when Miss Burnett happened to tell me
that she was dining that evening with Sir Alec Guinness and
Lord Olivier, I felt like saying 'Lawsy me, Carol, lucky old
you . . .'

At other times the bond can be sickly, or comic, or a bit
morbid, or even creepy. I went to a Democratic Party meeting in
Beverly Hills which reminded me almost eerily, in its sense of
inbred continuity, of the McCarthy era in Hollywood twenty
years ago. There were the very same writers and directors, I

swear, whom we used to see pale before the inquisitor's gaze; and there were their dauntless, loyal wives, no longer in dirndls and home-weave blouses indeed, but suitably beaded and denimed instead; and there was the same curl of pipe smoke in the air, with the same progressive smiles, and the same ladies went around getting signatures on petitions or propagating similar liberal causes – 'Can we persuade you to support the Council for Universal Rights?' – 'May I ask you to sign this petition on behalf of the Coalition for Handgun Control?' – 'You do *know* about CDC, don't you, *so* important we feel' – until the chairman called for silence, and there stepped handsomely to the rostrum, just as he might have braved Senator McCarthy's furies long ago, a young crusader of today's Los Angeles joustings whose name I momentarily forget.

The Los Angeles ethos is intensely infectious, and transmutes everything it touches. It can be great fun. The J. Paul Getty Museum of Art, for instance, which is housed in a dazzling re-creation of a Roman villa above the sea at Malibu, often excites the scorn of critics and connoisseurs, but delights people of more urbane taste. The Rolls-Royce motorcar, elsewhere in the world a symbol of dignity and reserve, becomes in Los Angeles, where it probably proliferates more than anywhere else, a young person's runabout, to swish up the drive to the Beverly Hills Hotel, or weave around the staid Cadillacs on the Palisades. Even the Californian cultists are easily Los Angelized, when they venture from their communes and mountain churches into the purlieus of the great city. The flaming sign on the Santa Ana Freeway announcing the Amazing Prophecy Center does not look in the least out of place, and I was not at all surprised to learn that America's largest incense factory, Spiritual Sky Scented Products Inc., was the property of the Hare Krishna community (acronymically ISKCON – International Society for Krishna Consciousness).

I visited the factory, as a matter of fact, to see just how easily the mantra and the head-knot would adapt to LA's style of capitalism, and found that fusion had easily been achieved. The lady at the reception desk was dressed in full Indianified costume, and the company memo pads ended their list of practical alternatives (Take Action/See Me/Call Me/File) with the hardly less clear-cut spiritual injunction, clean across the bottom of the page in vaguely Oriental lettering, 'HARE KRISHNA, HARE KRISHNA, KRISHNA, KRISHNA, HARE, HARE/HARE RAMA, HARE RAMA, RAMA, RAMA, HARE, HARE'. The plant manager was dressed more or less for Rotary, and told me that the Spiritual Sky line emphasized the incense America wants and loves – strawberry flavour especially: but when I pressed him on more spiritual matters, in no time at all he had pushed the *Wall Street Journal* aside and was enthusiastically explaining to me the principles of his Divine Master – rather wistfully, I thought, as though the management of Spiritual Sky was in the nature of a penance.

Just as often, though, the LA treatment only coarsens and degrades. It was no coincidence that so many of the Watergate acolytes were alumni of Los Angeles advertising agencies: the aerosol charm of John Dean, for instance, who entertained me most kindly to Dr Peppers in his Laurel Canyon hideaway, blends very easily into the ambience, and I suspect that Mr Nixon himself, if ever he turned up in Farmer's Market, would be ecstatically welcomed. 'Smartness', in the opportunist sense, the importance of image, the search for celebrity whatever its cause – all these are true LA characteristics, and are contagious. Many vegetarian restaurants, I am told, opening to a regular sacrament of organic ideals, soon degenerate into convenience foods, and even death of course becomes a packaged product up at Forest Lawn, where the Wee Kirk o' the Heather offers consolation in Time of Sorrow, and Companion Lawn Crypts provide the ultimate security of Reinforced Concrete. The TV game shows of Hollywood have evolved an entire language and ritual of falseness, from the stylized jumpings, handclappings and mock-bashfulness of the competitors to the palatial languor of the ravaged showgirls who act as ladies of the prize chamber.

For myself, I am left with an uneasy feeling even about Disneyland, where the most advanced technical resources, the most brilliant administrative systems, are used simply to animate a gigantic charade. The sham treads uncomfortably upon the heels of truth, and one begins to wonder whether a dummy castle from Snow White, a make-believe New Orleans restaurant, even a non-alcoholic mint julep, might not be as good, and as true, as the real thing. I found this inescapable illusion rather suffocating, and was revived, as I staggered from the King Arthur Carousel to the Casey Jr. Circus Train, through

Tomorrowland to the Bear Country, only by the presence of the peripatetic bands, blues, brass or Mexican, who really were undeniably alive and irreplaceable by electronics even in LA.

Saddest of all, for a visitor from over the water, is the spectacle of the liner *Queen Mary*, perhaps the most celebrated of all ocean steamships, which lies in the harbour of Long Beach in a condition of induced elation, as though she has been pumped full of stimulants. She has had the LA treatment with a vengeance. Her innards ripped out, her funnels replaced, part of her turned into a hotel, part into a museum, jazzed up, repainted, publicized, projected, she cost almost twice as much to turn into a tourist centre as she cost to build as a ship, and has been losing money ever since. Would it not have been easier, the municipality is sometimes asked, to build a new one? It would, they gravely reply, but then it would have lacked *curiosity quotient*.

Curiosity quotient! It is arguably better than scrapping her, I suppose, but still I thought the experience of the *Queen Mary* infinitely depressing. How silly, the mock-nautical uniforms! How pitiful the spectacle of that lifeless bridge! How drear, the prospect of nuptials in the Wedding Chapel (*Promenade Deck: Wedding Coordinators and Ordained Minister*)! This was the pride of the Clyde when I was a child, this was the ship which, speeding through the wolf packs in the grey Atlantic, safely took half a million Americans to the liberation of Europe! Now she lies there tarted up and phony, the victim of a culture which, in the intoxicating mastery of its know-how, so often uses it ignobly.

And, unexpectedly, when I examine my feelings about this tremendous and always astonishing city, I find them inextricably shot through with regret. This is not, I think, a usual reaction to Los Angeles, and I am moved to it partly because I come from a temporarily discomfited civilization myself – 'worrying the carcass of an old song', as the poet R. S. Thomas described us Welsh, 'gnawing the bones of a dead culture'.

Nobody driving down Wilshire Boulevard, say, or watching the surfers spring into the Pacific, could call the culture of LA dead. It is full of vitality still, full of fun and wealth. The refugees are still flocking to this haven beyond the deserts, the men of brilliance are still at work in labs and laboratories and studios from Malibu to Irvine. Almost every development of Western thought, from space research to comparative linguistics to Transcendental Lung Control, finds its niche, its expression and its encouragement somewhere in this metropolis. Surveyed in the morning from one of its mountain belvederes, Los Angeles really does look one of the classic cities, one of the archetypes. Its streets and houses and bridges and buildings seem to lie there *differently*, massed differently, differently integrated, sprouting here and there peculiarly with the clumps of their urban centres, and hung over already, as the sun rises over the deserts, with the particular chemical haze whose very name, smog, was a Los Angeles invention. Then it looks unmistakably a world city: and it will represent for ever, I think, the apogee of urban, mechanical, scientific man, rational man perhaps, before the gods returned.

For it is past its prime already. It has lost the exuberant certainty that made it seem, even when I first knew it, unarguably the City of the Future, the City That Knew How. None of us Know now. The machine has lost its promise of emancipation, and if L A then seemed a talisman of fulfilment, now it is tinged with disillusion. Those terrific roads, those thousands of cars, the sheen of the jets screaming out of the airport, the magnificent efficiency of it all, the image building, the self-projection, the glamour, the fame – they were all false promises after all, and few of us see them now as the symptoms of redemption.

There is one monument in L A which hauntingly commemorates this failing faith. It is the queer cluster of pinnacles called the Watts Towers, and it stands in one of the shabbier parts of town, way out on 107th Street, beside the railway tracks. Simon Rodia, an Italian immigrant, built these arcane artefacts single-handedly, taking more than thirty years to do it. He made them of cement, stuck all over with bits of glass and pottery, strengthened by frames of scrap metal and wound about with curious studded spirals, rather like precipitous roller coasters. When he had built them he surrounded them with an irregular cement wall, like a row of tombstones, so that the whole ensemble has the air of a temple or shrine, rather Oriental in nature.

It is very dusty there, and all around are the unpretentious homes of black people, so that you might easily suppose yourself to be in some African railway town, in the Egyptian delta

perhaps. Few cars go by. You can hear children playing, and
dogs barking, and neighbours chatting across the way. It is like
a simple country place, before technology arrived: and just as
the Watts riots of the sixties were a protest against the failure of
technique to give contentment to poor people, so the Watts
Towers, years before their time, were a symbolic *cri du coeur*
against the computer tyrannies to come.

Mr Rodia was a prophet: and when he had built his towers he
slipped away from Los Angeles once and for all, and went to
live somewhere quite different.

24

THE ISLANDERS

Manhattan, 1979

Manhattan is always different but always the same — shifting from day to day in fashion, trend or bigotry, constant in the fascination and excitement of its presence. When I went to New York in 1979 to write this essay I had been there every year for twenty-five years — it was my Silver Jubilee of Manhattan: but I found it fresh and fathomless as ever, and went home to Wales, as usual, in a condition of slightly intoxicated, and perceptibly sentimental, enthralment.

Sometimes, from high office windows in Manhattan, you can make out a faint white blob in the green of Central Park far below. It is like the unresolved blur of a nebula in the night sky: and just as through a telescope the fuzz in Andromeda resolves itself into M31, so that whitish object in the park, defined through binoculars, becomes a phenomenon hardly less spectacular. It is the polar bear in the Central Park Zoo, and even as you focus your lenses, bringing his indistinct physique into clarity, with a shaggy shake of his head he swings his great form vigorously from one extremity of his cage to the other. The bear lives alone in his compound down there, and I am told that he is a character of weird and forceful originality – sadly neurotic, some informants suggested, genuinely imaginative, others thought. He is a bear like no other, and it is not the fact of his captivity that makes him so, I am sure, but its remarkable location. Destiny has deposited that animal plumb in the middle of Manhattan: you might say he is the central New Yorker. He affects me profoundly, whenever I see him, and when I put my binoculars down, and only the suggestion of him remains, apparently inanimate among the trees, all around him in my mind's eye the marvellous and terrible island of Manhattan concentrically extends, ring after ring of cage, ditch or rampart, precinct limit and electoral boundary, Hudson, East River and Atlantic itself – the greatest of all the zoos, whose inhabitants prowl up and down, like victims of some terrific spell, for ever and ever within it.

For Manhattan really is an island, even now, separated from the mainland still by a channel just wide enough for the Circle Line boats to continue their pleasure circuits, and it is this condition of enclave that gives the place its sting. Like the bear, its citizens are heightened, one way or another, by their confinement. If they are unhappier than most populaces, they are merrier too. If they are trapped in some ways, they are brilliantly liberated in others. Sometimes their endless pacing to and fro is sad to see, but when the weather is right and the sap is rising, then it assumes an exhilarating rhythm, and the people of Manhattan seem to dance along their avenues, round and round the city squares, in and out the sepulchral subway.

Images of confinement certainly haunt me in Manhattan, but the first thing that always strikes me, when I land once more on the island, is its fearful and mysterious beauty. Other cities have built higher now, or sprawl more boisterously over their landscapes, but there is still nothing like the looming thicket of the Manhattan skyscrapers, jumbled and overbearing. Le Corbusier hated this ill-disciplined spectacle, and conceived his own Radiant City, an antiseptic hybrid of art and ideology, in direct antithesis to it. His ideas, though, mostly bounced off this vast mass of vanity. Tempered though it has been from time to time by zoning law and social trend, Manhattan remains a mammoth mess, a stupendous clashing of light and dark and illusory perspective, splotched here and there by wastelands of slum or demolition, wanly patterned by the grid of its street system, but essentially, whatever the improvers do to it, whatever economy decrees or architectural fashion advises, the supreme monument to that elemental human instinct, Free-For-All.

But the glowering ecstasy of it! No other city, not even Venice, projects for me a more orgasmic kind of allure. I do not mean the popular phallic symbolism of the place, its charged erections thrusting always into the sky. I am thinking of more veiled seductions, the shadows in its deep streets, the watchfulness, the ever-present hint of concealment or allusion. The clarity of

Manhattan is what the picture postcards emphasize, but I prefer Manhattan hazed, Manhattan reticent and heavy-eyed.

I like it, for instance, on a very, very hot day, a day when emerging into the streets from the air conditioning is like changing continents. Then a film of chemical vapour seems to drift around the city, fudging every edge, gauzing every vista. Exhausted, half-deserted, the island seems to stand stupefied in the haze: but sometimes flashes of sunlight, piercing the humidity, are reflected momentarily off windows or metal roofs, and then I am reminded of those uncertain but resplendent cities, vaporous but diamond-twinkling, which stand in the backgrounds of all the best fairy tales.

Conversely on a grey lowering day it is like some darkling forest. The tops of the buildings are lost in fog, and only their massive bases, like the trunks of so many gigantic oaks, are to be seen beneath the cloud base. I feel a mushroom feeling in Manhattan then, and the huddled scurry of the people on the sidewalks, the shifting patterns of their umbrellas, the swish of cars through pothole puddles, the blinking of the traffic lights one after another through the slanting rain, the plumes of steam which, like geysers from the subterranean, spout into the streets – all this speaks fancifully to me, here in *urbanissimus*, of clearing, glade and woodland market.

But best of all, for this reluctant and secretive beauty of the island, I like to walk very early in the morning down to Battery Park, the southernmost tip of it, its gazebo on the world, looking out across the great bay towards the Narrows and the open sea. This is a melancholy pleasure, for the shipping which used to make this the busiest basin on earth has mostly been dispersed now. Most of the Atlantic liners sail no more, the freighters mostly berth elsewhere around the bay, and of the myriad public ferries which used to sail like so many water insects to and from Manhattan, only the old faithful to Staten Island survives.

So early in the morning, the scene down at the Battery is not likely to be bustling. If it is misty, it is likely to be a little spooky, in fact. The mist lies heavy over the greyish water, muffled sirens sound, somewhere a sound-buoy intermittently hoots. Perhaps a solitary tanker treads cautiously towards Brooklyn, or a pilot boat, its crew collars-up against the dank, chugs out towards the Narrows. Early commuters emerge blearily from the ferry station; two or three layabouts are stretched on park benches, covered in rags and newspaper; a police car sometimes wanders by, its policemen slumped in their seats dispassionately, like men at the end of a shift.

It seems eerily isolated and exposed, and you feel as though the few of you are all alone, there at the water's edge. But as the morning draws on and the mist clears, something wonderful happens. It is like the printing of a Polaroid picture. The wide sweep of the bay gradually reveals its outlines, the Statue of Liberty appears unforeseen upon her plinth, lesser islands show themselves, and as you turn your back upon the water, glistening now in the freshening breeze, it turns out that the tremendous presence of Manhattan itself, its serried buildings rank on rank, has been looking over your shoulder all the time.

I was walking one day down Sixth Avenue (as New Yorkers still sensibly prefer to call the Avenue of the Americas) when I saw a lady taking a bath, fully clothed, in the pool outside the Time-Life Building. This struck me as a good idea, for it was a hot and sticky day, and I approached her to express my admiration for her initiative. I did not get far. When she saw me step her way she sat bolt upright in the pool, water streaming off her lank hair and down the clinging blue fabric of her dress, and screamed obscenities at me. It was unnerving. Shrill, wild and dreadfully penetrating, her voice pursued me like an eldritch curse, and everyone looked accusingly at me, as though I had insulted the poor soul, and deserved all the imprecations she could command (and her repertoire, I must say, was impressive).

Nobody, I noticed, looked accusingly at *her*. She was evidently mad, and so unaccusable. Confined like that bear on their own rock, the people of Manhattan are the most neurotic community on earth. The twitch, the mutter, the meaningless shriek, the foul-mouthed mumble, the disjointed shuffle – these are native gestures of the island. Pale and ghostly, violently made up or sunk in despair are thousands of its faces – clowns' faces, chalk white and crimson, or haunted faces that have survived concentration camps, or faces alive with a crazy innocence, like those of murderous infants.

Every great city has its bewildered minority – the confused are always with us. Manhattan, though, is the only one I know that sometimes seems on the brink of general nervous breakdown. Intensely clever, cynical, introspective, feverishly tireless, it has all the febrile brightness, alternating with despondency, that sometimes attends insomnia, together with the utter self-absorption of the schizophrenic. Few residents of Manhattan really much care what happens anywhere else. Backs to the sea and the waterways east and west, theirs is a crosstown outlook, focusing ever closer, ever more preoccupied, upon the vortex of the place – which is to say, themselves. 'Does dyslexia,' I heard an interviewer say in all seriousness on television one day, 'crop up in other parts of the country, or is it pertinent only to Manhattan?'

Lord Melbourne, when he was Queen Victoria's Prime Minister, was once asked by an anxious acquaintance for his advice on how best to cope with the problems of life. 'Be easy,' was all the statesman said. 'I like an easy man.' He would have to look hard for one in Manhattan, where the old gamblers' precept 'Let it ride' has long been rejected. Analysis, I sometimes think, is the principal occupation of Manhattan – analysis of trends, analysis of options, analysis of style, analysis of statistics, analysis above all of self. Freud has much to answer for, in this island of tangled dreams, and the women's movement has evidently liberated all too many women only into agonized doubt and self-questioning.

But actually, like most people New Yorkers like to be thought a bit crazy. When they had a poll in New York and Los Angeles, each city complacently claimed its own population to be madder than the other. I know a business corporation in Manhattan – I dare not mention its name – which seems to me to be run entirely, top to bottom, by people off their balance. The minute I enter its offices, an uneasy suggestion of collective haywire assails me. Concealed and unapproachable behind his monumental mahogany doors sits the president of this corporation of nuts, mad as a hatter himself, and in hierarchy of psychosis his subordinates hiss and fiddle their days away below. Sometimes a whole department is fired: sometimes a surprised and hitherto unnoticed employee is plucked from obscurity and made the head of a division for a month or two; sometimes the company, which deals (let us say) in commodity shares, suddenly invests a few million dollars in a Chattanooga umbrella factory, or a grocery chain in Nicaragua.

They have all been driven off their heads, I suppose, by the needling and hallucinatory pressures of Manhattan, the prick of ambition, the fear of failure: and in their eyes I see, as they contemplate the future of their lunatic careers, just the same fierce but loveless passion that one sees in the eyes of brain-washed cultists – a blend of alarm and mindless dedication, dimly tinged with tranquillizers.

I say hallucinatory pressures, because to the outsider there is much to Manhattan that seems surreal. This is not a place of natural fantasy, like Los Angeles – its spirit is fundamentally logical and rationalist, as befits a city of merchants, bankers and stockbrokers. But its daily life is spattered with aspects and episodes of an unhinged sensibility, of which I record here, from a recent two-weeks' stay on the island, a few by no means extraordinary examples:

Item: An eminent, kind and cultivated actress, beautifully dressed, is taking a cab to an address on Second Avenue. Cab-driver: 'Whereabouts is that on Second Avenue, lady?' Actress, without a flicker in her equanimity: 'Don't ask me, bud. You're the fucking cab-driver.'

Item: Sign at a Front Street garage: No GAS. DEALTH IN FAMILY.

Item: At the headquarters of the New York police, which is at Police Plaza, and is approached along the Avenue of the Finest, there is a functionary called the Chief of Organized Crime. I heard an administrator say to a colleague on the telephone there: 'You're going sick today? Administrative sick or regular sick?'

Item: A young man talks about his experiences in a levitation group: 'Nobody's hovering yet but we're lifting up and down again. We're hopping. I've seen a guy hop fifteen feet from the lotus position, and no one could do that on the level of trying.'

Item: Coming down in the hotel elevator at the New York Hilton is a delegate to the American Urological Association convention. He is on his way to a presentation on Pre-Lymph-adenectomy Staging of Testicular Tumours, and his name, I see from his lapel card, is Dr Portnoy.

Item: An aged court-appointed lawyer, down at the state courts, histrionically convinces the judge, with a florid wealth of legal jargon and gesture, that an adjournment is necessary, but spotting a row of hostile witnesses as he passes through the courtroom on his way out, loudly offers them a comment: 'Too bad, assholes.'

Item: Graffito in Washington Square: YIPPIES, JESUS FREAKS AND MOONIES ARE GOVERNMENT OPERATED.

Item: Four angry ladies are trying to enter St Patrick's Cathedral by the wrong entrance for the celebration of the cathedral's centenary, to be attended by three cardinals and eight archbishops. Their way is barred, but as the chanting of the mass sounds through the half-closed door, I hear them responding with a genuine *cri du coeur:* 'We must get in! We must! We're tourists from Israel!'

Item: The terrifyingly ambitious, inexhaustible girl supervisor at one of the downtown McDonalds. Over the serving counter one may see the glazed and vacant faces of the cooks, a black man and a couple of Puerto Ricans, who appear to speak no English: in front that small tyrant strides peremptorily up and down, yelling orders, angrily correcting errors, and constantly falling back upon an exhortatory slogan of her own: 'C'mon, guys, today guys, today . . .!' The cooks look back in pained incomprehension.

Item: I feel a sort of furry clutch at my right leg, and peering down, find that it is being bitten by a chow. 'Oh Goochy you naughty thing,' says its owner, who is following behind with a brush and shovel for clearing up its excrement, 'you don't know that person.'

Item: At nine in the morning, on a smart street in the East Seventies, a highly respectable middle-aged lady leans against the hood of a black Mercedes, meditatively scratching her crotch.

Item: It is night, and drizzling. I am crossing Park Avenue on my way home, and looking to my left to the mass of the Grand Central Terminal, see a sort of vision: piled on top of the New York General Building, and silhouetted floodlit against the monstrous Pan Am tower behind, the pinnacled cupola of the structure looks, just for a moment, like a shrine – a stupa, perhaps. I pause in astonishment, half expecting to hear mystical prayer bells sounding, until a passing cab, hooting its horn and showering me with mud from an adjacent gutter, scuttles me back to realism.

How small it is! Thirteen miles long from tip to tip, two and a half miles across at its widest point – at Eighty-sixth Street, I believe. It would be hard to be anonymous for long in Manhattan, if anyone well known ever wanted to be. When I was here last I went to see Mr Woody Allen's masterpiece *Manhattan*, the truest contemporary work of art I know about the island: after the show I went next door for a cup of tea at the Russian Tea Room, and there, large as life, toying with what I assume to have been a blini, was Mr Allen himself.

Sometimes it is hard to remember that this is one of the earth's most powerful cities, for in some ways it is oddly parochial. *The New York Times* is half a newspaper of international record, and half a parish magazine, with full obituaries of respected local insurance managers, and blow-by-blow accounts of the engagement of Miss Henrietta Zlyman to Edward Twistletoe III. Like all great metropolises, Manhattan is divided into lesser enclaves, each with its own personality and purpose, but the skinny shape of the island, the rigidity of its grid and the flatness of it all, make it impossible for any district to feel remote from any other. You can easily walk from Central Park to Battery Park in a gentle morning stroll; I boarded a bus recently with an acquaintance in the very heart of Harlem, all dingy tenements and apparently abandoned stores, and before he had finished telling me his war experiences we had arrived outside the Plaza Hotel. Besides, the great landmarks of the place, the Empire State Building, the twin towers of the World Trade Center, are so enormous that they are visible almost everywhere, and give the island a foreshortened sort of intimacy.

All crammed in like this, it is no wonder that the inhabitants of Manhattan sway to and fro, as though with minds linked, to the shifting tunes of fashion. No city in the world, I think, is so subject to the *Diktats* of critics, snobs and arbiters of taste. Manhattan feeds upon itself – intravenously, perhaps. A very public elite dominates its gossip columns and décors, the same faces over and over, seen at the same currently fashionable clubs and restaurants, Stork Club in one generation, Studio 54 another, drinking the statutory drinks, *kir* yesterday, Perrier today, using the same ephemeral 'in' words – when I was here last, for example, 'schlep', 'supportive', 'copacetic', 'significant others'.

I was taken one evening, at my own request, to the saloon currently the trendiest in town, Elaine's on Second Avenue. Everyone knows Elaine's. Secretaries hang about its bar, in the hope of being adopted by wild celebrities, young executives talk about it the morning after, and even the most intelligent of public people, it seems, literate directors and scholarly critics, unaccountably think it worth while to be seen there. No such phenomenon exists in Europe, for Elaine's is neither very expensive nor exactly exclusive – anyone can go and prop up the bar. I detested it, though: the noise, the jam-packed tables, the showing-off, the gush, the unwritten protocol which gives the best-known faces the most prominent tables, and banishes unknowns to the room next door. The beautiful people looked less than beautiful shouting their heads off in the din. The waiter resisted my attempts to have scampis without garlic (not liking garlic is *infra dig* in Manhattan).

I felt fascinated and appalled, both at the same time: but more surprising, I felt a bit patronizing – for all of a sudden, as I observed those bobbing faces there, wreathed in display or goggled in sycophancy, fresh as I was from my little village on the northwest coast of Wales, I felt myself to be among provincials.

Not a sensation I often get in New York. More often, when I am at large in this incomparable city, I feel myself to be among ultimates. *How're they gonna get me back on the farm?* This is, after all, The City of our times, as Rome was in classical days, as Constantinople was through centuries of Mediterranean history. This is everyone's metropolis, for there is no nation that has not contributed something to Manhattan, if only a turn of phrase or a category of bun. I went one day to the street festival which is held each May on Ninth Avenue, one of the most vividly cosmopolitan thoroughfares on the island, and realized almost too piquantly what it means to be a city of all peoples: smell clashing with smell, from a mile of sidewalk food stalls, sesame oil at odds with curry powder, Arabic drifting into Ukrainian among the almost impenetrable crowds, Yiddish colliding with Portuguese, and all the way down the avenue the discordant blending of folk-music, be it from Polish flageolet, Mexican harmonica or balalaika from Sofia.

Nothing provincial there! And if over the past 300 years the clambering upon this huge raft of refugees, adventurers, idealists and crooks from every land has given Manhattan always a quality of paradigm or fulcrum, so when it comes to the end of the world, I think, most people can most easily imagine the cataclysm in the context of this island. The great towers crumpling and sagging into themselves, the fires raging up the ravaged boulevards, the panicked rush of the people, like rats or lemmings, desperately into the boiling water – these are twentieth-century man's standard images of Doomsday: and in my own view, if God is truly going to sit one day in judgement upon the doings of mankind, he is likely to set up court on the corner of Broadway and Forty-second Street, where he can deal first (and leniently I am sure) with the purveyors of Sextacular Acts Live on Stage.

We live in baleful times, and it is a pity that Manhattan, that temple of human hope and ingenuity, should be obliged to fill this particular role of parable. There is no denying, though, that there often passes across the face of this city, like a shudder, a sense of ominous portent. I read one morning in the *Times* that a woman, walking the previous day down a street near City Hall, had been attacked by a pack of rats 'as big as rabbits'. I leapt into a cab at once, but Manhattan had beaten me to it: already a small crowd was peering with evident satisfaction into the festering abandoned lot from which the rodents had sprung. Already one of your archetypal New Yorkers had appointed himself resident expert, and was pointing out to enthralled office workers one of your actual rats, *almost* as big as a rabbit, which was sitting morosely in a wire trap among the piled rubbish. What became of the original victim, I asked? 'I guess she was some kind of screwball. She just drove off screaming . . .'

I would have driven off screaming too, if those rabbit-rats had attached themselves to me, but around the corner, almost within excretion distance of the rat pit, business was brisk as ever at the neighbourhood takeout food store. New Yorkers are hardened to horror, I suppose, and perhaps it is this acclimatization that gives their island its sense of fated obliteration. It might be designed for nemesis, and suggests to me sometimes an amphitheatre of pagan times, in which ladies and rats, like gladiators and wild beasts, are pitted against each other for the rude entertainment of the gods.

Everything comes on to the island: nothing much goes off, even by evaporation. Once it was a gateway to a New World, now it is a portal chiefly to itself. Manhattan long ago abandoned its melting-pot function. Nobody even tries to Americanize the

Lebanese or the Lithuanians now, and indeed the ethnic enclaves of the island seem to me to become more potently ethnic each time I visit the place. Nothing could be much more Italian than the Festival of St Anthony of Padua down on Mulberry Street, when the families of Little Italy stroll here and there through their estate, pausing often to greet volatile contemporaries and sometimes munching the soft-shelled crabs which, spread-eagled on slices of bread like zoological specimens, are offered loudly for sale by street vendors. Harlem has become almost a private city in itself, no longer to be slummed through by whities after dinner, while Manhattan's Chinatown is as good a place as anywhere in the world to test your skill at that universal challenge, trying to make a Chinese waiter smile.

So the lights blaze down fiercely upon a tumultuous arena: but its millions of gladiators (and wild beasts) are not in the least disconcerted by the glare of it, or daunted by the symbolic battles in which they are engaged, but are concerned chiefly to have swords of the fashionable length, to be seen to advantage from the more expensive seats, and preferably to face the lions at the same time as Jackie Onassis, say, or Dick Cavett if you like.

Back to the park. At the centre of the world's present preoccupation with Manhattan, for one reason and another, stands Central Park. 'Don't go walking in that Park,' they will warn you from China to Peru, or 'Tell me frankly,' they ask, 'is it true what they say about Central Park?'

The Park is the centre of the island too, no man's land amid the surrounding conflict of masonry – on the postal map it forms a big oblong blank, the only portion of Manhattan without a zip code. To the north is Harlem, to the south is Rockefeller Center, on one flank is the opulence of the Upper East Side, to the west are the newly burgeoning streets that sprout, teeming with artists, agents, Polish grocers and music students, right and left off Columbus Avenue. It is like a big rectangular scoop in the city, shovelled out and stacked with green. It covers 840 acres, and it is almost everything, to my mind, that a park should not be.

This is a heretical view. Central Park is enormously admired by specialists in planning and urban design. The architectural critic of *The New York Times* calls it the city's greatest single

work of architecture. It was laid out in 1856 by Frederick Law
Olmsted and Calvert Vaux, and ever since everybody has been
saying how marvellous it is. 'One of the most beautiful parks in
the world,' thought Baedeker, 1904. 'This great work of art,'
says the AIA *Guide to New York City, 1978.*

Not me. With its gloomy hillocks obstructing the view, with
its threadbare and desolate prairies, with its consciously contrived variety of landscapes, with its baleful lake and brownish
foliage, with the sickly carillon which, hourly from the gates of
its appalling zoo, reminds me horribly of the memorial chimes
at Hiroshima, Central Park seems to me the very antithesis of
the fresh and natural open space, the slice of countryside, that
a city park should ideally be.

Nevertheless the world is right when, invited to think of
Manhattan, it is likely to think first these days of Central Park.
If I deny its ethereal beauty, I do not for a moment dispute its
interest. It is one of the most interesting places on earth. 'It is
inadvisable,' warns the Michelin guide, 1968, 'to wander alone
through the more deserted parts of the park': but wandering
alone nevertheless through this extraordinary retreat, dominated on all sides by the towering cliffs of Manhattan, is to enjoy
one of the greatest of all human shows, in perpetual performance
from dawn through midnight.

You want tradition? There go the lumbering barouches, their
horse smells hanging pungent in the air long after they have left
their stands outside the Plaza, their Dutch trade delegates, their
Urological Association conventioneers, or even their honeymooners from Iowa, somewhat self-consciously sunk in their
cushions, and their coachmen leaning back, as they have leant
for a century or more, whip in hand to ask their customers
where they're from.

You want irony? Consider the layabouts encouched apparently permanently on their benches along the East Side, beyond
the open-air book-stalls, prickly and raggedy, bony and malodorous, camped there almost in the shadow of the sumptuous
Fifth Avenue apartment houses, and more tellingly still perhaps,
actually within earshot of the feebly growling lions, the cackling
birds and funereal carillon of the zoo.

You want vaudeville? Try the joggers on their daily exercise.
Doggedly they lope in their hundreds around the ring road,
generally cleared of traffic on their behalf, like migrating animals

homed in upon some inexplicable instinct, or numbed survivors from some catastrophe out of sight. Some are worn lean as rakes by their addiction, some drop the sweat of repentant obesity. Some flap with huge ungainly breasts. Some tread with a predatory menace, wolflike in the half-hour before they must present that memo about ongoing supportive expenditures to Mr Cawkwell at the office. Sometimes you may hear snatches of very Manhattan conversations, as the enthusiasts labour by – 'So you're saying (gasp) that since 1951 (pant) there's been no meaningful change whatever (puff) in our society?' Sometimes you may observe a jogger who has taken his dog with him on a leash, and who, obliged to pause while the animal defecates behind a bush, compromises by maintaining a standing run, on the spot, looking consequently for all the world as though he is dying for a pee himself.

But no, it is the sinister you want, isn't it? 'It is inadvisable to wander alone, despite the frequent police patrols on horseback or by car . . .' That is what Central Park is most famous for these days, and it is not hard to find. I have never been mugged in Central Park, never seen anyone else harmed either, but I have had my chill moments all the same. More than once, even as the joggers pad around their circuit, I have noticed perched distantly on the rocky outcrops which protrude among the dusty trees, groups of three or four youths, silently and thoughtfully watching. They wear dark glasses, as likely as not, and big floppy hats, and they recline upon their rock in attitudes of mocking but stealthy grace, motionless, as though they were fingering their flick-knives.

I waved to one such group of watchers once, as I walked nervously by: but they responded only by looking at each other in a bewildered way, and shifting their long legs a trifle uneasily upon the stone.

All around the city roars. Well, no, not roars – buzzes, perhaps. The energy of Manhattan is less leonine than waspish, and its concerns are, for so tremendous a metropolis, wonderfully individual and idiosyncratic. Despite appearances, Manhattan is an especially human city, where personal aspirations, for better or for worse, unexpectedly take priority.

Perhaps this is because, unlike either of the other global cities (for in my view there are only two, Paris and London) – unlike its peers, New York is not a capital. True, the headquarters of

the United Nations is down by the East River, but architecturally
it is the perfect reflection of its lacklustre political self, and one
hardly notices it. True too that the municipal affairs of this city,
being on so momentous a scale, are equivalent I suppose to the
entire political goings-on of many lesser republics. But it is not
really a political city. Affairs of state and patriotism rarely
intrude. Even the state capital is far away in Albany, and
Manhattan conversations do not often turn to infighting within
the Democratic Party, or the prospects of Salt III.

There is not much industry on the island, either, in any
sociological or aesthetic sense: few blue-collared workers
making for home with their lunch boxes, few manufacturing
plants to belch their smoke into the Manhattan sky. This is a
city of more intricate concerns, a city of speculators and advisers,
agents and middlemen and sorters-out and go-betweens. Many
of the world's most potent corporations have their headquarters
here, but their labour forces are mostly conveniently far away.
Fortunes are made here, and reputations, not steel ingots or
automobiles.

The pace of New York is legendary, but nowadays in my
opinion illusory. Businessmen work no harder, no faster, than
in most other great cities. But New Yorkers spend so much time
contemplating their personal affairs, analysing themselves,
examining their own reactions, that the time left for business is
necessarily rushed. Do not suppose, when the Vice-President of
Automated Commercial leaves his office in such a hurry, that he
is meeting the Overseas Sales Director of Toyuki Industries:
good gracious no, he is leaving early because he simply must
have it out face to face with Brian about his disgraceful
behaviour with that Edgar person in the disco last night.

More than any other place I know, to do business in New
York you must understand your colleagues' circumstances. They
often need worrying out. There are some tell-tale signs indeed,
like tribal tattoos – short hair for Brian and Edgar, for example,
droopy moustaches and canvas shoes for aspirant literary men,
rasping voices and nasal intonations for girls who hope to get
into television, hands in trouser pockets for Ivy League executives. But you should take no chances. The tangles of Manhattan
marital and emotional life, which provide inexhaustible hours
of instruction to the social observer, set the tone of this place far
more than torts, share prices or bills of lading.

There is hardly a citizen of Manhattan, of any race, creed or social class, who does not have some fascinating emotional imbroglio to relate – and hardly a citizen, either, who fails to relate it. Nitter-natter, chit-chat, *you would hardly believe it, so I said never, so she said absolutely* – sibilantly across this city of gossip, from Wall Street clubs to bars of Harlem one seems to hear the tide of confession and confidence, unremitting as the flood of the traffic, rattly as the clang of the subway trains which now and then emerges from grilles beneath one's feet.

Is this inbreeding? Certainly there is something perceptibly incestuous about Manhattan, now that the diversifying flow of immigration has abated. This is no longer the lusty stud of the world. Ellis Island, through whose lugubrious halls so many millions of newcomers passed into the land of fertility, is only a museum now, and ethnically Manhattan has lost its virile momentum. You feel the migratory thrust far more vividly in Toronto, and most of New York's contemporary immigrants are hardly immigrants at all, in the old risk-all kind, but are Puerto Ricans joining their relatives, or Colombians cooperatively financed by the drug-rings of Jackson Heights.

They are seldom inspired, as their predecessors were, by any flaming spirit of release or dedication, and they very soon fall into the Manhattan mode. 'Well it's like I say, see, I got this lady I used to know back in Bogotá. She says to me, "Leon," she says, "I wantya to know, I'm fond of you, truly I am, but there's this problem of Juan's baby, see?" "To hell with Juan's baby," I says, "what's Juan's baby to me?" And she says, "Leon honey," she says, "listen to me . . ." '

'Give me your tired, your poor, your huddled masses yearning to breathe free . . .' An occasional Russian dissident appears in New York these days, to endure his statutory press conference before being whisked away to CIA debriefing or associate professorship somewhere. But the loss of the grand old purpose, so stoutly declaimed by the Lady of Liberty out there in the bay, means that Manhattan is recognizably past its prime.

Every city has its heyday, the moment when its purpose is fulfilled and its spirit bursts into full flower, and Manhattan's occurred I think in the years between the Great Depression, when the indigents squatted in Central Park, and the end of the Second World War, when the GIs returned in splendour as the

saviours of liberty. In those magnificent years this small island,
no more than a fantastic dream to most of the peoples of the
world, stood everywhere for the fresh start and the soaring
conception. Manhattan was Fred Astaire and the sun-topped
Chrysler Building! Manhattan was the Jeep and Robert Benchley!
Manhattan was rags-to-riches, free speech, Mayor La Guardia
and the Rockettes!

No wonder nostalgia booms on Broadway. Those were the
days of the American innocence, before responsibility set in,
and every dry and racy old song of the period, every new Art
Deco furniture boutique, is an expression of regret. European
Powers pine for their lost glories with bearskin parades or
jangling cavalry: New York looks back with *Ain't Misbehavin'*, or
the refurbishing, just as it was, of that prodigy of Manhattan
gusto, Radio City Music Hall (whose designer reportedly had
ozone driven through its ventilator shafts, to keep its audiences
festive, and toyed with the idea of laughing gas too...). Fortunately the old days come quickly in a city that is not yet 300
years old, and the authentic bitter-sweetness is relatively easy
to achieve. I was touched myself by the furnishing of a restaurant
equipped entirely with the fittings of one of the old Atlantic
liners, those dowagers of the Manhattan piers, until I discovered
that the ship concerned was the *Caronia*, whose launching I
remember as clear as yesterday.

The memories of that time are legendary already, and moving
fast into myth. Nothing in travel stirs me more than the dream
of that old Manhattan, the Titan City of my childhood, when the
flamboyant skyscrapers soared one after the other into the
empyrean, when John D. Rockefeller, Jr., pored over the plans
for his Center like a modern Midas, when the great liners
stalked through the bay with their complements of celebrities
and shipboard reporters, and the irrepressible immigrants toiled
and clawed their way up the line of Manhattan, from Ellis Island
to the Lower East Side to the Midtown affluence of their
aspirations. Its monuments are mostly there to see still, newly
fashionable as the buildings of the day-before-yesterday are apt
to become, and sometimes even now you may stumble across
one of its success stories: the waiter proudly boasting that, since
arriving penniless and friendless from Poland, he has never
been out of work for a day – the famous publisher, in the

penthouse suite of his own skyscraper, whose mother landed in Manhattan with a placard around her neck, announcing her name, trade and language.

Rockefeller Center is the theatre of this mood. Raymond Hood, the creator of its central structure, the RCA Building, was reminded one day that he had come to Manhattan in the first place with the declared intention of becoming the greatest architect in New York. 'So I did,' he responded, looking out of the window at that stupendous thing, jagged and commanding high above, 'and by God, so I am!' The magnificent brag, the revelatory vision, the ruthless opportunism, the limitless resource – these were the attributes of Rockefeller Center, as of Manhattan, in the heady years of its construction: and when at winter time they turn the sunken café into an ice rink, then in the easy delight of the skaters under the floodlights, some so hilariously inept, some so showily skilful, with the indulgent crowd leaning over the railings to watch, and the waltz music only half drowned by the city's rumble – then I sometimes seem to be, even now, back in those boundless years of certainty.

If the conviction is lost, the abilities remain. This is the most gifted of all the human settlements of the earth, and there are moments in Manhattan when the sheer talent of the place much moves me. I happened to be in the Pan Am Building recently when an orchestra of young people was giving a lunch-time concert in the central concourse. This is a common enough event in Manhattan, a place of inescapable music, but somehow it seized my imagination and twisted my emotions. No other city, I swear, could provide an interlude so consoling. The brilliant young players were so full of exuberance. The audience listened to their Brahms and Vivaldi with such sweet attention. The music sounded wonderfully tender in the heart of all that stone and steel, and seemed to float like a tempering agent down the escalators, through the bland air-conditioned offices, of that great tower of materialism. ('How beautifully they play,' I remarked in my delight to a man listening beside me, but in the Manhattan manner he brought me harshly down to earth. 'They gotta play beautifully,' he replied. 'Think of the competition.')

The cities of Europe have mostly lost their artists' quarters, swallowed up now in housing estates or ripped apart by ring roads. In Manhattan, Bohemia flourishes still, in many an eager alcove. This is a city of the streets and cafés, where human contact, carnal or platonic, is still easy to arrange, where no young artist need feel alone or benighted for long, and where no ambition is too extravagant. Manhattan probably has more than its fair share of artistic phonies, and SoHo, currently the most popular painters' quarter, certainly exhibits an adequate proportion of junkyard collages or knobs of inadequately sandpapered walnut labelled 'Significant Others 3'. But tucked away in the attics, cheap hotels, apartment blocks and converted brownstones of this island a myriad genuine artists and craftsmen are at work, impervious to trend and disdainful of sham.

I like to spend Sunday mornings watching the alfresco circus down at Washington Square, the gateway to Greenwich Village, where wandering musicians and amateur jugglers compete for the attention of the sightseers with virtuoso frisbee throwers, classical in their skills and gestures, impromptu demagogues, chess players, itinerant idiots and Rastafari bravos. Often and again then, when I am sitting on my park bench watching this colourful world go by, I spot a fellow practitioner of my craft, alone on *his* bench with *his* notebook, and as our eyes meet I wonder if I ought to feel compassion for him, as the struggling artist from his austere garret somewhere, or envy, as the author of tomorrow's runaway bestseller.

Contrary to the world's conceptions, New York is rich in people of integrity. In a city of such attainments it has to be so. This is a city of dedicated poets, earnest actors and endlessly rehearsing musicians. Draft after draft its writers are rejecting, and there are more good pianists playing in New York every evening than in the whole of Europe – smouldering jazz pianists in the downtown clubs, crazy punk pianists on Bleecker Street, stuffed-shirt romantic pianists in the Midtown tourist spots ('Would you mind lowering your voice to a whisper, please, during Mr Maloney's renditioning?'), smashing student pianists practising for next year's Tchaikovsky competition, jolly young pianists accompanying off-Broadway musicals, drop-out pianists, drunk ruined pianists, mendicant pianists with instruments on trolley wheels, Steinway pianists flown by Concorde that afternoon for their concerti at Lincoln Center.

So I am never really deluded by the charlatan inanities of New York. I disregard the fatuous interviewers and repellent respondents of what we are gruesomely encouraged to think of as NBC's Today Family. I sneer not at the sellers of Instant Ginseng. I am not deceived by the coarse-grained editors, hag-ridden by their own accountants, or the ghastly company of celebrities. 'Creativity' is so degraded a word in Manhattan that I hesitate to use it, loathing its translation into salesmen's acuity or publicity gimmick. But creative this place truly is: not in the old audacious style perhaps, but in the quieter, introspective, muddled but honest way that is more the Manhattan manner now.

It would seem inconceivable to Hood or John D., Jr., let alone Commodore Vanderbilt or Pierpont Morgan, but actually in 1979 Manhattan feels a little old-fashioned. The Titan City has come to terms, and recognizes that everything is *not* possible after all. They build more thrilling buildings in Chicago now. They do more astonishing things in Houston. There are more aggressive entrepreneurs in Tokyo or Frankfurt. It is no good coming to Manhattan for the shape of things to come: Singapore or São Paulo might be more reliable guides. In the days of the Great Vision the New Yorkers built an airship mast on the top of the Empire State Building almost as a matter of course, sure that the latest and greatest dirigibles would head straight for Manhattan: it was years, though, before New York was reluc-tantly persuaded, in our own time, to allow supersonic aircraft to land at JFK.

Manhattan is no longer the fastest, the most daring or even I dare say the richest. For a symbol of its civic energies now, I recommend an inspection of the abandoned West Side Highway, the victim of seven years' municipal indecision, which staggers crumbling on its struts above a wilderness of empty lots, truck parks and shattered warehouses, the only signs of enterprise being the cyclists who cheerfully trundle along the top of it, and the railway coaches of the Ringling Bros., Barnum and Bailey Circus which park themselves habitually underneath.

The falter came, I believe, in the fifties and sixties, when Manhattan began to see *laissez-faire*, perhaps, as a less than absolute ideology. Doubts crept in. The pace slowed a bit. The sense of movement lagged. All the great ships no longer came in their grandeur to the Manhattan piers; the New York airports were far from the island; today even the helicopters, which were for a couple of decades the lively familiars of Manhattan, are banned from their wayward and fanciful antics around the

skyscrapers. Bauhaus frowned down upon Radio City Music
Hall, in those after-the-glory years, and most of Manhattan's
mid-century architecture was, by Hood's standards, timid and
banal. The truly original buildings were few, and worse still for
my taste, the swagger-buildings were not built at all.

When, in the early 1970s, the World Trade Center was erected
in a late spasm of the old hubris – the two tallest towers on earth
then, beckoning once more the world across the bay – all
Manhattan groaned at the change in its familiar skyline, and to
this day it is hard to find a New Yorker willing to admit to
admiration for that arrogant pair of pylons. The fashionable
philosophy of smallness strongly appealed to New Yorkers, in
their new mood of restraint, and nowadays when citizens want
to show you some innovation they are proud of, they generally
take you to a dainty little kerbside park with waterfalls, or
Roosevelt Island, an itsy-bitsy enclave of sociological good taste.
Suavity, discretion and even modesty are the architectural
qualities admired in Manhattan now, and the colossal is no
longer welcomed.

And believe it or not, *quaintness* approaches. Mr Philip
Johnson's latest building is to be crowned with a decorative
device like the back of a Chesterfield sofa: so does old age creep
up, all but unsuspected, upon even the most dynamic organisms
– Time's A-Train, hurrying near! Manhattan is no longer critical
in the atomic sense: 'No Nukes' is a proper slogan for this gently
decelerating powerhouse.

It is not a sad spectacle. I find it endearing. If New York has
lost the power to amaze, it is gaining the power to charm. They
did not mean it seriously, when they called this Little Old New
York, but the phrase is losing its irony now. Old Manhattan
inevitably becomes – small geographically it always was – little
and old in the figurative sense, in the cosy familiar endearing
sense. Manhattan telephone operators, who used to be mere
human mechanisms, call one 'dear' nowadays: and at the New
York Hilton, that very shrine of impersonal efficiency, there is
somebody down in the kitchens who actually recognizes my
voice, every time I go there, and sends me up my breakfast with
kind endearment and inquiries after my family.

It happened that when I was in Manhattan, Bonwit Teller, for
generations one of the smartest stores on Fifth Avenue, closed

its doors to make way for a building development. I went along there on the last day, and what a sentimental journey that was! Tears came to saleswomen's eyes, as they pottered for the last time along the atrocious hats, unsellable ceramics, belts and bent coat hangers which were all that remained of their once-delectable stock: and an elderly customer I buttonholed by the elevators seemed almost distraught – something beautiful was going out of her life, she said, 'a bit of New York, a little bit of me'.

Bonwit's was quick to remind us, in the next day's *New York Times*, that they have plenty of stores elsewhere, but still the event really did touch some heart-chords in New York. Senti-mentality, eccentricity, Earl Grey tea – all these are signs of a society growing old, but doing it, on the whole, gracefully. There is much that is jaded or curdled, of course, to the culture of Little Old New York. Violence really is a curse of the place, circumscribing the lives of hundreds of thousands of people, and blighting whole districts of the city – when the donor of the East River Fountain was asked why it had not been spouting recently, he said he assumed it was clogged wtih corpses. More people in Manhattan, as it happens, suffer from human bites than from rat bites – 764 recorded in 1978, as against 201 from the rats.

Yet I am of the opinion all the same that Manhattan, whose very name is a byword for the mugging, the fast practice, the impossible pressure and the unacceptable vice, has become in its maturity the most truly civilized of the earth's cities. It is where mankind has, for good or for bad, advanced furthest on its erratic course through history, and in unexpected places, in unforeseen situations, its mellowness shows.

I spent a few hours one night with a squad car of the Fifth Precinct, operating out of Elizabeth Street on the Lower East Side, and found it, to my astonishment, a curiously gentlemanly exercise. I am not overfond of policemen as a breed, and have heard the worst about New York's Finest, but I can only report that my experiences that night were altogether disarming.

My pair of cops were textbook, almost comic-book, figures: burly fellows as you would expect, bulging slightly at the belt, with guns sagging heavy at their hips and that peculiar akimbo sort of gait, as though they are about to enter a Japanese wrestling bout, which is peculiar to American policemen. Our

calls too were as you might foresee; a potential suicide on the
Brooklyn Bridge, some kids starting a fire, a molester in a
tenement house, an elderly householder shot through the head
by a thirteen-year-old robber. We progressed around town,
within limits as closely defined as a fox's hunting territory, with
the proper alternation of creep and crash, now nosing insidiously into back alleys, where the junkies stared blankly at our
passing, now switching our yelper on and exploding through
the traffic in our battered sedan as though wild horses were
carrying us.

But I was surprised, whenever we got there, by the moderation
of these Fifth Precinct heavies. I have ridden with big-city
policemen in many countries, Bolivia to Hong Kong, and these
fellows seemed to me the nearest of them all to the neighbourhood cops of long ago. The Brooklyn jumper turned out to be a
merry fellow, brandishing a bunch of flowers above his head,
who said he was merely responding to the Challenge of the
Waters, and was given a lift to somewhere less stimulating. The
kids were putting out their fire by the time we reached them,
and we did not interfere. At the scene of the shooting the local
population of Puerto Ricans, Italians and Colombians, far from
melting into the night when we and eight other police cars
appeared helter-skelter on the scene, howling and flashing,
crowded seriously around to help, and were treated I thought
with rough but sensible courtesy.

A lucky night? Untypical cops? Perhaps, but nevertheless my
night down at the Fifth Precinct, cruising from Chinatown to
Mafialand, from Ratner's restaurant still aglow to the seafood
joint where they show the bullet holes that killed a Godfather
seven years ago – my night down there left me indefinably
beguiled and conciliated by Manhattan. I stopped off at an all-
night café on my way uptown, and had a pancake. There were
a couple of grotesquely painted old ladies in there, looking as
though the funeral parlour cosmetician had prematurely had a
go at them, and a slob distastefully wiping the last of the egg off
his plate with a piece of greasy bread, and two or three night-
workers mildly chatting up the waitress, and an obvious
Englishman, in a striped tie, grinning and bearing it through
the jet lag, the time change and the behaviour patterns of the
Manhattan midnight.

*

They used to say of it that it would be a fine place when it was finished. I think in essentials they have completed it now. They are no longer tearing down its buildings, and throwing up new ones, with the fury of their youth. Whole districts are no longer changing character year by year under the impact of the immigrants. Manhattan has jelled, I think. A feeling not of complacency but perhaps of wry experience pervades Little Old New York now: when, in the Russian Tea Room that day, I caught the eye of Mr Allen, truly the laureate of Manhattan in its silver age, his expression was nothing if not *wistful*.

Actually it is Woody Allen, not that bear, who should be encaged in Central Park, to stand as a focal symbol for peregrinating Welsh essayists. But let me end anyway with one more visit to the Park, that zipless blank at the heart of Manhattan, for a lyrical *envoi* to this piece. I chanced one day, off the joggers' circuit, to come across a young black man fast asleep upon a bench below the lake. His overcoat was thrown over him, his boots were placed neatly side by side upon the ground. His head upon his clasped hands, as in kindergarten plays, he was breathing regularly and gently, as though bewitched.

Even as I watched a grey squirrel, skipping across the green, leapt across his legs to the back of the bench, where it sat tremulously chewing, as squirrels do: and suddenly, almost at the same time, there arose one of those brisk gusts of wind, tangy with salt, which now and then blow a breath of the ocean invigoratingly through New York.

A scatter of leaves and fallen blossoms came with it, flicked and eddied about the bench. The squirrel paused, twitched again and vanished. The black man opened his eyes, as the breeze dusted his face, and seeing me standing there bemused, smiled me a slow sleepy smile. 'Be not afeared,' I said ridiculously, on the spur of the moment, 'the isle is full of noises.'

'Yeah,' the man replied, stretching and scratching mightily in the morning. 'Bugs, too.'

25

A DREAM

Moscow, 1957

❧

When I went to Moscow to write this piece the mummified corpse of
Stalin still lay beside Lenin in the Kremlin mausoleum. Wishing to keep
the essay up to date, when it was reprinted in book form in 1963, I did
what the Russians had done, and removed him.
   Now I've put him back again. I hope they never do.

Through an ambuscade of aircraft the traveller stumbles – more
aircraft, it seems, than he has ever set eyes on before, with their
fierce noses and high tails shining dully in the snow, hulking
and unfamiliar, like great predatory pike: but inside the stuffy,
ill-lit reception hall a line of prickly porters, in brown quilted
jackets and fur hats, lounges and slouches on benches, while an
official in a blue cap peers myopically at documents, turning
them this way and that for a better grasp of their purport, like
a country policeman in a farce.

A fusty crowd of passengers, muffled in wrappings, hangs
about the Customs desk: a fat, broad-faced woman in tears, her
child tugging at the strap of her handbag; a sallow man in a
velvet hat, arguing over a suitcase of brocades; a covey of
Chinese, dignified and double-breasted; a welter of thick-set,
sweaty, colourless men with badges in their lapels, and elaborate
medals dangling from their chests. Among them all the traveller
warily passes, a shuffling, heavy-breathing porter carrying his
bags behind, and into the car that waits outside; and so down
the dank, snow-muffled road, through a landscape numb with
cold, he is driven towards the city.

Thin flurries of snow are chased by the wind across the road.
The windows of the car are thick with ice, frost, and condensa-
tion. Blurred in a haze of winter, as if seen through a toper's

eyes, are the places along the route. There are shambled lines of shacks and shanties, painted an ancient peeling blue, with rickety verandas and precarious porches, knee-deep in snow, invested by old outhouses, fences, dog-houses, bits of masonry. There are clusters of small houses, tightly huddled together for warmth and comfort, as if they have heard the howling of wolves. There are wide, desolate acres of snow-encompassed land, cruel and grubby, supervised by brooding firs, and crossed perhaps by a solitary old woman in a trailing tattered coat and a green kerchief, bundled with packages and buckets, and pushing her way like a lemming towards some unseen homestead in the wood.

Sometimes a gaunt old horse hauls a sledge lop-sidedly down the road, piled high with baskets and packing-cases; or a car ploughs past with a puff of oily exhaust and a whiff of crude petrol; or a great rough-hewn lorry, painted a sombre green and wrapped around the bonnet with quilted fabric, rumbles darkly through the trees; and presently there appear through the misted windscreen the first tokens of the city. A suburban trolley-bus slides alongside, painted a bright blue and yellow, its windows so steamy that only a blur of head-scarves and wrinkled faces can dimly be seen, or the pink tip of a child's nose pressed against the glass. The traffic thickens, the empty countryside falls away, and soon there looms out of the fitful snowfall a monstrous parade of buildings. Huge, square, and forbidding they appear, of no definable style or period, like so many vast eight-storey breeding-houses. They look shuttered and deserted, but for a bleak light here and there, and they rise sheer and stern on each side of the road, window after window, block after block, mile after mile, like enormous piles of ammunition boxes in some remote and secret dump. Only a few squat women move in and out of their vault-like doors, and the television aerials, standing awry on their roofs, seem sad but lovable impertinences.

Immensely wide is the street that strikes through this gloomy cavalcade, and presently the rhythm of the buildings shifts, like a train crossing the points. Dreadful symmetry gives way to a jumble of old and new and indeterminate: a sagging, classical portico behind high walls; a rickety cul-de-sac of single-storey chalets, the plaster and lath peeling to show the criss-cross wood beneath; a bridge across a frozen river, its ornamental urns stacked with sculptured rifles, swords, trumpets and machine guns. The traveller rubs his window with his fur hat, and sees that the city has closed in upon him.

Not a drop, not a hint, not a memory of colour enlivens its frozen outskirts. All is brown and grey and stacked with snow. The stocky pedestrians of the place are swathed in greatcoats, furs and high boots, and move stuffed and bundled along the pavements, their children so encased in hoods and sheepskin that only their eyes appear like gems among the wrappings. Machines bustle everywhere, clearing away the sludge – jolly little motor-sweepers, like benign weasels, and huge clanking devices with spindly arms, like lobsters, and suction chutes, and tall, frowning snow-ploughs; and among them, wearing padded jackets over white aprons, an army of rugged women sweeps, shovels, and picks, leaving an intricate meshed pattern of brushes on the pavement, and an obbligato of swishing and chipping constantly on the air.

From an iron grille in the ground a plume of steam arises, and in its vapour crouches a flock of birds – half a dozen proud but shabby pigeons, a few rapscallion sparrows. A line of small boys paces on skis through the trees of a garden, and an old philosopher with flaps over his ears sits defiantly on a bench reading a book, the snow like white fur upon his coat collar. Across the vast crossroads a stream of huddled figures endlessly plods, hurried along by the chivvying of whistles and the testy gestures of belted, padded, high-booted, fur-hatted policemen. The city feels at once curiously empty and claustrophobically crowded: empty because its buildings are pallid and aloof, like monuments to dead scientists; crowded because to the movements of the scurrying citizenry there is something dark and inexorable, as though nothing could even staunch its sheer weight of numbers, as though it is impelled not by pleasure, industry, ambition, or even duty, but by irresistible physical instincts – like birds migrating, or small black salmon fighting their way upstream.

But now there appear, in glimpses among the office blocks, weird and spectral skyscrapers, solitary above the rooftops, ornamented strangely with spikes and pinnacles, like the pavilions of Eastern satraps; and just as the dusk begins to fall the traveller sees before him, raised upon an eminence, a huge and haunting fortress. Ancient turreted walls protect it, and a wide,

icy river lies beneath its gates; and within it there shine clusters
and globules of gold, complicated bell-towers, citadels, palaces,
weathervanes, emblems of power and politics, a mound of
cathedrals and barracks and florid watch-towers, an immense
straggling tessellated rampart, a dome with a gigantic flag
streaming arrogantly in the wind.

In the square beneath this chill marvel he steps from his car;
and joining a silent queue of citizens, he passes between a pair
of sentries, rigid as idols, their collars turned up around their
cheeks, their boots glistening, their small eyes hard and unshift-
ing. Slowly, meditatively, like mutes, the queue shuffles
between granite portals into a bare and massive building.
Officers in long grey greatcoats peer watchfully from its
shadows, and only the cries of a heedless baby break the silence
as the crowd, bareheaded and awe-struck, presses clumsily
down the granite steps into the stomach of the edifice. Silently,
silently it lumbers on, with a pulse of breathing and a swish of
thick clothes and an awkward clatter of boots on stone: until at
last the traveller, hemmed in willy-nilly among the pilgrims,
finds himself within an inner chamber, like a dungeon. Four
silent soldiers stand there with their rifles, and the endless
queue winds its way around the room like a fascinated viper,
button to button, breath to breath, gazing always at the crystal
box that stands in the centre.

A pair of dead men are embalmed there among the bayonets,
bathed in an unearthly light, waxen and preternaturally clean.
One has a short beard and a high-domed head. The other's
moustache is coarse and bushy, and the jacket of his pale blue
uniform is heavy with medals. Not a word, not a sigh, not a
cough escapes the crowd as it passes these cosmetic relics. An
occult sense of ritual pervades the place, as in the eerie tomb-
heart of a pyramid. The traveller, caught in the fustian momentum of the queue, is carried as in a dream out of the chamber
and up the broad steps into the evening light: and already he
feels clinging to his person, trapped in the folds of his coat and
the turn-ups of his trousers, impregnating his hair like tobacco
in a railway carriage, creeping beneath his fingernails, smarting
in his eyes, the odour and essence of Moscow.

Moscow in winter is hardly a dream, and not exactly a
nightmare, but has more the quality of a hangover: blurred,

dry-mouthed and baleful, but pierced by moments of almost painful clarity, in which words, ideas, or recollections roll about in the mind metallically, like balls on a pin-table.

It is a graceless but obsessive city, the capital of an alien Asiatic world. Among its avenues of ugly buildings, stamped with the inexpressible emptiness of Stalinist taste, the muffled multitudes shove their way with hungry gusto: not indeed mindlessly, as myth would have it, but with a special technique of ill manners, a kind of self-induced trance in which the existence of anybody else on the pavement is erased from the consciousness, as a yogi dismisses the blistered crowd around him. Nobody can push more effectively than a Muscovite: but drab and docile are the queues, all the same, that trail away from the milk counter in the central market, or wait in suffocating proximity, each man breathing stertorously down his neighbour's neck, for their hats and galoshes after the opera. No elegance or style is left twitching in the streets of Moscow. This is the metropolis of the common man, and he eats his bortsch with a proud snuffle.

Through the dreary proletarian pall, though, crooked mysteries gleam. Some are the mysteries of Communism: mummied philosophies and deifications, medallions of Lenin as a baby, a dead physicist lying in state upon his bier, a wilderness of pamphlets and slogans and Five-Year Plans, the shifting mosaic of strange faces that makes this an imperial city – Mongols and Kazakhs and bland Chinese, scarred Africans, wide-eyed Indians, lean men from Central Asia, with knobbly sticks and crinkled lambskin hats.

Some are the mysteries of ancient State: the spiked medieval helmets of the Kremlin Treasury, the gorgeous saddle trappings and the royal sledges, gold in piled elaborate formality, splendid silver from England, jewellery of minute ingenuity, thrones of ivory, sceptres, golden cocks, owls, pheasants, railway trains, ships in golden eggs, galleries of armour, all shining and glinting in their cases while the tourists, their feet muffled in felt overshoes, as in a mosque, pad in obedient groups behind their guide.

Some are the mysteries of religion – the religion of Leninism, which has already etherealized that eminent political scientist, or the religion of Tsarist Russia, still ornately surviving beneath its onion domes. Church service on Sunday morning is still veiled in strangeness and suffering. Outside the door an old man with a forked beard feeds a gaggle of mangy pigeons: inside a million Muscovites seem to occupy the nave, crammed so tightly that a sudden genuflection sends a ripple across the church. Far, far away the vestments of a priest sometimes flicker in the candlelight, and always drifting around the pillars and the ikons loiters a cadence of hidden choirs. Near the door the corpses of two old ladies, pale but peaceful, lie encouched in flowers. In a side chapel a bespectacled priest with long golden hair, sitting on a kitchen chair beside the altar, accepts a stream of murmured confessions and entreaties, the women pressing round him like dwarfs around a magician.

Strange are the encounters of Moscow, like incidents in a fevered fancy. A man in clumping boots and huge leather gloves will introduce himself in a champagne bar as a Brigadier of Communist Labour, and ask after the welfare of the comrade plasterers in England. A gay girl in the Lenin Library will slip you an irreverent witticism about Socialist realism. A female judge in a divorce court will burst into tears at the memory of her orphaned childhood. Two youths in slinky coats will solicit you for pound notes, fountain pens, *Life* magazine, chewing gum, nylon shirts or gramophone records. A charming renegade, springing out of the night, will eat caviare in your hotel room, talk for an hour or two about Proust, Evelyn Waugh and Wiltshire, and vanish again like a perfumed phantom. Moscow is full of innuendoes, hints of espionage, suspicions, the threat of imminent portentous confidences.

Sometimes a sense of suffocation overcomes you, and you feel yourself so far from the sea, in the heart of something so swollen and incalculable, that the blood throbs in your head and your mind sags. In the immaculate subterranean halls of the underground you may feel like this, stifled by gigantic symbolisms and frescoes of dancing milkmaids; or lost among the myriad textbooks, tracts, collected works of Lenin, portraits of bemedalled demi-gods, economic treatises and inspirational posters of a bookshop; or wandering among the awful symmetries of Moscow University, Big Brother's *alma mater*, a brain factory, a production line where 25,000 students labour like so many ants in a 32-storey heap (33 reading rooms, 5,754 sleeping chambers, 80 Members of the Academy of Sciences, 20 Merited Sciences, a million books, 50,000 trees, an assembly hall with 1,500 seats and 11 floors of storage space – 'The best university in the world,' as an Intourist pamphlet puts it, 'can only be seen in Moscow').

Sometimes you may feel frightened: not simply by the suggestion of hidden microphones and secret police, or the strained isolation of the foreign residents, herded into their ghettoes, or even by the sense of stark power that emanates from this dismal but impressive city; but by a profound sense of alienation, as though you belonged to some unrelated visiting species. Your conversations, however cordial, never really bridge the gulf of ideology. Your informant, kindly and hospitable, will suddenly assume a tone of quite unexpected arrogance. Behind the inquiries of the Brigadier of Communist Labour there lurks not hostility exactly, but a sense of inescapable misunderstanding, as though at some predestined point both your languages and your conceptions will diverge, never to be reconciled. You can never get to grips with the truth in Moscow. It slithers away from you into the snow, and even its tracks are obliterated by armies of passing footfalls.

But sometimes you may, nevertheless, catch a glimpse of the very heart, the core of this city's mysteries, as the man with the hangover analyses with cheerless clarity the exact mixture of drinks that was his undoing. It may well be at the Bolshoi, while some gigantic Russian epic is being ferociously enacted, with rolls of kettle-drums and clashes of armour, a mammoth chorus open-throated, a clutch of heroes swelling in the foreground, with a passage and repassage of knights, horses, serfs, a frenzy of conical helmets and chain mail, banners dramatically waving, flames issuing from a backcloth, smoke, flashing beacons, the orchestra in a quivering *fortissimo*, the conductor wiping his sweating bald head, the enormous audience gripping its seats or craning from the high gilded balconies above the chandelier – then, in the middle of it all, you will glance across your neighbour's shoulder to the great State box in the centre: and there will be sitting the most powerful man on earth, looking bored and rather glazed, a slight sad smile playing around the corners of his mouth, his wife, in a bun and brown sagging dress, demure and attentive at his elbow.

You need not wait for the last act. Go home and sleep it off.

26

HOWZAT? AND MR MORGAN

Port of Spain, 1958

In 1958 I went to write about the West Indian Federation set up by the retreating British as a post-imperial political device. The Federation did not last long, but Trinidad, in particular, seemed to me essentially impervious anyway to changes of constitution or regime.

If you walk across the Savannah in the dying heat of evening, you may sometimes hear the strains of unaccompanied music, and know that young Mr Morgan is practising his violin. The Savannah is a wide green common on the northern side of Port of Spain, in Trinidad, where the tropical hills come sidling down to the sea, and around its perimeter there stands a company of legendary Trinidadian mansions. One is gorgeously Gothic, one exotically Moorish, one predominantly blue: but the most stylish of them all is No. 25 Maraval Road, where Mr Morgan lives. It is a big white house surrounded with balconies, like an eccentric gunboat on the China Station, and it is encrusted with every kind of ornament, towers and turrets and filigree and wrought iron and balustrades and flagstaffs and weathercocks and all possible fractions of elaboration.

In the Moorish house there lives an archbishop, in the Gothic castle an old plantation family; but it is characteristic of Trinidad that among the inhabitants of No. 25 should be young Mr Morgan, who came from England only a few years ago and who loves to play his violin in a cool vaulted upstairs chamber. Port of Spain is a city of endless tumbling variety, mingled races, haphazard collusions, surprises and incongruities; gilded with the histories of the Western world, with a past of piracy, slavery and war, and a present ranging from razzle-dazzle politics to the British Council. Mr Morgan may sound an improbable figure, up there with his music-stand, but he is only an agreeable chip in a gaudy and multitudinous mosaic.

As you wander on through the Savannah, with his music faintly in your ears, you may sense some of the gusto and exuberance of this heterogeneous society. Here is the piazza of Trinidad. In the empty grandstand of the racecourse a big Negro in a straw hat sprawls across the seats in indolent splendour, but below him on the grass all is movement, bustle and vivacity. Wherever you look, from the hills to the city, they are playing cricket. To be sure, they are playing the game all over the island, in numberless unmapped clearings in the bush, overhung by lugubrious banana trees or gorgeous flamboyants: but this is the very heart of Trinidadian cricket, where the game is played today with more dash and delight than anywhere else on earth. There may be thirty or forty games, all at the same time. The thud of the balls echoes like muffled fireworks across the green, and wherever you look there are the crouching fielding figures, the big stylish black batsmen, a game suddenly collapsing in hilarious laughter, or the poised theatrical expectancy, all white eyes and quivering arms, that follows the magical cry of 'Howzat?'

Some of these sportsmen are grand and mannered, with spotless whites and rolled wickets; but they trail away through immeasurable gradations of clubmanship to the raggety small boys on the edge of the field, with an old bit of wood for a bat, and a stone for a ball, and the wicket-keeper peering with breathless expectancy over a petrol can. Whatever the style, the game is pursued with panache. Balls, stones, and fieldsmen hurl themselves indiscriminately across your path. Wild cries of scorn or enthusiasm punctuate your progress. 'Him's out! Him's out!' shout the small boys in delight, and the young man with the pipe murmurs 'Pretty, very pretty shot.' Many a strand of culture or tradition contributes to the texture of Port of Spain, and one of the strongest is that tough old umbilical, cricket.

Not all the cricketers are black. Many of these citizens are Indian by origin, and many are a *mélange* in themselves, part European, part African, with a touch of Chinese and a Hindu grandparent on the mother's side. Racial rivalries are still potent, especially between brown and black, and sometimes you may catch a hint of them on the Savannah. An Indian father, for example, shoos away a small black boy anxious to play kites with his son. 'Go away, sonny,' he says crossly, 'this is a private game we are playing, you see, we do not want other people coming and playing here.' The black boy gazes stubbornly into the middle distance. He is wearing an old Army forage cap, much too big for him. 'I'se not playing with you anyway,' he says. 'I'se playing here all by myself. This ain't no private garden. I'se just flying my kite right here where I belong.' And you can see a spasm of annoyance cross that Hindu's smooth face, a spasm that runs through the society of Trinidad, and gives an extra vicious animation to the politics of the city.

There are white people on the Savannah, too. The girls playing hockey on the south side, watched by an audience ranging from the maternal to the frankly salacious, well represent the shades of allure once conceived by a local competition promoter: 'Miss Ebony and Miss Mahogany, Miss Satinwood and Miss Allspice, Miss Sandalwood, Miss Golden Apple, Miss Jasmine, Miss Pomegranate, Miss Lotus and Miss Appleblossom.' Here and there a weathered white West Indian plays long-stop or lounges in the grass, and sometimes you may even see an elderly imperial couple, in khaki shorts and linen skirt, exercising themselves doggedly across the green. Beside the botanical gardens the Governor-General's house still looks exceedingly British, but only very rarely do you hear the strident voice of anti-white nationalism. There seems no public resentment against so diffident a pigment as ours, and the loiterers will grin at you pleasantly as you pursue your watchful navigations between the pitches.

Often they will do more than merely grin, for the Trinidadian is a great talker. He may want to talk about religion. 'You have to understand that we are Sunnis; it's all a matter of orthodoxy, we do not agree about the succession, you see.' Or: 'My friend, I come here not to play games but to meditate. I come to think, to try to understand, you get me?' Or they want to talk politics. 'It's all a matter of race, man. This man's a dictator, that's quite clear. He's got no experience. A man like Bertie, he's got politics in his blood. That's the truth, man.' Or: 'Where do you belong? England? I've got two brothers and an aunt and a cousin in Birmingham. They live 102 Middens Lane, Birmingham 2. Sure, they like it fine, making plenty money!' Or here, as everywhere in the Western world, you may hear the time-honoured cry of the taxi-man, leaning across the railings beside the road. 'You want a car, sir? I take you all round the island, Pitch Lake,

Benedictine Monastery, Airport, Calypso, Limbo Dance, Night Clubs? Here's my card, sir! That's my name. Cuthbert B. Harrison!'

And finally, a climax to your wanderings, you may find yourself embroiled in the counter-marchings of an embryo steel band, twenty boys in home-made uniforms beating on cans and tin plates and chanting rhythmically. On their sailor jackets the words 'Brass Boys' are hazily embroidered, and they prance there in the evening sunshine like black leprechauns, banging away at their plates, singing their boisterous but monotonous ditty, round and round in a vigorous long-legged barefoot circle. The cricketers play their ancient game; the kites stream above the Savannah; an English lady waits patiently for her dog beside the racetrack; the Negro in the grandstand stirs, tilts his hat over his eyes and goes to sleep again; and in the middle of it all this noisy rite exuberates, the shining lithe legs kick to its clattering rhythms, and the white teeth flash in the sunshine.

Port of Spain is a tolerant, cosmopolitan, relatively well-educated city; but one sometimes feels that for all the stroke-play and the intelligence the real essence of the place is contained in these raw and raucous celebrations. Certainly there are moments when the music of Mr Morgan's violin, still riding the breeze uncertainly, seems the melody of a retreating world, just as the intoxicating turrets and baubles of his house are memorials to a Trinidad of long ago.

27

END OF THE LINE

Puerto Montt, 1961

They say now that in the early 1960s Puerto Montt, at the southern end of Chile, was a bolt-hole for Nazi war criminals, but I never found any, and rather admired the German community there as a matter of fact. I would never have made an investigative reporter.

I bet you've never heard of Puerto Montt, and I don't blame you: for there are, as it happens, not many places on the face of the earth much farther away from everywhere else. You can beat round the Horn to get here, if you like, or you can pound down the spine of Chile in a train from Santiago, but whichever way you travel, Puerto Montt is likely to strike you as being a very long way indeed, a very long, strange, wet, windy way from home. No first fine careless raptures here, no honey still for tea: if you feel inclined to home thoughts from abroad, come to Puerto Montt.

It stands huddled in winter damp at the head of the Ancud Gulf, 700 miles south of Santiago, and it is in more than one sense the end of the track. Below Puerto Montt the Chilean archipelago stretches desolately on, another 1,200 miles of it, mostly forested, roadless, wild and cut about with fjords, until it reaches the sheep, oil and gold settlements at the bottom of the earth – Punta Arenas, on the Magellan Strait, and China Creek, where they are drilling for oil on the edge of the Antarctic.

This cold, grey and windswept world begins at Puerto Montt. Here the railway trains turn and go home again, here the Pan-American Highway peters out at last, and here the battered old coasters, tall-funnelled and dented, plough away past Chiloe Island for the remotest south.

*

How do you see it? Birch-bark Indian? Cold Conrad? Pata-
gonian Baroque? It is none of these. It is a German colony with
aboriginal grace-notes, set in a sort of volcanic Norway on the
South Pacific shore. Puerto Montt was founded in the first half
of the nineteenth century, when the Chileans moved across the
Bio-Bio river into the lands of the fierce Auyracanian Indians:
and it still faintly possesses the shambled pride of a frontier
town, a hint of a cuss and swagger, the snort of a railhead.

Behind there stretches a magnificent hinterland of lakes,
mountain trails and Andean summits. Below the bleak coastline
sprawls away in mist and drizzle. High above the town, veiled
now in cloud and vapour, the great volcano Osorno, crowned
with the perpetual snows, stands in splendid menace. It is a
heavy landscape, but suggestive; grandiose, but sly.

Upon it the German Chileans have faithfully imposed a little
image of their origins. The first colonists came here in 1842, as
a memorial in the plaza tells us, and they have remained to this
day, through all the ups and downs of European fortune,
inalienably German. People call this part of Chile, northwards to
Osorno and Valdivia, the German Commonwealth, so long and
so diligently have the Germans colonized it, and so strong is the
flavour they have stamped into its soil. They are not many in
numbers – 35,000, perhaps – but they are strong in character,
and one can only admire the tenacity with which they have
down the generations, without overt arrogance or reserve,
preserved their mores and their identities.

Puerto Montt itself, for instance, is pre-eminently a town of
scrubbed tables and common sense, thrift and business diligence. Its houses are mostly faced with unpainted shingles, very
Nordic and sensible, and here and there stand structures in the
Alpine manner, all high-pitched roofs and quaint balconies. The
big new hotel beside the waterfront is a vision of the Bavarian
highlands, and even the municipal pigeons inhabit a little
mountain chalet on a pedestal beside the sea. The church in the
main square is infinitely clean, quiet and austere. The West
German consulate has its offices above a hardware store in
which half the goods are Chilean-made, and virtually all the rest
German.

Blonde bland girls serve you in the shops of Puerto Montt.
Big expressionless men drive about in pick-ups. In the Olympia
Café, opposite the Farmacia Doggenweiller, there is a large

coloured poster of Hamburg, and on many a wall are chalked slogans in favour of two local political aspirants, Klein and Muhlenbrock. There is no false reticence about it all, no half-conscious instinct to submerge, such as seems to soften the edges of many British and American communities in South America. These people are Germans and proud of it, for all their Chilean citizenship, and it will be a long, long time before their roots are lost at last.

But their ascendancy is not complete, for around its perimeter Puerto Montt reverts to its environment, loses its trimness and stolidity, and is shot through with darker racial strains, Indian and Latin, swarthy faces and shaggy hair and twinkling boys with runny noses.

There are men with long raggety ponchos about, and floppy black hats, and sometimes somebody clatters by on a muddy pony, and often there creaks through the streets a small covered wagon with an arched canvas roof, such as you see swaying across the landscapes of the Western legend. An old man with a barrel-organ plays outside the tobacconist's kiosk on the esplanado: he has a cage of canaries on top of his instrument, and he looks so brown, wrinkled and anachronistic, surrounded there by solemn children in the afternoon, that he reminds me of the gaunt Neapolitan organ-men you see in daguerrotypes of old London.

Most of all it is the sea, the tumbled grey western sea, that brings a strain of wilderness into Puerto Montt, tempers its German order, and makes the wanderer feel so peculiarly remote. The Pacific always strikes me as a pallid, unlovable sort of ocean, and when it is associated with cold, dank and unpainted wood it seems a thing of empty disenchantment, not worth trying to understand, like one of those spurious mysteries that are really not mysteries at all.

In the bay of Puerto Montt some old freighter is commonly lying, streaked with age and weariness, lop-sided among her lighters as she loads for the Magellan Straits or Patagonia. In the fishing harbour around the corner the hulking southern schooners lie side by side, stinking of oil and bilge, and sometimes you see one towed out into the fairway by four men in a rowing-boat, like an old galleon off to the Indies. There is a huddle of landing-craft in the harbour, and a grey dredger, and along the green Angelmo inlet, like a soggier Falmouth, many a boat lies bottom-up in a yard, or is propped despondent on a slipway.

And wettest, strangest, most southern, most remote, more alien than any melon-flower are the sea creatures of Puerto Montt, dredged through the rain out of the Pacific. There are heavy eels with muscular flanks, big flat fish like slabs of fat, giant clams, crinkled oysters by the million, mountains of spiky urchins, glistening and globular. Down at the fishing harbour cheerful black-eyed men unload these queer objects from their rowing-boats. There on the shingle they pile their wooden drays with oysters and urchins, and there and then the people of Puerto Montt, like hungered animals driven to the seashore, crack open the oysters with their knives, or carefully extract with tongue or finger, like cats exploring the last segment of a saucer, the slobbery insides of urchins. There is something disturbingly elemental about this process, if you try it for yourself: it makes you feel, as you suck out the intestines of your dying mollusc on the beach, a bit like a scavenger crab.

Funny sort of place, you are probably saying. All those Germans, and feeling like a crab! Well, it's probably not so strange if you live here, and all its lights and shades are probably heightened, its rains made wetter, its Teutons more Teutonic, its sea-urchins pricklier and its land-urchins snottier, its ponchos more frayed, its steamboats more tumbledown, if you are seeing it for the first, and almost certainly the last, time in your life.

Anyway, few travellers stay long in Puerto Montt. Some turn up their collars for the southern desolations, where seven days of the year are normally tempestuous, twenty-five stormy, ninety-three squally, and 189 rainy or overcast. Some return, soaked or sated, in a Pullman coach to Santiago. And some like me, impelled by an irresistible homing instinct, turn their faces east, and struggling through the lakes and mountains of the southern Andes, make for Argentina. For Puerto Montt, 41°51′ South, 73°West, is distinctly the end of the Grantchester line.

28

RIO!

Rio de Janeiro, 1961

I dare say this exuberant piece is a little too exuberant, but coming to Rio de Janeiro for the first time after a long and sometimes difficult journey around the South American republics did wonders for my adrenalin. Anyway, though Brazil remains the perennial Country of the Future, I have found no reason to revise my reactions since.

When I was once hanging around an airfield in Patagonia, hoping to thumb a lift to the north, I noticed a small group of people, dressed apparently for *après-ski*, who seemed to dominate the waiting-room with a kind of steely radiance. They looked very rich, and very brassy, and very thrusting. Their children were ill-mannered but intensely vivacious, their women were gimlet-eyed but seductive, their men had a feline Italian elegance to them: and unexpectedly, when I offered a smile in their glittering direction, one and all suddenly, brilliantly, delightfully smiled back. I asked where these magical creatures were making for, and was answered in one short tingling word: 'Rio!'

Angels they are not, the people of Rio, but instantly I felt like an old Pope in a slave market, for to me there seemed something remote and romantic about their manner of effervescent, if not reckless, audacity. It is this spirit of excitement, this animal crackling of the spirits, that sets their city apart from its South American peers, and makes it such a shot in the arm, such a haunting tune in the head. Rio is not, as legend has it, one perpetual Mardi Gras, thumping and blaring in false noses all night long. It is a place of deep and humane variety, full of fun indeed, but tinged also with a high-strung melancholy. Here you may well be deafened by the sambas blazing down

Copacabana Beach, but you may also stumble across some elderly grey Negro, in dungarees paled by many a scrub, plucking upon his guitar melodies of a very different kind, half African, half Portuguese, part New World, part Old, sad as an east wind, soft as any courtier's lyric, and played with such grave and sophisticated intellectualism that you may feel yourself, down there by the harbour-front, in the presence of some remarkable inheritance, some old and unassailable attitude of mind.

For Rio is a manner of thought: not just a spectacle, not just a song and dance, but a particular approach to the problems of human progress. In this city you suck your milk out of the coconut with an impeccably hygienic straw: and whether you are discussing economic philosophy with some whiskered academic, or holding hands in the dim of a night-club dawn – whether you are twanging your guitar in the Dorian or the Lydian mode, you will find that here, by some happy freak of the time mechanism, the clock always stops at midnight.

Everything they say about it, all the same, is factually true. Never did a city better live up to its reputation, or more handsomely justify the picture-postcard flattery. In its splendour of situation, encouched among bays and humped hills, it has only half a dozen rivals on earth – Hong Kong perhaps, Venice, Wellington, San Francisco, Naples, Sydney, possibly Beirut, Cape Town at a pinch. Its brilliant beaches, lined with parades of skyscraper hotels and patrolled by gaudy bird-shaped kites, have become the very emblem of sunshine hedonism – to my own taste ineffably boring, but to those who enjoy the salacious torpor of a rich sandy foreshore, incomparable in their kind. Its climate, sometimes desperately hot but often softened by sea mist, gives it a sensual, heavy-lidded, perfumed temperament. Its old culture, inherited equally from Portuguese gentlemen and Muslim slaves out of Africa, makes it much more than just a pleasure-drome. The miserable hovels of its slums, perched in sad incongruity above the waterside highways, or crouched hangdog among the apartment blocks, remind us that it is a city in the round, where every kind of man lives and makes love, and women in rags can look across a pavement to see the ripple of Balenciaga. The squalid indigence of its countryside, only twenty miles from Copacabana, rams home the truth that it is only the beautiful pinnacle of a vast, half-ignorant, disease-ridden, mostly empty, partly unexplored hinterland. Rio is all things to everyone. It fulfils every preconception.

It is an urgent, overcrowded city, invested in the rear by the Brazilian jungle, still creeping gloomily down its hillsides, and giving to some imaginative visitors a spectral impression of impending doom. Its topography is cramped and awkward. It is sprawled about the big bay of Guanabara, big enough to shelter half the navies of the world, and all around it stand mountains, some in massive forested ridges, some in sudden bumps and protrusions at the water's edge. If you stand beneath the gigantic hilltop figure of Christ, where the tourists buy their pictorial crockery or their cases of pickled Brazilian beetles – if you stand up there on the peak called Corcovado beneath the outstretched arms of the statue, you may see how sinuously Rio weaves its purlieus among the contours, sometimes slinking behind a mountain, sometimes huddling beneath a ridge, sometimes charging clean through a hillside in a pair of masterly tunnels. The waterfront of Rio is all curves, all unexpected coves, lined with trees and tall white buildings, cut off one part from another by high ground or inlets. The roads of Rio are a congested clamour. The waters of Rio stream with shipping, from the chugging Niterói ferry-boats to the big Brazilian carrier lying like a grandee beyond Flamengo. Even the skies of Rio are full of animation, for never did a city plunge so enthusiastically into the air age, so that the municipal airport lies slap in the middle of town, beside the water, and there are four hundred services a week to São Paulo alone.

But if it is sometimes frantic, it is also handsome, in a curled and burnished taste. São Paulo to the south is genially plebeian, a haven, a labour market and a gold mine. Brasília across the mountains is doggedly futuristic, airily above class or controversy. But in Rio it is easy to accept the unlikely fact that Brazil was once an Empire of its own, and that up the road in Petropolis a pretender to the imperial throne still sits hopefully in a florid palace. We call it Rio indeed, but its proper name is São Sebastião do Rio de Janeiro, and its origins are nothing if not high-flown. It does not feel an old city, though in fact it was founded in 1560. Its impatient gusto has torn down most of the old structures, and long ago discarded the old design, leaving only an occasional gilded church among the office blocks, or a splendid theatre high and dry among the traffic jams. Its manner, though, is seldom blatant, and more than most cities it feels organic to its setting. This is a place naturally clothed, as the Scottish wanderer John Robertson said in the early 1800s, 'with richness and beauty altogether marvellous'. The modern architecture of Rio is not often ugly, and is sometimes magnificent. Its elderly suburbs do not feel unwanted or humiliated, but are allowed to age there quietly among their palms, like rather cantankerous, but still affectionately regarded relatives. The famous mosaic pavements of the city blend as happily with glass and concrete as they did with sculptured stone and whirligigs. Almost nothing feels intrusive, from the incomprehensibly abstract war memorial on the waterfront to the famous cable car swinging hungrily across the bay to the restaurant on top of the Sugar Loaf.

For the spirit of this city is tolerant and sanguine to a fault, and makes you feel that nothing is unwelcome, and nothing altogether impossible. Here you can be, by and large, what you want to be, behave how you like, wear a frock-coat to dinner or a Jamaica shirt, a mink stole or a bikini. Rio takes you as you are, impelled by the conviction that in a community of such endless and pulsating variety, every little helps. Of course this magnanimity has its seamier concomitants – greed, exploitation, corruption, extravagance, materialism, ostentation. Even the transient visitor to Copacabana, searching desperately for a hotel room, will soon detect the advantages of greasing a Rio palm. Somehow, though, one is not affronted by these weaknesses, for all the fiddlings and coarser ambitions of the place are blunted, softened and made innocent by the warm tropical air of Brazil, which brings to this city's affairs a faint languorous suggestion of *dolce far niente* – not enervating enough to prevent the making of fortunes or the beating of drums, but sufficiently soothing to make you feel that here, more than in places of more rigid principle, humanity still lingers on. For Rio is, as a hard-boiled oil-man once observed to me, a very benediction among cities, like a morning of English summer among days of the year, or an apple pie among puddings.

The sceptics will scoff, and of course this is the romantic's view of Rio. It is true that there is to this city a certain never-never feeling, just as there is to Brazil as a whole a certain *naïveté* or childish enthusiasm. It is not exactly power that you feel in Rio, immense though the resources of this city are, but a sense of heady appetite – a looking-glass appetite, where you may shrink or grow by a nibble or a sip, sing wild songs or consort with strange knights. Brazil has been the Country of the Future for several centuries now, and Rio is its mirror. The overwhelming impact of the place is one of always impending euphoria, as though things are just about to be all for the best in practically the best of all possible worlds. Some people liken it to a supremely talented dilettante, perpetually about to fulfil the promise of youth, mincing down the years with a novel always at the back of his mind.

But Rio cares not what they say. It is never put out, never discouraged, always hopeful, always sure. It has far more faults than I have cared to enumerate, but I loved it from the start, and I think its carping critics, sniffling at its overdrafts and deploring its excesses, cannot see the oaks for the nettles. Perhaps, like Brazil itself, it lacks some niggling virtues of common sense, but it glories in that grandest of historical qualities, style. Whatever it does is big, whatever it thinks is generous. Great God! I will swap you a dozen prim and thrifty boroughs for one such lovely greatheart!

29

THE CITY STATE

Singapore, 1974

Singapore seems to me one of the most interesting, if hardly one of the nicest, places on earth. In the early 1970s it was only beginning to emerge as a great economic force in the world, but it already gave me a strong unnerving feeling that I was visiting the future.

And on from thence, I misquoted to myself as I boarded the aircraft in Hong Kong, and on from thence to Singapore: and though the Lion City is hardly a garden of the sun, at least it is distinctly golden, and possesses a mingled allure of the rapacious, the aggressive, the repellent and the extraordinary that any true pilgrim would relish. We live in a world of alliances, alignments and conformities: for the professional traveller there is nothing more agreeable than to reach, like the desert caravans of old, a place that is altogether on its own, ramparted, defiant and *sui generis*. Such a place, like it or not, is undeniably the Republic of Singapore. It is like nowhere else. It lives adventurously. It is equally admired and detested. It glitters in the anticipation. It stands on the sea's edge, ostentatiously. It is the last of the city-states – or perhaps, gnomically speaking, the first.

No Florence, though, or Mantua. Flat, steamy, thickly humid, the island lies there in its hot seas, fringed with mangrove swamps, and from the air it looks as it always did, a slightly desperate place that ought to be uninhabited. It looks an invented place, and so of course it is: for it was created by the British virtually out of nothing, to consolidate their command of the eastern trade. Only a handful of Malays, Chinese farmers and peripatetic seamen lived uncomfortably on Singapura when

Stamford Raffles bought it from Chief Temonggong and Sultan Tengku Long of Johore: the island was brought to life by the alchemy of Empire.

The artefacts of the British still show down there, adjusting geography as they so often did. There is the Johore Causeway, still the one link with the Malay peninsula, which the imperialists built to connect the island with their protectorates upon the mainland. There is the naval base upon the Johore Strait, one of the last great military works of the British Empire. There the island roads converge, as they do in many another imperial island, upon the sprawl of the seaport around its harbour. There are the jostling sampans still, like a log-jam in the Singapore river, and there are the ranks of ships in the roadsteads, fussed about by launches, tugs and bum-boats, that the magnetism of Empire first attracted to this fulcrum of the eastern seas.

For most Britons of a certain age, I suppose, Singapore remains Raffles's island to this day: but it is poignantly true that although no possession of the old Empire was more dashingly acquired, romantically conceived, or successfully developed, still in historical terms Singapore remains a figure of all that was fustiest and snobbiest in the colonial Empire, all that went with baggy shorts and ridiculous moustaches, with servant problems and Sunday sing-songs at the Seaview, with tennis clubs and beer and meeting for elevenses at Robinson's – with everything that was most bourgeois about the declining Empire, and in the end with everything that was most ineffectual. Singapore was the archetype of Somerset Maugham's Empire, Noel Coward's Empire – an Empire that had lost its purpose, its confidence and its will: when it fell to the Japanese in 1942, in effect the Empire fell too, and the idea of Empire too.

When I landed in Singapore a homing instinct led me direct to the core of this dead colony, the downtown expanse of green called the Padang, and there without surprise I discovered that the imperial ghosts live on. There was the warm nostalgic smell of mown grass. The last post-prandial members of the Singapore Cricket Club were still sitting with their gin-slings on the veranda, white linen hats over their eyes. There stood the spire of the Anglican cathedral, fretted but still handsome in its close, with small Anglican-looking cars parked outside its offices, and large Anglican-looking ladies coordinating arrangements in its porch. Ineffably conceited barristers, direct from Lincoln's Inn, adjusted their wing-collars or tilted their wigs beneath the colonnade of the Supreme Court: civil servants with briefcases hurried preoccupied into the great offices of Government from whose windows, during a century of British rule, expatriate administrators looked out with pride or loathing across the tropic green.

Away to the west, over Anderson Bridge, the lumpish structures of imperial capitalism still breathed the spirit of the thirties, so that I half-expected to see Oxford bags and monocles emerging from their revolving doors, or wives in pink cloche hats dropping in on Reggie. Away to the east stood the glorious palms of Raffles Hotel, that grand caravanserai of Empire, the Shepheards of the East, where the Maughams used to drink and the Cowards fizz, where the gin-sling was invented, where there was a Free Dark Room for Amateur Photographers, and Hotel Runners Boarded All In-coming Steamers, where Admiral Skrydloff and the Duke of Newcastle stayed, where generations of Malayan planters intrigued their leaves away, and not a few planters' wives began their tearful journeys home to mother.

It is all there still. There are no Britons in those offices of Government. Those barristers are mostly Indian. The Finest Organ in the East no longer plays for Lady Tumsbury's charity balls, at the Victoria Memorial Hall. The spin-drift ensigns of the regiments have been removed from the cathedral. Even Raffles, in an uncharacteristically philistine moment, recently lowered the ceilings of its vast bedrooms, where the old iron fans used to creak and swirl through the nights of exile or ecstasy. Yet those ghosts wander there still, mostly dead but sometimes alive, and the ethos of the dying Empire, threadbare, raffish, gone to seed, well-meaning, lingers there forlornly.

It was from the Padang that the humiliated tuans and their wives, mustered by the Japanese, began their cruel march to Changi Prison and often to death: and if I closed my eyes, I thought, I could still hear their voices in the sunshine, courageous or querulous, insisting upon water for the dogs or bursting bravely into 'There'll Always Be An England'. The British Empire went out with a whimper, assiduously though we have disguised the fact even to ourselves, and in Singapore especially it faded away in pathos – or worse still, bathos, for the generals were second-rate, the songs were banal, the policies were ineffectual, and even the courage was less than universal.

I find this mixture very moving – the imperial energies debased and enervated, like a very exclusive sport when the masses take it over. Singapore fell partly because its defence was timid and inept, but partly because its rulers did not wish to put at risk the lives of their indigenous subjects: it was an attitude flaccid but not altogether ignoble, and translated to a wider sphere, it meant that the Empire had outlived itself. My *Whitaker's Almanack* for 1945 records Singapore as being 'temporarily in hostile Japanese occupation': but though that 'temporarily' proved true, and the British did raise their flag again above the Padang, still things could never be the same again. The good of Empire, like the bad, depended upon force and the will to use it: by 1945 the British had lost that will for ever, and for that matter the force too.

In a masochistic moment I determined to visit the exact spot where, on 15 February 1942, was sealed the fate of Singapore and thus of the British Empire – which Churchill himself, only a year or two before, had conjectured might last a thousand years. The Japanese had then captured most of the island, but had only penetrated the outskirts of Singapore City: short of fuel and ammunition, they were exerting their will upon the hapless British more by bluff than by superior power. They were on a winning streak, the British unmistakably on a losing: at seven o'clock that evening General Percival, wearing his steel helmet and long shorts, walked along the Bukit Timah road to meet General Yamashita at the Ford Motor Company factory, and surrender Raffles's island to the Great East Asia Co-Prosperity Sphere.

The factory has not much changed since then. The buildings are still modest, low and rather drab, and the man at the gate still raises his barrier with that faintly military manner so characteristic of lesser functionaries under British colonial rule. Inside, the offices have been shifted around somewhat, and separated with glass partitions, and the room in which the surrender was signed has been divided into two. Nevertheless, they said, as they showed me into a fairly gloomy, wood-panelled and teak-furnished executive chamber, this was the very place where the surrender was signed. Even the furniture was the same. Here sat Percival and his three staff officers, hangdog and exhausted, hopelessly, almost obsequiously asking for more time. Here sat the bullish Yamashita in his medal ribbons and open-necked shirt – 'All I want to know is, do you surrender unconditionally or not? Yes or no?' The fans whirred heavily above their heads, and as the sun began to set the dim electric lights came on: in the long silences Percival stared helpless at his papers, Yamashita's fingers drummed the table-top. Japanese war correspondents and military photographers jostled all around the table, Yamashita's generals sat impassive beside him. I could see the tired eyes of the British officers, flinching in the flare of the flash-bulbs, as Percival accepted the terms with a limp 'Yes', and the papers were signed – Yamashita in a bold flourish, Percival in a cramped schoolboyish hand with what I would surmise to be a Conway Stewart 2s 6d fountain pen.

I felt ashamed to be there, and sorry, and I wished poor General Percival happier campaigning in his afterlife – 'He looked so pale and thin and ill,' said General Yamashita later, before they hanged him for his war crimes. Did many British visitors come to see the room? I asked the Ford people. Not very many, they said, very few in fact: but seldom a day went by without a coachload of Japanese tourists stopping at the factory gate, while their guide pointed out the historic window, and the Canons clicked.

Singapore is a harbour, and when the British went, the harbour stayed. One afternoon I rented a sampan, and chugged with a couple of friends to an offshore island called Sakijang Bendera, which looked enticing on the map. It took a long time to get there. The ignition keys were missing. The engine wouldn't start. The boatman remembered some unfinished business on the next pier but one. The sampan, though sturdy, was not swift. Spray got in our eyes, oil got on our skirts, the heat blazed mercilessly down, warming the water like a tepid bath and blurring the horizons in mirage. Once a tropical storm burst violently over us, and sometimes the boatman made despondent grunting noises, as though he wished he had never come.

But this is the best way to experience the harbour of Singapore – sweating, soaked, oiled, delayed, slightly irritated. These are the conditions of the place, and best illustrate its origins and meanings. Raffles chose the island as his new entrepôt because he recognized it as the ideal staging-post on the Oriental shipping routes, commanding the narrow straits by which shipping must pass from the Indian Ocean to the China Sea. Here, 100 miles north of the Equator, the Indian, the Chinese and the Polynesian worlds meet, and the great trade routes converge. It is Conrad country, where the seamen of every nation clamber ashore for their pleasure at Connaught Pier, the coasters labour in from Borneo and Java, and the original Bill Bailey ignored all requests to go home from his celebrated bar in Cuppage Road. The average noonday temperature of Singapore is 87°F, and the population is a heady mixture of the races, packed tumultuously around the great port as in a huge bazaar.

All about us, as we proceeded jerkily across the harbour, ships and islands lay: the islands green with palms and mangroves, and suggestive with the remains of fortifications: the ships anchored row by row, like a city of ships, some high in the water, some deep with merchandise, from Monrovia and from Panama, from Liverpool and from Yokohama; and from their rails the wan faces of sailors looked down upon us like prisoners, sometimes offering us a listless wave, or chewing gum like camels. The water was thick and scummy, the ships all looked rusty, it rained again, and when we got to the island an adamant official said we were forbidden to land there, owing to its being a quarantine station for *highly* infectious diseases – '*deadly* diseases, Madam, I cannot allow you to run the risks'. I enjoyed every minute of the trip, and thought it admirably demonstrated for me the brutal continuity of Singapore.

Actually hardly anybody in Singapore seems to think about history at all. The reason for this is that though the Malays originally owned Singapore, the British developed it and the Japanese conquered it, it was always the Chinese who really ran it. Year by year, generation after generation, they drifted down the line of the peninsula from their Chinese homeland, intuitively attracted by the opportunities of Singapore, until they far outnumbered Britons and Malays alike, and provided most of the island's muscles, and much of its brains. The Chinese are not habitually interested in the past, and the result is that Singapore essentially lives for the day, and does not much bother about history. The statues of Raffles and other imperial worthies survive unmolested, but lacklustrely, as though nobody is quite sure who they are: and the Singapore Museum, so painstakingly built up by the imperialists, seems to have fallen into a genteel but unloved decline.

The Chineseness of Singapore is a quality of the overseas Chinese, and thus stands to the central Chinese tradition, I suppose, rather as Australianness stands to England. It is very different from the ethos of Hong Kong, whose citizens stand in everyday contiguity to China, and see the shores and hills of their heartland every day of their lives. Singapore is 1,500 miles from China, and the vast majority of its inhabitants have never set eyes on the country. In Hong Kong one feels China beckoning her children home across the Sham Chun river: in Singapore one senses only the steelier, less emotional genius of China in exile.

China in Singapore is not beautiful. No great monuments give it grandeur. Its architecture is a muddle of styles East, West and unclassifiable. Its faces are, to Western eyes, parchments of bland reticence. Its colours are greyish, greenish, wooden, sun-bleached colours. Its shapes are higgledy-piggledy. It seems beyond number and beyond control, yet it seems to move, too, with an inner deliberation, an innate expertise, that gives it an almost conspiratorial air, very different to the jolly push and roguery of Hong Kong.

Three quarters of Singapore citizens are Chinese, and in effect this is a great Chinese city, one of the greatest. Everything that is most vigorous about it is Chinese-sponsored, from the skyscraper to the corner boutique, from the exquisite cuisine of the great restaurants to the multitudinous eating-stalls which, miraculously as the sun goes down, spring up in the streets and car parks of the city. The grave bewigged judges of the Supreme Court, impeccable though their Oxford English may be, and remote their acquaintance with Peking and Soochow, are really as Chinese as Mao himself. The sampan man in the harbour, though he lives and moves against a background of equatorial sleaziness, is no more than a transplanted junk man from the austere grey Yangtse. Nine of the twelve Cabinet Ministers in the Singapore Government have Chinese names, and even now most Singapore citizens over thirty, say, if you ask them their nationality, will say Hokkien, Cantonese or Hakka.

There is in fact a Chinatown, in the heart of the downtown city. Once it was a racial enclave created by British town-planners in the cause of communal harmony; now it is merely a quarter even more thickly Chinese than all the rest. They are going to pull it down soon, for it is old-fashioned, untidy and picturesque, and already its nooks are being whittled away, and its crannies given logic: but I often strolled through it during my stay in Singapore, walking there across the green from Raffles Hotel, and spending an hour or so loitering around the waterfront of the Singapore river, which forms the promenade of Chinatown. Everyone was kind to me, for the Singapore Chinese seem to have, like Scots or Yankees, gentle natures beneath dour fronts, and in the Chinese way nothing is particularly private down there, and nobody minds you poking about.

So I pottered here and there among the go-downs, feeling always the pulse of profit, and I trod the precarious gangplanks to the lighters in the river, and I peered over the shoulders of the tally-men, intent at their ledgers in the shady warehouse doors. It was blazing hot whenever I was there, and all the earnest motion of the waterfront made it seem hotter still: so that often I took a few moments off from my investigations, and sat on a doorstep in the shade, fanning myself with my hat, while the local grandmothers mumbled incoherently but benevolently beside me, and the barefoot children gathered around as for a bedtime story. 'Lady hot?' the passing labourers would say, and sometimes they would answer their own questions with a grin, humping their sacks upon their backs, or staggering beneath the load of a girder – 'very hot, too too hot today . . .'

Behind the waterfront the Chinese do their shopping. Here the food markets sprawl among the narrow streets, and deal in exotica like dried frogs and snake flesh, laid out beneath their tattered awnings in flamboyant exhibition. There are panoramas of fruit, oranges, papayas, rambutans, limes, pears from Japan, apples from South Africa and the legendary durian, which smells so bad and tastes so scrumptious. There are eggs caked in mud, and bundles of dried fish, and indefinable herbs, and vegetables unknown to man, and cages of grasshoppers. The market women eyed me wrinkled and amused as I stood aghast before these marvels, and made witty remarks to each other in Hokkien: but the shoppers spared me hardly a glance, for they were choosing their victuals with a scholarly concentration, calculating the density of turnips, contemplating the specific gravity of carp, comparing the metabolisms of goose liver and pickled crab, before with decisive gestures they solved their several equations, and stuffing liver, noodles, pressed duck and sharks' fins into their blue and yellow plastic shopping bags, hastened home to make the soup.

Though fun for foreigners, little of this is actually remarkable. It is standard Chinadom, more or less, as it exists more or less anywhere in the Chinese world. Singapore Chinatown does have a few distinctive quirks – the ornate carved clubhouses of the hongs, once gangsters' mobs, now charitable societies, or the sad street of the about-to-die, where the withered faces of the terminally sick look wistfully to the street below from their rented chambers above the coffin-shops. Mostly, though, this is a fairly ordinary community of the overseas Chinese. It has the organic strength of the commonplace, and it feels absolutely inextinguishable, as though no natural calamity, no historical force, could ever wrest it from the island, or wrench the go-down capitalists from their abacuses upon the quays.

The classic view of Singapore is from Mount Faber, a hillock which stands to the west of the harbour. Everyone goes up there to see the view. The hill was named for a nineteenth-century colonial engineer, otherwise only remembered for his sensible demand that the Singapore river be deepened, when his bridge over it proved too low to let the lighters through. In British times the indefatigable wives of colonial secretaries and directors of public works came up here to paint their water-colours, and nowadays the practitioners of Tai Chi, the ritual exercises of the Chinese discipline, pursue their craft on the summit. Not long ago Mount Faber was almost rural, with only a bumpy way worn to the summit by the wheels of landaus: now there is a tarred highway to the top, and a dramatic cable-way links it across the water to the newly developed resort island of Sentosa, on the whole the least inviting tourist project I know.

When I first went to Singapore it was the Raj that chiefly showed from Mount Faber, and filled my sketchbook pages, as it had filled Lady Timsbury's, with its domes and steeples. In those days the Padang and its buildings looked the embodiment of authority: its law courts and office blocks were like policemen linking arms to control the crush of the crowd behind, and keep it off the green. Then the crowd was about 800,000 strong: today it is more than two million, and has so overwhelmed that stately cordon that the policemen hardly show. Dome and portico,

Raffles and Empress Place are humiliated by the thickets and shafts of the new skyscrapers – gleaming, rectangular, terrifically ostentatious and none more than ten years old. New Singapore seems to be sprouting there before your eyes, and its proliferation of gaudy curtain-walls, its frenzy of penthouses and observation decks, defied my sketchbook pen, and made me turn the other way in desperation, and attempt a dispirited rendering of Sentosa.

They are a nasty kind of skyscraper – very rich, very arrogant, very vulgar, more like Centre Point than the Seagram Building. But they are more than mere show. They truly represent, as potently as the old Padang, a political energy: the new insular dynamic, born by defiance out of danger, which has made Singapore something new in the world for a second time, and created on this steamy island a new kind of state.

When the constituent parts of the British Empire were left to find their own place in the world, blessed one by one with a grant-in-aid and a farewell visit from royalty, Singapore was left more in the cold than most. It existed only as a cog in the imperial machine, one of the four Straits Settlements which were governed as crown colonies around the perimeter of the Malay protectorates (the others were Penang, Malacca and Labuan). It was a predominantly Chinese island in a region profoundly suspicious of the Chinese, a non-Islamic community in a strongly Muslim part of the world. Attempts to incorporate Singapore in the Malaysian Federation soon failed, the Malaysians having no wish to be dominated by the Singapore Chinese; relations with the Indonesians to the south were very nearly warlike; in 1965 Singapore declared itself a sovereign republic, 'founded upon the principles of liberty and justice', with a flag of a crescent moon with five white stars, and the motto 'Let Singapore Flourish'. A city-state was born, recognizably in the tradition of the merchant-princes, with a total area of 225 square miles, but an energy that made it, by 1974, the fourth busiest port on earth.

It is not, I think, an attractive republic, but it certainly has spirit. Though its relations with its neighbours are easier now, it is still a tense, tight little state, with the same prickly and defensive excitement as Israel, say, or Iceland – a backs to the wall, let 'em all come, chips down excitement. It is a noisily

opinionated state, strong on hand-outs, short on tact, or sympathy – a harsh and cocky state, setting its own standards,
choosing its own styles, and working so hard that its living
standards are claimed to be the highest in Asia, excepting only
Japan's. There are very few clubs in modern Singapore; there
are no beggars at all; the railway trains may not arrive punctually,
for they come over the Johore Causeway from Kuala Lumpur
and Bangkok, but I am quite sure they *leave* on time.

It is no coincidence that the new Singapore, like the old, is
the creation of one man. There is no room here for committee
government: until the war Singapore was an absolute depen-
dency of Britain, and the Governor was in effect omnipotent –
'Well,' said His Excellency Sir Shenton Thomas, when told that
the Japanese Imperial Army had invaded Malaya, 'I suppose
you'll shove the little men off!' I never saw Lee Kuan Yew when
I was in Singapore, but like everyone else I felt I knew him well,
from his frequent appearances on television, his well-known
political opinions, and the sensation of his ubiquitous power.
Physically, it is true, I sometimes confused him in my mind
with Willy Brandt, to whom he bears a paradoxical Orientalized
resemblance: but metaphysically I saw him clear, for he is
perhaps the last in the line of Western-educated Chinese
autocrats, a man built for greater power, the commands of
armies or the marshalling of provinces, who is obliged by
history to channel his brilliant and perhaps bitter abilities into
the narrow arena of a state less populous than Wales.

'The first 150 years of Singapore', says a commemorative
history published in association with the Singapore International Chamber of Commerce, 'open and close under the aegis
of a great man: Raffles . . . pointing the way: Lee Kuan Yew for
today.' Connoisseurs of sycophantic history, or for that matter
of post-imperial commerce, will recognize the tone of this
remark. It is the tone of a wary citizen, brought up in the liberal
tradition of the West, who finds himself subject to a very
different kind of authority, and is playing it cautiously. I have
heard it in many corners of the old Empire, Ghana to St Lucia,
and if I observe that it seldom seems to have done anybody
much good for long, I am not implying that Lee Kuan Yew is
just another petty despot. He is by all accounts a cultivated and
charming man, with a Cambridge law degree and a witty mind:
but he is nevertheless, if not actually a dictator, at least an

authoritarian, at the head of a one-party state, and in his
Singapore you will detect most of dictatorship's symptoms,
good, bad and disturbing.

Like many autocracies, Lee Kuan Yew's is very logical.
Singapore has no natural resources, except its human ones, and
it lives by its abilities. It makes things out of other people's
substances, it loads and tranships other people's cargoes, it fuels
and mends other people's ships and aircraft, it insures and
disposes other people's goods, it gives advice, it banks money,
it shows itself to visitors from elsewhere. Like many another
former imperial entrepôt or dockyard – Malta, Gibraltar, Hong
Kong – it sets out to perform, as a freelance, the offices it once
performed, as a staff member, for the British Empire. This is a
precarious status. Lee Kuan Yew believes that to preserve it, the
whole state must be resolutely directed towards a kind of
communal expertise. There is no time for argument. There is no
room for dilettantism, nostalgia or party politics. Prosperity is
the single aim of the state, and it can be retained only by
rigorous discipline and specialization, under the unchallenged
authority of an intelligent despotism. Political stability, reasons
Lee Kuan Yew, equals foreign confidence, equals investment,
equals money for all, which is all the average citizen wants of
life and statesmanship.

In some ways this is a Puritan ethic, and both Cromwell and
Mao would approve of many of Lee Kuan Yew's policies.
Singapore is clean, relatively honest, apparently undecadent.
Litter on the streets is savagely punished, drugs are mercilessly
kept out, the rock culture is pointedly discouraged. Newspapers
must toe the official line or disappear, and dissenting politicians
too are apt to find themselves in trouble, or even prison. All this
makes of course for the usual autocratic drabness. Nothing is
more *boring* than a one-party state, and nothing is more
dispiriting than to wake up at Raffles Hotel, settling down to
papaya, toast and marmalade, and to find that there is nothing
to read but the *Straits Times*, a newspaper rather less outspoken
than *Little Women*.

Everywhere in Singapore nowadays one feels the imprint
of a single and implacable intelligence. At the University the
arts faculties are being encouraged to die on their feet, as use-
less parasites of a technical society. At the cinema black
blobs expunge unsuitable passages of film, as messengers of

degeneration. At the airport young visitors are to be seen shepherded in embarrassment towards inner chambers, to have their hair cut. Beside the Anderson Bridge a hideous concrete chimera, half-lion, half-dolphin, adequately symbolizes both the republic's self-image and its aesthetic standards. Nothing, one feels in Singapore, is being left to chance: serendipity is the very last of this republic's virtues. Singapore is a living-machine, highly functional, with the ornamentation reduced to a mini-mum, and an inflexible foreman at the controls.

It is all very deliberate, very rational. Take industry. Since the entrepôt business is always vulnerable, and depends upon the economic circumstances of others, Singapore has deliberately turned itself into a manufacturing state – and not just any old manufactures, but specifically sophisticated products which less highly skilled labour forces cannot manage. Young people are being educated towards this specific end, a new industrial city has been built on the most modern lines in the swamp country of the south-west, and already industry is more impor-tant to Singapore than the entrepôt trade of tradition.

Or take congestion. Since the land area is so small, the new Singapore is rebuilding itself on revolutionary lines. It is not simply that buildings are going higher. In Singapore entire social complexes are being concentrated within single blocks, containing not only hundreds of shops, offices, flats, but hotels, theatres, garages, swimming-pools, the whole entity pulled together by the inescapable escalators, perpetually packed and often visible from the street outside, which remain in my mind as the kinetic emblems of the republic. The population is being rehoused in equally concentrated complexes, and so Singa-pore takes on an altogether new appearance, more or less unique to itself, and more truly futuristic than anywhere else I know.

Or take tourism. This is very important to Singapore, and the Government adeptly adjusts some of its principles to accom-modate it, especially as, except for shopping and Sentosa, there is practically nothing in Singapore for a tourist to do. When it comes to tourism Lee Kuan Yew's asceticism is modified, and all is indulgent luxury. There is the customary duty-free shop-ping, of course, without which no tourist haven can respectably survive. But there is also a carefully cherished ambience of the sybaritic. 'Instant Asia', the local publicists call Singapore, but it is an opulent kind of Asia. There are said to be more first-class hotels on Orange Road, once the epitome of colonial suburbia, than in the whole of Australia, and everywhere the travel agents proliferate, the foreign exchanges thrive, soft music sounds from hotel mezzanines and wildly extravagant foods are served in preposterously garish décors.

It really is a new world – as new as the world that Raffles created, within this same cramped ground of experiment. Singapore's is a purely modern, technological society, without slack or sentiment: semi-communal, half brain-washed, materialist to the point of philistinism, but healthy, rich and enterprising. I expect it will crack one day, like most autocracies, when Lee Kuan Yew finally exceeds himself, succumbs to *folie de grandeur*, grows old or even dies, if death has not been banned in Singapore by then. In the meantime, the republic does not lose a moment. In every corner of Singapore, one feels, at every moment of day or night, the planners are planning, the excavators are churning, the steam-hammers chug and the ideologues prepare their next injunctions – 'hard work, thrift and grit', is what the Finance Minister demanded in a recent budget, and Lee Kuan Yew would undoubtedly add discipline too.

I often asked Singapore people if they were happy under this forceful regime, and once one of my hosts asked a similarly simplistic question of me. We were eating a delectable *poh piah* (eggs, squid, shrimp, chilis and mixed greens wrapped up in a thin pancake) at a stall in Hokkien Street, where the night looked down at us through the glare of Chinatown, and the sweating cooks laboured half-naked, towels around their necks, over their blazing stoves. 'You do a lot of travelling,' said my friend, 'so tell me, is Singapore a good idea?'

A good idea? I looked at him blankly, searching in vain for some Confucianist retort, like 'The wise boatman does not measure the current', or 'What use is the scroll without the brush?' I did not know what to say. The impact of the new Singapore is so powerful, so diametrically opposite to the bourgeois pragmatism of the old, that my sensibilities were rather numb. Was it a good idea? I certainly found it stimulating. The neo-Fascist vigour of Singapore is undeniably fun, if only because one feels that despite that chaste veneer it is fundamentally amoral. The futuristic imagination of the place is undeniably exciting. I myself rather relish that sense of zealous and unswerving purpose, not fortunately having to share the purpose myself. I find Lee Kuan Yew vicariously attractive as a person, but then I am often attracted by cultured authoritarians. Singapore is excellent as theatre, if rather tedious as real life.

But as to the idea of it, I felt disqualified to judge. Though I am by no means an addict of universal democracy, and recognize that our own dear Empire was at least as despotic as Lee Kuan Yew, still I am too much a child of my time and my background to enjoy the taste of autocracy. I believe in man's full and free self-expression. But even as I thought over my reply, I began to feel like an old-school music-lover trying to come to terms with electronic music. Could I be behind the times, in so distrusting the idea? Was this ruthless specialization, this cutting away of dead wood, this discarding of wasted energies, necessary for human survival? Could Lee Kuan Yew be right, in claiming that in Singapore at least, the rich man was happier than the free? How long would you pine for liberty if you had never sampled it?

Twice in a single journey I had been tempted towards these heresies – once looking across the Chinese frontier from Hong Kong, and now toying with my *poh piah* in Hokkien Street. It was not because I was weak in my allegiances: it was because I felt I was experiencing, if only vicariously, something new in the world – a new energy of the East with which, sooner or later, the Western peoples will come to grips, if not physically, at least philosophically. It is a sort of mystic materialism, a compelling marriage between principle and technique which neither capitalism nor Soviet Communism seems to me to have achieved.

The great tourist experience of Singapore used to be a visit to Change Alley, the dark covered bazaar, hardly wide enough to stretch one's arms in, through whose gauntlet of Indian shop-keepers and money-changers generations of sailors and globe-trotters picked their bemused and gullible way. I did it once or twice for old times' sake, stepping into the alley's shadows out of the glare and hustle of the quays, and enduring once more the immemorial banter of the bazaars, that leitmotiv of Empire. 'You wanta change money? You want souvenirs? Look lady, very good silk, real silk. Where you from? You got dollars? You got pounds? Look here, very cheap – come and look, no need to buy, have a cup of coffee with my father!'

Nowadays, though, the excitement of Change Alley comes at the far end of it, where it debouches into Raffles Place. Half-way through I was tempted sometimes to think that nothing changes in the Orient after all, or ever will: but the moment I emerged from that clamorous trap, and saw as in fantasy the new towers of Singapore shining in the sunshine, then I knew I was seeing something new in the world: the city-state, within its island ramparts, brazen and self-assured. It was like emerging from a tunnel under the walls, to surface within some extra-territorial civilization, where everything was shinier and brassier than life, and new kinds of people were genetically reared.

I knew my reactions then. Let me out! I cried in my waking dream. Let me out! Where's Reggie?

30

ON THE TABLELANDS

Spanish Cities, 1963

❧

In 1963 my American publishers, out of the blue, invited me to spend six months in Spain, and write a book about it. I hardly knew the country, and its impact upon me was terrific — especially that of the old cities of the high interior, Salamanca, Segovia, Avila, Toledo, which this piece describes. It was not a comfortable place: General Franco was still in power, and though this is purely a descriptive essay perhaps you may discern something of his autocracy's cold presence between my lines.

The stern tablelands that form the heart of Spain are like sounding-boards for the spirit. Though your voice often falls flat upon a dry soil, or is whisked away by the bitter wind, ideas seem to echo and expand, visions form in the great distances, and man, all alone in the emptiness, seems only the agent of some much greater Power. No wonder the Spaniards, at once oppressed and elevated by the character of the place, have built upon this plateau some of the grandest of all human artefacts, the cities of the centre. They are grand not so much as collections of treasures, or gatherings of people, but as things in their own right: all different, all indeed unique, all instantly recognizable for their own savour and design, but all touched by this same resonance of setting, and thus, one feels, by something nobler still. Let us visit four of them, and see how powerfully this combination of variety and inner cohesion contributes to the presence of Spain.

Salamanca, on the western edge of the *meseta*, is made of sandstone. One does not often specify the raw material of a city, but Spain likes to be explicit: Santiago is granite, Salamanca is sandstone. It is the calmest of the famous cities of the tableland, set more tranquilly than most beside the River Tormes, insulated by age and culture against the fierce intensity of the country. Salamanca is above all a university city – 'Mother of the Virtues, the Sciences, and the Arts' – and though its scholarship has long been shrivelled, its colleges decimated in war or emasculated by autocracy, still it has the special poise that marks a place both learned and long admired.

You approach it, if you come the right way, by foot across a fine Roman bridge, and this in itself is a kind of sedative. The bridge is old, stout, and weather-beaten; the river below is wide and steady; groves of larches and poplars line the banks; and if you pause for a moment at the alcove in the middle, you will find that life around you seems wonderfully simple and assured, as though the big trucks pounding along the ring road are only some transient phenomenon from another civilization. In the thicket immediately below the bridge, perhaps, a solitary student is deep in his book at a trestle table, supported by a bottle of pop from the shanty-café along the path, and inspired by flamenco music from the radio beneath his chair. Downstream the bourgeoisie washes its cars in the river water. Across the river a small boy canters around on a pony. A mill-wheel turns at the weir upstream; sheep graze the fields beyond; in the shallows an elderly beachcomber is prodding the mud with a stick.

Raise your eyes only a little, and there above you, scarcely a stone's throw away, stand the two cathedrals of Salamanca – so close is the Spanish country to the Spanish town, so free from peevish suburbs are these old cities of the interior. It is rather like entering Oxford, say, in the Middle Ages. The city is the heart and the brain of its surrounding countryside, so dominant that the olive trees themselves seem to incline their fruit towards its market, and the mules and asses pace instinctively in its direction. Yet the physical break is instant, and complete. One side of the river is the country, the other side is the city, and there is no straggle to blur the distinction.

Almost immediately, too, the meaning of Salamanca becomes apparent, and you seem to know by the very cut or stance of the place that this is a city of scholars. Here is the old courtyard of the university, where generations of students have written their names in flowery red ochre; and here are bookshops, those

rarities of contemporary Spain, heavily disguised with magazine racks and picture postcards, but still recognizably university
shops; and here is the great medieval lecture-room of Luis
de León, still precisely as he knew it, still bare and cold
and dedicated, with his canopied chair just as it was when,
reappearing in it after four years in the cells of the Inquisition,
he began his lecture with the words 'Dicebamus hesterna die . . .'
– 'As we were saying yesterday . . .'

Salamanca University was founded in the thirteenth century,
and for four hundred years was one of the powerhouses of
European thought. Columbus's schemes of exploration were
submitted to the judgement of its professors. The Council of
Trent was a product of its thinking. The concept of international
law was virtually its invention. The first universities of the New
World, in Mexico and Peru, were based upon its statutes. It was
while serving as Professor of Greek at Salamanca that Miguel de
Unamuno, driven out of his mind by the atrocities of the
Spanish Civil War, rushed into the street one day shouting
curses on his country, later to die of grief.

Around this institution, over the centuries, a noble group of
buildings arose, and stands there still in golden splendour. The
gorgeous plateresque façade of the Patio de las Escuelas, with
its dizzy elaborations, its busts of Ferdinand and Isabel, and its
lofty inscription – 'The King and Queen to the University and
the University to the King and Queen' – is a reminder of the
importance of this place to the State, the Crown and the Church
throughout the grand epoch of Spanish history. The New
Cathedral, pompous and commanding, was opened in 1560 to
express the grandeur of a university that then boasted twenty-
four constituent colleges, 6,000 students, and sixty professors of
unsurpassed eminence. One of the most delightful buildings in
Spain is the House of the Shells, built at the end of the fifteenth
century for a well-known Salamanca sage, and covered all over
with chiselled scallops. And nothing in Europe better expresses
a kind of academic festiveness than the celebrated Plaza Mayor,
the drawing-room of Salamanca: its arcaded square is gracefully
symmetrical, its colours are gay without being frivolous, its
manner is distinguished without being highbrow, and among
the medallions of famous Spaniards that decorate its façade
there have been left, with a proper donnish foresight, plenty of
spaces for heroes yet to come.

It is a lovely city, but like many lovely Spanish things, it is sad. Its glories are dormant. Its university, once the third in Europe, is now classed as the seventh in Spain, and seems to have no life in it. Few outrageous student rebels sprawl in the cafés of the Plaza Mayor, no dazzling philosophical theories are emerging from these libraries and lecture-rooms. Expect no fire from Salamanca. The Inquisition dampened it first and in our own time Franco's narrow notions have fatally circumscribed it. The genius of this tableland is not friendly to liberty of thought, and it will be more than a four-year hiatus, this time, before some grandly independent thinker, free as reason, can climb the steps to a Salamanca rostrum once again, and begin his lecture: *'Dicebamus hesterna die . . .'*

There is sadness too in Avila, though of a different kind. This is a soldier's city, cap-à-pie, and when you approach it from the west over the rolling plateau almost all you see is its famous wall: a mile and a half of castellated granite, with eighty-eight round towers and ten forbidding gates. It looks brand new, so perfect is its preservation, and seems less like an inanimate rampart than a bivouac of men-at-arms, their helmeted front surveying the *meseta*, their plated rear guarding some glowing treasure within. It looks like an encampment of Crusaders on the flank of an Eastern hill: a city in laager, four thousand feet up and very chilly, with the smoke rising up behind the walls where the field kitchens are at work.

But inside those watchful ranks, no treasure exists. Avila is like an aged nut, whose shell is hard and shiny still, but whose kernel has long since shrivelled. Its main gate is by the mottled cathedral, whose apse protrudes into the wall itself, and around whose courtyard a dozen comical lions – the only light relief in Avila – hold up an iron chain, their rumps protruding bawdily over the columns that support them. At first the shell feels full enough, as you wander among the mesh of medieval streets inside, through the arcades of the central plaza, and down the hill past the barracks; but presently the streets seem to peter out, the passers-by are scarcer, there are no more shops, the churches tend to stand alone in piles of rubble, and the little city becomes a kind of wasteland, like a bomb-site within the walls, several centuries after the explosion.

Avila was always a mystic city, but this wasted presence gives it a gone-away feeling. The snow-capped sierra stares down at it, the plain around seems always to be looking in her direction, the little River Adaja runs hopefully past its walls; but when you knock at its gate, there is nobody home – and even those knights-at-arms turn out to be made of stone, and are floodlit on festival days. The life of the city has escaped the ramparts, and settled among the shops and cafés of the modern town outside; and from there, sitting with an omelette at a restaurant table, or wandering among the country buses, you may look up at the Gate of Alcazar and the city walls, and think how false, indeed how slightly ludicrous, a defensive posture can look when there is nothing at all to defend.

So emaciated does the old part of Avila feel today that sometimes it is difficult to imagine how virile it must have been in her palmy days. Was it really here that St Theresa was born, that most robust of mystics, whose very visions were adventure stories, who jogged all over Spain in a mule wagon, and who did not even scruple to answer back Our Lord? ('That's how I treat My friends,' she once heard a divine voice remark, when she was complaining about a flooded river crossing, and unperturbed she retorted: 'Yes, and that's why You have so few!') Was it really in this pale outpost of tourism that young Prince Juan, only son of the Catholic Monarchs, was trained to rule the earth's greatest empire – only to die before his parents, and thus pass the crown to the house of Austria, to Philip II and his successors of the Escorial? Was it really in Avila, this city without a bookshop, that the great Bishop Alfonso de Madrigal, the Solomon of his time, wrote his three sheets of profound prose every day of his life – to be immortalized in the end by an alabaster figure in the cathedral that shows him half-way through his second page of the day? Was it here in Avila that the martyr St Vincent, having stamped upon an altar of Jupiter, was beheaded on a rock with his two loyal sisters?

It all feels so remote, so long ago, so out of character: in the Civil War, the last great historical event in which Spain played a part, Avila fell bloodlessly to the Nationalists, and never thereafter heard a shot fired in anger. For me it is like a superb plaster cast of a city, all hollow. There is only one place in Avila in which the pungency of the past really seems to linger, and that is the crypt of the Church of San Vicente, just outside the walls on the eastern side. Here you may see the very rock on

which that family of martyrs died, and beside it in the wall
there is a small sinister hole. On 27 October 303, St Vincent
was executed, and his body was thrown to the dogs who
prowled and yapped about the rock. A passing Jew paused to
make fun of the corpse, but instantly there flew out of that small
hole in the rock face an angry serpent, which threw itself upon
the Hebrew and frightened him away. This episode was gratefully remembered by the Christians. For several centuries it was
the custom of the people of Avila, when they wished to take an
oath, to crowd down the steps of the crypt of San Vicente, and
place their hands in that orifice as they swore; and to this day it
is easy to see them down there in the dark, beside that rough
old rock – awe-struck peasant faces, queer hats and thonged
sandals, a smell of must, earth, and garlic, a friar to supervise
the solemnities and the slow words of the oath echoing among
the shadows.

The Jew was so glad to escape with his life that it was he who
built the church upstairs, and an inscription beside his tomb in
the west transept tells the tale. As for the serpent, when Bishop
Vilches took a false oath at the hole in 1456, out it popped again
and stung him.

A world away is Segovia, and yet it stands only forty miles to
the north-east, in the lee of the same mountains. If Avila is only
a shell, Segovia is all kernel: it feels the most complete and close-
knit of the Castilian cities, as though all its organs are well
nourished, and nothing is atrophied. The gastronomic speciality
of Avila is a little sweet cake made by nuns; but the speciality of
Segovia is roast suckling pig, swimming in fat and fit for
conquerors.

Segovia is the most beautifully organized of cities. It is a
planner's dream. It lies along an elongated rocky knoll, with the
sparse little River Clamores on the south side, and the more
affluent Eresma to the north, and to get the hang of it you should
first walk up to the little Calvary which stands, lonely and
suggestive, on a hillock beside the Avila road. From there you
can see the whole city in silhouette, and grasp its equilibrium.
Very early in the morning is the best time, for then, when the
sun rises over the plateau, and the city is suddenly illuminated
in red, it loses two of its three dimensions, and looks like a
marvellous cut-out across the valley. In the centre stands the tall

tower of the cathedral, the last of the Gothic fanes of Spain. To
the left there rise the romantic pinnacles of the Alcazar, most of
it a nineteenth-century structure in the Rhineland manner, all
turrets, conical towers, and troubadour windows, properly
poised above a precipice (down which a fourteenth-century
nanny, when she inadvertently dropped the baby, instantly
threw herself too). And at the other end, forming a tremendous
muscular foil to this fantasy, there strides across a declivity the
great Roman aqueduct of Segovia, looking from this distance so
powerful and ageless that it might actually be a strut to hold the
hill up. Between these three bold cornerposts – fortress, church,
and aqueduct – Segovia has filled itself in with a tight, steep,
higgledy-piggledy network of streets, sprinkled with lesser
towers, relieved by many squares, and bounded by a city wall
which is often blended with houses too, and looks, from your
brightening Calvary, rather like the flank of a great ship. It
seems, indeed, to sail across its landscape. It looks like a fine old
clipper ship, there in the morning sun, full-rigged, full-blown,
ship-shape and Bristol-fashion.

A sense of strength or defiance infuses it. It was in the Alcazar
that Isabel, recently proclaimed Queen of Castile, found herself
besieged by a furious mob, but rode so bravely into the thick of
it, alone upon her charger, that the crowd fell back subdued by
her very presence. It was in the Alcazar too that the daring King
Alfonso the Wise actually ventured to doubt, poring over his
books one day, whether in fact the sun moved round the earth:
instantly, such was the effect of this proposition, there was a
flash of lightning, and the King, hastily dismissing the whole
idea from his mind, ever afterwards wore a rope of St Francis
around his waist, a perpetual penance for a rash thought. It was
in the queer little Church of Vera Cruz, beneath the castle, that
the Knights Templar performed their secret rites of chivalry,
standing vigil over their arms all night, in all the mysterious
splendour of seneschal, gonfalon, and accolade. It was the image
of Our Lady of Fuencisla, in the Carmelite convent, that was
officially made a Nationalist Field-Marshal in the Civil War; she
still carries a Marshal's baton, and it is said that when Hitler
was told the story, he swore that nothing on earth would induce
him to visit Spain. Even the calamities of Segovia have a
boisterous air: the old palace of the Alcazar, which was burnt
down in 1862, was destroyed, it is said, by the cadets of its

artillery school, because they wanted the school to be moved to
Madrid. Even its miracles are thoroughgoing: one night in
November 1602 an intense light shone over the convent of Santa
Cruz, and the crowd that hastened there was gratified to find an
eminent Dominican theologian, Melchor Cano, lost in prayer
upon his knees, but suspended a good four feet above the level
of the ground.

The finest sight in Castile, is how Segovians sweepingly
define the first appearance of their city, and I agree with them:
there can be few urban compositions on earth to equal the
impact of Segovia, when you cross the last ridge on the
approaching road, and see its bulk riding there above the fields.
For myself, though, I remember with less pleasure a stroll I took
inside the city on my first evening there. It was a wet night, the
lamplight shining damply on the streets, and as I wandered
aimlessly through the drizzle I came upon a small plaza down
the hill from the cathedral, called in the vernacular the Place of
the Sirens. It is set upon a flight of steps, rather like the Scala
d'Espagna in Rome, and feels like some slightly overpainted
opera set – so theatrical that you almost expect it to revolve
beneath your feet, to carry you onstage. To its left stands the
lovely Romanesque atrium of San Martin, with a tall square
tower above it; in its centre there stands the effigy of a well-
known Segovian patriot, waving a flag; on the right, as you
climb the steps, there is a row of enchanting small houses, ferns
and flowers dripping over their balconies; above the rooftops
there looms a four-square fortified palace, where Wellington
stayed when he took Segovia; and at the top of the steps there
is a small courtyard, enclosed on three sides by walls.

It was very shadowy in this yard that night, and I could not
see very well. The street lights behind me, reflected in the
puddles, only made the darkness darker. On the left-hand side,
however, close to the wall, I could just make out two squat,
plump stone shapes, crouching in the dark; and when I cautiously stumbled over to them, I found them to be a pair of
queer primitive animals, with snouts, tails, and very solid
bellies. Were they pigs? Were they lions? Were they gods? Were
they devils? Nobody really knows, but I took no risks that
evening, and hastily backed away from them: I was in Segovia,
a city of spirit, and I thought they might bite.

*

Lastly Toledo, which stands to Spain as Kyoto to Japan – a repository of all that is proudest, oldest, and most private in the national consciousness. When you think of Old Spain, you think of Toledo – 'a clear and illustrious nightmare', as the poet Garcilaso de la Vega once irreverently described it. Toledo was once the capital of Spain, and is still the seat of the Spanish Primate, and within its walls the Castilian, Jewish and Moorish cultures, productively coexisting for several centuries, created a rich and tolerant civilization of their own. Everybody knows what Toledo looks like, from El Greco's famous idealization of the place, and even the most determinedly flippant tourist, taking an afternoon excursion from Madrid, usually feels it necessary to cast an eye over this celebrated city, provided of course she can get back by cocktail time.

If you believed the old travellers you would imagine Spain to be one uninterrupted desert, absolutely denuded of vegetation; but Toledo is one city that really does live up to their descriptions – 'girdled in', as Augustus Hare put it, 'by the indescribable solitude of its utterly desolate hills'. It stands only forty miles from Madrid, but there *is* a kind of indescribable solitude to its flavour, and the desolation of its hills, if scarcely utter, still is severe. If Segovia often feels like a flat backcloth, Toledo is heavily in the round. It is built on a rocky mound in a bend of the Tagus, and is thus surrounded on three sides by a deep gorge, with shingle and grey rock running down to the water's edge. The river runs fast here, with a clutter of old stone mills and two excellent bridges; a castle stands sentinel across the stream; harsh grey hills are all about: the setting of Toledo is all abrasion – nothing soft, nothing amusing, nothing hospitable. This is the Spanish character at its most intractable. If a city can be said to look like a person, then Toledo looks just like one of those El Greco characters who were in fact conceived here – towering, handsome, humourless, sad, a little bloodless.

The Church dominates this city, and reminds us that the Archbishops of Toledo have often been men more powerful than the State itself: the formidable Cardinal Jiménez de Cisneros not only paid all the expenses of an expeditionary force to Africa, but actually led it himself, in the crimson. On the flank of Toledo's hill stands the fortress of the Alcazar, still recognizably large enough to hold, as it used to, two thousand horses in its subterranean stables. Unmistakably dominating it, though, its tower rising effortlessly above a tawny muddle of roofs and minor pinnacles, stands the cathedral. At night it is floodlit, and then the great luminous finger of this church, peremptory against the sky, makes even the transient sceptic think for a moment about immortality.

Inside the city, too, things of the spirit seem pre-eminent. They may be Jewish devotions that are remembered, in the haunted synagogues of this once-great Jewish city. They may be Muslim, in the adorable little mosque now called Cristo de la Luz – a tiny Córdoba, with its own small copse of horseshoe arches and its silent dusty garden. They may be memories of the Mozarabs, those Christians who retained their faith throughout the Moorish occupation, and thus kept alive the ancient liturgy of Gothic Christianity. When Toledo was recaptured from the Moors in 1085, a dispute arose as to whether the old Mozarabic rites should be retained, or replaced by the Gregorian rites from Rome – adopted in northern Spain during the years of the occupation. The issue was put to trial by fire. The rival prayer books were placed simultaneously in the flames, but the Roman was whisked to safety by a heavenly wind, while the Mozarabic simply did not burn; and because of this stalemate, which both sides claimed as a victory, the old Gothic ritual is still celebrated, every day of the week, in one chapel of Toledo Cathedral. (They keep the door closed during the service, and when I chanced to open it one day I found myself almost at the priest's side on the steps of the altar: so severely did he turn to stare at me, so disapprovingly did his acolytes look up, so long and empty did the chapel extend behind him, that I instantly closed that door again, and allowed the Mozarabic ritual to continue its survival without me.)

But Roman or Gothic, Gregorian or Mozarab, above all it is Spanish Catholicism, that imperial creed, that is honoured and reflected in this imperial city. This is the city of the Toledo blade – 'a sword of Spain', as Shakespeare called it, 'the ice-brook's temper'; nowadays the swordsmiths make matador's swords and paper knives, but once they were kept busy making swords for Christian knights. In the Church of Santo Tomé there hangs El Greco's celebrated picture *The Burial of Count Orgaz*, which epitomizes the alliance between God and the Spanish ruling classes. Count Orgaz was a Toledan so distinguished for piety that when he died the young St Stephen and the old St

Augustine personally descended from Heaven to bury him. The painting shows them doing so, but more striking than their saintly figures are the Spanish gentlemen who stand behind. They look sorry indeed, but not surprised: they seem to represent a class of society that expects miracles as a matter of policy, and they are watching the saints at work rather as they might watch, with a certain patronizing interest, the technique of any foreign expert sent to do a job under reciprocal arrangements. To the right of the picture a priest appears to be checking the operation in some instruction handbook. High above, Philip II, though still alive when the painting was done, is already among his peers in Heaven. It is a beautiful picture, most richly composed, most haunting in portraiture, given an unexpected twinkle by El Greco's signature – Domenico Theotokopouli – delicately embroidered on the hem of a page's handkerchief; but it seems to record not an instance of divine grace but the payment of a national due.

You may sense the same air of high collusion all over Toledo. At one end the Church of San Juan de Los Reyes, above the bridge of San Martin, is a resplendent monument to the Reconquest. Its architecture, the most delicate and elaborate kind of Gothic, is like a smile of gentle triumph across the prostrate art of the infidel, and upon its golden walls there hang the chains of Christian captives released from Moorish camps and galleys. At the other end of the city the ruined Alcazar is a memorial, in many Spanish minds, to the last of the Crusades. 'The heroic epic,' said a message from the young women of Burgos to the defenders of the fortress in 1937, 'which your valour for God and Spain has written in our glorious Alcazar will be the pride of Spanish chivalry for ever': seventy priests had been murdered in Toledo, and when the Army of Africa fought its way in at last, the main street ran with blood, several wounded men were killed in their beds in hospital, and forty anarchists, trapped in a seminary, set fire to the building and burnt themselves to death.

And surveying all, the culmination of this city, Toledo Cathedral stands like a vast testimonial of Spain's divine destiny. The streets of Toledo are unbelievably tortuous, so narrow that along most of them a car cannot pass, and even a hand-trolley of oranges blocks the way; but when you have manoeuvred your baffled way along them, have discovered the unremarkable outer walls of the cathedral, and have entered its unobtrusive cloister gate, then the immense expanse of the interior, its nave of seven bays and its twenty-eight chapels, seems to express the ultimate escape of the Spaniard from himself, via glory, to infinity. 'Valour for God and Spain' fills this great church like incense; and as witness to the working relationship between the two you may be shown a small white stone, preserved behind a grille, upon which Our Lady actually set foot during a royal visit in 666.

Soldiers, saints, heroes and great churchmen seem to populate Toledo Cathedral, and when there is a service at the high altar, with all the swift formality of its ritual, the bowing priests, the genuflecting servers, the bewigged attentive vergers, the clink of the censers, the gorgeous shimmer of copes and jewelled monstrances, the exchange of plainchant between altar, *coro* and thundering organ – when the heart of the cathedral is filled with the sights and sounds of that tremendous spectacle, this really does feel like the nerve-centre of some formidable war machine, a bunker or a Pentagon, disposing its unseen forces in distant strategies. From the transept ceilings the Cardinals' hats hang rotting like battle-flags. In the Chapter House the faces of all the archbishops look back at you from their portraits like generals in a war museum. In the treasury the silver spheres, rings, breastplates, censers, and crucifixes glitter beneath their bright lights like State jewels. Above the high altar there stands the figure of a mysterious shepherd who, sent by God to help Spain, guided the Christians to victory over the Moors through the mists of Las Navas de Tolosa in 1212; only King Alfonso VIII saw the face of this man, and the King it was, we are told, who carved the figure.

It is a great hall of triumph, a victory paean for the Christian culture. A superb assembly of treasures here upholds the Christian ethos – grilles by the great Spanish masters of wrought iron; sculpture and stained glass by virtuosos from Holland, Italy, and France; paintings by Rubens, Velázquez, Van Dyck, Goya, El Greco, Bassano, Giovanni Bellini; multitudes of stone angels, tombs of kings and prelates, sudden shafts of sunlight through stained glass, a vast, tumbled, restless, infinitely varied museum of the faith. Nothing in Christendom, I suspect, better expresses the militancy of the Church than the *retablo* or reredos of Toledo, which rises in serried magnificence from the high

altar to the roof. It is fretted everywhere with stone canopies
and niches, and in a series of elaborate stone tableaux, like the
set of an experimental theatre, tells the New Testament story;
with an endless profusion of detail, and an inexhaustible
imagination – with saints on guard at each flank, and angels
fluttering everywhere – with gleaming gold, and blue, and a
glow of old stone – with an almost physical movement upwards,
up through the sweet mystery of the Nativity and the splendour
of the Ascension, up through a glittering field of stars in a deep
blue sky – up to the very rafters of the cathedral, where your
dazed eye reaches at last the supreme symbol of Calvary,
portrayed there in immense tragic grandeur at the very apex of
Christian Spain.

With such a cause, one feels, with such a champion, no
Christian soldier could lose. We are, however, in Spain, where
the last victory is death itself – 'Viva la Muerte!' was the battle-
cry of the Falange in the Civil War. A few feet away from
that glorious reredos there stands the tomb of the Cardinal-
Archbishop Portocarrero, Viceroy of Sicily, Cardinal Protector
of the Spanish Nation, Regent and Primate of Spain. He died in
1719, and has been described as 'incapable, obstinate, and
perfectly selfish'; but on his tomb, by his own orders, there was
inscribed the dry Spanish epitaph *Hic Jacet Pulvis, Cinis, et Nihil*
– 'Here Lies Dust, Ashes, Nothing'.

Incomparable old cities of the interior! No other towns on
earth are anything like them. They have no peers, no rivals, no
imitators. A circle a hundred miles across would contain them
all; but you can stand ten thousand miles from their walls, close
your eyes and think of Spain, and see them clear as sunlight
still.

31

AN AFRICAN EXHIBITION

Swaziland, 1970

In the new Africa that was still, in the early 1970s, emerging from colonial times, Swaziland played a peculiar and fascinating role, being an extraordinary mixture of négritude and political compromise, tradition and opportunism. I found it distinctly bewildering: so, I suspect, did some of the Swazis.

On a weekday the dirt road from Mbabane to Piggs Peak, in Swaziland, is very quiet. An occasional car announces its approach with a plume of dust across a distant ridge. Women pass in twos or threes on their way to market. There are a few of those solitary wizened wanderers, sunk in meditation, who seem to stride perpetually across the expanse of Africa. The hills around are sparsely populated, and until one reaches the forests of the north the landscape is bare and for the most part apparently deserted.

But at the weekend, when the tourists drive in from Johannesburg, things are different. Then the road bursts raucously and inexplicably to life, and Africa performs brilliantly all along your route. Jostling vivacious boys sell wooden birds and animals. Chorus lines of infants in palm-leaf skirts suddenly burst into dance routines. Adorable naked babies scramble precariously over rocks in the middle of mountain streams, while their mothers gossip over the washing. Blind men walk with their hands held high above their heads, goatboys herd heroically bearded goats. Every sort of costume asserts itself, from the indefinably tribal, accoutred with feathers, beads and shields, to the sober-sided, mission-school, Sunday morning three-button suit.

The air seems to sizzle. Smiles gleam, hands wave, colours

clash, children dance, dust billows, goats scamper, bicycles wobble, and if ever you stop for a moment, in the most isolated and abandoned corner of your route, in a flash, by the sorcery of this continent, a black boy uncurls or uproots himself from the ground, or detaches himself from a rock, or emerges from the river shallows, to come and have a look at you.

In all Africa there is no more vividly African place than Swaziland: and this sudden flaring of an entire landscape, like the magic appearance of the spring flowers when the rain falls at last, is like a spontaneous ritual of Africanness – *négritude*, as the African intellectuals say – both marvellous and perturbing to experience.

Perturbing not because it is unfriendly, but because it suggests to Western sensibilities so many mysteries. To the innocent from another culture Africa is a half-closed book. We see only the outward signs of the inner genius – only the display that gives expression to the instinct, only the forms which have been evolved over the centuries to reflect or mask the intricacies of religion, social order and artistic sense which lie at the roots of *négritude*.

For most of us the first and simplest mystery, in the Balkanized Africa of the 1970s, is the mystery of where anywhere is. Swaziland is easier than most, first because it has never changed its name, secondly because it forms a neatly identifiable little enclave within the frontiers of the South African Republic. Until 1968 it was a British Protectorate, its African integrity jealously guarded by London against the encroachments of apartheid. Now it lives, willy-nilly, in compromise. It is an independent kingdom ruled by His Majesty Sobhuza II, with its own parliament, armed forces and diplomatic representatives: a black African State officially dedicated to the ideal of racial equality. But squeezed as it is between the Republic on three sides and Portuguese Mozambique on the fourth, it has had to come to terms with white supremacy. A customs union links it with South Africa, Swaziland getting 0·53033 of the joint customs income. South African money is current in Swaziland, South Africa provides most of the tourist trade, and many South Africans, Boers and British, live in the country – my favourite Swazi address is that of H. S. Herbst, Killarney, Hhohho.

You might suppose that all this might create awkward anomalies. The powerful republic, though, looks with a fairly approving eye upon the minuscule kingdom. For private citizens of South Africa Swaziland provides not only magnificent scenery, but the more direct allures of legal gambling and accessible pornography, both verboten at home. And for the South African Government, Swaziland stands as a living example of apartheid in its loftiest sense – a separate Negro State within southern Africa, ruled by a black king along traditional tribal lines: just what, in the manifestos of the apartheid theorists, separate development is really supposed to mean.

Swaziland indeed is almost like an exhibition country, clothed in that meticulous decorum which the British brought to their possessions and protectorates everywhere. Its two principal towns, Mbabane and Manzini, are trim garden settlements, with prominent post offices and cosy places for coffee. Its central landscapes are mountainous, dotted here and there with hygienic-looking kraals. Its southern regions are flat ranchlands, hot and empty, prickled with scrub. Its western reaches are covered with a particularly disciplined kind of forest – one of the largest man-made forests on earth, scrupulously categorized in blocks, and functionally centred upon a large sawmill. Swaziland is a layered, staked sort of country, logically disposed, as though it has been organized for demonstration purposes.

Consider almost any valley of central Swaziland, off the tourist routes and away from the towns, any fine morning before lunch. It is likely to offer one of those views that have no particular culmination or focal point – no foreground monument, no snowline behind – but is like a diorama in a museum, diligently filling its frame. Patches of mealie give green body to the scene, with clumps of tall reedy grass here and there, and the hills are slabbed with grey basalt, the colour and apparently the texture of elephant hide. Birds with long black floppy tails fuss about the place; dragon-flies waver over the passing stream; from the dark trees huge seed-pods hang, like sacks of bird-food.

Gently across this setting move the Swazis – at a leisurely, companionable pace, for they are not an urgent people. Two bullocks, perhaps, are hauling a sledge piled with logs, preceded by a small girl in blue carrying an axe, encouraged by a man with a huge whip of ox-hide, followed by a couple of women with enamel pots on their heads and blanketed babies on their backs. Unattended donkeys potter in their trail, infant boys supervise a goatherd on their flank, and the whole scene seems poised in time – neither modern nor archaic, neither primitive nor progressive, but simply organic, like the birds or the basalt slabs, to this particular little piece of Africa.

The Swazi heart beats bravest in the Ezulwini valley, between Mbabane and Manzini. The valley slopes away gently to the south, surveyed from either side by austerely handsome hills, and it is the shrine of everything most necessary to Swazi tradition, prosperity and self-respect – the Kyoto, Stratford-on-Avon and Las Vegas of Swaziland, all in one. Here is the Royal Swazi Hotel and Casino, for example, which contributes so lavishly to the kingdom's wealth. Here are the spanking Parliament buildings bequeathed by the British, an earnest of democratic intention though thoughtfully fitted, in their more vulnerable offices, with bullet-proof glass. Here is the office of the Swazi National Council, the headquarters of tribal authority, providing a traditional counter-weight to the political parties up the road. Most important of all, here is the royal kraal of Lobamba, the ceremonial capital of the Swazi nation, which houses a few score of the King Sobhuza's unnumbered wives, and the highly influential State functionary called the Queen Mother (not the King's mother at all – in fact one of his senior wives).

The King is inescapable in his kingdom. His picture hangs in every Government office and almost every shop. His princely relatives are found in every capacity, Prime Minister to telephone operator. His royal activities fill the columns of the morning paper, and dignify the bulletins of Radio Swazi. His name or honorific is attached to schools, hotels, roads, fields of experimental agriculture. Everything is opened by him, dedicated to him, patronized by him. His power, though not absolute, is distinctly persuasive. He is, though now in his seventies, a very active and diligent ruler, and he is unquestionably the most remarkable spectacle in Swaziland.

I first saw him at the offices of the National Council, attended by a functionary called The Eye Of The King. His subjects fell on their knees, or even on their faces, as he passed, but he offered me a kindly greeting, and I looked him Jeffersonianly in the eye. I shall never forget the moment. He has the most remarkable, most twinkling, most pungent, most mischievous, altogether most entertaining face in the world. He seems to radiate an amused but a resolute complicity, as though he knows what a preposterous charade life is, but is determined to make the best of it. He was dressed that day in European clothes, as he generally is: when he wears his tribal costume, a stunning assembly of feathers, bright textiles and talismanic brooches, the impact must be terrific.

I was not deceived by the monarch's merry eye. I knew him to be an able and worldly politician, tempered by long contact with the British, educated in South Africa, well-travelled and urbane. At the same time his roots are deep in that African underworld to which I must always remain a stranger. He is only one generation removed from the days of royal smelling-outs in Swaziland, when his ferocious father King Bubu discovered his enemies by the divinations of witch-doctors, and generally had them killed. The royal kraal at Lobamba is still run on the old lines – not with witchcraft, though the art still flourishes in Swaziland, but with an unchanged devotion to the old traditions, and an almost complete rejection of Western values or conveniences.

The men of the royal guard, who keep watch over it, are strangely uniformed in kilts and skins, and are sometimes old: quavering and suspicious sentinels, their hair waxed or buttered, carrying knobkerries and wearing badges engraved with the King's lion symbol. They receive the foreign visitor warily, and this is perhaps wise, for I can see that the royal kraal must sometimes stir a progressive, or at least a feminist spirit in many visitors from abroad. It is a large compound of round thatched huts, surrounded by a stockade of sticks and reeds, in the centre of which, like a queen bee in her hive, the Queen Mother occupies a small masonry building. The other queens live alone, a queen to a hut, doing their own cooking. Nobody knows how many wives the King has, scattered as they are among several different kraals: when I asked a member of the bodyguard a hazed look came into his eyes as he tried unsuccessfully to compute a possible total – 'in accordance with age-old traditions', as an official pamphlet discreetly puts it, 'King Sobhuza has a number of wives.'

Yet when I arrived at the kraal not one was to be seen, only a sprinkling of raggety children – 'some of them the King's children,' said the guide, 'some of them not'. We walked through the maze of little mud alleyways in silence. We saw the cattle kraal in which, once a year, is performed the sacred reed dance, when the maidens of Swaziland are displayed *en masse* for the royal inspection. We saw the hut in which the Queen Mother, assisted by the King, conducts the Rain Ceremony in times of drought – a hut so tremendously sacred that my companions would talk only in whispers in its proximity. We saw the tumbledown building from which a previous Queen Mother, during a period of regency, had governed the destinies of all the Swazis. But we saw no queens. It was blazing hot, lunch-time approached, and I was preparing to return disappointed to the Royal Swazi Hotel, when we saw across an open yard a solitary hunched female figure, swathed in draperies, squatting outside the door of a hut.

A small boy crouched at her side, and perhaps fifteen feet away from her one of the royal guards was standing in a half-bowed posture, exchanging some words with her. 'She is an old queen,' said my interpreter. 'Nobody may approach a queen closer than that. The small boy must accompany her everywhere, even to, if you will forgive me for saying, the lavatory. No queen may ever leave the royal kraal. Once chosen to be queen she must remain in this kraal for ever. The boy may be one of the King's sons, or he may not be. Some are, some are not.'

I stood for a moment dazed by this flow of information, and aghast at the thought of life confinement in that hot dusty harem, and the interpreter paused for a minute too before adding a last and convincing clincher.

'All those who are the King's sons', he said, 'have very noticeable faces.'

If phenomena like these baffle the Western visitor, they are prosaic enough to the Swazis, whose most difficult problem must be how to reconcile their ambitions for material progress with their reverence for tribal culture. I was not surprised to learn that the incidence of mental illness is high in the country kraals. This is partly because so many men are always at work in the Transvaal mines, leaving behind a lonely and frustrated women-folk. It is partly because of the continuing pressures of witchcraft. But it is chiefly no doubt because of the clash of old and new in this complex little country. The Swazis are related to the Zulus, and speak more or less the same language, but they seem to lack the confident fire of that formidable and ferocious people: they are gentler, more easy-going, finer-strung perhaps, and so more vulnerable to the anxieties of change.

The condition is half vivacity, half malaise, and makes for constant anomalies. I think, for instance, of a respectably dressed girl, in blouse and skirt with white shoulder bag, whom I noticed outside my window one blazing noonday. She looked like a competent shorthand-typist, and she was strolling down the pavement rather as though she was wondering whether to have a salad somewhere, or make do with a milk shake. As she approached my window, however, and entered the shade of a solitary small tree, suddenly she collapsed gently and gracefully upon the ground – in one movement removing her shoes, placing her bag beneath her head as a pillow, and casting off every suggestion of Western manners. In a moment she was fast asleep, like a cat on a rug: and half an hour later, when the sun had shifted over the tree and offices were reopening after lunch, I saw her springing just as suddenly back to life – without the need to straighten her skirt or even tidy her hair, immaculate and self-composed she walked out of my sight from one life-style into the next.

Or by contrast I think of a hotel in the forest country of the north where the strictest forms of *Western* traditionalism are rigidly sustained – in reaction perhaps to the insouciance with which so many young Africans switch from world to world. I arrived there after dark, and stopped before I entered to breathe the ecstasy of the Swazi night – a soft astringent wind on my face, like a skin-tonic – tumultuous frog-croaks from some woodland pool – smells of pine, sawn wood and dust – urgently above my head, flashing and winking like electronic devices, the insistent stars of Africa. All my senses were ravished, but the moment I crossed the threshold of the hotel I was returned to an all too familiar earth. Ladies Are Requested, said a sign upon the wall, Not To Wear Slacks In The Dining-Room. Parents Are Requested To Keep Their Children Quiet After Dinner. Formal was the service there, wholesome was the food, and at six in the morning inexorably down the corridor I heard the door-tap of the man with the morning tea – nearer and nearer as I lay there, like a prisoner in the condemned cell, until he entered my own room with a resolute 'Good Morning' and opened the curtains to blind me with the morning sun (but I could not go to sleep again anyway, for I knew he would be back in a few minutes for the crockery).

And I think last of the Royal Swazi Casino, where *négritude* meets materialism with a glittering vengeance. This is an exceedingly luxurious place, with its own spa (there are mineral water taps in the bedrooms), its own golf course, its continental chefs and its European croupiers – black operators, it is thought, would somehow alter the *feel* of roulette. The Royal Swazi is strong on conventions, offering a constant stream of South African business groups full conference facilities in the morning, golf in the afternoon, booze and grub in the evening and gambling all night. It is probably the best run resort complex in the whole of southern Africa, besides being the only casino south of Victoria Falls.

Yet vividly through it all stalks the genius of the country, horned and painted. Little Swazi boys scurry cheerfully around the gambling machines in the lobby. King Sobhuza II has been known to visit the tables. And the lawnmowers are driven by men in glorious Swazi costume, perched on their seats like warriors on the move, their multi-coloured draperies flying in the wind as they chug tremendously between the croquet lawn and the fifteenth hole.

Royal people in Swaziland are buried in mountain caves, holy places shunned by ordinary Swazis as spirit-haunted. Such cave-sepulchres exist in several hills above the Ezulwini Valley, sheltering the ghosts of many royal generations – their bones for the most part long since crumbled into dust, only their charisma remaining.

One group is to be found in the hills a few miles south of Mbabane, near the head of the royal valley, and the European who owns the land kindly gave me permission to go and visit them. I would have to find my own way, he said. No Swazi would go near the place – it would be the worst of bad luck – all the rules were against it. But I would find it easily enough anyway. 'Just keep climbing. All the way up you'll hear the sound of a river away to your left. When you get to the spot where the sound of the river stops, then you'll be somewhere near the caves.'

I met nobody on the walk up, though I heard the chopping of an axe somewhere in the woods, and won a contest of wills with

an obstructive herd of cows. Always to my left, as he had said,
I heard the rush of water far below: until quite abruptly, when
I had passed through the woods to the open hillside beyond,
and stood there in a little rocky glade, I realized that the noise
had stopped. The silence was disconcerting. I never felt myself
in a more haunted spot. Presently I found the dark entrance of
a cave in the hillside, half-blocked with rubble and brambles:
and as I stood there braving the resentment of the dead I saw in
my mind's eye the cortège which had once laboured up that
hillside to take the royal corpse inside – the body embalmed in
a black ox-hide, the head shrouded with the bladder of a black
goat, the hands holding twigs from ritual shrubs – brought up
here secretly on a moonless night, lying on a wooden bier, and
entombed there in the cavern with a black tethered goat, never
to be seen again.

On my way down I began to feel rather queer, and the next
two days I spent violently ill in my bedroom. One should respect
the rules, in Africa.

32

OVER THE BRIDGE

Sydney, 1983

When I first wrote about Sydney, in 1958, I disliked the city so much that it was five full years before the last furious response reached me from Australia. By 1983, after half a dozen visits, I may have mellowed a bit, and the city certainly had: I was rather disappointed to find local reactions to this essay almost entirely friendly (but then this time I did not describe Sydney's society ladies, as I had in 1958, as looking 'steely, scornful and accusatory, as though they are expecting you – which Heaven forbid – to offer them an improper suggestion . . .').

'Kev. *Kev*! Time you got going.'

'Jeez, Sandra, it's raining out there.'

'TV says it's fining up. You're not crook are you, Kev? It's all that booze you know, Kev, you know what the doctor said, cut down on the booze he said, no wonder you're crook in the mornings, the human body can take only so much . . .' But Kev has slipped out by now, and with his office gear slung in his back-pack is away, and up the steps, and half-way along the approach to the great bridge.

If he was crook, he is crook no more, for the TV was right, the rain clears as if by magic, and all the glory of the winter morning unfolds over the water as he breaks into his jog along the sidewalk. He is joining the stream of life itself! To his right the suburban trains clatter, the commuter cars lurch in fits and starts towards the city. To his left ferries bustle across the harbour, the first hydrofoil is streaking in a foamy curve towards the sea, the very first yacht is slipping from its moorings, and a tug is on its way, riding lights still burning, to meet the towering freighter just appearing around the headland.

On the harbour bridge there are already plenty of people

about. He overtakes briskly walking businessmen with briefcases and identical moustaches. He is overtaken by huge athletes
in sweatbands and sloganed shirts. Archetypal schoolboys loiter
their way, satchels dangling, reluctantly towards their education. An elderly lady in a mackintosh cries 'Grand to see the sun
again!' in an exaggeratedly Irish brogue. Another pack of giants
comes panting and sweating past. Another covey of schoolboys
kicks a pebble here and there. Ahead of him, between the
massive pylons of the bridge, the city towers are beginning to
gleam in the sun, and there is a flashing of upper windows, and
a fluttering of flags in and out of shadow, and a golden shine
from the observation deck of the tallest tower of all.

It is as though the innocence of the morning has infected the
whole scene, and made everything young. A pristine vigour is
on the air, very fresh and good for you, like orange juice. By the
time Kev reaches his office on the seventeenth floor, he feels
he's never drunk a tinny of Foster's in his life: and looking back
upon the scurrying ferries of the Circular Quay, the flying white
roofs of the Opera House, the traffic still streaming across the
bridge, the rising sun and the water and the green parklands all
around, silently he congratulates himself once more, as he does
every morning as a matter of principle, upon his great good
fortune in being born an Australian.

The city he surveys is a very concentrate of that condition.
The whole matter of Australia, history, character, reputation,
attitude, finds its best epitome in this particular corner of the
great land mass, where Sydney stands beside its fjord-like
harbour. When the world thinks of Australia, it thinks of that
bridge, that Opera House, that wake-frothed and yacht-flecked
harbour. When the world thinks of an Australian, it thinks,
more or less, of Kev.

Australian society is overwhelmingly urban, and Sydney is
Australia *urbanissima*. Canberra is the capital, Adelaide is a
delight, Perth holds the America's Cup, Melbourne people
believe their city to be at least as mature, civilized and unutter-
ably lovely, but only Sydney has the true metropolitan presence.
An enormous spread of surburbia around an intensely packed
downtown, it stands upon its marvellous haven in the stance of
proper consequence. A glittering business quarter makes one
feel it is keyed in to the Wall Street–London–Zurich–Hong Kong

circuit of profit. The inescapable presence of virtually the whole
Australian Navy, moored beside its dockyards or glamorously
returning from sea with ensigns flying and radars twirling,
gives it a front-line air. It is equipped with all the statutory
metropolitan tokens – city marathon, revolving restaurant,
supine veiled figure by Henry Moore, breakfast TV and Bahai
temple.

Its stature really resides, though, not in its universality, not in
its membership in the league of big cities, but for better or
worse, like it or not, in its unchallengeable Australianness. It is
a metropolis *sui generis*. Take its looks for a start. Architecturally
Sydney is no great shakes. Its suburbs are at best pleasantly
ordinary, enlivened only, here and there, by wrought iron and
engaging terracing. Its downtown is handsome but unexceptional, the usual cubes, cylinders, plazas and mirror-walls
of contemporary urbanism surrounding the usual clumps of
nineteenth-century florid. It has no elegant set pieces of civic
planning, and has crudely degraded its waterfront on Sydney
Cove, the site of its beginnings and still the focus of its life, by
building an express-way slap across it.

Yet it is one of the most beautiful cities in the world,
specifically because it is Australian. That winding, nooky,
islanded, bosky harbour thrillingly reminds one always that
Sydney stands on the shore of an island totally unlike anywhere
else on earth. The pale pure light of the Sydney winter seems to
come straight from the bergs and ice mountains of Antarctica.
The foliage of Sydney's parks and gardens is queerly drooped
and tangled, apparently antediluvian fig trees overshadow
suburban streets, and the perpetual passing of the ships through
the very heart of the city gives everything a tingling sense of
remoteness. The water goes down the plug-hole the other way
in Australia, and it really is possible to imagine, if you are a
fancifully minded visitor from the other hemisphere, that this
metropolis is clinging upside-down to the bottom of the earth,
so subtly antipodean, or perhaps marsupial, is the nature of the
scene.

The supreme Sydney experience, for such a traveller, is a walk
on a brisk sunny morning around the headland called Mrs
Macquarie's Chair, through a complex of park and garden beside
the harbour. Except only for Stanley Park in Vancouver, this
seems to me the loveliest of all city parklands, but its loveliness

is of a sly, deceptive kind. It is like a park in the mind. The grass is almost too vividly green, the trees look curiously artificial, parakeets squawk viciously at each other in the shrubbery. The shifting scene around you, as you walk the park's perimeter, seems more ideal than actual – water everywhere, and those grey warships at their quays, and glimpses of Riviera-like settlements all around, and a sham castle in a garden, and the inescapable passing of the ferries.

And slyest of all is the prospect as you round the point itself, where the families are spreading their picnics on the grass, and a solitary ibis is burrowing for edibles in a rubbish can; for there suddenly like an aery fantasy the Sydney Opera House, most peculiar of architectural masterpieces, spreads its white wings in the sunshine, light as some unsuspected water-bird, with the massive old harbour bridge, a beast to its insubstantial beauty, all brutal heft above.

Those two unforgettable structures, the one rooted so power-fully in the bed-rock, the other aspiring to the state of levitation, represent the nature of this city more than aesthetically. Upon Sydney's foundation of absolute British Australianness has been superimposed a prismatically ethnic superstructure, making this city, formerly one of the most homogeneous and stodgy in the world, a fascinating mix of the complacent and the tentative, the almost immovable and the practically irresistible.

Once it used to suggest nowhere else. Now it is full of alien allusion. It reminds me often of Stockholm. As Sydney is to the south, Stockholm is to the north, and Sydney's Australia is Stockholm's Scandinavia – I am not surprised that the Danish architect of the Opera House clearly had in his memory, as he planned his prodigy, Stockholm's Town Hall upon an inlet of another sea. The light of this southern fjord is not unlike the light of the Baltic; a pallid freshness is common to both cities; sitting snugly out of the sunlight in Sydney's Strand Arcade, all fancy balustrades and tesselated paving, sometimes I almost expect to see the shoppers shaking the snow from their galoshes, breathing in their hands to restore the circulation, and ordering themselves a schnapps.

At other moments Sydney reminds me of somewhere in Central Europe: any Saturday morning in the plush water-side suburb called Double Bay, for example, when the rich immigrants assemble in the street café of the Cosmopolitan, talking loudly in Ruritanian, or deep in the financial pages of the *Sydney Morning Herald*. Like the bourgeoisie of old Prague or Budapest they while the hours away in chat and exhibitionism – here four men with coats slung over their shoulders, smoking small cigars and passionately arguing about President Benes – here a couple of leathery ladies, furred and proudly diamonded, sitting in lofty silence over aperitifs – a young poseur in a deer-stalker hat, smoking a cigarette in a long jade holder, a gaggle of Double Bay socialites in the swathed ragbag fashion, faintly Martial Arts in suggestion, rampant in Sydney at the moment.

Lebanese proliferate in Sydney, and Greeks, and Philipinos, and Indonesians. The Vietnamese, they tell me, are shifting out of the western suburbs towards East Sydney. Maori gays, gossip picturesquely maintains, are taking over Bondi. The Spanish Club advertises itself with a picture of Don Quixote and Sancho riding out of a golden Outback. Sydney's Chinatown booms with investment from Hong Kong, and the Chinese taste for unexpectedly mixed foods seems to have infected the entire municipal cuisine, so that perfectly true-blue Aussie resturants are likely to offer you hot buttered pumpkin and orange soup with peppercorns floating in it, or quail in a sauce made of red wine and bacon. The Sydney Municipal Board sometimes likes to announce itself in all the languages of its tax-paying citizenry – 'MESTSKÁ RADA SYDNEY' or 'SYDNEY VÁVOSI TANÁCS' – and these arcane proclamations, attached to some lumpish municipal pile of mid-Victorian imperialism, pungently illustrate the state of things.

Still dominant nevertheless, as the bridge looms high over the Opera House, stand the likes of Kev. The flow of immigration has softened, eased and illuminated Sydney, but it came too late ever to displace the original blood-stream of this city. Half a century ago 98 per cent of Sydney people were of British descent, and it is they, the Old Australians, who still set the anthropological tone. Sit long enough among the Ruritanians at the Cosmopolitan, and some beefy young Ocker will arrive to steal the scene and drink his beer out of the bottle. Go to *La Traviata* at the Opera House, and my, what an unexpectedly hearty and robust chorus of ladies and gentlemen will be attendant upon Violetta in the opening act, their crinolines and Parisian whiskers delightfully failing to disguise physiques

born out of Australian surf and sunshine, and names like
Higginson and O'Rourke – while even La Traviata herself, as
she subsides to the last curtain, may seem to you the victim of
some specifically Australian variety of tuberculosis, since she
looks as though immediately after the curtain-call she will be off
for a vigorous set of tennis with the conductor, or at least a
grilled lobster with orange sauce and caramel.

Such is the strength of Kev's sub-species, into which the
children of all those immigrants, too, are inexorably mutated.
Years ago, waiting for the Manly ferry, I caught the eye of a
young Italian working at a coffee-stall, and I remember distinctly
the wiry black Latinate quality of his person. I went down there
again the other day to see if he was still about, and found him
not just aged and plumped, but altogether altered by the Kev
Effect – his face pulled into a different shape, his sparkle
replaced by something more wary or blunted, or perhaps
dreamier. And when he spoke, the last traces of Neapolitanism
were all but hidden beneath the virile twisted vowels of
Australian English.

Language they say is the badge of nationality, and above all
else it is the language of Sydney that binds this fissile society
into a recondite unity. It is many years since the writer Monica
Dickens, at a Sydney signing session, inscribed a volume to
Emma Chissett, misunderstanding a lady who wanted to know
the price of the book, but fundamentally the vernacular has not
changed: 'Emma Chissett?' I make a point of asking now, when
I want to buy something, and the shop assistants never give me
a second glance, taking my dinkum Aussiness for granted, and
frequently confiding in me their grievances about the train
service from Parramatta.

Or from Woop Woop perhaps, an imaginary township which
has become a Sydney generic for the back of beyond. Sydney
English is full of such fantasies and in-jokes, and consciously
perpetuates itself in self-amusement, hardly a year passing
without another new dictionary of the argot. Usages change
constantly – out goes *she'll be apples* ('it'll be OK'), in comes
throwing a mental (losing one's temper) – and there is almost
nobody in Sydney, schoolboy to sage, who is not eager to
discuss the present state of the vernacular. Why do Sydney
women end all their sentences, even the most definite, with a
rising interrogative inflexion? Because they're so put down they

daren't say anything for sure. What's the true definition of an Ocker? 'A man who watches the footy on TV with a terry-towel hat on his head and a tinny of Foster's balanced on his belly.'

The language makes the man, and makes the city too. Without his language your Sydney citizen (he no longer calls himself a Sydneysider) might be taken for a Scandinavian, a Californian or even sometimes an Englishman: with it even a second-generation immigrant can be mistaken for nobody else, and the fizz and the fun of the tongue reflects Sydney's particular strain of constancy. The pubs of this city are loud with jazz and rock music, deafening the packed saloons within, blaring over the sidewalks. Often the thump of it drives the customers into a frenzy, and the bars are full of strapping young Ockers throwing their hands above their heads, whoopeeing and beating their enormous feet. They are not at all like roisterers of Europe or America, partly because they all seem to be, like that opera chorus, in a condition of exuberant physical well-being, partly because the tang of their language pervades everything they do, and for a time I thought their burly disco to be something altogether new out of Sydney, an Australization specifically of the 1980s.

But emerging half-shattered one day from the Observer Inn, having weaved a perilous way among those flailing limbs and stomping size 14s, I chanced to see, in a shop down the road, a print of early Sydney settlers living it up 150 years ago. They wore floppy slouch hats and check shirts, were heavily bearded, and were probably celebrating their recent release from hard labour in the prisons: but they were kicking their legs about in that self-same Sydney fandango, in just the same heavyweight high jinks, and were yelling their songs and cheerful obscenities, I am sure, in similarly rank and entertaining distortions.

For even Sydney has a past. It began in the 1780s with the arrival of the first British convicts, put ashore here in their chains to serve as the reluctant and incongruous Founding Fathers of Australia. It ended in the 1950s with the mass landings of the European immigrants, disembarking after their government-subsidized passages to transform Australia from semi-emancipated colonialism into Pacific cosmopolitanism. By then the penal colony had developed into a city of great but somewhat unlively character, chauvinist to an almost comical degree, with an elite of often snobby and vulgar monarchists, and a labour force so powerful that unionists everywhere called this the Worker's Paradise. In those days any Sydney matron worth her social salt boasted of her distant connection with the Earl of Mudcastle while the Sydney proletariat was as rough, as ready, as truculent, as contemptuous of Earls and as militantly Irish as a self-respecting proletariat ought to be.

Today that society has mostly gone underground. If you want a symbolic demonstration of it, try going to the subterranean railway station beside the Town Hall: for there behind the trendily creeper-covered walls of the sunken plaza, all waterfalls and canopies, the station itself survives as a very museum of the Old Australia – brass knobs, bakelite switches, Instructions to Employees in copperplate script behind brass-framed glass, bare electric bulbs lighting up to announce the next train to Pymble or Hornby. The Sydney railways are very Old Australia. So are the ferries, and the pubs, and the memorials to kings and queens and Robbie Burns. The granddaughters of those well-connected matrons still curtsey with a preposterous zeal when Prince Charles drops by. Go-slows on the Woop Woop line, heavy-jowled men with placards demanding a Fair Go For Aussie Ships, recall the heyday of the Worker's Paradise. The old beery machismo has not been entirely subsumed in white wine and unisex hairdressing.

More importantly, out of the Old Australia comes Sydney's sense of order and fair play, which underpins the shifting vigour of this city. 'KINDNESS AND COURTESY' is still the motto of Double Bay School, and to a remarkable degree the old values obtain. You might expect this haven on a creek at the bottom of the world to be a seamy, wild and reckless place, and of course Australians, like city people everywhere on earth, talk with dismay of rising crime rates and drunken driving. By most standards, though, Sydney is good as gold. The streets are much safer than most, the traffic is generally demure enough, even jay-walkers look guilty, and the city comports itself, at least to visitors, with unfailing *politesse*.

These are legacies based, *au fond*, upon Parliamentary democracy and the Common Law, and their survival is a tribute to their strength: for what has happened all around them, in the last three decades, is nothing less than a social revolution. Sydney has become a different city, different in style, in aspiration, in loyalty, in taste. A generation ago, it seemed to me, the very core of the Sydney ethos was the memory of the sacrifices its men had made in the two world wars, fighting in a cause almost quixotically remote to them, yet made poignantly real by their devotion to Crown, Flag and Empire. The heroic ordeals of Gallipoli and Alamein stood somewhere near the root of the civic pride, and the Returned Servicemen's League was sacrosanct and inescapable.

But on a recent winter Sunday I revisited the great war memorial in Hyde Park which was the shrine of those epic memories, and found its tragic magnetism dispersed. It stood there still of course, grey, powerful and sombre among the trees; the sad sculpted soldiers still looked down, sitting like thoughtful gods around the parapet; but the people in the park somehow seemed to shy away from its presence, as though it had been put out of their minds by some process of re-education, or sealed up, with all its toxic energies, like an expended reactor.

It seems only proper that the motto of another Sydney school, 'I Hear, I See, I Learn', should translate into Latin as *Audio, Video, Disco,* for the young have boisterously discarded the old image of Sydney, and have remoulded it again in their own. Today this city is one of the world's great promises, a pledge of better things, living in a state of ill-defined but perpetual expectancy.

It is a very young city: not just young in manners and accomplishment, but exceedingly young in person. Sometimes indeed it seems to be inhabited chiefly by schoolchildren, children kicking pebbles across bridges, children racing fig-leaves down the channels of ornamental fountains, children clambering like invading armies all over the Opera House, or mustered in their thousands in the New South Wales Art Gallery. They seem to me a stalwart crew. 'Now this is a Picasso,' I heard a teacher say in the gallery one day, 'I'm sure you all know who Picasso was.' 'I don't,' piped up a solitary small Australian at the back, and I bowed to him as the only absolutely honest soul in sight.

It is a city attuned to young ideas – 'Barefoot shoppers', sensibly decrees one of the grandest department stores, 'must not use the escalators ' – and its youthfulness is so pervasive as to be almost hallucinatory. The magistrate in the petty sessions court looks like a second-year law student, the prosecuting attorney might just have invested in his first motor bike, and surely the accused, who is charged with public indecency, has not yet reached the age of puberty? As for the Stock Exchange, it appears to be run by several hundred athletes, helped by a few go-go girls in miniskirts, and the old men in the public gallery upstairs, ostensibly examining the shares board through their binoculars to see how Consolidated Metals are doing, look to me less like speculators than plain voyeurs.

The youthfulness of Sydney, like all youthfulness, is a little schizo, being half brash, but half timid. In a posh Sydney hotel, for instance, or an upstage Sydney restaurant, customers tend to behave with a detectable sense of reverence, talking in undertones to each other and gratefully accepting the wine-waiter's recommendation – it would be a *maître d's* delight, were it not for the fact that in Sydney even that insufferable guild behaves with a becoming inhibition. Australians always used to be accused of inferiority complex, and though their image in the world is very different now, still Sydney has not reached the free fine assurance of absolute civic maturity – 'When I go to California', a very attractive and intelligent Sydney girl said to me, 'I feel like a mouse.'

And the mouse instinct erupts sometimes, of course, as it always does, into absurd expressions of self-assertion. Sydney people are far less vulnerable to criticism than they used to be – this used to be one of the prickliest of all the world's cities – but they are hardly less sensitive to the patronizing or the aloof. In Europe, one Sydney intellectual told me severely, ignorance about Australian affairs was abysmal, *abysmal* – why in London, he had been assured, reputable art critics had never even heard of Brett Whiteley!

'Brett Who?' I could not resist inquiring (remembering the boy in the art gallery) for this aspect of the Sydney style can be a bit relentless. One is told a little too often of the Whiteley genius, one tires of the gossip about the Sidney Whites and the Patrick Nolans; yes, one did realize that the author of *Schindler's Ark* was a local man; for myself I feel lucky to have missed the recent Sydney fashion show, about which I heard so much, which featured a ballet performance to aboriginal music, songs with flute accompaniment against a background of wrecked cars, and some extreme examples of the Bundled Jap look.

But then youth, hope and silliness go together, in cities as in people, and it is the hope that counts. The hope is what Kev unconsciously feels, as he jogs over the bridge in the morning, and what nearly every stranger feels too, on a first foray into the streets of Sydney. How young and strong the city! How magnificent the promise! One forgets sometimes that even in the Land of Oz, youth is not eternal . . .

The Reeperbahn or 42nd Street of Sydney is King's Cross, a mile or two south-east of Sydney Cove. This used to be an entertaining Bohemian quarter, but has degenerated lately into a nasty combination of squalor and pathos. Among the usual Reeperbahn company of pimps, pornographers, strippers, tattooists and transvestites, bathed in the conventionally sinful half-light, gaped at by the inevitable visitors from Woop Woop, through King's Cross after midnight there now move some more heart-rending figures: child-prostitutes, hardly in their teens, desperately made up and not very expertly soliciting the passing drunks and lechers.

John Gunther the great reporter used to ask, wherever he went in the world, 'Who runs this place?' It is my practice to ask who (or in print, perhaps, *whom*) I ought to be sorry for. In some cities – think of Calcutta, think of Johannesburg! – the question is superfluous. In many another the tender heart is wrung by terrible poverty, or political oppression, or general gloom of environment. In Sydney there is hardly any abject poverty. Politically the people of this city are free as air, socially they are as emancipated as anyone on earth. Their town is clean and mostly safe, their climate is a dream, and though they grumble a good deal about the effects of recession, and frequently go on strike, by the standards of the world at large they live magnificently.

So who should I be sorry for? Sydney people are puzzled by the question, and sometimes can't think of anyone at all. Sometimes they reply with jokes about unsuccessful football players or politicians in eclipse. 'Me,' says Kev, but he does not mean it. A few propose those poor children of King's Cross, there are vague references sometimes to derelicts ('derros') or exploited immigrants. And in the end it occurs to most people that I should give a thought to the abos, the aborigines, whose names are all around one in Sydney, in Woolloomooloo, in Parramatta or in Woop Woop, but whose physical presence is but a wisp or a shadow in the thriving city.

Most of the aborigines of these parts were exterminated, by imported disease or by brute force, within a few decades of the first white settlement. Yet two centuries later a few hundred cling to their roots in Sydney, at the very site of the European coming. They are called 'coories' here, and like the water of the harbour, like the exotic foliage of the parks and headlands, they are a reminder of stranger, older things than Kev and his kind can conceive. To some Australians the aborigines are a blot on the conscience, to others just a pain in the neck: still, in the end most people thought the coories were worth feeling sorry for, and feel sorry for them I did.

Though their community has produced some celebrities in its time, notably boxers, they live mostly in more luckless quarters of the town, and do not show much as a rule. As it chanced however, while I was in Sydney this time they celebrated Aboriginal Day. The aboriginal flag of gold, black, and yellow flew, to the consternation of Old Australians, side by side with the national flag on Sydney Town Hall, and a march through town was announced, to be followed by a rally at Alexandria Park. Alas, all this went sadly awry. Nobody seemed to know where the march was to begin, or when somebody pulled the flag down from the Town Hall, not everyone seemed to have mastered the rally chant – 'What do we want? Land rights! What have we got? Bugger all!' – and the arrangements ran so late that when the time came for speeches everyone had gone home. 'They are a *random* people,' was the convincing explanation I was given, when I asked if this was true to coorie form.

By the time I reached Alexandria Park Aboriginal Day seemed to have fizzled out altogether, and all I found was a small huddle of dark-skinned people around an open bonfire, surrounded by litter on the edge of the green. They greeted me with a wan concern, offering me beer out of an ice-bucket, sidling around me rather, and occasionally winking. A small thin boy with cotton wool stuffed in one ear wandered here and there leading a black puppy on a string. Others kicked a football about in the gathering dusk, and around the fire a handful of older men and women looked sadly into the flames. A strong smell of alcohol hung over us, and the man with the bucket urged me quietly, again and again, to have one for the road, dear. Had the rally been a success? I asked. 'Yeah,' they said, and looked into the fire.

I *did* feel sorry for them. They were like last wasted survivors from some primeval holocaust, those memories of their own civilization were aeons ago expunged. Did they have a Sydney all their own, I wondered, long ago near the beginnings of time? Did their flag fly braver then? When I said good-bye and drove away ('Go on, dear, just one') the lights of the downtown tower blocks were shining in the distance: but in the shadows at the edge of the park the bonfire flames were dancing still, and the frail figures of the indigenes moved unsteadily in the flicker.

One morning I went to Iceland, the skating-rink, to watch the Sydney people skating. They did it, as they do most things, very well. Their tall strong frames looked well on the ice. Once more I was struck by the Scandinavian analogy, so Nordic does an Australian look when you put him in cold circumstances, but eventually my attention was gripped by a figure who, it seemed to me, could be nothing else but Aussie.

He was about five years old, blond, lively, tough and unsmiling. He could not, it seemed, actually skate, but he was adept at running about the rink on his blades, and his one purpose of the morning was to gather up the slush that fell off other people's boots, and throw it at passing skaters. This task he pursued with skilful and unflagging zeal. Hop, hop, he would abruptly appear upon the rink, and picking a lively target, staggering his way across the ice, inexorably he would hunt that victim down until *slosh!* the missile was dispatched – and hobble hobble, quick as a flash he was out of the rink again, gathering more material.

I admired him immensely. He hardly ever fell over, he seldom missed, and he did everything with a dexterous assiduity. When I asked him his name he spelt out GORGE with his finger on the rail of the rink; when I asked him if he was enjoying himself he just nodded grimly; and in my mind's eye I saw him thirty years from now, exploding into a company meeting perhaps, with an irresistible take-over, or relentlessly engineering the resignation of a rival under-secretary. I kept my eye firmly on him as I walked out of Iceland, for instinct told me he was assembling slush for me.

Australia was not built by kindness, nor even by idealism. Convicts, not pilgrims, were its Fathers, and Sydney remains rather steelier than it looks. It is not a very sentimental city, and not much given I fear to unrequitable kindness. There is a certain kind of Sydney face, especially among women, which at first sight looks altogether straight, square and reliable, but which examined more carefully (surreptitiously if possible, over the edge of a newspaper from the next table) reveals a latent meanness or foxiness inherited surely, I tell myself in my romantic way, from the thuggery of the penal colonies.

Here are a few graffiti I have jotted down in Sydney: 'CHINKS HIRED, YOU'RE FIRED'. 'WHITE BUT UGLY'. 'THE POLICE KILLED LYOL TITMARCH'. 'NO SCABS OR ASIANS'. 'TURKISH MURDERERS'. Behind the pleasant façade of this city, harsher things are always happening. Inexplicable political scandals excite the newspapers. Numberless Royal Commissions investigate improprieties. Through this apparently egalitarian society stalks a handful of gigantic capitalists, with tentacles that seem to extend into every cranny of city life, and make you feel that whatever you are doing, whether you are buying an ice-cream or booking an airline ticket, you are making the same rich Australians richer yet. Immigrants say that your older Ocker is a terrible bigot still, and even now they tell me a foreign accent often gets snubs and indignities – and not only a European accent, for the favourite Sydney witticism of the day is the New Zealand Joke ('How d'you set up a New Zealander in a small business?' 'Give him a big one, and wait').

Sydney people strike me as essentially cautious or suspicious in their social attitudes. They lack the gift of spontaneous welcome or generosity. They are too easily embarrassed. Invariably smiling and helpful though this citizenry seems, and quite exceptionally polite, I sometimes think that if I were in real trouble, friendless, destitute and passport-less in the streets, I might feel less abandoned in Manhattan. I considered making the experiment as a matter of fact, and presenting myself on the Circular Quay to beg passers-by for my ferry fare: but I remembered that look in the eye of the ladies at the next table, and lost my nerve.

Even now, two centuries after the event, a streak of bad

origins is still apparent in Sydney. Truth will out! It has been smudged in the historical memory – if you can believe the Australians, none of the transported convicts ever did anything worse than poach a squire's salmon, or tumble his daughter in the hay. It has been romanticized, too – in the figure of the larrikin for instance, the Sydney street urchin of ballad and anecdote who used to strut picturesquely about these streets in bell-bottom trousers and pointed shoes, fighting merry gang wars and picking pockets. Today it has been varnished over with layer upon layer of gentility and sophistication, but it is there all the same, and if you want to see it plain, try going to the park on a Sunday afternoon, when the Sydney soap-box orators give vent to their philosophies, and the hecklers to their interruptions. In most countries I love these arenas of free expression – they are rich in picaresque episode and eccentricity, and sometimes even in wisdom. I left Sydney's Speakers' Corner though, with a shudder. The free speech was too grossly free, too crudely spiteful, sexist and foul-mouthed. The arguments were bludgeonly, the humour was coarse, and all around the soap-boxes there strode a horribly purposeful figure, wearing a beret tipped over his eyes, and holding a sheaf of newspaper, whose only purpose was to shout down every speaker in turn, whatever the subject or opinion, with a devastating loutishness of retort – never silent, never still, hurling offensive gibes at speaker and audience alike with a flaming offensive energy.

Now where, said I to myself, have I seen that fellow before? And with a pang I remembered: GORGE the indefatigable ice-slosher, up at the ice-rink.

After lunch one day (Warm Salad, new to me, with Chicken Liver) I met Kev in the elevator, with three of his friends from the office. They stood there in silence, sometimes shifting on their feet. 'I've just eaten', I ventured for conversation's sake, 'a plate of Warm Salad,' but it did not make them smile. They looked at me anxiously, trying hard to think of a reply. 'Good,' managed Kev himself at last, and with relief, murmuring polite and embarrassed excuses, they left me at the seventeenth floor.

Away to the west of Sydney, over a long innocuous hinterland of suburbs, neither ugly nor beautiful, neither poor nor rich, with Lebanese laundries, and pubs with names like the Gladstone Arms or the Lord Nelson, and ladies in flowered house-coats exercising their dogs at lunch-time, and pizza houses with blown-up pictures of Vesuvius behind their counters, and streets called Myrtle Street and Merryland Road – out there beyond the Western Suburbs you can see the outline of the Blue Mountains. Snow falls up there sometimes, and log fires burn in resort hotels: and beyond them again, beyond Orange and Dubbo, there begins the almost unimaginable emptiness of Australia, extending mile after mile after mile of scrub, waste and desert into the infinite never-never of the aborigines. Nearly all Australia is empty. Emptiness is part of the Australian state of things, and it reaches out of that wilderness deep into the heart of Sydney itself, giving a hauntingly absent sense to the city, and restricting the responses of advertising executives in elevators.

The scrub is always near. The splodges of green everywhere make this metropolis feel, even now, like an interloper in the wasteland, and people commute daily into Sydney from country that is almost virgin bush. Only just outside the metropolitan limits, up on the Hawkesbury River, are communities that still cannot be reached by road, to which the mail goes out each day on a chugging river-boat, nosing its way among the creeks and channels, between woodlands where wallabies leap and koalas ruminate, to be unloaded on rickety wharfs at hamlets of shacks and bungalows, and hobbled away with by aged oystermen – the air-conditioned towers of Sydney itself hardly out of sight beyond the gum-trees!

The sea everywhere, insidiously entering the city in a myriad inlets, seems a vacuous kind of ocean, which seldom brings the tang of a salt breeze into the downtown streets, and often looks to me indeed like fresh water all the time. The history of Sydney, like the history of Australia, is essentially blank, very little of interest ever having happened here, and there is a sort of bloodlessness even to the very success of the place, and a pallor to its style, and a curious suggestion of muffle even at rush-hour, which reminds one repeatedly of that immense desolation beyond the hills.

This sensation preoccupies many Australian artists, and affects me very strangely. Sometimes in Sydney I feel I am not looking directly at the city at all, but seeing it through glass, or perhaps reflected in a mirror. Its edges seem oddly ill-defined when I am in such a mood, its pellucid light is lacking in refraction, without the opacity of dust, breath, history and regret that hangs on the air of most great cities. The wind seems to have been filtered through some pale mesh of the south. Even the seafood, however imaginatively garnished with strawberries or avocado, seems to lack the tang of the deep sea and the tides. Even the Australian language sometimes sounds to me echolike, as though it is reaching me from far, far away, or out of another time.

Sydney can be exhilarating, but it is a *moderate* exhilaration. It can stir the heart, but not quite to the point of ecstasy. You do not dance along these streets, or thrill to the beat of the place. Its faces, in repose, are neither kind nor cruel, but just expressionless. People seldom seem surprised in Sydney, and for that matter they are seldom very surprising themselves: though it is astonishing that so grand a place should exist down here at all, so handsome, so complete a metropolis on the edge of nowhere, still it never gives the impression, as other young civic prodigies do, that it has burst irresistibly out of the sub-soil into life.

Here are two old Hungarians walking on a Sydney beach. They wear hats, camel coats and signet rings. They came here half a lifetime ago out of the shambles of Europe, and they have lived happily ever after. They escaped the murder of war and the miseries of Communism to prosper in this peaceful haven of the Antipodes. Their wives are taking coffee at the Cosmopolitan – remember the two in furs, silent over their Camparis? Their sons, daughters and grandchildren are probably out in their boats. They are very lucky, and know it. 'We are very lucky,' they say. 'Sydney is a beautiful city. Australia is the Best Country in the World.' They do not say it *con amore*, though, or even *cantabile*. They seem unlikely to kiss the soil they walk on, or raise their hands in gratitude to the Australian dream. 'Let us hope the world stays in peace,' they simply conclude, as if to say, let's hope our luck lasts out – just give us ten more years, O God of the Southern Sun!

Most people like Australia, but in this city of the numbed reflex, the blank eye, few will open their hearts about the place: just as Kev and his colleagues in the elevator, I feel sure, must have bottled up some frightfully witty retorts about the Warm Salad.

*

Far up the coasts of Sydney, north and south of the Sydney Heads that form the spectacular portal of Australia, comfortable villas of the well-to-do lie encouched in fig-trees, gums and lawns of buffalo grass. They are seldom ostentatious houses. They are not like the garden palaces of Cap d'Antibes, or the monastically enclosed pads of Hollywood. Though it is true that the Sydney *jeunesse dorée* is given to things like flying by seaplane to take lunch in suburban restaurants, or giving birthday parties for favourite Ferraris, still history, temperament and politics have combined to ensure that this is not a city of conspicuous consumption. Its extremely rich are seldom visible, if only because they are in Europe or California; and its glossiest mansions cannot be seen either, because they are country houses set in 25,000 acres of sheep country somewhere over the hills. All this gives the city an air of calm stability: the very idea of economic collapse, still less revolution, seems preposterous, as I look out of my hotel window now to see the white yachts at play in the harbour, yet another laughing horde of schoolchildren storming the terraces of the Opera House, and Kev at his window in his shirt-sleeves, preparing himself psychologically for the long jog home.

Short of another world catastrophe, I think, this place has reached its fulfilment. This is it. It will probably get richer, it will certainly get more Asian, but aesthetically, metaphysically, my bones tell me I am already seeing the definitive Sydney, the more or less absolute Australia. A few more tower blocks here, an extra suburb there, a louder Chinatown, more futuristic ferryboats perhaps – otherwise, this is how Sydney is always going to be. That bland pallor of personality will survive, that seen-through-a-glass quality, and visitors from the north will always be able to fancy, as they look out at the harbour's odd foliage and wide skies, that they have been deposited upside-down on the obverse of the world. The strain of shyness, the old streak of the brutal, will be held in balance still: another zealot will always be collecting sludge at the ice-rink, another generation of satisfied entrepreneurs will ask destiny for just another decade of happiness, just long enough to live out their lives in the Best Country in the World.

I have been at pains to draw the warts of Sydney in, but on the whole, I have to say, few cities on earth have arrived at so agreeable a fulfilment. Those old Hungarians are right – they are very lucky people, whose fates have washed them up upon this brave and generally decent shore. But just as no man is a hero to his valet, so no city is a paragon to its inhabitants, especially at the end of a hard day in the office, and by 5.30 Kev's morning euphoria has long worn off. The ferries down there are jammed to the gunwales with commuters. The bridge looks solid with traffic. It is drizzling again. Bugger it, Kev remembers, tonight's the night for Andrew and Marge – avocados again, you can bet your life, and they'll probably bring that snotty brat Dominic to crawl around the table. 'Night, Mr Evans.' Night Avril, silly cow. 'Night, Kev.' Night, Jim, you pot-bellied Ocker. 'Just before you go, Kev, heard this one? There's this New Zealander . . .'

Jeez this rain is miserable. Get out of the road, you silly sod. Christ, who dreamed up that Opera House? (We all know who paid for it, don't we.) Avocado and prawns, you can bet your life. What was that woman on about in the elevator? Warm salad! Shit! Look at that traffic! Look at that madman in the Fairmont! Who'd live in a town like this, I ask you. Warm Salad! We must all be bloody loonies . . .

'Kev! Kev, is that you? Marge and Andrew are here, dear, and they've brought little Dominic with them.'

33

SECOND PRIZE

Toronto, 1984

❧

In 1984 Toronto celebrated its sesquicentennial (Sesquicentennial, sb., US: a hundred and fiftieth anniversary). *The Canadian magazine* Saturday Night *invited me to mark the occasion by writing a portrait of the city, and this is what I gave them. Canadians are nothing if not* fair.

As I waited for my bags at the airport carousel I considered the faces of my fellow arrivals. They mostly looked very, very Canadian. Calm, dispassionate, patiently they waited there, responding with only the faintest raising of eyebrows or clenching of gloved fingers to the loudspeaker's apology for the late delivery of baggage owing to a technical fault, edging gently, almost apologetically, inwards when they spotted their possessions emerging from the chute. They looked in complete command of their emotions. They looked well fed, well balanced, well behaved, well intentioned, well organized, and well preserved. Sometimes they spoke to each other in polite monosyllables. Mostly they just waited.

But like a wayward comet through these distinctly fixed stars there staggered ever and again a very different figure: a middle-aged woman in a fur hat and a long coat of faded blue, held together by a leather belt evidently inherited from some earlier ensemble. She was burdened with many packages elaborately stringed, wired and brown-papered, she had a sheaf of travel documents generally in her hands, sometimes between her teeth, and she never stopped moving, talking, and gesticulating. If she was not hurling questions at those expressionless bystanders in theatrically broken English, she was muttering to herself in unknown tongues, or breaking into sarcastic laughter.

Often she dropped things; she got into a terrible mess trying to get a baggage cart out of its stack ('You – must – put – money – in – the – slot.' 'What is slot? How is carriage coming? Slot? What is slot?'); and when at last she perceived her travelling accoutrements – awful mounds of canvas and split leather – erupting on to the conveyor, like a tank she forced a passage through the immobile Canadians, toppling them left and right or barging them one into another with virtuoso elbow-work.

No, I have not invented her – touched her up a little, perhaps, as I have heightened the characteristics of the others, in the interests not so much of art as of allegory. I don't know where she came from, whether she was in Canada to stay or merely to visit her favourite married nephew from the old country, but she represented for me the archetypal immigrant: and she was arriving at the emblematic immigrant destination of the late twentieth century, Toronto, whose citizens are certainly not all quite so self-restrained as those passengers at the airport, but which is nevertheless one of the most highly disciplined and tightly organized cities of the Western world.

I watched that first confrontation with sympathy for both sides: and though I lost sight of the lady as we passed through customs (I suspect she was involved in some fracas there, or could not undo the knots on her baggage), I often thought of her as we both of us entered Toronto the Good in its sesque – sesqua – sesqui – well, you know, its one hundred and fiftieth year of official existence.

There are moments when Toronto offers, at least in the fancy, the black and terrible excitements of immigration in the heyday of the New World. I woke up the very next morning to such a transient revelation. A lowering mist lay over the downtown city, masking the tops of the great buildings, chopping off the CN Tower like a monstrous tree trunk; and under the cloud the place seemed to be all a-steam with white vapours, spouting, streaming with the wind, or eddying upward to join the darkness above. Lights shone or flickered through the haze, the ground everywhere was white with snow, and the spectacle suggested to me some vast, marvellous, and fearful cauldron, where anything might happen, where villains and geniuses must walk, where immediate fortunes were surely to be made, where horribly exploited Montenegrin seamstresses probably lived in unspeakable slums, and towering manufacturers swaggered in huge fur coats out of gold-plated private railway cars.

The mist cleared, the cloud lifted, even the steam subsided as the first spring weather came, and it was not like that at all. Toronto has come late in life to cosmopolitanism – even when I was first here, in 1954, it seemed to me not much less homogenous than Edinburgh, say – and as a haven of opportunity it is unassertive. No glorious dowager raises her torch over Lake Ontario, summoning those masses yearning to breathe free, and conversely there are no teeming slums or sweatshop ghettos, still less any passionate convictions about new earths and heavens. I heard no trumpet blast, no angel choirs perform, as I took the streetcar downtown.

The promise of Toronto, I presently realized, was promise of a more diffuse, tentative, not to say bewildering kind. On a modest building near the harbour-front I happened to notice the names of those entitled to parking space outside: D. Iannuzzi, P. Iannuzzi, H. McDonald, R. Metcalfe and F. Muhammad. 'What is this place?' I inquired of people passing by. 'Multicultural TV,' they said, backing away nervously. 'Multi-*what* TV?' I said, but they had escaped by then – I had yet to learn that nothing ends a Toronto conversation more quickly than a supplementary question.

Multiculturalism! I had never heard the word before, but I was certainly to hear it again, for it turned out to be the key word, so to speak, to contemporary Toronto. As ooh-la-la is to Paris, and *ciao* to Rome, and *nyet* to Moscow, and hey you're looking *great* to Manhattan, so multiculturalism is to Toronto. Far more than any other of the great migratory cities, Toronto is all things to all ethnicities. The melting-pot conception never was popular here, and sometimes I came to feel that Canadian nationality itself was no more than a minor social perquisite, like a driving licence or a spare pair of glasses. Repeatedly I was invited to try the Malaysian vermicelli at Rasa Sayang, the seafood pierogi at the Ukrainian Caravan, or something Vietnamese in Yorkville, but when I ventured to suggest one day that we might eat Canadian, a kindly anxiety crossed my host's brow. 'That might be more difficult,' he said.

A whole new civic ambience, it seems, has evolved to give some kind of unity to this determined centrifugalism – I never knew what a heritage language was either, until I came to Toronto

– but I soon got used to it all. I hardly noticed the street names in Greek, or the crocodiles of schoolchildren made up half and half, it seemed, of East and West Indians. I was as shocked as the next Torontonian, three days into the city, to hear a judge tell a disgraced lawyer that he had betrayed not only the standards of his profession but also the trust of the Estonian community. I was not in the least surprised to see a picture of the Azores as a permanent backdrop for a Canadian TV news-cast, or to find the ladies and gentlemen of the German club swaying across my screen in full authenticity of comic hats and Gemütlichkeit. 'My son-in-law is Lithuanian,' a very WASPish materfamilias remarked to me, but I did not bat an eyelid. 'Only on his father's side, I suppose?' 'Right, his mother's from Inverness.'

But multiculturalism, I discovered, did not mean that Toronto was all brotherly love and folklore. On the contrary, wherever I went I heard talk of internecine rivalries, cross-ethnical vendet-tas, angry scenes at the Metro Guyanese political rally, compet-ing varieties of pierogi, differing opinions about the Katyn massacre, heated debates over Estonian legitimacy, the Coptic succession, or the fate of the Armenians. There turned out to be a darkly conspiratorial side to multiculturalism. I have never been able to discover any of those writers' hangouts one is told of across the world, where the poets assemble over their beers; but in Toronto I felt one could easily stumble into cafés in which plotters organized distant coups, or swapped heavy anarchist reminiscences. (It costs only twelve dollars to broadcast a thirty-second announcement in Korean on CHIN, Toronto's multi-lingual radio station: how much, I wondered, as a headstrong nationalist myself, for an inflammatory exhortation in Welsh?)

But actually, this is not the sort of fulfilment I myself wanted of Toronto. I am not very multicultural, and what I chiefly yearned for in this metropolis was the old grandeur of the North, its size and scale and power, its sense of wasteland majesty. Fortunately now and then I found it, in between the Afro-Indian takeaway, the Portuguese cultural centre, and the memorial to the eminent Ukrainian poet in High Park. Here are a few of the signs and symbols which, at intermittent moments, made me feel I was in the capital of the Ice Kingdom.

Names such as Etobicoke, Neepawa Avenue, Air Atonabee, or the terrifically evocative Department of the North.

Weekend breaks to go fishing in the frozen lake at Jackson's Point (All Huts Stove-Heated).

The sculpted reliefs on the walls of the Bay Street postal office, thrillingly depicting the state of the postal system from smoke-signals and an Indian-chased stage-coach to an Imperial Airway flying-boat and Locomotive 6400.

High-boned faces in the street, speaking to me of Cree or Ojibawa; 'Raw and Dressed Skins' in a furrier's window, taking me to forests of fox and beaver.

The great gaunt shapes of the lake freighters at their quays, with huge trucks crawling here and there, and a tug crunching through the melting ice.

The fierce and stylish skating of young bloods on the Nathan Phillips rink, bolder, burlier, faster, and more arrogant than any other skaters anywhere.

And best of all, early one morning I went down to Union Station to watch the transcontinental train come in out of the darkness from Vancouver. Ah, Canada! I knew exactly what to expect of this experience, but still it stirred me: the hiss and rumble of it, the engineers princely in their high cab, the travel-grimed gleam of the sleeper cars, 'Excelsior,' 'Ennishore' – the grey faces peering out of sleeper windows, the proud exhaustion of it all, and the thick tumble of the disembarking passengers, a blur of boots and lumberjackets and hoods and bundled children, clattering down the steps to breakfast, grandma, and Toronto, out of the limitless and magnificent hinterland.

These varied stimuli left me puzzled. What were the intentions of this city? On a wall of the Stock Exchange, downtown, there is a mural sculpture entitled 'Workforce', by Robert Longo: and since it expresses nothing if not resolute purpose, I spent some time contemplating its significance.

Its eight figures, ranging from a stockbroker to what seems to be a female miner, do not look at all happy – the pursuit of happiness, after all, is not written into the Canadian constitution. Nor do they look exactly inspired by some visionary cause: it is true that the armed forces lady in the middle is disturbingly like a Soviet Intourist guide, but no particular ideology seems to be implied. They are marching determinedly, but joylessly, arm-in-arm, upon an undefined objective. Wealth? Fame? Security? The after-life? I could not decide. Just as, so Toronto itself has taught us, the medium can be the message, so it seemed that for the Stock Exchange workforce the movement was the destination.

Well, do cities have to have destinations? Perhaps not, but most of them do, if it is only a destination in the past, or in the ideal. Toronto seems to me, in time as in emotion, a limbo-city. It is not, like London, England, obsessed with its own history. It is not an act of faith, like Moscow or Manhattan. It has none of Rio's exuberant sense of young identity. It is neither brassily capitalist nor rigidly public sector. It looks forward to no millennium, back to no golden age. It is what it is, and the people in its streets, walking with that steady, tireless, infantry-like pace that is particular to this city, seem on the whole resigned, without either bitterness or exhilaration, to being just what they are.

Among the principal cities of the lost British Empire, Toronto has been one of the most casual (rather than the most ruthless) in discarding the physical remnants of its colonial past. In Sydney, in Melbourne, in Wellington, even in Cape Town, not to mention the cities of India, the imperial memorials remain inescapable, sometimes even dominant. In Toronto they are all but overwhelmed: a lumpish parliament, a university, a statue or two, a mock castle, a few dull buildings forlornly preserved, tea with cream cakes at the Windsor Arms, and on the face of things that's about it. Nobody could possibly mistake this for a British city now: it comes as a queer shock (and a degraded one, for a republican like me) to see the royal coat of arms still above the judge's bench in a Toronto court of law.

On the other hand there is no mistaking this for a city of the United States, either. If that lady at the airport thought she was entering, if only by the back door, the land of the free and the home of the brave, she would be taken aback by the temper of Toronto. Not only do Torontonians constantly snipe at all things American, but this is by no means a place of the clean slate, the fresh start. It is riddled with class and family origin. Humble parentage, wealthy backgrounds, lower-class homes and upper-class values are staples of Toronto dialogue, and the nature of society is meticulously appraised and classified. Think of buying a house in Gore Vale? Don't, it's 27 per cent service industry employees. Deer Park? Nineteen per cent executive – that's better!

For it is not a free-and-easy, damn-Yankee sort of city – anything but. Even its accents, when they have been flattened out from the Scots, the Finnish, or the Estonian, are oddly muted, made for undertones and surmises rather than certainties and swank. There is no raucous equivalent of Brooklynese, no local cockney wryness: nor will any loud-mouthed Torontonian ocker come sprawling into the café, beer can in hand, to put his feet up on the vacant chair and bemuse you with this year's slang – Sydney has invented a living language all its own, but nobody has written, so far as I know, a dictionary of Torontese.

It is as though some unseen instrument of restraint were keeping all things, even the vernacular, within limits. One could hardly call authority in Toronto Orwellian – it seems without malevolence; but at the same time nobody can possibly ignore it, for it seems to have a finger, or at least an announcement, almost everywhere. Where else could it be said of a work of art, as it says on a plaque beside the Flatiron mural in Toronto, that it was initiated by the city of Toronto and Development Department, Urban Design Group, the project being coordinated by an Arts Administrator? Imagine! 'Commissioned by the Chapel Improvement Board of the Holy Vatican, supervised by the Sistine Executive Subcommittee . . .'

If authority in Toronto is not admonishing you to save energy it is riding about on motor-bike side-cars looking for layabouts; if it is not hoisting one flag outside city hall it is hoisting another outside the Ontario parliament; in the middle of shopping streets you find its incongruous offices, and no one but it will sell you a bottle of Scotch. I have heard it address criminals as 'sir' ('I'm going to send you to prison, sir, for three months, in the hope that it will teach you a lesson') and say 'pardon' to traffic offenders (Offender: 'Well, hell, how'm I supposed to get the bloody thing unloaded?' Policeman: 'Pardon?'). Yet it is treated by most Torontonians with such respect that if the bomb itself were to be fizzing at the fuse on King Street, I suspect, they would wait for the lights to change before running for the subway.

Toronto is the capital of the unabsolute. Nothing is utter here, except the winters I suppose, and the marvellous pale expanse of the lake. Nor is much of it crystal clear. To every Toronto generalization there is an exception, a contradiction, or an obfuscation. A kind of cabalistic device, like a spell, tells the baffled stranger the frequency of services on the Harbourfront courtesy bus, and a fine example of the true Toronto style, I thought, was this announcement at the city hall skating-rink: 'Hours of Operation. Monday through Saturday, 9 a.m. until 10 p.m. Sunday, 9 a.m. until 10 p.m.'

What's that again? Sometimes I felt I could never quite get to grips with Toronto. For instance in many ways it appears to the stranger, even now, almost preposterously provincial. Appearances count, conventions apply, theatre-goers attend matinées dressed, if not for weddings, at least for gubernatorial luncheon parties. Toronto critics indulge themselves in childish vitriolics, like undergraduates in university magazines. Toronto preoccupations can be loftily local. (Torontonian: 'I suppose you're going to meet William Davis.' Me: 'Who's William Davis?' Torontonian: 'My God. Do you know what I mean when I say "The Dome"?')

Yet it is not really provincial at all. It is a huge, rich and splendid city, metropolitan in power – not only much the biggest city in Canada but a money centre of universal importance. Mighty capitalists reside here! Millions and millions of dollars are stacked! The world's tallest freestanding structure is in this city! The world's largest cinema complex! The world's biggest freshwater yacht club! Mary Pickford was born in Toronto! Insulin was invented! A housewife whose name I forget wrote 'I'll Never Smile Again!'

Provincial indeed! No wonder those eight stalwarts of the Stock Exchange mural, clutching their stethoscopes, their briefcases, and their picks, are marching so irresistibly towards – oh, I was going to suggest the dawn, but I see they're facing west. Towards Spadina Avenue, then.

And why not? Toronto is Toronto, and perhaps that is enough. I look out of my window now, on a bright spring afternoon, and what do I see? No Satanic mills, but a city clean, neat, and ordered, built still to a human scale, unhurried and polite. It has all the prerequisites of your modern major city – your revolving restaurants, your Henry Moore statue, your trees with electric lights in them, your gay bars, your outdoor elevators, your atriums, your Sotheby Parke Bernet, your restaurants offering (Glossops on Prince Arthur Avenue) 'deep-fried pears stuffed with ripe camembert on a bed of nutmeg-scented spinach'. Yet by and large it has escaped the plastic blight of contemporary urbanism, and the squalid dangers too.

Only in Toronto, I think, will a streetcar stop to allow you over a pedestrian crossing – surely one of the most esoteric experiences of travel in the 1980s? Only in Toronto are the subways quite so wholesome, the parks so mugger-less, the children so well behaved (even at the Science Centre, where the temptation to fuse circuits or permanently disorient laser beams must be almost irresistible). Everywhere has its galleria nowadays, Singapore to Houston, but none is quite so satisfying as Toronto's Eaton Centre – just like one of the futuristic cities magazine artists liked to depict in the 1930s, except that instead of autogiros passing beneath the bridges, only lovely sculpted birds float down from the high vaulting . . .

Toronto citizens, who seem to be at once defensively cap-à-pie, as though always expecting you to make fun of them, and relentlessly self-critical, as though afraid you might think them smug, often say that compared with a European city theirs doesn't offer much to *do*. 'Oh when I think of Paris,' they say, or, 'Goodness, when we were in New York we went to a theatre almost every night . . .' They do not, however, often recall evenings of cultural delight in Brest or Indianapolis. Only the greatest of the world's cities can outclass Toronto's theatres, cinemas, art galleries and newspapers, the variety of its restaurants, the number of its TV channels, the calibre of its visiting performers. Poets and artists are innumerable, I am assured, and are to be found in those cafés where writers and painters hang out, while over on the Toronto Islands, though permanently threatened by official improvements, a truly bohemian colony still honourably survives, in a late fragrance of the flower people, tight-knit, higgledy-piggledy, and attended by many cats in its shacks and snug bungalows.

I spent a morning out there, guided by a genial and gifted littérateur, taking sherry with a charming English lady ('Now you won't be *too* hard on Toronto, will you'), watching the pintail ducks bobbing about the ice and the great grey geese pecking for worms in the grass; and seen from that Indianified sort of foreshore – the city's 'soul-kingdom', the poet Robert Sward has suggested – the achievement of Toronto, towering in gold and steel across the water, seemed to me rather marvellous: there on the edge of the wilderness, beside that cold, empty

lake, to have raised itself in 150 years from colonial township to
metropolis, to have absorbed settlers from half the world, yet to
have kept its original mores so recognizable still!

For it is in many ways a conservative, indeed a conservationist
achievement. What has *not* happened to Toronto is as remarkable
as what *has* happened. It ought by all the odds to be a brilliant,
brutal city, but it isn't. Its downtown ought to be vulgar and
spectacular, but is actually dignified, well proportioned, and
indeed noble. Its sex-and-sin quarters, where the young prostitutes loiter and the rock shops scream, are hardly another
Reeperbahn, and the punks and Boy Georges to be seen parading
Yonge Street on a Saturday night are downright touching in
their bravado, so scrupulously are they ignored.

If 'multiculturalism' does not key you in to Toronto, try
'traditionalism'. It is a potent word too. The Toronto weekend,
once notorious for its Presbyterian severity, still seems to me
more thoroughly weekendish than most – especially as, having
whiled away Saturday morning with the huge weekend editions
of *The Globe* and the *Star*, you can lie in on Sunday with the
mammoth *New York Times*. The Toronto Stock Exchange, at
least as seen from the visitors' gallery, is marvellously cool and
gentlemanly. It costs up to $8,000 to get into the Royal Canadian
Yacht Club; the club's two private launches were built in 1898
and 1910 respectively. And though some of the Toronto rich
build themselves houses, on the Bridle Path for instance, of
almost unimaginable ostentation, to judge by the realty adver-
tisements most Torontonians aspire to nothing less decorous
than mock-Tudor, neo-Georgian, or sham-Château – 'Gracious,
grand and affordable', with elegant libraries, gourmet kitchens,
and 'classic fluted columns to punctuate the expansiveness of
sunken conservatories . . .'

The real achievement of Toronto is to have remained itself. It
says something for the character of this city that even now, 150
years old, with 300,000 Italian residents, and 50,000 Greeks,
and heaven knows how many Portuguese, Hungarians, Poles,
Latvians, Chileans, Maltese, Chinese, Finns, with skyscrapers
dominating it, and American TV beamed into every home –
with condominiums rising everywhere, and a gigantic Hilton
dominating the waterfront, and those cheese-stuffed pears at
Glossops – it says something for Toronto that it can still be
defined, by an elderly English lady over a glass of sherry, with

a Manx cat purring at her feet and a portrait of her late husband on the sidetable, as 'not such a bad old place – don't be too hard on it!'

So this is the New World! Not such a bad old place! Again, for myself it is not what I would want of a Promised Land, were I in need of one, and when I thought of that woman at the airport, and tried to put myself in her shoes, wherever she was across the sprawling city, I felt that if fate really were to make me an immigrant here I might be profoundly unhappy.

Not because Toronto would be unkind to me. It would be far kinder than New York, say, or Sydney down under. It would not leave me to starve in the street, or bankrupt me with medical bills, or refuse me admittance to discos because I was black. No, it would be a subtler oppression than that – the oppression of reticence. Toronto is the most undemonstrative city I know, and the least inquisitive. The Walkman might be made for it. It swarms with clubs, cliques and cultural societies, but seems armour-plated against the individual. There are few cities in the world where one can feel, as one walks the streets or rides the subways, for better or for worse, so all alone.

All around me I see those same faces from the airport carousel, so unflustered, so reserved; I caught the eye once of a subway driver, as he rested at his controls for a few moments in the bright lights of the station, waiting for the guard's signal, and never did I see an eye so fathomlessly subdued – not a flicker could I raise in it, not a glint of interest or irritation, before the whistle blew and he disappeared once more into the dark. It takes time, more time than a subway driver has, for the Toronto face, having passed through several stages of suspicion, nervous apprehension, and anxiety to please, to light up in a simple smile. Compulsory lessons in small talk, I sometimes think, might well be added to those school classes in Heritage Languages, and there might usefully be courses too in How to Respond to Casual Remarks in Elevators.

Sometimes I think it is the flatness of the landscape that causes this flattening of the spirit – those interminable suburbs stretching away, that huge plane of the lake, those long grid roads which deprive the place of surprise or intricacy. Sometimes I think it must be the climate, numbing the nerve ends or even the sheer empty vastness of the Toronto sky, settled so conclusively upon the horizon, wherever you look, unimpeded by hills. Could it be the history of the place, and the deference to authority that restrains the jay-walkers still? Could it be underpopulation; ought there to be a couple of million more people in the city, to give it punch or jostle? Could it be the permanent compromise of Toronto, neither quite this or altogether that, capitalist but compassionate, American but royalist, multicultural but traditionalist?

Or could it be, I occasionally ask myself, me? This is a city conducive to self-doubt and introspection. It is hard to feel that Torontonians by and large, for all the civic propaganda and guidebook hype, share in any grand satisfaction of the spirit, hard to imagine anyone waking up on a spring morning to cry, 'Here I am, here in T.O., thank God for my good fortune!' I asked immigrants of many nationalities if they liked Toronto, and though at first, out of diplomacy or good manners they nearly all said yes, a few minutes of probing generally found them less than enthusiastic. Why? 'Because the people is cold here.' 'Because these people just mind their own business and make the dollars.' 'Because the neighbours don't smile and say hullo, how's things.' 'Because nobody talks, know what I mean?'

Never I note because the citizenry has been unkind, or because the city is unpleasant: only because, in the course of its 150 years of careful progress, so calculated, so civilized, somewhere along the way Toronto lost, or failed to find, the gift of contact or of merriment. I know of nowhere much less merry than the Liquor Control Board retail stores, clinical and disapproving as Wedding Palaces in Leningrad. And even the most naturally merry of the immigrants, the dancing Greeks, the witty Poles, the lyrical Hungarians, somehow seem to have forfeited their *joie de vivre* when they embraced the liberties of this town.

Among the innumerable conveniences of Toronto, which is an extremely convenient city, one of the most attractive is the system of tunnels which lies beneath the downtown streets, and which, with its wonderful bright-lit sequences of stores, cafés, malls and intersections, is almost a second city in itself. I loved to think of all the warmth and life down there, the passing crowds, the coffee smells, the Muzak, and the clink of cups, when the streets above were half-empty in the rain, or scoured by cold winds; and one of my great pleasures was to wander aimless through those comfortable labyrinths, lulled from one

Golden Oldie to the next, surfacing now and then to find myself
on an unknown street corner far from home, or all unexpectedly
in the lobby of some tremendous bank.

But after a time I came to think of them as escape tunnels. It
was not just that they were warm and dry; they had an intimacy
to them, a brush of human empathy, absent from the greater
city above our heads. Might it be, I wondered, that down there
a new kind of Torontonian was evolving after all, brought to life
by the glare of the lights, stripped of inhibition by the press of
the crowds, and even perhaps induced to burst into song, or
dance a few steps down the escalator, by the beat of the canned
music?

'What d'you think?' I asked a friend. 'Are they changing the
character of Toronto?'

'You must be joking,' he replied. 'You couldn't do that in a
sesquicentury.'

He's probably right. Toronto is Toronto, below or above the
ground. And you, madame, into whatever obscurely ethnic
enclave you vanished, when we parted at the airport that day,
have they changed *you* yet? Have they taken you up to Bloor
Street to rig you out in mix 'n' match? Have they taught you not
to push, or talk to yourself, or hurl abuse at officialdom? Are
you still refusing to pay that customs charge, or have they
persuaded you to fill in the form and be sure to ask for a receipt
for tax purposes? Are you happy? Are you homesick? Are you
still yourself?

Whatever has happened to you, destiny has not dealt you a
bad hand in bringing you to this city by the lake. You are as free
as we mortals can reasonably expect, there are dumplings on
your dinner plate and a TV in your living-room, if not classic
fluted columns in a sunken conservatory. Your heart may not be
singing, as you contemplate the presence around you of Toronto
the Good, but it should not be sinking either. Cheer up! You
have drawn a second prize, I would say, in the Lottario of Life.

34

A TOWN THE ARTISTS LOVED

Trouville, 1964

In 1964 I wrote a series of articles, for the American magazine Life, *about famous European resorts. This happy assignment introduced me to Trouville, which remains for me still, as it seemed then, the quintessence of seaside pleasure, and an art form in itself. You can keep your Acapulcos!*

I had to look up Trouville on the map, but when I got there I knew it at once – not from any specific book or painting, but from a whole temper or even genre of art. There lay the long empty foreshore, with only a few shrimp-catchers knee-deep in its sand pools; and there along the boardwalk strolled a group of those women that Boudin loved, blurred and shimmery in flowered cottons; and the beach was lined with a gallimaufry of villas, gabled, pinnacled or preposterously half-timbered; and three fishing boats with riding sails chugged away offshore; and over it all, over the sands and the estuary and the distant promontory of Le Havre, there hung a soft impressionist light, summoned out of moist sunshine, high rolling clouds and the reflection of the sea. I knew the scene at once, from Monet and Bonnard and Proust. The English were the modern inventors of the salt-water resort, and made it fashionable to frequent the beaches; but the French first saw the beauty of the seaside scene, and transmuted into art all its perennial sights – the slant of that white sail, the stoop of that child beside his sand castle, the preen of the great ladies along the promenade.

This particular aesthetic was born in Trouville. It was among the earliest of the French seaside resorts, for a time it was the grandest, and at the back of our minds it is half familiar to us all.

*

Not far below the Seine estuary a little river called the Touques arrives unobtrusively at the English Channel, flowing through the lushly wooded landscape of Normandy, and surrounded at its mouth by a superb sandy beach. At high tide along this shore the sea rises to the very edge of the fields and orchards; at low tide an immense plateau of gold and sea shells is exposed, with chunks of black rock jutting out to sea, and a million infinitesimal crustaceans hopping about in the shallows. On the right bank of the Touques, almost at its mouth, there stood at the beginning of the nineteenth century the isolated village of Trouville – once a commercial port of some importance, later overtaken by better situated rivals and reduced to the status of a minor fishing station. The Channel here abounds in mackerel, eel, hake, turbot, sole and every kind of shellfish; a packet boat connected Trouville with Le Havre across the estuary; the village pottered along in picturesque modesty, with no great claim to fame, and not much hope of fortune.

In this condition the artist Charles Mozin discovered it in the 1820s. In a long series of affectionate paintings he portrayed every detail of Trouville in its pristine days: the few villas beside the sand, the horsemen plodding across the river at low tide, the brawny fisherwomen, the bright sails of the boats along the quays, the colonnaded fish market beside the waterfront, and above all the limpid hush that seems to have hovered over the little town. His pictures, not very distinguished examples of the romantic school, are mostly forgotten now: but they were exhibited in Paris, and they introduced the world to the charms of a coastline hitherto considered bleak, blighted and impossibly primitive. Other artists followed Mozin to Trouville, and writers too, and presently the great caravan of fashion found its way to the Normandy shore, and made the name of Trouville synonymous, for a brief but gorgeous heyday, with the pleasures of the Second Empire.

It was a full-blown sort of climax. Napoleon III's regime began brilliantly, matured lavishly, and died in humiliation. Under its aegis, all the more sumptuous arts flourished. Romanticism flounced through its rich decline. Fashion went in for ribbons, crinolines and massive flowered bonnets. Sainte-Beuve presided over a sparkling school of literary criticism, painters like Courbet and Manet were bringing a daring new splendour to realist art. Led by the Empress Eugénie, herself a creature of infinite sensuality, the Second Empire fell upon Trouville like some overwhelming rich aunt, all scent and furbelows. The boardwalk was laid upon the sands, and above it, beneath the bluffs, a parade of hotels and villas arose – very assured, very opulent, with parasols, and wicker chairs on their verandas, and whirligigs on their eaves. At the point where the river reached the sands, they built a huge casino, a regular monument of a place, with opulent assembly rooms in the latest style, and carriage drives fit for any imperial barouche.

Trouville became a catalyst of the grand and the quaint. Where the fishing quay ended, the village began. The port remained a little port, but to the new resort came the Emperor himself and all of his racy, glamorous but not always very reputable court. The Empire set a seal upon Trouville, and the taste and style it engendered in this place have remained ever since part of the French artistic consciousness. Flaubert, Dumas, Victor Hugo, Boudin, Rossini, Gounod, de Musset and Dufy all felt the spell of the little town. Whistler stayed there with Courbet, Monet with Boudin, and nearly half a century after the fall of the Empire Trouville contributed its elements to the Balbec of Marcel Proust, where the sea looked like a painted fan through the windows of La Raspelière, where Albertine and her friends of the little band idled on the boardwalk, and where the Narrator himself pursued his introspections in 'that Pandora's box, the Grand Hotel'.

So I recognized it all: the sea and the sand from the painters, the style from the history books, and the very stance of the hotel manager from the pages of *A la Recherche du Temps Perdu*. Trouville has not much grown since Proust's day – or even since Eugénie's. The countryside behind it remains delectably unspoiled, with its famous stud farms hidden away among the elms, and strong emanations of milk, fruit and rough cider. The combination of green grass and sand, meeting at the foreshore, still makes the view from the beaches feel like one of those glimpses you get from the deck of a ship, when the passing landscape seems close but altogether unattainable, as though you are seeing it through plate glass. Across the estuary Le Havre has spread down its peninsula with oil tanks and tall apartment blocks, but its very hint of power and bustle, seen distantly across the water, only heightens Trouville's sense of detachment.

History is kind to pleasure-places, and Trouville has been spared by the wars. Long ago the English corsairs used to raid it, but in modern times nobody has much harmed the town. A plaque in one of the churches gratefully records the fact that the invading Prussian armies of 1871 never came farther than Honfleur, fifteen miles up the coast. In the last war, though the Allies bombed the German defences on the neighbouring hills, and fifty-six citizens of Trouville lost their lives in the Resistance, nevertheless when the liberating Belgians marched in, all was in reasonable order. This impunity means that Trouville, not so far along the shore from Utah Beach or Arromanches, has a curiously preserved or pickled air. It is a period piece, more perfect than most. Its balance of commerce and pleasure has been scrupulously maintained, and you can enjoy today almost the same mixture of sensations that the courtiers and the artists enjoyed a century ago. The core of the town remains the Casino. This has aged a little since its ceremonial opening, and has rather gone down in the world. Part of it is a cinema, part of it a salt-water spa, part a night club, part a waxwork show, part a fire house, part a shabby kind of tenement. As an architectural whole, nevertheless, it is still imposingly snooty, and looks faintly exotic – like a vast Mongol marquee, perhaps, with bobbles and domes and flagstaffs, and its own name in large and ornate letters above the entrance.

On my first evening in Trouville I made my way to the steps of this old prodigy and, leaning against a marble pillar, surveyed the town before me. The square outside the Casino, dotted with trees and used as a car park, is asymmetrical, and this splaying of its form makes it look exactly like one of those panoramic postcards popular among our great-grandmothers, in which several negatives were tacked together, and the view came out peculiarly elongated, smaller at the edges than in the middle. From this distorted apex I could see both halves of Trouville. To my left lay the beach and all it represents, the pride, the old grandeur and the space. To my right, the fishing boats were lined up beside the quay, bright awnings ornamented the shop fronts, and all was cluttered intimacy. Both styles were essential, I realized that evening, to the art form that is Trouville; and it is the confrontation of the two, set against the light and scale of the foreshore, that gives the aesthetic of the seaside its especial tangy charm.

I looked to my right first, towards fisherman's Trouville – still as in the 1820s, any romantic's delight. The tide was high, and the upper works of fishing smacks lined the river boulevard – tangled structures of rope and rigging, hung with flags, buoys, lifebelts, nets and paintpots, and undulating slightly at their moorings. Here and there a crew was unloading its catch in crates upon the quay, while the fish merchant gravely calculated the value, a huddle of housewives knowingly discussed the quality, a few tourists looked on with the glazed fascination that dead fish inspire in almost everyone, and several small boys in their blue school smocks wormed and giggled through the crowd. There were men angling, too, with heavy rods and voluminous canvas satchels. There were porters lounging around the *poissonnerie*, in stained overalls and nautical caps. High-wheeled carts were propped against walls, there was a noise of hammering from a boatyard, and the fish stalls down the street glistened with crabs, lobsters, jumpy things like big water fleas, twitching eels, clams, oysters and mackerel with a cold bluish tinge to their flanks.

For Trouville is still a working town: and behind its waterfront, workaday good sense fills the tight mesh of streets at the foot of the hill. There are shops that sell nets and tackle; shops lusciously flowing with the fruits, vegetables and cheeses of Normandy; trim cafés full of mirrors and tobacco smoke; a couple of big chain stores; and up in the grounds of the hospital, overgrown with ivy and embellished with archaic saintly figures, the original church of Trouville, thirteen paces long from door to altar, in whose reverent obscurity the fishing people worshipped for several centuries before the first tourist set eyes upon this place. All the stubborn variety of French provincial life stirs along those streets. Trouville is rich in tough twinkling old ladies, eccentrically dressed and wheeling their groceries on basket trolleys, and in those shabby but courteous old gentlemen of France who might be anything from dukes to retired milkmen, and wear high starched collars in the middle of August. But there are many laughing representatives of the new French generations, taller, gayer and more confident than we have ever known French people before, with beautiful children in the back seats of small family cars, and a sense of bright emancipation from a fusty past – figures from that rich young France which is, as D. W. Brogan has observed, 'something that Europe and the world have not seen for a century'.

Fisherman's Trouville is never torpid. It admirably illustrates those aspects of the French genius which are unalterably organic – close always to the earth, the sea, the marriage bed and the neighbour's gossip. The Duchesse de Guermantes, the ineffably aristocratic chatelaine of Proust's great novel, loved to tell country anecdotes in a rustic accent: and it is this ancient attachment to earthy things, so vital a part of the French artistic energy, that the right-hand view from the Casino best expresses.

Then I looked to the left, and there lay another France in esplanade. Exuberantly the hotels and villas clustered about the beach – none of them young indeed, but all of them gay, like jolly old gentlefolk, in lace and grey toppers, out to enjoy themselves. It was an elaborate age that made Trouville famous, and the buildings of this resort are flamboyantly individualist. Some are gloriously encrusted with coils, domes and flourishes of classicism. Some are expensively faced in Normandy half-timber, and stand incongruously beside the sands like farmhouses on Fifth Avenue. Others go to wilder excess, and are built like castles, like fairy palaces, even in one case like a Persian caravanserai. The rooftops of this Trouville are punctuated with golden birds, pineapples, crescent moons, spindles, metal flowers and urns, and all the way up the hillside among the trees the mansions stand in majesty, unabashed by shifts of taste or society, and still looking, behind their ornamental gates and protective shady gardens, almost voluptuously comfortable.

Not much has changed since the great days of the resort. The bright little tents that people put up on the beach are made of nylon nowadays, but with their suggestion of eastern dalliance still recall the enthusiasms of Delacroix or Gautier. Cars are not admitted to the beach, so that the long-celebrated boardwalk, however crowded it becomes in high summer, is still quiet and leisurely. Nobody has erected a skyscraper hotel, or built a bowling alley, and severe instructions affixed to flagstaffs govern the decorum of the sands. The miniature golf course, beside the Casino, is a very model of genteel entertainment, admirably suited to the inhibitions of elastic-sided boots and bustles: with its painted wooden windmill for knocking balls through, its tricky inclines and whimsical hazards, it seems to ring perpetually with the silvery laugh of ladies-in-waiting, and the indulgent banter of colonels. As for the unexploded mines and bombs which occasionally turn up along these shores, Trouville officially classifies them as *'Objets Bizarres'* – and what a fine old-school sniff infuses those fastidious syllables!

The Second Empire was scarcely an empire really, but it loved the imperial trappings, and stamped the grand manner upon Trouville. Two nineteenth-century churches overshadow the little fishermen's chapel, and are full of superior memories. In one, a large but indistinct painting has nothing to indicate either its subject or its artist, but only a plaque to tell us loftily: 'Presented by the Emperor'. In the other stands an altar given by the Comte d'Hautpool and his wife the Princesse de Wagram – Napoleonic titles which, for all their splendour, remind us that the ruling class of this extravagant period was never quite the real thing, but rested upon the pedigree of a Corsican adventurer. The florid style of the Empire is everywhere in Trouville, and when the regime collapsed with the defeat of Napoleon III at the Battle of Sedan, the great days of the resort ended too; it was here that the fiery Eugénie stepped aboard an English yacht and sailed away into exile.

Finally I walked behind the great mass of the Casino (looking, as the evening drew on, just as humped and portentous as Bonnard had painted it fifty years before) and across the narrow river I saw another, larger, more glittering city on the other side. The Duc de Morny, half-brother of the Emperor himself, was paradoxically the originator of Trouville's decline. In the 1860s this enterprising speculator cast *his* eye across the Touques, and saw that the sand on the other side was just as golden, the climate just as sparkling, the sea the same stimulating sea – and the landscape entirely empty. Trouville had reached its peak of fashion; Parisian elite was beginning to hanker for somewhere more exclusive; in a few years, upon the impetus of the duke, there arose on the left bank of the Touques the excruciatingly posh resort of Deauville.

Today it is the smartest watering place in northern France, and it looked to me that evening, from the backside of Trouville's Casino, like a vision of another age. Its clientele nowadays is richer and more cosmopolitan than Trouville's. Its casino has a turnover twice as great. Its street lights come on fifteen minutes earlier. Its race meeting is one of the most important in Europe.

No fishermen's cafés soil its elegant promenades, and only yachts and speedboats sail into its basin. It is all resort. Today if you want to explain where Trouville stands, you can best say that it's over the bridge from Deauville.

So there is a certain pathos to the prospect from the Casino at Trouville – but pathos of a gentle, amused kind. Trouville does not feel humiliated. It is this small town that the artists loved, its image, variously interpreted down the generations, that has entered all our sensibilities – Trouville's sands and sails we all dimly recognize, Trouville's ludicrous mansions that ornament the album pages, Trouville's bright light that gleams so often, with a tang of Channel air, from the walls of so many galleries. In Trouville the sun, the sea, the fishing folk and the high society became an inspiration, and created a tradition of art.

So I did not mope that evening. I crossed the square to my hotel, accepted the bows of Proust's page boys, left a note inviting Whistler and de Musset to join me for a drink at *Les Vapeurs*, and asked the maid to clean my best shoes, in case I bumped into the Empress at the Casino after dinner.

35

A BALEFUL PARABLE

Vienna, 1983

∞

I first knew Vienna at the very end of the Second World War, but for nearly forty years I never wrote about it. When at last I did, though I gratefully recognized the city's pleasures, I simply could not bring myself to like it. It is no place for a Welsh republican.

Nothing so becomes a city as a street-car (or a tram, as we Europeans prefer it), especially if it has a single cyclopean headlamp on its front, and a couple of flags fluttering on its roof, and is connected by sundry pipes and couplings with a trailer-car behind. What weight! What responsibility! What reassurance!

And nowhere does the tram fulfil its municipal functions more staunchly than in the city of Vienna, for here it must trundle its way, day in day out, come war come peace, through a state of affairs utterly alien to the instincts of any self-respecting trolley: fantasy is piled upon fantasy in Wien, Österreich, pretence is compounded by delusion, introspection repeatedly degenerates into complex, and the whole adds up to a baleful parable of the urban condition. In some ways Vienna is the most intensely civic of great cities, the most complete and compact, the most preoccupied with its own civicness – a fifth of the entire Austrian population, after all, lives within this peculiar capital. In other ways it transcends mere city status altogether, and is more a temperament or a sensibility, embodying as it does an inexpungable repertoire of doubts, regrets and ambiguous prides – was it not within living memory the seat of the Habsburgs, the Imperial Capital of Austria-Hungary, the root of all that the word 'Empire' came to mean to the world before the wars?

Steadily notwithstanding, small flags flying, the trams clank their way around town: they are painted in strong and sensible colours, and look rather barge-like, as though they ought to be stirring up bow-waves along the track in front of them.

Down upon their diligent passings stare the structures of the Ringstrasse, the boulevard which, in the nineteenth century, replaced the ancient ramparts around the inner city of Vienna. Now as then, the Ringstrasse unforgettably dramatizes the false and footling values of this city, and it has given its name to a whole genre of Viennese art and thought – the Ringstrasse genre. Like some mad architect's dream fulfilled, its buildings rise one after another preposterously into view, Gothic or Grecian or Baroque, plastered in kitsch or writhing with classical allusion, capped by spires, monstrous domes and silhouetted effigies, clumped with goddesses, chariots, gross escutcheons, caryatids, piles of sculpted trophies – here a titanic opera house, here a refulgently Attic Parliament, a university more utterly academic than Princeton, Padua, Cambridge and the Sorbonne put together, museums as overwhelmingly museumy as museums possibly could be, and dominating the whole ensemble, half-way round the ring, the immense pillared sprawl of the Hofburg, the palace of the Habsburgs until their removal after the First World War, which seems to lie there all but exhausted, as well it might, by the weight of so much consequence.

Vienna is all consequence. It stands at the far end of the Alps like a grandiloquent watchman of history. Its streets lead not just to suburbs or provincial towns, but to ancient satrapies and fields of action: the Ostautobahn strikes grandly out for Budapest and Prague, Triesterstrasse will take you, if you persevere, direct to Dalmatia, and at the end of Landstrasse, as Metternich once observed, Asia itself begins. Everything around here is designed for consequence. The Danube passes a mile or two from the Ringstrasse, crossed by strategic bridges, commanded by castles. Flatlands just made for tanks or cavalry sweep away almost from the suburbs to the marshlands of the east. The spire of St Stephen's Cathedral, plumb in the middle of the inner city, stands as a mighty marker to guide or warn the tribes, the caravans and the warring armies.

God-made then for consequence, long ago the city came to

worship it. Under the aegis of the immemorially self-important Habsburgs, the Viennese became the archetypal sychophants of history, and made of their city one vast tribute to the vulgarity of class. How could they help it? For centuries they revered as their models of behaviour men who not only called themselves, in all seriousness, Their Imperial, Royal and Apostolic Majesties, but also claimed to be Kings of Jerusalem, Dalmatia, Bohemia, Transylvania, Croatia and Galicia, Grand Dukes of Tuscany, Princely Counts of Tyrol, dukes of a score of dukedoms and lords of lordships without number. These walking Social Registers, these Grand Panjandrums of Central Europe, were the presiding spirits of this place almost into modern times, and their silly standards and superstitions linger inescapably still.

It reminds me of Beijing. Beijing too has torn down its medieval walls to make way for pompous squares and thoroughfares, it too apparently depends for its self-assurance upon childish charades of grandeur, and it is also haunted by the ghosts of dead autocrats. Franz Josef, the last of the great Habsburgs, was the Mao of nineteenth-century Austria, the Helmsman of Vienna, the Great Father, and like Mao he has left behind him a host of followers who may deny their loyalty to his ideology, but who are subject by hereditary brainwash to his values. Watch now – stand back – here come a couple of Ministers down the steps from the Council Chamber in Parliament, portly important men, deep in portly and important matters of State – and swoosh, like a rocket from his office leaps the porter, buttoning his jacket – out of his door, panting heavily, urgently smoothing his hair, down the steps two at a go, *bitte, bitte!* – just in time, my goodness only just in time to open the door for Their Excellencies, who acknowledge his grovel only with slight inclinations of their heads, so as not to interrupt the flow of the discourse, as they lumber out beneath the figures of Minerva and her attendant sages to their waiting limousine.

Where sundry passers-by look almost inclined to bow and curtsey themselves, to see those dignitaries so lordly! In manners as in symbolisms, Franz Josef's convictions of hierarchy seem to colour everything in Vienna still. Though this is the capital of a republic, and a Second Republic at that, it abounds in princes and archdukes, not to mention mere counts or baronesses, glittering in restaurants with sleek golden hair and predatory half-Magyar faces, elegantly cordial at cocktail parties ('If you're ever in Carinthia, we happen to have a little place down there . . .'), or sometimes to be glimpsed, if young enough, driving around the Ringstrasse in racy Italian cars for all the world as though they should still be dressed in the shakoes, plumes and dangling scabbards of White Hussars.

And below the aristocrats, the social order is marshalled still in self-perpetuating gradations of esteem and respectability. The style of the imperial bureaucracy, established to administer a dominion that extended from Switzerland to Albania, now orders the affairs of a powerless neutral republic of 7½ million souls. People grumble constantly about the size, the slowness, the fussiness, the not unknown corruption, the ornate arcanum of it, but still one feels they are themselves oddly complicit to its survival. It is the last blur of their greatness. It is Franz Josef himself living fuzzily on, honoured still by all Vienna's myriad ranks of social and official import, all its Excellencies and Herr Professors and Frau Doktors and guilds and orders and infinitesimal nuances of protocol – the allegiance symbolized every morning, to this day, by the awe-struck deference that attends the morning exercises of the Imperial Lipizzaner horses, cantering round and round their palatial riding school, and followed obsequiously by a functionary with a shovel to remove their noble defecations.

Vienna feeds upon its past, a fond and sustaining diet, varied with chocolate cake or boiled beef with potatoes (Franz Josef's favourite dish), washed down with the young white wine of the Vienna Woods, digested, and re-digested, and ordered once more, over, and over, and over again . . . If it reminds me sometimes of Beijing, sometimes it suggests to me the sensations of apartheid in South Africa. The city is obsessed, and obsessive. Every conversation returns to its lost greatness, every reference somehow finds its way to questions of rank, or status, or historical influence. Viennese romantics still love to wallow in the tragic story of Crown Prince Rudolf and his eighteen-year-old mistress Marie Vetsera, 'the little Baroness', who died apparently in a suicide pact in the country house of Mayerling in 1889. The tale precisely fits the popular predilections of this city, being snobbish, nostalgic, maudlin and rather cheap. I went out one Sunday to visit the grave of the little Baroness, who was buried obscurely in a village churchyard by command of Franz Josef, and was just in time to hear a Viennese lady of a certain age explaining the affair to her American guests. 'But in any case,' I heard her say without a trace of irony, 'in any case she was only the daughter of a bourgeois . . .'

I often saw that same lady waiting for a tram, for she is a familiar of Vienna. She often wears a brown tweed suit, and is rather tightly clamped around the middle, and pearled very likely, and she never seems to be encumbranced, as most of us sometimes are, with shopping bags, umbrellas or toasters she has just picked up from the electrician's. If you smile at her she responds with a frosty stare, as though she suspects you might put ketchup on your *Tafelspitz*, but if you speak to her she lights up with a flowery charm. Inextricably linked with the social absurdity of Vienna is its famous *Gemütlichkeit*, its ordered cosiness, which is enough to make a Welsh anarchist's flesh creep: the one goes with the other, and just as it made the people of old Vienna one and all the children of their kind father His Imperial, Royal and Apostolic Majesty, still to this day it seems to fix the attitudes of this city as with a scented glue – sweetly if synthetically scented, like the flavours you sometimes taste upon licking the adhesives of American envelopes.

There is nothing *tangy* to this city, except perhaps the dry white wines. There is no leanness to it. Even the slinkiest of those patricians, one feels, is going to run to fat in the end, and the almost complete absence, in the city centre, of any modern architecture means that a swollen sense of inherited amplitude seems to supervise every attitude. Though Vienna is ornamented everywhere with eagles, the double-headed eagle of the Dual Monarchy, the single-headed eagle of the Austrian Republic, nowhere could be much less aquiline. Vienna an eyrie! It is more like a boudoir birdcage, and when one morning I saw a seagull circling over the pool at Schönbrunn Palace it was like seeing a wild free visitor from some other continent.

Wildness, freeness, recklessness – not in Vienna! I went to a minor police court one day, and noticing one of the accused studying a road map between hearings asked him if he was planning an escape. 'No,' he said, 'I am deciding the best route to visit my aunt at Graz.' The famous Big Wheel of the Prater funfair, that beloved image of the Viennese skyline, moves with such a genteel deliberation that I felt like kicking it, or scrawling scurrilous graffiti on its benches: the Vienna Woods which are said to have inspired so many artists in their passion for the Sublime represent Nature about as elementally thrilling as a rectory rock garden.

But who would want it otherwise, in this city of the coffee-house, the white-tie Wholesalers' Ball and the merry tavern evening with accordion accompaniment? Vienna is an elderly, comfortable, old-fashioned city. If you want excitement, a student of my acquaintance told me, you must either go to Munich or work up a peace demonstration. More immediately to hand than in almost any other city, Vienna possesses all the sensations and appurtenances of metropolitan existence, the stream of the sidewalk traffic, the great green parks with ponds and cafés in them, the opulence of long-established stores, the plushy banks and crowded theatres, the consoling lights of restaurants gleaming on wet pavements, the glimpses of opera audiences spilling out for gossip and champagne in the inter-mission, the bookshop after bookshop down the boulevards, the hotels rich in lore and private recipes, the memorials to heroes and historical satisfactions, the newspaper kiosks selling *Le Monde* or *Svenska Dagbladet*, the grand steepled hulk of the cathedral above its square, the buskers in pedestrian precincts, the winking TV tower, the sleepless trams . . . Yet as no other city can, Vienna somehow mutates this glorious distillation of human energy and imagination into something irredeemably domestic and conventional.

I walked one day into the Karlskirche, the most spectacular of Vienna's Baroque churches, which has a dome like St Peter's, a couple of triumphal columns dressed up as minarets, and two subsidiary towers roofed in the Chinese manner. Inside I found a wedding in progress. It was magnificent. The great church seemed all ablaze with light and gilding, rococo saints floated everywhere, the bride and groom knelt side by side before the high altar, and flooding through the building came the strains of a Haydn string quartet, marvellously played and amplified to a crisp and vibrant splendour. Yet all that glory was subtly plum-pened or buttoned by Vienna, for when I looked at the faces of the congregation I saw no exaltation there, only a familial compla-cency, satisfaction with the decorum of the arrangements only slightly tinged by the thought that dear Father would have played that *adagio* with a little more finesse.

For yes, if there is one art that has the power to make *Gemütlichkinder* of them all, it is the inescapably Viennese art of music. To Beethoven, Mozart, Haydn, Liszt, Schubert, Brahms, Bruckner, Mahler and any number of Strausses the Viennese feel a cousinly and possessive relationship. 'I hate going to concerts,' I rashly announced to a Viennese companion over dinner one evening, and our rapport was never quite the same again: and ah! how I grew to dread the quivering pause in the garden of the Kursalon – conductor with bow and violin raised above his head, orchestra poised expectant over their strings, audience frozen with their spoons half in, half out of their ice-creams – that preceded, twenty or thirty times a day, the fruity melody and relentless beat of the Viennese waltz!

I made a pilgrimage, all the same, to the grave of Beethoven in the Grove of Honour, at the central cemetery, the *Zentralfried-hof*. Mozart is commemorated there too, if only retrospectively, his body having unfortunately been dumped in an unmarked pauper's grave, and Johann Strauss the Elder is lapped by cherubim nearby, and Hugo Wolf the *Lieder*-writer, than whom no single human being has ever plunged me into profounder despondency, is among the shrubberies round the corner. Beethoven's tomb was easy enough to find because it had so many wreaths upon it, including one laid that morning, with visiting card attached, by Professor Hisako Kocho, President of the Folk Opera Society of Oita Prefecture (telephone Oita 5386). Yet even this grand sanctuary did not make my heart race, or inspire me to heroic yearnings: for with the gilded lyre upon its headstone, its Old German lettering and its generally metro-nomic or Edition Peters manner, it reminded me horribly of piano practice.

At night however lights are reflected in the overhead wires of the tram-cars, and seem to slide eerily around the Ringstrasse of their own accord, like beings in a separate field of animation, lighter, faster, airier, more sly, than any No. 2 to Franz Josefs-Kai. Perhaps that well-known Viennese Herr Professor Freud used to contemplate them, as he strode on his long meditative walks: certainly it was from the generic psyche of Vienna that he drew his definition of the subconscious – that part of every human, every city, which lies concealed beneath the personality, or is revealed only by shimmering glints on street-car wires.

The most celebrated contemporary citizen of Vienna is not an analyst of trauma, but a scourer. Policeman lounging feet up on the stairs outside, files of data stacked macabre around him, Simon Wiesenthal the Nazi-hunter sits in his office above Salztorstrasse, close to the old Jewish quarter and the Gestapo HQ, endlessly considering the darkest categories of *Angst*. Around him are framed testimonials from grateful institutions – he is an Award-Winning Nazi-hunter – but few of them come from societies in Vienna. Hundreds of the most virulent Nazis, he says, still live unscathed in these parts – one much-respected builder of churches not only constructed the Auschwitz gas chambers, but *repaired* them, too. Dr Wiesenthal is by no means sufficiently *gemütlich* for the Viennese. There was an attempt on his life not long ago, and the city authorities very much wish, he tells me, that he would go somewhere else: in the meantime they put that slovenly policeman on his door, and another one, toting an automatic rifle, stands just in case outside the Synagogue in Seitenstettengasse.

I have to say that for a few hours after visiting Dr Wiesenthal I saw the face of Eichmann all around me – that peaked but ordinary face which I remember so exactly from the court-room at Jerusalem years ago, and which Hannah Arendt characterized for ever as expressing 'the banality of evil'. Nothing could be more unfair, I know, to the people of Vienna. Half of them are too young to remember Nazidom anyway, and the others, though if we are to believe Dr Wiesenthal they include a far higher proportion of war criminals than survive in any German city, were doubtless the victims above all of their *genii loci*. It was the presence of Vienna, after all, that first incited Adolf Hitler himself to his grandiose dreams of sovereignty – like an enchantment out of the Arabian Nights, he thought the vainglorious horror of the Ringstrasse.

But even if I dismiss from my mind the image of that lady in the brown suit, braided and blonde in those days, greeting the stormtroopers with rose petals from the pockets of her dirndl, still I cannot dispel the feeling, as I walk these streets, that I am promenading one great conglomeration of neurosis.

The reasons for it are not hard to conjecture – the crippling social legacies of the monarchy, the relentless pressures of *Gemütlichkeit*, historical humiliation, geographical exposure – drive down Metternich's Landstrasse now, and in an hour you are on the frontiers of Czechoslovakia or of Hungary, where the sentinels of the Eastern world, weapons over their shoulders, stand with the great steppes at their backs.

No wonder this is a Freudian city in every sense. Not only is Freud's house in Berggasse maintained as a shrine, where you may buy mounted photographs of his original Couch, or fancy yourself summoning dreams for interpretation in the very room where the Oedipus complex was first isolated. Not only that, but everywhere in the city you feel around you the ideas, the idioms and the subject matter of Freud's vision: Father Figures tower in royal and apostolic statuary, libidos search for discos or Prater prostitutes, repressions wander arm-in-arm on Sunday afternoons down the beckoning avenues of *Zentralfriedhof*. It is as though at heart this whole famous metropolis, through its bows, smiles and proprieties, would like nothing so much as to flop down on a sofa in tearful revelation – in the presence, of course, of a properly *gemütlich* and well-qualified Herr Dr Professor.

And the last and most marvellous flowering of the Viennese genius, that surge of styles, ideas and mannerisms which orchestrated the decay and collapse of the Habsburgs, was itself a distinctly neurotic blossoming. No lyric joy of liberation seems to have inspired the new artistic forms by which the architects, the painters and the composers of this city rebelled against the old order of things. The temple of their revolution was the art gallery called the Secession House, built by the architect Josef Olbrich in 1898 and still as good as new: but it was officially opened by the Emperor anyway, and with its squat hunched form and its dome of gilded laurel-leaves looks rather like a mausoleum from that Grove of Honour (though I dare say the Secessionists themselves, whose text was Ver Sacrum, Sacred Spring, thought it looked like a pumproom). There was not, it seems, much fine careless rapture to this renaissance, to the venomous furies and gold-encased women of its paintings, to the alternate swirls and severities of its ever more loveless architecture.

But it did have a daemonic fire to it, and this strain of tormented or inverted genius lingers today like a reflected glow of the city's inner conflicts. I find it more haunting, if less dazzling, than the excesses of Ringstrasse, for it shows itself more obliquely, in art as in life: a sudden tangle of decoration, a blank façade of concrete, the sunken eye of a man in the subway, a woman's twisted face – wrenched by stroke? by bitterness? – as she sits alone over her coffee. For all its comfort, for all its beauty, for all its wealth and self-esteem, Vienna does not feel to me a happy city. Its citizens seem to be still working out, in their various ways, the very same doubts and frustrations which those artists expressed with such disturbing power in the last days of the old regime.

They often fail. The suicide rate has always been high in Vienna. 'He died like a tailor,' is supposed to have been Franz Josef's odious comment on the fate of his son and heir at Mayerling, and so he acknowledged how commonplace, how workaday, was the self-destructive urge among his children the citizens at large. Death is a born Viennese, and nowhere is he more *gemütlich*, as it happens, than in the crypt of the Church of the Capuchins, where the corpses of the Habsburgs themselves are stored: for there is a small workshop down there too, for the restoration of imperial sarcophagi, and if you look through its window you may see a gigantic casket emptied of its contents, having its lid repaired perhaps, or its supporting angels re-capitated, and looking for all the world like a car in for its 6,000-mile service, or a lawnmower parked among the buckets and hose-pipes of the garden shed.

I was walking up Kohlmarkt one morning when there appeared beneath the carriage arch of the Hofburg, stalking into the city with a slow imperial swagger, a well-known eccentric of Vienna, nicknamed Waluliso. He was extremely thin, spectral almost. Dressed all in white, as in a toga, he wore an imperial laurel round his brow, and carried a long staff to which streaming banners were attached. As he walked he shouted high-pitched slogans, slip-slopping in his sandals out of the great shaded archway into the sun. Nobody seemed surprised. A policeman chaffed him, a youth on a bicycle slowed down to pat him affectionately on the shoulder: but he gave me a nasty shock, emerging there so abruptly, so white, so skeletonic, so like the ghost of an All-Highest gone off his head with the folly of things, and sprung from his crypt to confuse us.

Actually the trams all but killed me once. In some parts of the Ringstrasse they alone run against the flow of the traffic, and looking to the right to make sure I was not run down by an archduke in an Alfa, I was all but squashed by a trolley-car

coming up from the left. *'Achtung! Achtung!'* screamed several
ladies in brown tweed suits, but they forgave me my stupidity
– had not Dr Waldheim, they reminded each other, Secretary-
General of the United Nations, almost met his end in the very
same way, on that very same street?

Inevitably people have seen Freud's Death-Wish exemplified
in this city, so preoccupied with the past, the tomb, and how
the mighty fall. It seems to me though that Vienna is adept at
transferring that Wish to others. It is fateful not so much to itself
as to the rest of us. It prospers well enough in its neuroses – it
is we who suffer the traumas! Viennese Modernism hardly
touched the surface of Vienna with its shapes, but everywhere
else it was to cause a tragic alienation between architecture and
public taste. Viennese Atonalism may seldom be heard in
Vienna's own *Musikverein,* but everywhere else it long ago made
life's hard pleasures harder still. Viennese Communalism,
expressed in the vast housing estates so dear to sociologists of
the 1930s, turns out to have been a step towards the universal
miseries of the Social Security tower block. The anti-Semitism
of Vienna pushed us all towards the Final Solution, the Zionism
that was born there has left many a young body, Jewish and
Gentile too, dead along the path to Israel. Freud himself, though
until twenty years ago, I am told, his name was scarcely
mentioned at psychiatry seminars in Vienna, long ago left the
rest of the world irrevocably addled by his genius.

Is there any city more seminally disturbing? It is as though
Vienna has been a laboratory of all our inhibitions, experiment-
ing down the generations in new ways of confusing us. Perhaps
rather than all our Death-Wishes it expresses all our schizo-
phrenias? I rather think it may, you know, for as I stepped back
from the track that day just in time to avoid extinction – *Achtung!
Stop! Comes the tram!* – I looked up at the passing streetcar and
distinctly saw there, just for a moment, my own face in its
slightly steamed-up window. We exchanged distant smiles, as
between Id and Ego, or dream and wake.

36

FROM A POLISH WINDOW

Warsaw, 1957

❦

I had a great deal of fun in Poland in 1957, but on my last night in Warsaw I was seized by an overwhelming sadness: and shutting myself up in my hotel bedroom, I wrote this heartsick polonaise.

Seen across the hours from a hotel window in the depths of winter, Warsaw could only be Warsaw, for nowhere else on the face of the earth breathes quite the same fusion of atmospheres. Room 221 in the Bristol Hotel is heavily but quite cosily Victorian, with a wicker mat hung in incongruous ornamentation on one wall and a bright if unadventurous abstract on another. Outside the door two dear old pudgy housemaids sit habitually on the floor in white caps, aprons and carpet slippers, sibilantly gossiping, and down the corridor the immense glass lift, like a cage for a phoenix, slides in magnificent lurches to the foyer, its voyagers slipping a few zlotys to the operator as they leave. There is a violent smell of cooking on the landing, and downstairs you may just hear the tapping of a progressive American playwright's typewriter – he spent last evening with a group of eminent sociologists, and is busy working up his notes.

It is a fusty, old-fashioned, plush but mournful hostelry: but outside the window Warsaw is nothing if not spacious. The sky is grey, immense, and unmistakably Central European. The snow lies thick and sullen on the broad streets. Down the hill only a thin winding stream of water forces a way through the frozen Vistula. The air, to a visitor from England, seems slightly perfumed with petrol and boiled potatoes, but feels nevertheless like country air, blown out of forests and endless plains and Carpathian ravines; and when you first lean from your window in the icy morning you will hear the clatter of horses' hooves and the triumphant crow of a cold but irrepressible cock. Below you then the first citizens of the morning intermittently appear: an elderly lady with a jolly black dog, a covey of merry schoolchildren, entrancing high-boned faces peering through their fur hoods like fox cubs through the bushes. Long carts full of snow go by, with a column of big lorries, and even an antique barouche trundles with creaks and squeaks towards its cab-rank; and presently Warsaw is wide awake, the sun is wanly shining, and the observer in Room 221 can watch the world of the Poles pass by.

It is not altogether a drab world, for the Poles have forced many concessions out of their Communist masters. The citizenry that now pours down the pavement is not badly dressed – colourlessly, perhaps, by Western standards, but well shod and warmly coated. Sometimes a young beauty steps by almost ludicrously glamourized, slinking skilfully in the Bardot manner, in the finest nylons and the most preposterously frivolous of fur hats. Sometimes a peasant stumps down the street in thick but threadbare serge and mighty boots. Mostly the people look less arresting than workmanlike, as though they are more concerned with keeping warm and getting to the butcher's first than with turning heads or charming the boss's daughter.

The shops across the way might not win prizes in Fifth Avenue or Regent Street, but have more sparkle to them than you might expect (weary though the queue may be at the grocer's, and tiresome the shortage of meat). A surprising variety of inessential imports glitters bravely among their displays – American cigarettes, French sardines, Hawaiian pineapples, Florida fruit juice, tinned coffee from England, tea from Madras, olives from Argentina, things that look like bottled gooseberries from Bulgaria, Chinese jams (in bottles shaped like illustrious mandarins of the eighth degree). A bright parade of foreign books shines in the bookshop down the road, from a picture book of Oxford that almost breaks the homesick heart to an empirical range of American paperbacks. You can even buy French perfumes in Warsaw, if you happen to prefer them to the local product, and have an indulgent husband.

The cars that pass in increasing but still moderate profusion mostly look beetle-backed and froward, but now and then one of the smart new Russian limousines appears, not a bit Socialist-

realist, and sometimes an opulent Mercedes-Benz slides by, or
a delicate Fiat. Agatha Christie is probably on at one of the
theatres. You can read the Manchester *Guardian* at the Grand
Hotel. The buses are made in France. Just down the road is the
headquarters of the British and Foreign Bible Society. Nostalgic
you may be for Tom Quad or Times Square, but in Warsaw
there are still tenuous links with home.

And even from Room 221 you can see something of the
character of the Poles, for they move with a special kind of
vigour, almost jaunty, and they have strong and interesting
faces. Warsaw is haunted always by sad memories, but there is
nevertheless a liveliness, a jollity, a gaiety in the air that springs
only from the hearts of the Poles. A gleam of wrinkled humour
lightens the eye of the elderly chambermaid when she arrives,
some hours after lunch, to make your bed. Polish conversation,
for a visiting Briton anyway, is infinitely easy, entertaining and
somehow familiar. Sometimes in the street below a rip-roaring
jovial drunk will stagger through the snow, bawling witticisms
and singing bawdy songs. They are not an aloof, remote or
inscrutable people, the Poles; they might do well, I sometimes
feel, in Ireland.

At other moments, though, Warsaw feels a long, long way
from Galway; and as the evening draws on, and the progressive
playwright closes his typewriter and leaves for a séance with
seven eminent philosophers, you may notice a stream of citizens
moving intently towards the church which, with its twin angels
sustaining the cross on its golden ball, stands in ornate confidence beyond the park. They walk with an air of functional
resolution, very different from Ballycommon on Sunday morning, and slip into the church hurriedly, as though they have
work to do there, crossing themselves for all the world as a
worker clocks himself in at the factory; and if you are patient
you will see them emerging again a few moments later, buttoning up their coats, putting on their thick gloves, and hastening
away towards the trolley-bus. They look as though they have
stopped at a petrol station to get fuel for the evening; and they
even remind me – not with irreverence, only sympathy – of
addicts on a lost weekend, stocking up at Joe's Bar on Fourth
Avenue.

Then the night falls on Warsaw, chill and early, and the dim
lights of Eastern Europe reluctantly awake. The view from your

balcony grows grim and depressing, with the presence of the harsh frozen Vistula always behind your back and only a trickle of prepossessed traffic enlivening the streets. The coffee-shops and restaurants hide their identities behind curtains and closed doors, and few bright lights entice you towards the theatres. The thump of a jazz band may reach you across the snow, but the city feels obscurely muffled and padded, and the gaunt square buildings of the new Warsaw lie there unsmiling in the cold.

Raise your eyes above the rooftops, though, above the chimneys, above the angels with their golden ball, and there you will see the big red light on the Palace of Culture and Science, presented to Poland by the Soviet Union, and towering above this grey city like a vast watchman in the dark. And perhaps at the same time if you listen hard enough, closing your ears to the clang of the trams and the rumble of the passing cars, you may hear from some distant student attic the thin thrilling strains of a Chopin polonaise, riding the cold night air like an invocation.

But probably not. I must not romanticize. 'Room service? A cup of coffee, please, two aspirins, and a cable form. That's it, bless you, Room 221.'

37

THE ARK OF THE MYTH

Wyoming, 1975

Looking for the Lost American Innocence became almost a literary industry in the late 1970s, but when I wrote this essay the quest was relatively new. I had been greatly depressed by the Watergate scandal, and the exposure of President Nixon, and I really did go to Wyoming in search of older American values. Did I find them, or were they mythical themselves?

I had long missed, like everyone else, the American innocence. When I first went to the States, in the 1950s, it flourished still in Norman Rockwell's world of sundae, prom and *Saturday Evening Post*; it flickered momentarily, I think, in the successive debuts of beats, hippies, flower people and Jesus freaks; but for myself I had lately only felt its presence, and fitfully, even then, among the harbourmen of New York City, in whose company, on tugs and pilot boats, flats and oil barges, I had been making some agreeable excursions. It was one of these men, lounging on one side of his pilot-house while I ate a bar of Hershey's Tropical Chocolate on the other, who reproached me for despondency. 'Look, why belly-ache? If ya don't like the city, go some place else. This place ain't everywhere. We can't help it. We grew up this way. Get out of the place. Go to the Rockies or some place – but like I say, don't belly-ache . . .'

I cherished his advice, and when the opportunity arose I booked a ticket to Wyoming, hoping to find in that remote hinterland something real in America still: for I had seen, in a statistical chart about the origins of celebrated movie actors, that while twenty-three of the most famous had been born in New York State, and fifteen in Michigan, and eleven in California, the only State in the Union unable to claim a single star was The

Equality State (whose population is rather smaller than Coventry's, and whose area is rather larger than the entire United Kingdom's).

I had reached the conclusion that the downfall of the Americans had been insincerity. This is of course no news to old-school British sceptics, who have been saying for 200 years that Americans can't be trusted. But it was not exactly dishonesty that I found so inescapable in the America of the 1970s, nor even hypocrisy: it was that loss of innocence. It was a habit of deception so ingrained, so universal it seemed, that the Americans did not notice it in themselves. It was a national frame of mind. The pioneers had doubtless invented the false fraternity of America merely in order to survive. The American need to be loved was originally a withdrawal symptom of revolution. Capitalism had made the Republic itself a kind of advertising campaign. And all these elements had lately been compounded by the illusory quality of life in modern America: the combined hallucinogens of drugs, of electronics, of racial dogma, of political corruption and persiflage, which had whittled away at reality and made everything suspect, whether it be an interview with a bank manager or an argument for the preservation of Alaskan wilderness.

A worldly American friend of mine, when I told him what the tugboat man had suggested, assured me that if anything the American delusion was less profound than its British equivalent. If you stripped an Englishman of his veneer you eventually reached a core of infinite complexity: but beneath the American layers there survived, he swore, more shy by far than any English inhibitions, yearning, ancient, unfulfilled, a purity unsuspected. 'Pure white,' he thought, 'virgin white at the centre.' I could only say that very different colours showed: introspective purples, crooked reds, greens for envy and acquisitiveness, black for urban crime, and a muddy, greeny, yellowy mish-mash colour for all that anxious groping, doped with hash and addled with psychiatry, with which young America stumbles pitiably towards nowhere in particular.

'But go by all means', my friend fastidiously added, 'if the West attracts you': and so I rented myself a car in Denver, a city all agog, as it happened, with newspaper revelations about downtown pornography, and drove across the State line into

Wyoming. I stopped for a coffee and a salad on the way north, and the women at the counter showed me with a mock-shudder a headline in one of the local newspapers that day. I found it encouraging, on the whole. 'TEN MORE BALD EAGLES', it said, 'FOUND POISONED IN WYOMING PITS.'

'Cheyenne, our State capital', the tourist lady told me educationally, 'is essentially a railroad city, but I don't suppose, dear, railroads interest you.' There she was wrong. My images of the American naivety were inextricably linked with railroads. I had never thought the Pilgrim Fathers innocent, let alone Washington or Jefferson, and the kind of simplicity I coveted dates, I think, from the days of the Western expansion. While the patrons of American railroads were seldom child-like, the men who made and ran them do seem to have been, by our fallible standards, a genuine, rough-and-tumble lot of people, and the American railway mystique has always been a benevolent abstraction. It evokes sentimental nostalgia, a weakness I enjoy. Even now, I am told, hobos and hitch-hikers are kindly treated by the railroad men, as their tradition demands, and hardly a freight train passes in the West without a few unauthorized riders behind its steel doors.

It is true that Cheyenne is a railroad town still. One hears the wail at night sometimes, as the Irish might say, and the main downtown street demonstrates its origins by running parallel with the Union Pacific track, which pre-dated it. Everyone told me with pride that Cheyenne had been frightfully sinful in its youth, when the mobile camp of construction workers ('Hell on Wheels') reached this site with the advancing rails. Even by railroading standards, they said, it had been a wild town, with its perilous saloons and its brazen brothels, its hordes of speculators and promoters, its gunmen, its hunters and trappers, its opportunist lawyers and its tented thousands of Chinese and Irish labourers. The Civil War had just ended then, and America was in a violent mood. By 1869 Cheyenne was ambitiously described as 'the gambling centre of the world', and during the same year its unofficial committee of vigilantes, administering the justice of the frontier, executed at least a dozen offenders.

'Oh,' said the lady in mild surprise, 'in that case you must go and see our reconstruction of Hell on Wheels, with the locomotive, *Big Boy* . . . Authentic Relic', she continued, relapsing into

her brochure voice, 'of the Railroad Era.' But it was a sorry
reflection, I thought, of those rumbustious origins. Hell on
Wheels turned out to be a folksy enclave of novelty shops and
sideshows, surrounded by canvas awnings and closed anyway
for the season. *Big Boy* was the biggest railway engine ever built
anywhere, a vast black mechanism with nineteen wheels on
each side: but it stood forlornly on a petty line of track in a park,
Hell on Wheels flapping depressingly behind, and seemed so
absolutely of the museum or the Rotary Club that I could scarcely
conceive those pistons ever pumping, still less hear a cuss from
its cab.

So I proceeded to the Union Pacific station itself, at 16th and
Central, for nearly a century one of the main depots on the trans-
continental run, where the Denver Pacific and the Colorado
Central met the great UPRR – 'travellers will here take a dinner',
says my *Trans-Continental Railroad Guide* (1881), 'in comfortable
style at one of the best kept hotels between the two oceans.'
Alas, as a citadel of the old values it too lacked conviction. It
seemed to be on its last legs. Trains *did* come, they told me, but
they took a lot of hanging around for. The station was officially
open from 10 to 5, and still possessed an office magically
inscribed 'Special Agent', and housed the last of the overland
stage-coaches from Julesburg, Co., propped outside the ticket
booths: but its mahogany fittings badly needed love and feather
dusters, and so silent were the tracks, so endlessly into the
distance did the lines of the Union Pacific extend in absolute
hushed desertion, so utterly absent were porters, trolleys, mail-
bags or homing pigeons in wicker baskets, that it looked to me
as though never again would a train hiss to a halt at Cheyenne,
to disgorge from its high steps that nervous, gauche and lovely
girl of whose inevitable arrival the late-night movies long ago
forewarned us.

But there was life of a sort outside the platforms. At one of the
ticket windows a shabby line of men waited, standing first on
one leg, then on the other, sometimes removing their Stetsons
to scratch the tops of their balding heads, or passing coffee
around in squashy plastic cups. These were the redundant of
the railroad. 'They'll never close the track, never, for the freight,
see, but in the meantime here's some of the boys without a job.'
The boys politely made way for me as I edged to the head of
their queue to peer through the ticket-window: and what I saw

behind was curiously disillusioning. It is true that one man wore an eye-shade, like the telegraph operators of old, but in most respects the scene back there, in the private quarters of Cheyenne depot, looked less Western than Oriental. It reminded me of Madras. It was a cameo of officialdom, framed in dockets, files, chits in triplicate. It looked old and tired. Everybody looked up when I appeared at the window, and offered me *babu* smiles. 'Anything I can do for you? You looking for someone?' But it was not what I was hoping for, the innocence was absent, so I shook my head sadly and drove out of town.

I went to the Indian country, but soon got tired of Indians. 'I am tired of Indians,' said I to the kindly cicerone who showed me round the Bradford Brinton Memorial Ranch House, near Sheridan, fearing she might draw my attention to yet more portraits of squaws or shamans, pre-Raphaelite impressions of tepee ceremonials, or (worst of all) bead artefacts. She looked startled. It was not, I think, the opinion that perturbed her, it was simply its expression. European visitors to the West are not generally tired of Indians, and American visitors would not dream of saying so.

Part of the unreality of America, it seemed to me, was its retroactive conscience. Americans suffered allegedly lacerating pangs about matters they could not mend, and for which they were blameless anyway, and their guilt over the fate of the Indians was the prime example. It was doubly false. For one thing no living American was conceivably to blame, and for another the Americans did not really feel guilty in an actual or personal way, but merely found it morally or perhaps ecologically fashionable to appear so. Integral to the American innocence had been a guileless violence, generally acceptable by the morality of the time, and its denial now was part of the national lie. How could the Americans feel guilt about the fate of the Sioux or the Modocs? I certainly did not feel in the least guilty about Amritsar, say, being unthought of at the time, never having heard of the massacre until twenty-five years after the event, and possessing neither the inclination nor the technique to massacre anybody anywhere.

This particular American indulgence struck me as especially sickly in Wyoming, where I did not doubt the persecution of the Indians would be continuing still, were it not for the fact that the white people, from the wickedest rich landowners to the liliest academic progressives, were no longer troubled by them. For in this State the theme, vocabulary, and flavour of the Indian presence cannot be evaded. I went to Greybull, which commemorates an old grey buffalo of Indian legend, and Crowheart, which remembers Chief Washahue of the Shoshones, dying there with a Crow warrior's heart upon his spear, and Spotted Horse, and Medicine Bow, and Ten Sleep; and I inspected the reconstructed buildings of Fort Laramie, white and spanking in the sunshine, once the storied Army headquarters of the Indian wars, now so aggressively repentant that even the wild creatures within its perimeter are officially protected, and the moment I entered its central enclosure an impertinent rabbit sprang at me.

There were memories of those wars everywhere, for Americans to tear their hair and beat their breasts over. Some I found very moving. I knew nothing, for instance, of the Fetterman Massacre, but I felt I understood its import when, driving down the empty road between Sheridan and Buffalo, I saw its commemorative obelisk upon a ridge. Here the impulsive Colonel Fetterman, contemptuous of Indian tactics, led his force of seventy-nine soldiers from Fort Phil Kearney to escort a wagon-train of timber from the hills. On this grand bare windswept ridge, just before Christmas 1866, with the savage Big Horn Mountains splendidly to the east, and the wide plateau of the Wind River extending southwards snow-white and bitter – on this spot his column was ambushed, so the obelisk told me, 'by an overwhelming force of Sioux under the command of Red Cloud'. 1866! In New York in 1866, they started to build Brooklyn Bridge. In England, in 1866, Newman published the *Dream of Gerontius*. In Brisbane, in 1866, they first lit the General Post Office with gas lamps. But in Wyoming, on 21 December 1866, Red Cloud fell upon the 18th United States Infantry, and there were no survivors.

All over Wyoming I was reminded of those old adventures, by cryptic memorials, the names of old forts, the sites of old battlefields – the Wagon Box Fight in Big Piney Creek, the Crazy Woman Fight in Johnson County, or the Dull Knife Battle of 1876, from whose carnage the surviving Cheyenne Indians, their wounds staining the snow, crept half-naked across the hills to seek refuge with Crazy Horse. But the Wyoming Indians of today are a distinctly unexciting people. In the pamphlets I was shown in Cheyenne they were dressed up for festival, feathered, gaudy, bold, with horses and pipes and painted tepees. Off-duty, so to speak, they proved less virile, and seemed to me an argument less for the advantages of peace than for the stimulants of war: for it was not of course the US Cavalry who destroyed the Indians, but the peacemakers, the improvers or rationalists of their day, the nineteenth-century ecologists, who herded them logically into reservations, and put the fire out.

There is only one reservation in Wyoming, the Wind River. I visited the Shoshones and Arapahoes there, vaguely hoping to find, I think, that those long-defeated tribes might be the custodians of an older relationship between man and nature, and that one day they would, like the possessors of some royal strain or talisman, emerge into their own again. But if they possessed the old panaceas, one would not know it. The Wind River Indians are taciturn, not to say surly, representatives of the old race. Even one of their own white officials admitted to me that he found them heavy going – especially, he hastily added, lest I should think him racialist, after a few years among the perfectly charming Navajos of the south. There is a large café and community hall at Fort Washakie, the agency head-quarters, and I went for a cup of coffee there hoping to enjoy an informative chat with the girls at the counter. But they were not a chatty crew. Expressionless they served me, desultorily they exchanged monosyllables with their Indian customers, more bigoted than ever did I leave their reservation, vowing I would buy not another basketwork bag, admire no more antique pictographs, express no further interest in a folk-ceremony, nor ask one more diplomatic question about the communal collection of huckleberries so long as I remained in the State of Wyoming – whose motto, by the way, is Equal Rights, and whose State Flower is the Indian Paint Brush – 'A strange little flower', as Addie Viola Hudson has put it, 'with a sun-kissed nose,'

> Without any perfume, yet red as a rose.
> Did some Indian maiden plant you here
> Or are you the symbol of blood that was shed
> In the footprint left by the hoof of a deer,
> In the feud of the white man, and the red?

Nor at first was I much beguiled by the Old Western evocations of the State. Wyoming has been a tourist trap almost since the first pioneers passed this way. Among the earliest travellers in these parts were Major Sir Rose Price and Mr William S. Baillie-Grohman, sportsmen from England, and even in the roughest days of Hell on Wheels and the Cattle Barons, dudes found their way here to shoot their buffalo and write their travel memoirs. By now history, myth, reality and tourist exploitation are inextricably confused, and at first I thought that even here, in these half-empty landscapes, in these snug ranching towns, along these terrific treeless highways, the corrosion of fraud was inescapable.

There is a lot of sham. There are silly tourist ranches, and phoney saddlers, and ghost towns preposterously resurrected, and ludicrous Wild West enthusiasms, like the collection of old Burnham's Beef, Wine, and Iron bottles. The Old West breeds its own degradations, and Wyoming often parodies itself not merely for the tourists, but for itself. I winced each time I heard the phrase Old Timer, and hurried sickened and distraught from the well-known Wyoming spectacle called the Wild Life Exhibit, which turned out to be a revolting assemblage of 100 stuffed animals and 600 sets of antlers, slaughtered personally by Mr Dale Warren of Dubois – 'Kids [as his publicity says] Just Love our Baby Fawn, Baby Bear and Baby Seal', all unhappily murdered young.

Aesthetically the memory of the Old West can be distressing, in garish water-colour or mawkish ode:

> Out where the handclasp's a little stronger,
> Out where the smile dwells a little longer,
> That's where the West begins . . .

while the public humour of Wyoming might be described in architectural terms as Rustic Commercial:

> Grab the Tab
> Pay the Tariff
> Come Back Soon
> Or We'll Send the Sheriff.

Wyoming is a great place, too, for slogans: 'The Can Do Country – Stop Roaming, Try Wyoming – Healthy, Wealthy, Growing Wyoming – Wonderful Wyoming'. Since 1936 Wyoming car number-plates have carried a publicity picture of a bucking bronco, with a whooping cowboy up, and this is far more telling an insignia of the State than the Great Seal with its scrolls and banners, or even the State Flag with its somnolent buffalo.

The patron saint of tourist Wyoming, or perhaps the managing director, is Buffalo Bill, Colonel Cody. I got very tired of him, too. He was the original hallucinogenic American, for what was genuine in him and what was pretence seems to have been unresolvable. The house where he was born is at Cody, in the north-west of the State, but that celebrated town, now a shrine to his memory, was not in fact his place of birth. It seems that in 1895 a few speculators thought of founding a new town in Wyoming. 'Horace and I had a talk, and we concluded that as Buffalo Bill Cody was probably the best advertised man in the world, we might organize a company and make him president . . .' Colonel Cody not only agreed, but suggested that the town should actually be named after him. 'This did no harm to us, and it highly pleased the Colonel.'

To clinch the arrangement Cody's birthplace was brought there from Iowa, and instantly Cody, Wyoming, became a prosperous tourist destination. It was probably the first municipality to capitalize the Western legend, which thus coexisted there in fantasy and in fact, and it has thrived ever since. A vast, emotional, and rather beautiful statue of the colonel dominates the town; he is pointing the way ahead with his rifle, leaning in his saddle to encourage the timid pioneers out of sight behind, while his horse, heroically neighing (it was modelled from life in Manhattan), raises its left forefoot in a graceful and fortunately symmetrical pose. There is an enormous Buffalo Bill Museum, a Vatican of the Western ethos, and diverse lesser monuments to the Colonel flourish, like the Irma Hotel he built for his daughter Irma, and the Cody Stampede on Independence Day, and Buffalo Bill Day on 26 February, and Buffalo Bill souvenir counters, and Buffalo Bill coffee-shops, and Buffalo Bill's birthplace, of course, its Iowan origins forgotten now and its manner breezily indigenous. 'Cody Lives!' cried a graffito I saw on a wall in town; and by golly, so he does.

Yet it came to me that the varnish was thin, and could be flaked away. There were often moments when the real and the spurious overlapped, but they did not synthesize. I became aware that a gap separated the two, and that in Wyoming the communal self-delusion was at least incomplete. A distinction existed still, as it seldom did in New York, between the way people behaved privately, personally, and the way they acted in their public personae. The transcendentalism was in check. Self-awareness survived.

I sensed this first, unexpectedly, among townspeople, not in Cheyenne but in the smaller ranch and market towns which speckle the map of Wyoming. In area this is the ninth largest of the American States, but in population only Alaska is smaller. The 315,000 people of Wyoming are scattered among nearly 98,000 square miles of territory, so that miles of open country divide one little town from the next: aromatic, sage, snow and sunshine country, sprinkled at that time of the year with sweet small flowers, tracked by the hoofs of wandering cattle, bounded always by the distant line of Teton or Big Horn. Reaching a Wyoming town after a few hours' drive across the magnificent range is like reaching a particularly trim and comfortable oasis, for though it will naturally display most of the physical symptoms of the American norm, still its isolation, and the beauty that surrounds it on every side, gives it a satisfying unity and compactness.

At one such place, Lander in Fremont County, I visited the Pioneer Museum, which is run by the county Pioneer Association. This body is presided over by dignitaries called the Esteemed Patriarch and the Esteemed Matriarch, whose photographs hang honoured at the entrance, and the excellent small museum is attended by ladies scarcely less matriarchal or esteemable. During my visit a schoolmistress was taking a group of children round the exhibits, and I heard her drawing their attention to a chair that stood in a corner of the gallery. It was made all of bleached white horn, legs, seat, back and all, and looked impressive but comfortless. 'That is an example', she was saying, 'of the craftsmanship of the very first pioneers to come to Fremont County. Isn't that beautiful, children?' Yes ma'am, most of them dutifully murmured, but after the main body had passed on to the Shoshone relics, a section of the museum I preferred to circumvent, I noticed a pair of laggard urchins trailing along behind. They had not heard their teacher's eulogy of the chair, but they too paused as they passed it, and inspected it with no less admiration. 'Jeez,' one said to the other. 'Take a look at that, Elk!'

I respected their expertise, and adopted their assessment as a synonym for the true in Wyoming. Elks abound in the State, and in all its homelier aspects I came to think of it as Elkin country. Elkin its splendour, elkin its charm, elkin I suspect its streak of country ruttishness, which tends to express itself in hawkish car stickers – *'They'll take my gun away from me when my dead hands are too cold to hold it'*, or *'I'm fighting poverty, I work'*. There is a kind of triumphal arch of elk antlers in the town square at Jackson, Wyoming, very apposite I thought, and it must have been elks they were referring to in a notice I saw upon a stockade near Pinedale: 'KEEP OUT, MEAN ANIMALS'.

The present Esteemed Patriarch of Lander, I was told, was by origin part English, part French, and part Sioux, and was the very first child ever to ride through town in a perambulator. These little Wyoming settlements are very new. The cliché that America itself is 'young' is, of course, preposterously out of date. It is one of the older nations now, and there are places in New England and the South that feel almost as ancient and stubborn as Little Ruttleborough on the Marsh. But this is one of the American hallucinations – the queer old-young flavour of it, the nation like so many of its matrons a weird cosmetic blend of decay, protean vigour, bluff and self-persuasion. Wyoming, though, needs no silicones. Wyoming really is young – a State since 1890 – and Wyoming people talk about the original heroes of this frontier as we in Britain might recall well-remembered village characters of our childhood.

There was 'Old Lady' Boland, for instance, who ran a hotel in Lander for many years, who was well-known all over western Wyoming, and who crops up often in conversation still. What does Mrs Ada Piper, 90, think of Old Lady Boland? 'Not much of a lady,' says Mrs Piper conclusively. Nobody is sacred in those parts, I was relieved to discover, and if I really tried I could even induce this citizenry to make disrespectful noises about Buffalo Bill. Butch Cassidy and the Wild Bunch, Cattle Kate, Flat Nose George the Train Robber – they remember them all without rancour or sentimentality, just ornery human critters like the rest of us, some good, some bad – 'take Cattle Kate, now, they hanged her up there in Spring Creek Gulch, and some folks say she was real bad, but my Auntie Norah she knew her intimate, and she used to say there weren't nobody she'd sooner bake a pie with, not nobody . . .'

I discovered in these little towns a kind of urbanity based not upon sophistication, but upon frankness. To the garage man, the laundry woman, the girl in the pharmacy, the motel reception clerk, there was an attitude of inquiry which much comforted me. Off the main road the Wyoming townsman still looks you straight and interested in the eye, as though not many strangers come his way. Make a remark and he'll offer another. 'Look at your poor thumb,' said I to a cobbler who was mending a strap for me, and whose thumb looked as though it had been, over several generations, repeatedly squashed in vices. 'You don't need to fret about it,' he immediately replied, 'I give it a bang once in a while just to keep it awake.' In the post office at Medicine Bow, where Owen Wister set the immortal exchange of lines that culminated in 'When you call me that, *smile*' – in the false-fronted post office at Medicine Bow, almost next door to the Virginian Hotel and opposite the open range, the post-mistress gave me some handy advice about buying stamped envelopes. 'If you buy an envelope here I lick it for you, if you buy it some place else you do your own licking.' At Como Bluff, near a celebrated fossil field, there is a hut which claims itself to be the oldest building on earth, because it is made of fossilized dinosaur bones, and on this eccentric structure I saw a sign which trenchantly exemplified, I thought, the elkin directness of Wyoming: 'HONK HORN IF YOU WANT IN FOSSIL CABIN'.

The aristocrats of such a little town are the ranchers, in whose lives it plays the part that Andover, say, or Market Harborough play in the lives of country gentlemen in England. The cattle ranchers are the swells of Wyoming – they used often to be the villains, too, in the days when they ruthlessly harassed small-holders and sheep-herders rash enough to settle in the territory. They live splendidly, many of them, in lovely country houses in the lee of the hills, with rose gardens and grand connections in the East – in England too, sometimes, for parts of Wyoming were settled by English milords.

I caught a pleasing glimpse of this society in the coffee-shop of a hotel at one mid-Wyoming town. The hotel lobby had not been encouraging. A fat, curled, eye-darkened, menacingly powdered moll eyed me unlovingly from the reception desk; chewing check-shirted figures leant against walls brooding; two or three reptilian elders with sticks and greasy Stetsons sat slumped in armchairs grunting; there was a clock on the wall with a face in the pattern of a Kennedy silver dollar, and a haze of cigar-smoke drifted among the apotheoses of Western life and re-enactments of Shoshone legend that hung upon the walls.

But I braved it all, and found a very different segment of society dominating the coffee-shop. The first thing that struck me about the group of ranchers lunching there was how fast they talked. That America contains more bores than all other countries put together is of course irrefutable: but it is not because Americans say boring things, only that they talk so slowly. This must reflect, I think, a fundamental defect of American educational method, for some of the slowest talkers and most excruciating bores of all, I have observed, have been Harvard men of exquisite instruction.

These Wyoming squires, though, talked fast, and with a nice mixture of cultivated and idiomatic English. They seemed altogether without self-consciousness: edgy, lean, rather brilliant people I thought. They struck me as *finished* men, who had never been reconstituted in the American melting-pot, but had always been themselves. Many of the Wyoming ranching families were certainly well-off from the start: early settlers around Sheridan, for instance, included English army officers who had first gone to the West buying horses for the British cavalry. The cattle barons of the 1880s and 1890s were men of means and style – one of the first Powder River ranches was stocked at the beginning with 25,000 head of cattle – and when Theodore Roosevelt visited the State in 1910 he was given what was described as a characteristic Wyoming dinner: trout, pike, grouse, prairie chicken, roast elk with currant jelly, and champagne.

The ranchers still have a reputation for arrogance, but spared as they have been the miseries of the race struggle and the distortions of the social rat race, they seem to me more truly gentlemanly than most of the Virginia snobs or New England pedigree men who consider themselves the only American patricians. The men in the coffee-shop talked shop mostly, but it was marvellously racy or colourful shop: those darned heifers, getting the helicopter repaired, thirty miles of wire, Idaho mares, the Chinese grain market, 'if Ed says it's going to rain you can bet prime ribs it won't', and they parted, after coffee but no cigars, with courteous goodbyes to me and easy

informalities to each other – 'Thanks a lot', 'You bet, Sam', 'Be
seein' ya', 'Love to Sue, now . . .'

And so I came, circumspectly, to those theatrical archetypes
of the American West, the cowboys. Much of the innocence had
gone, I believed, with the decline of craftsmanship in the States,
and with the consequent disappearance of a whole class of
American working men – petty officer Americans, foremen
Americans, the sort who never let you down, or forgot their
tools. For a time the kind survived in the garage men of America,
in the days when cars were still cherished as machinery, and
American males appeared to have an instinctive affinity with
them. Some have been socially promoted, and are to be glimpsed
grandly accoutred as the captains of American airliners. Some
survive among my friends the New York harbour men. I have
occasionally met one on a construction project far away, extending telecommunications in Persia or supervising the electrifi-
cation of Siam. And a few thousand, I suppose, like Celts in
Cornwall or pine martens in Wales, can be seen flourishing still
in enclave, pure-bred and unmistakable, upon the ranges of
Wyoming.

I approached them, as I say, with suspicion, for I feared the
worst of them. Surely, after so many decades of the fancy, the
rot had set in on the fact! But my very first encounter with
Wyoming cowboys, on the road near Laramie, wonderfully
reassured me. It seemed to me a genuinely romantic spectacle,
in the grand manner. Their sheep and cattle were loitering in
hundreds along the highway, straggling and nibbling up a hill,
and the cowboys too seemed in no hurry at all. They did not
nag. They were not fussed. They sat their horses with a divine
assurance, all muscle, no bone, drooping rather, languorously
chewing sometimes, with their Stetsons not too rakish, their
gear moderately gaudy, and their posture one of lordly self-
satisfaction. I loved them, and will not pretend to deny the
frisson I derived from the elegant condescension of their greet-
ings, as I nosed my car through the livestock and drove on aglow
to Rock River.

The cowboys give to the Wyoming scene a style, at once
sensual and aesthetic, to which most Americans are anxiously
and I fear irrevocably alien. It was the cowboys, I realized now,
not the redundant railwaymen or morose Arapahoes, who were

the guardians of that lost identity: they, almost alone among their 180 million compatriots, still seemed at ease with their environment, their history, their jobs and themselves. Some of course are bad. They like guns and murder bald eagles. When they drive home from work in the evenings (for many now live in the towns), with their saddles in the backs of their cars, their mode does slightly shift away from High Chapparal towards Easy Rider. They often wear dark glasses, too, which gives them a slightly sinister air. But in casual encounter and conversation there can be no gentler or more polished working men. They are the nearest thing to a white American peasantry, I suppose, and they possess a timeless rural grace.

Often these magnificent people befriended me. Once they invited me to come on down and watch the branding: and I left the car, and scrambled down the bank to the fence below, and there I found an Indianified cowboy very slowly walking his horse around an enclosure lassoing bullocks by their hind legs – a performance of some grandeur, almost stately, with a measured tread of the horse and a theatrical swank to the tilt of the horseman's head. One by one he picked his steers and dragged them, helplessly kicking, over to the branding pit, where heat sizzled from oxygen cylinders, the air smelt of scorched flesh, and a couple of elderly ranch-hands nonchalantly branded them. They greeted me rather as stall-holders welcome passing visitors to village fêtes – graciously, that is, almost protectively, and informatively. Stall-holders are inclined to tell you about dry-rot in the church tower, or trace the ancestry of Sir Charles at the Manor. Cowboys put you in the picture about cattle. 'Take the Lazy Y Brand, that means a letter Y lying on its side, see, kinda layabout. U Lazy A, that means a letter U and a sideways A. The Hildebrand outfit, they brand Upside Y Lazy 3 – that's a letter Y upside down and a number 3 backside up. We have all sorts – E Slash 4, Lazy Diamond R – you get the hang of it in time, same as you get the hang of most anything . . .'

Or sometimes they merely walked their horses up to me, as I picnicked in the sage, or sat sketching in my car, or took my morning walk through the scented countryside, picking flowers for my notebook or trying to analyse the dappled colour-patterns on the hills: and then, after we had exchanged pleasantries, and told each other where we came from, and explained what we were doing, sometimes they would slide lithe from their saddles

and join me for a few minutes, looking over my shoulder at a
sketch, accepting a slice of cheese, or simply sharing the pleasure
of the place and the moment – not a talkative presence usually,
but one so natural, kind and unembarrassed that a silence was
never awkward, and the parting came organically, like the end
of a good meal, just before satisfaction moved towards surfeit.

This reminded me very much of Spain: and just as in Spain,
in the bitterest expanses of the high *meseta*, the Spaniard
commands the scene with his dignity, so it seemed to me that
the cowboys in Wyoming, with their Castilian tact and splendour, needed no pretence. They were themselves, uncompro-
mised. I thought it a happy irony, in the end, that I seemed to
have found the last American reality in the very ark of the
American myth.